Shojo Beat

Rasetsu

Vol. 4

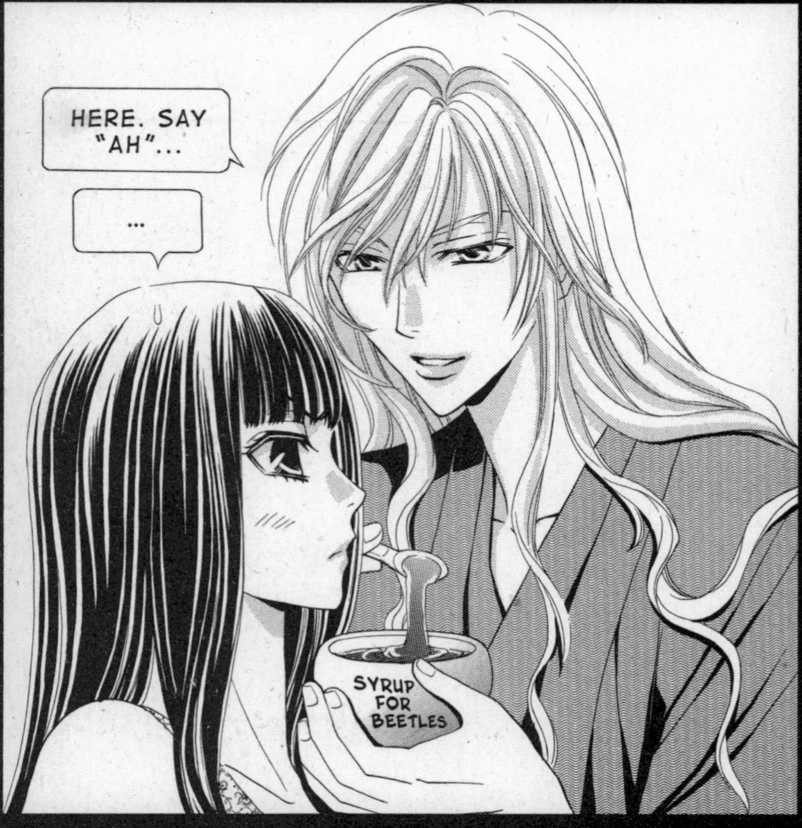
HERE. SAY "AH"...
...
SYRUP FOR BEETLES

Story & Art by

Chika Shiomi

Characters

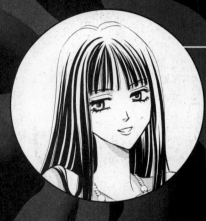

Rasetsu Hyuga

A powerful 18-year-old exorcist, Rasetsu has a flowerlike mark on her chest—a memento left by a demon. Rasetsu eats lots of sweets to recharge her psychic powers. She's currently looking for a boyfriend.

Yako Hoshino

An ace psychic who controls water, Yako was headhunted by Rasetsu. He still has feelings for the spirit he was in love with in high school…

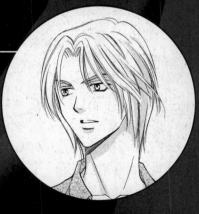

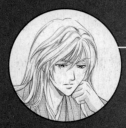

Hiichiro Amakawa

The chief of the agency where Rasetsu and Yako work. A very powerful psychic.

Kuryu Iwatsuki

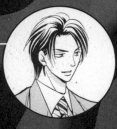

A psychic who uses *kotodama* (spiritual power manifested through words). His power works on humans and animals alike.

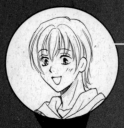

Aoi Kugi

Does administrative work for the agency. Ever since Yako came to the office, however, he's been left with nothing to do.

Story

The Hiichiro Amakawa Agency deals with exorcisms, and Rasetsu and Kuryu are psychics who work there. One day, Yako visits their office because he needs help with a possessed book. Rasetsu recognizes Yako's supernatural powers and tries to recruit him. He eventually joins the agency and learns that Rasetsu is actually cursed by a malevolent spirit. However, Yako doesn't know that the only way for Rasetsu to break her curse is to find true love, so he derides her for seeming hell-bent on finding a boyfriend… Later during an exorcism, Yako says that Rasetsu reminds him of sunlight. Now Rasetsu finds herself thinking about him all the time…!

Rasetsu

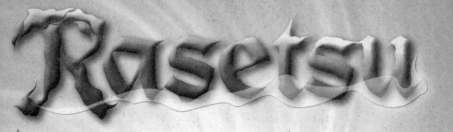

Volume 4

Contents

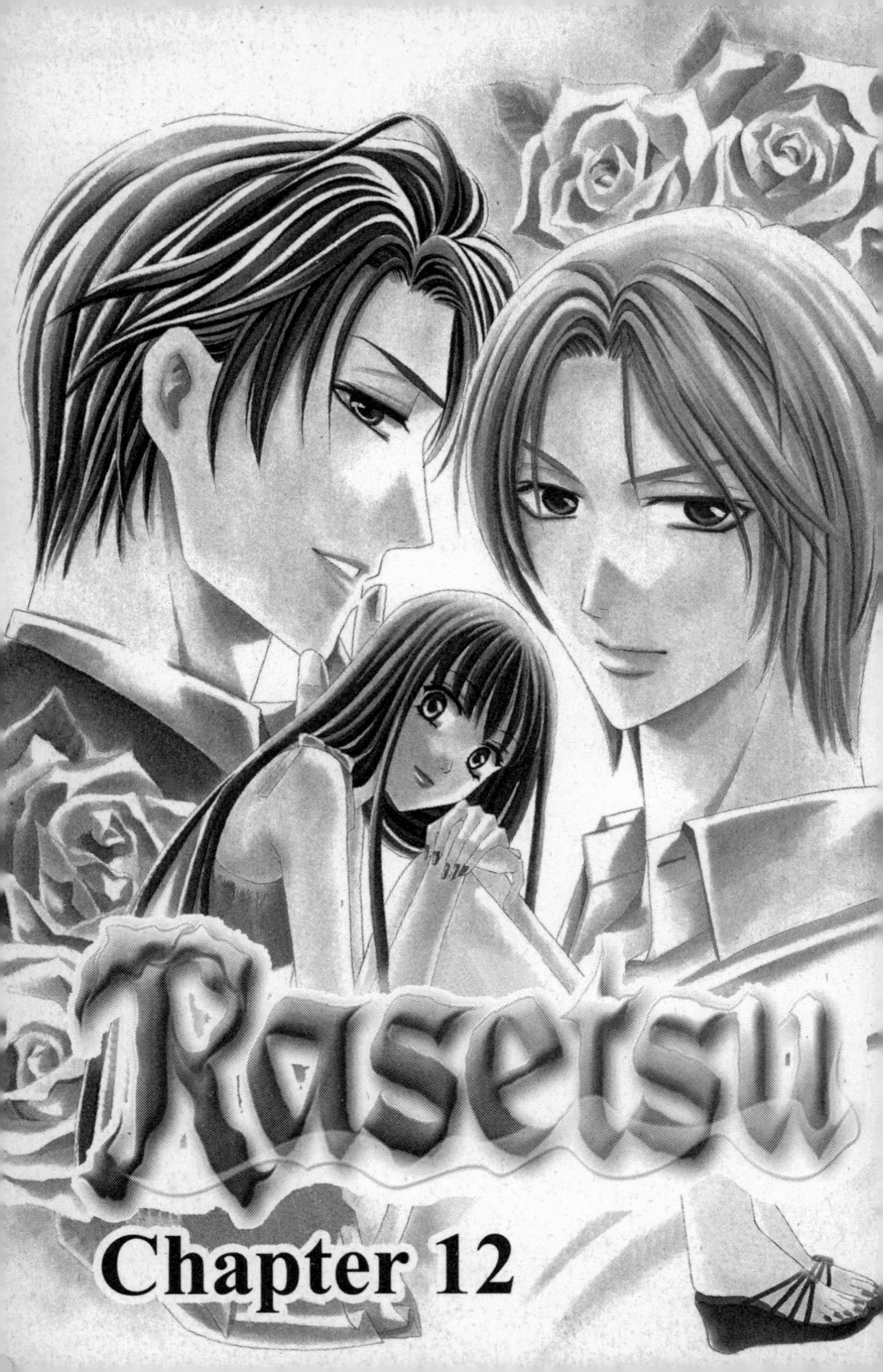
Rasetsu
Chapter 12

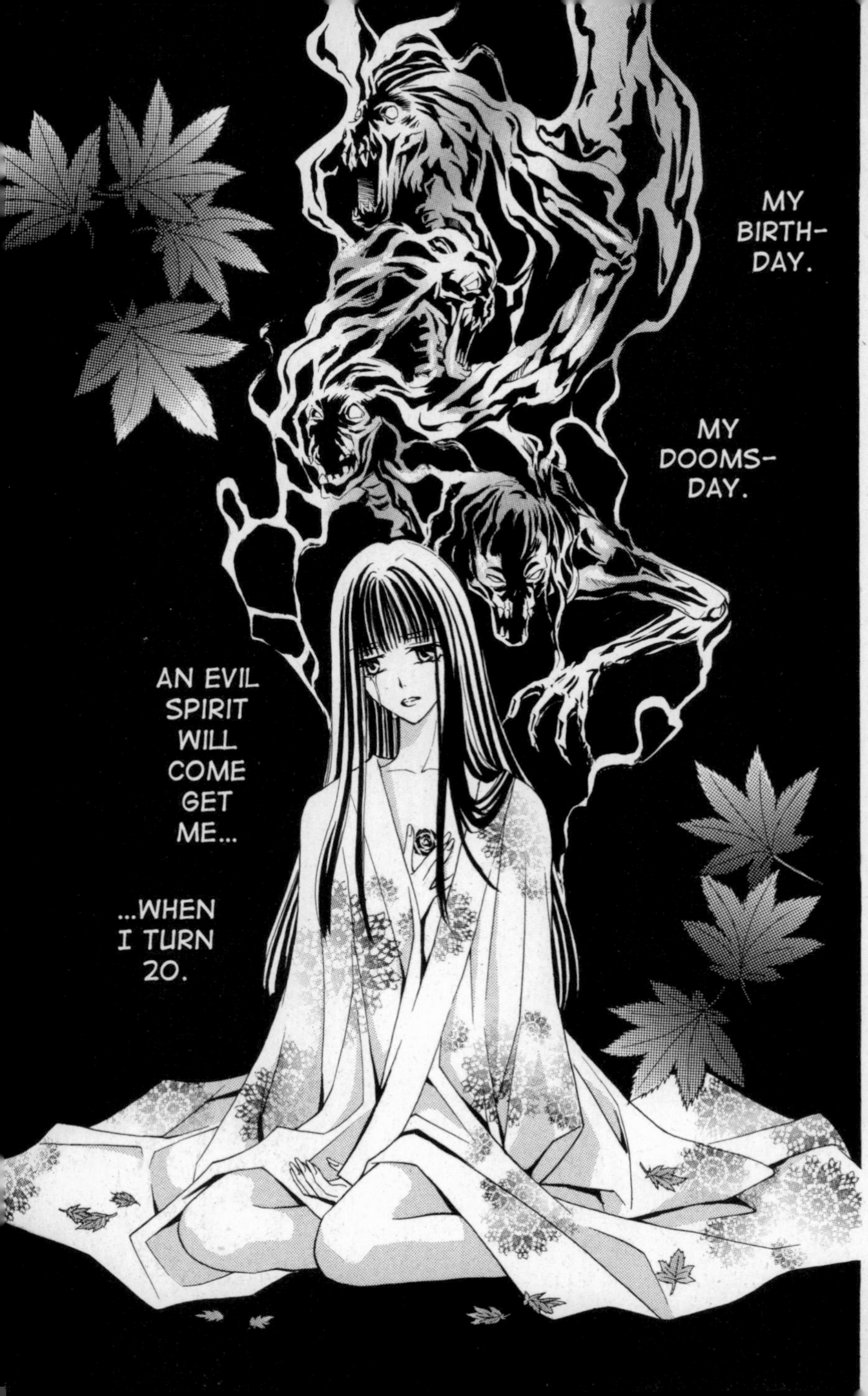
MY BIRTH-DAY.
MY DOOMS-DAY.
AN EVIL SPIRIT WILL COME GET ME...
...WHEN I TURN 20.

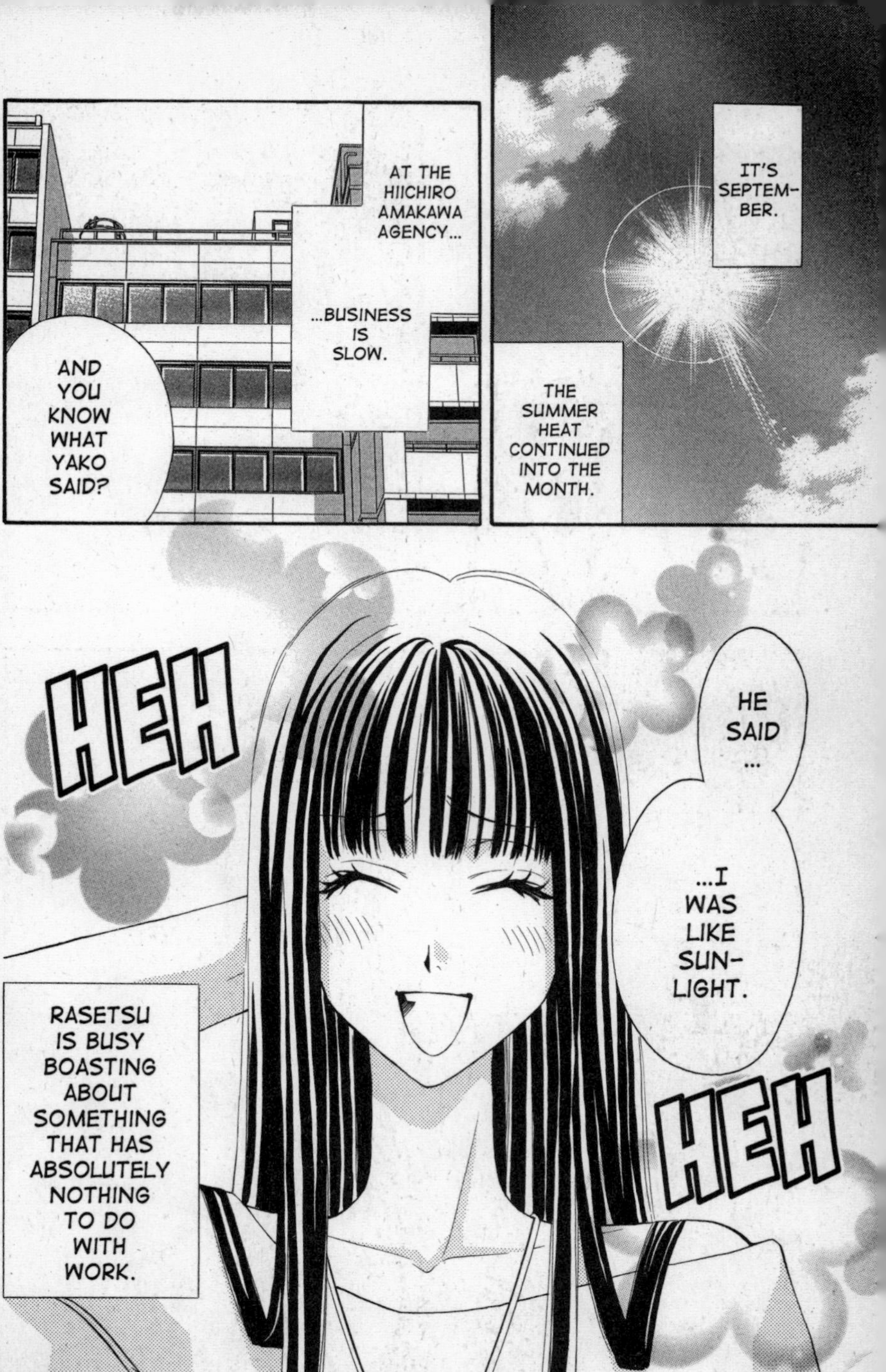
IT'S SEPTEMBER.
THE SUMMER HEAT CONTINUED INTO THE MONTH.
AT THE HIICHIRO AMAKAWA AGENCY...
...BUSINESS IS SLOW.
AND YOU KNOW WHAT YAKO SAID?
HE SAID...
...I WAS LIKE SUNLIGHT.
HEH
HEH
RASETSU IS BUSY BOASTING ABOUT SOMETHING THAT HAS ABSOLUTELY NOTHING TO DO WITH WORK.

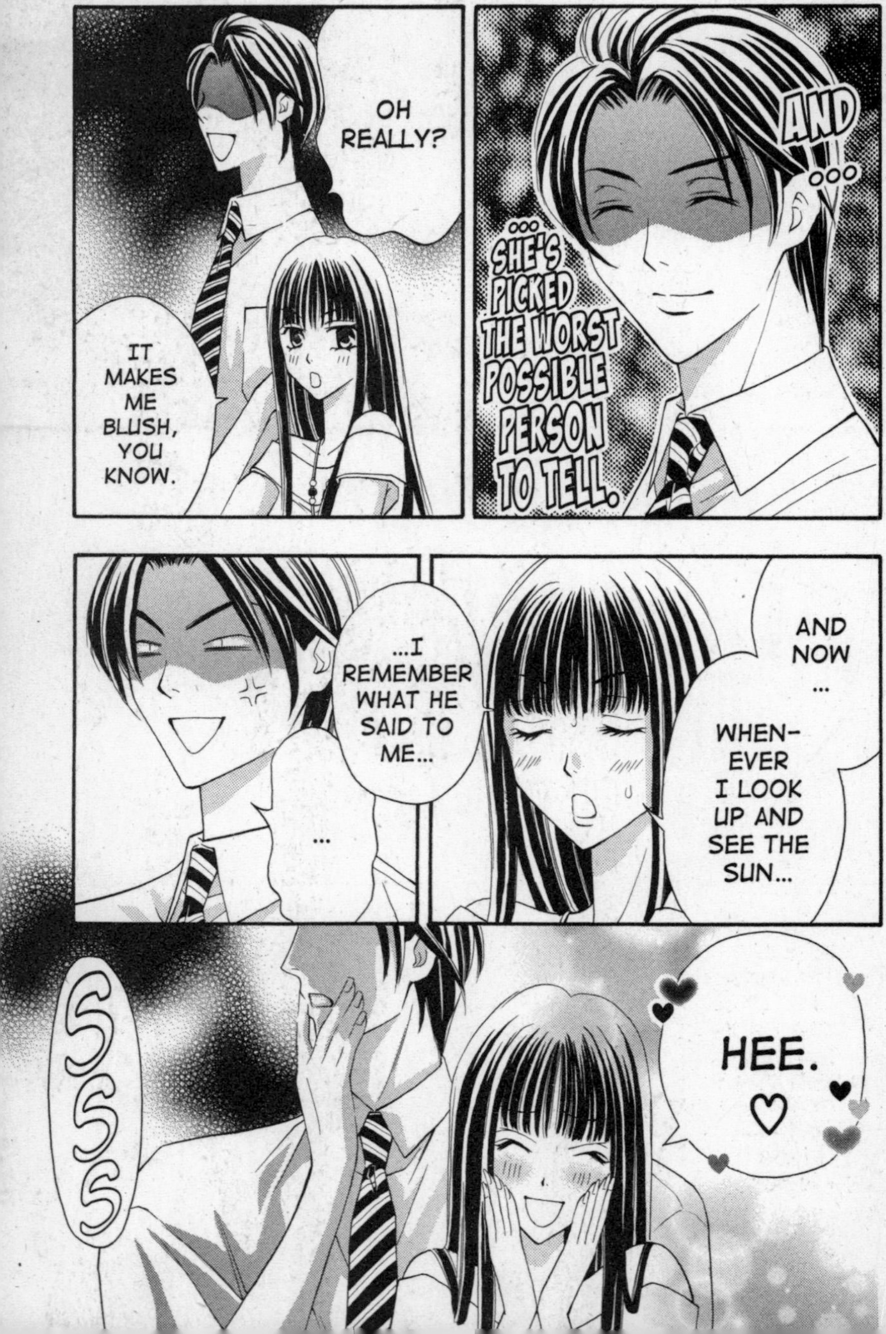
AND...
...SHE'S PICKED THE WORST POSSIBLE PERSON TO TELL.
OH REALLY?
IT MAKES ME BLUSH, YOU KNOW.
AND NOW...
WHEN-EVER I LOOK UP AND SEE THE SUN...
...I REMEMBER WHAT HE SAID TO ME...
...
HEE. ♡
SSSS

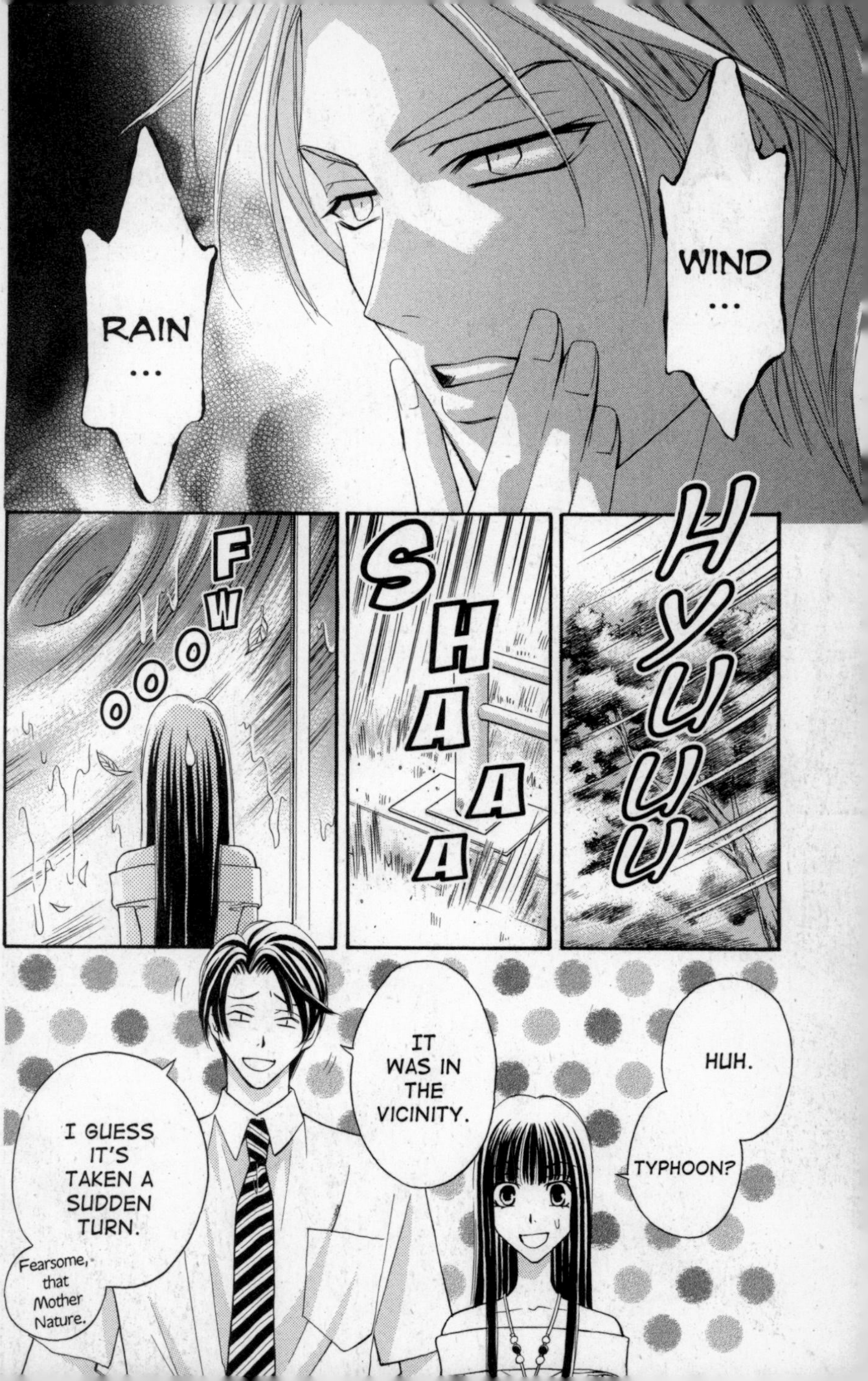
WIND ...
RAIN ...
HYUUUU
SHAAA
FWOOO
HUH.
TYPHOON?
IT WAS IN THE VICINITY.
I GUESS IT'S TAKEN A SUDDEN TURN.
Fearsome, that Mother Nature.

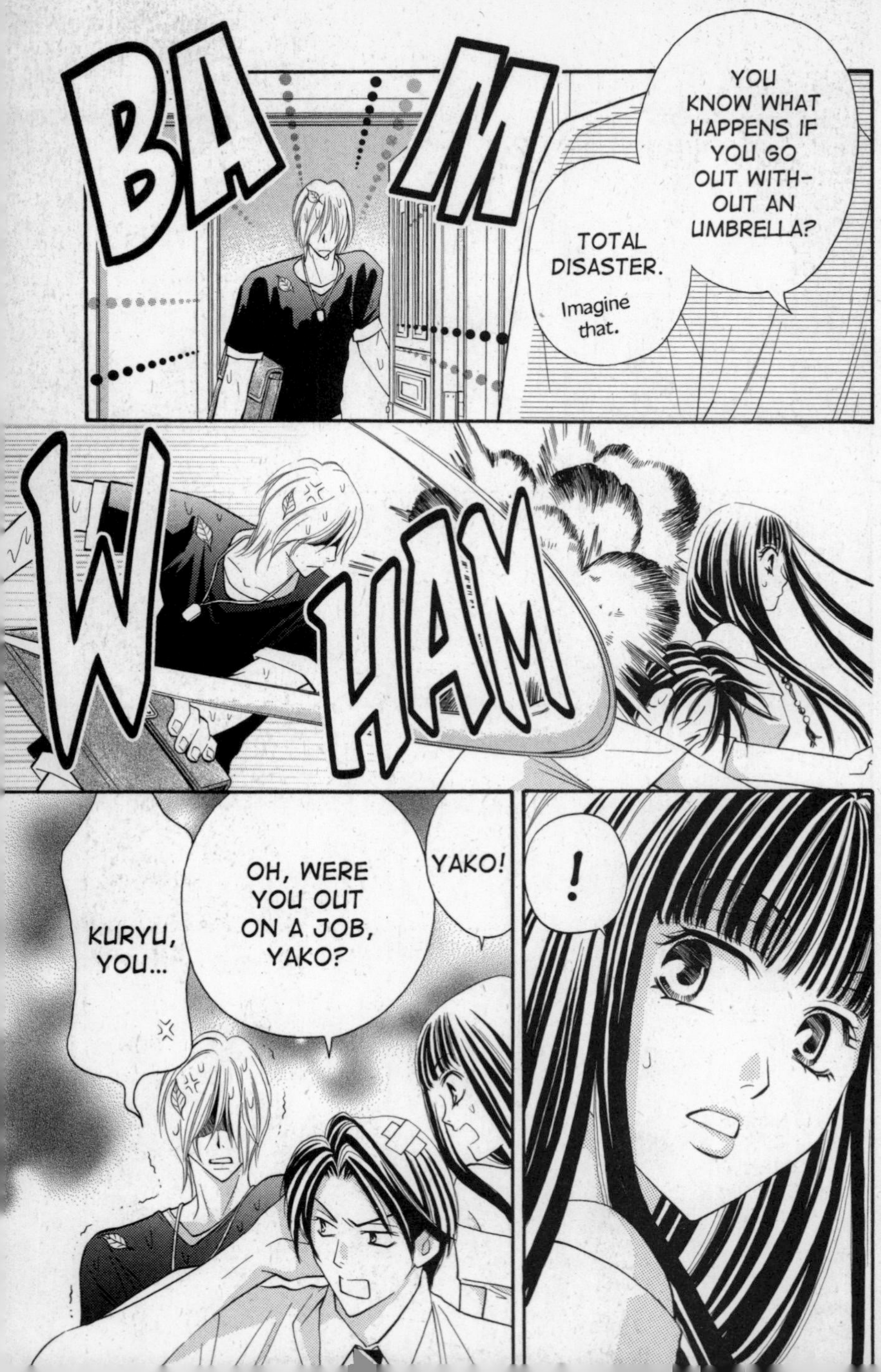

YOU KNOW WHAT HAPPENS IF YOU GO OUT WITH-OUT AN UMBRELLA?
TOTAL DISASTER.
Imagine that.
BAM
WHAM
!
YAKO!
OH, WERE YOU OUT ON A JOB, YAKO?
KURYU, YOU...

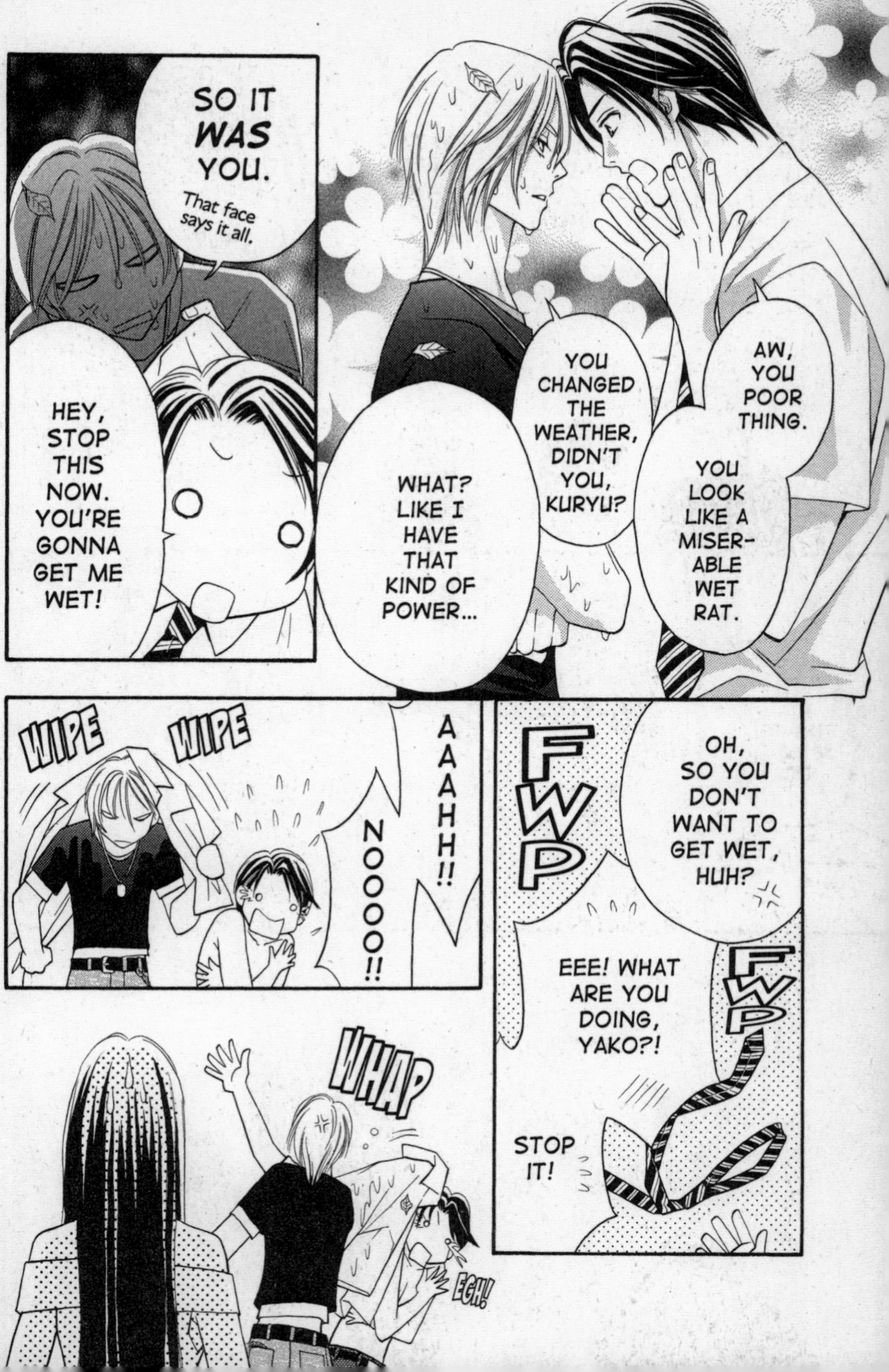
AW, YOU POOR THING.
YOU LOOK LIKE A MISER-ABLE WET RAT.
YOU CHANGED THE WEATHER, DIDN'T YOU, KURYU?
WHAT? LIKE I HAVE THAT KIND OF POWER...
SO IT WAS YOU.
That face says it all.
HEY, STOP THIS NOW. YOU'RE GONNA GET ME WET!
FWP
OH, SO YOU DON'T WANT TO GET WET, HUH?
FWP
EEE! WHAT ARE YOU DOING, YAKO?!
STOP IT!
AAAHH!!
NOOOO!!
WIPE
WIPE
WHAP
EGH!

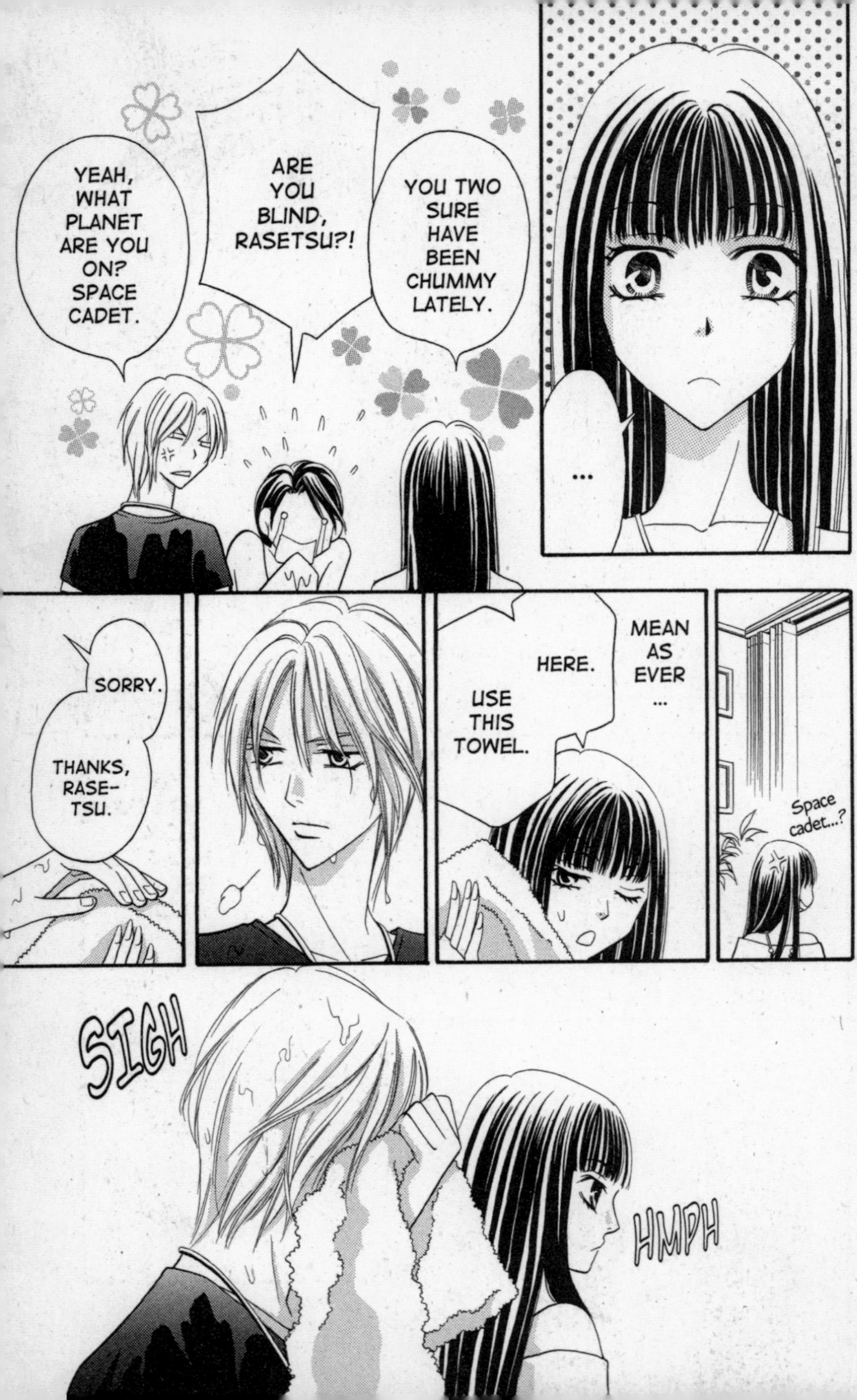
...
YOU TWO SURE HAVE BEEN CHUMMY LATELY.
ARE YOU BLIND, RASETSU?!
YEAH, WHAT PLANET ARE YOU ON? SPACE CADET.
Space cadet...?
MEAN AS EVER...
HERE.
USE THIS TOWEL.
SORRY.
THANKS, RASE-TSU.
HMPH
SIGH

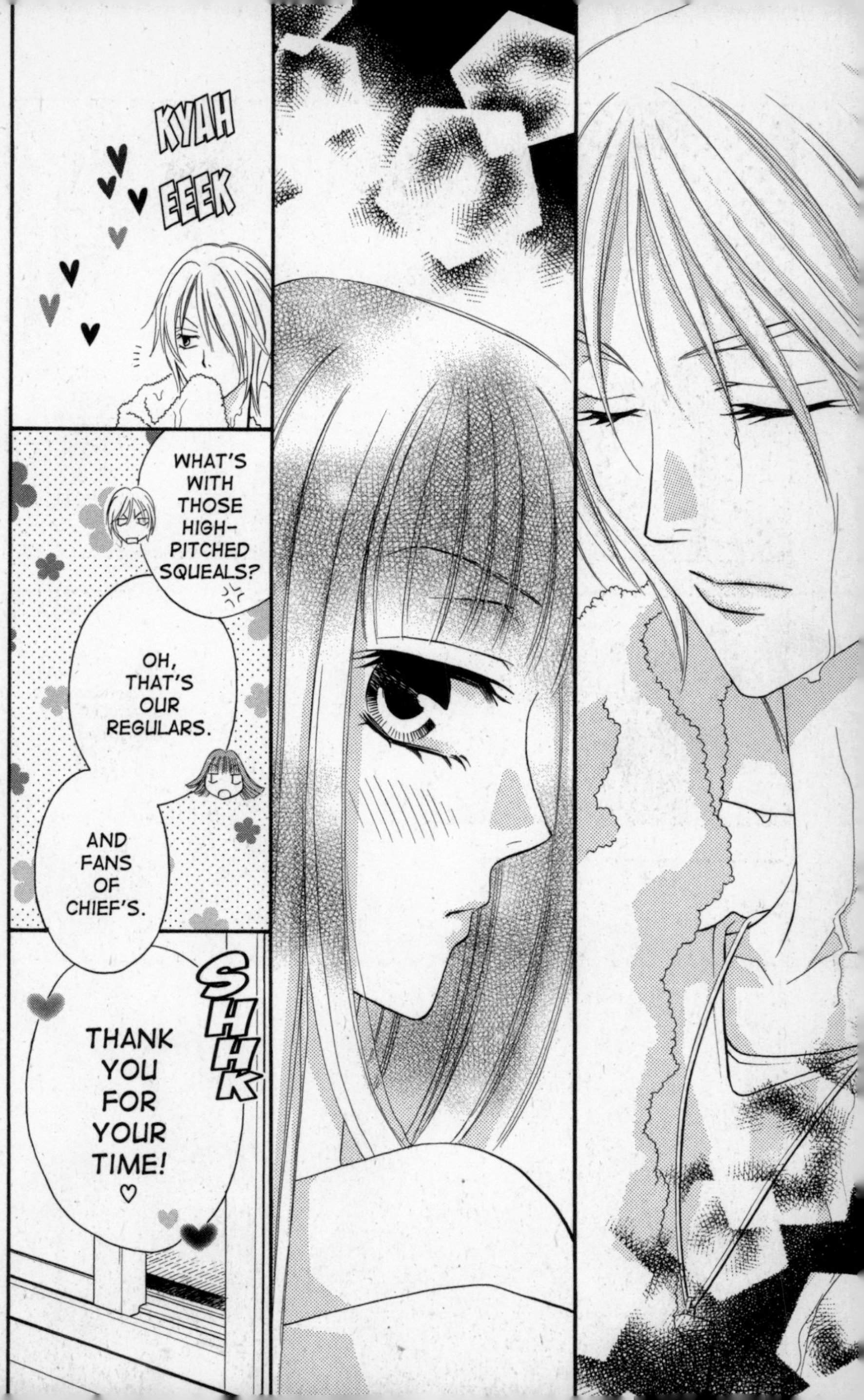
KYAH
EEEK
WHAT'S WITH THOSE HIGH-PITCHED SQUEALS?
OH, THAT'S OUR REGULARS.
AND FANS OF CHIEF'S.
SHHK
THANK YOU FOR YOUR TIME! ♡

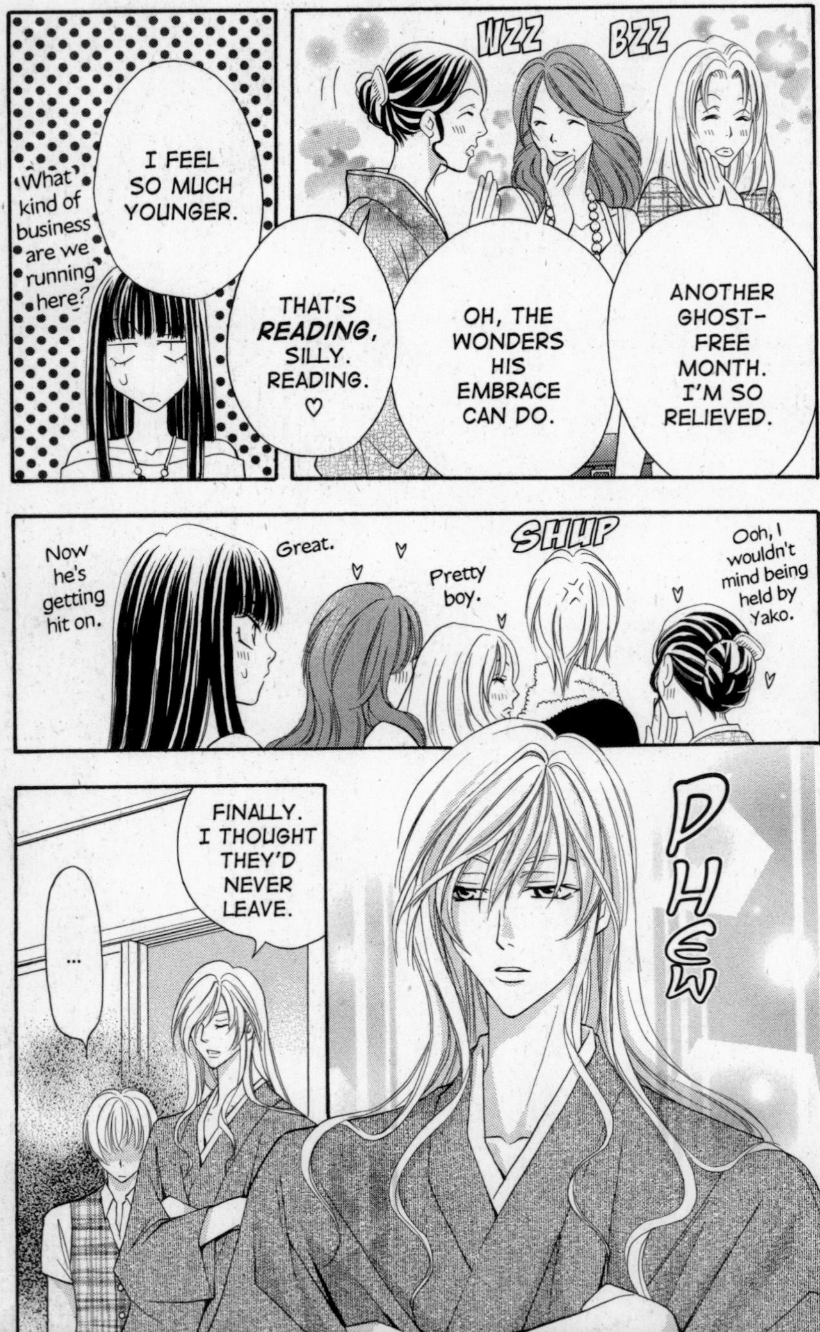
WZZ
BZZ
ANOTHER GHOST-FREE MONTH. I'M SO RELIEVED.
OH, THE WONDERS HIS EMBRACE CAN DO.
THAT'S *READING*, SILLY. READING. ♡
I FEEL SO MUCH YOUNGER.
What kind of business are we running here?
SHUP
Ooh, I wouldn't mind being held by Yako.
Pretty boy.
Great.
Now he's getting hit on.
DPHEW
FINALLY. I THOUGHT THEY'D NEVER LEAVE.
...

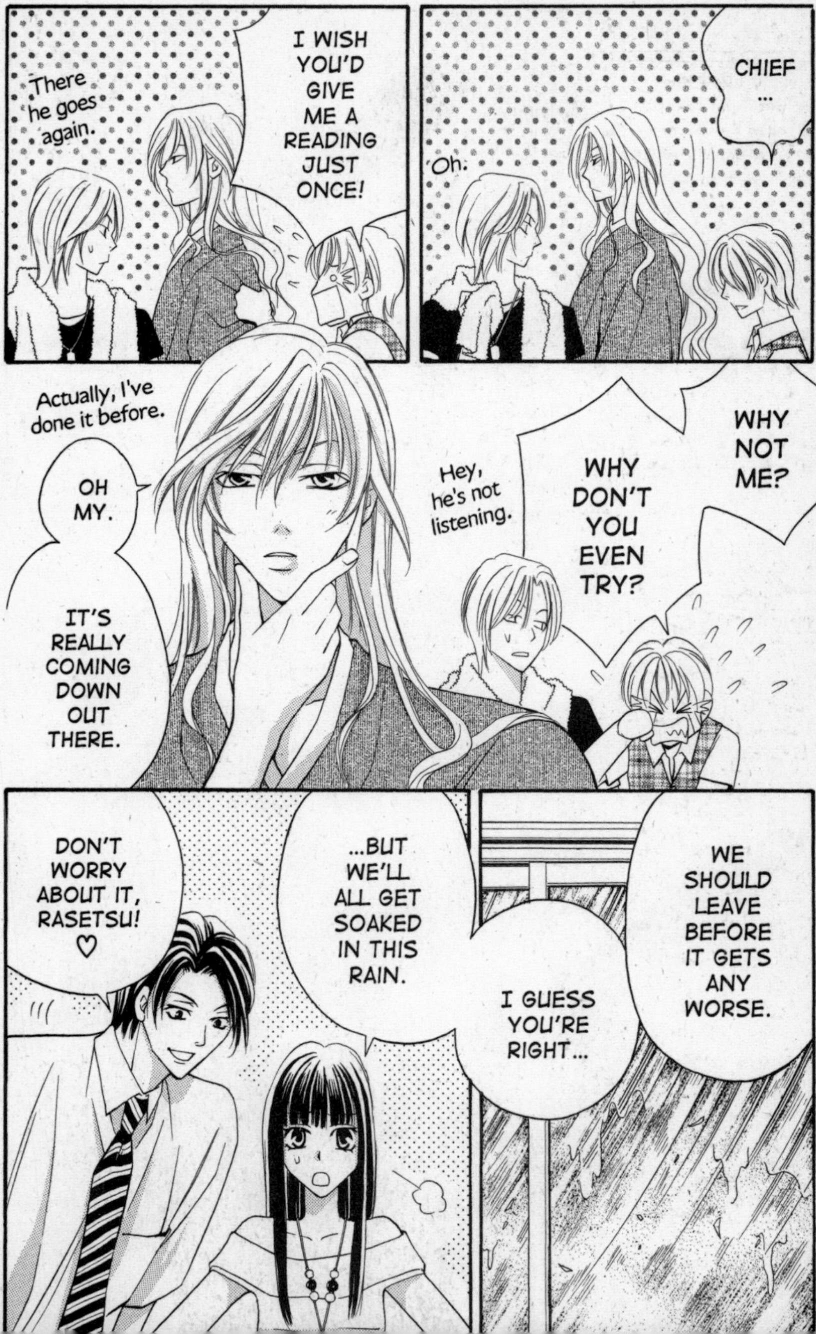
CHIEF ...
Oh.
I WISH YOU'D GIVE ME A READING JUST ONCE!
There he goes again.
WHY NOT ME?
WHY DON'T YOU EVEN TRY?
Hey, he's not listening.
Actually, I've done it before.
OH MY.
IT'S REALLY COMING DOWN OUT THERE.
WE SHOULD LEAVE BEFORE IT GETS ANY WORSE.
I GUESS YOU'RE RIGHT...
...BUT WE'LL ALL GET SOAKED IN THIS RAIN.
DON'T WORRY ABOUT IT, RASETSU! ♡

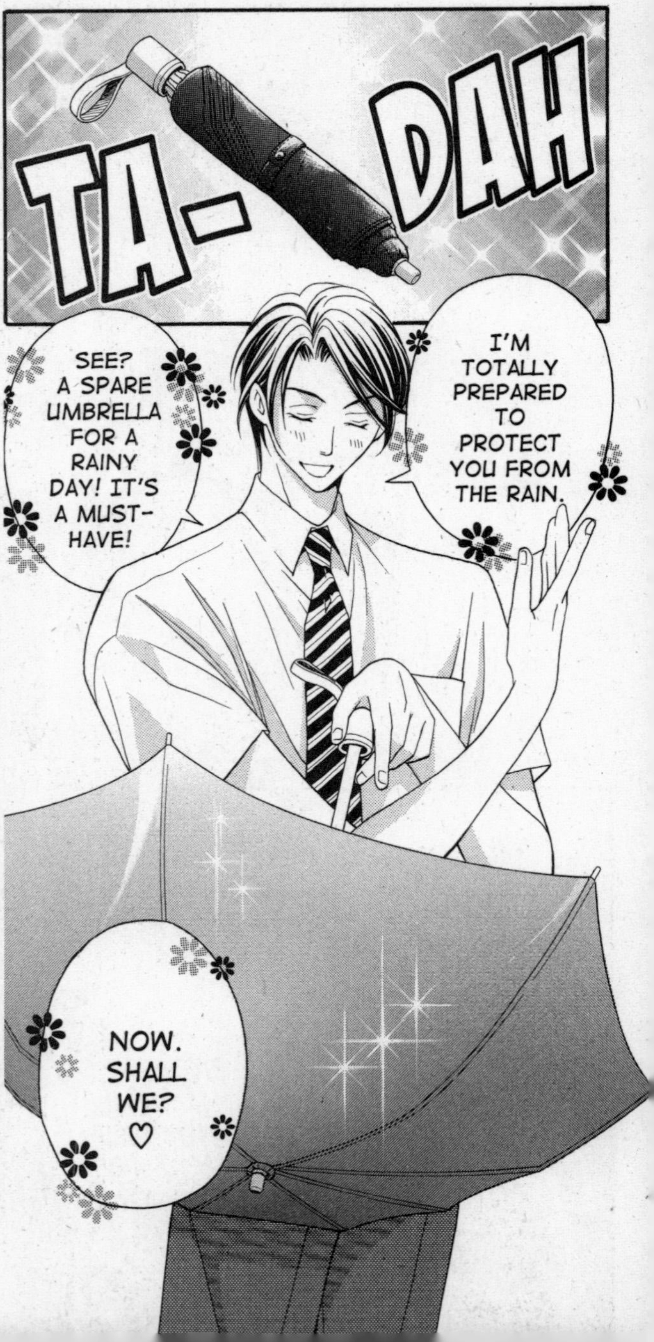
TA-DAH
I'M TOTALLY PREPARED TO PROTECT YOU FROM THE RAIN.
SEE? A SPARE UMBRELLA FOR A RAINY DAY! IT'S A MUST-HAVE!
NOW. SHALL WE? ♡

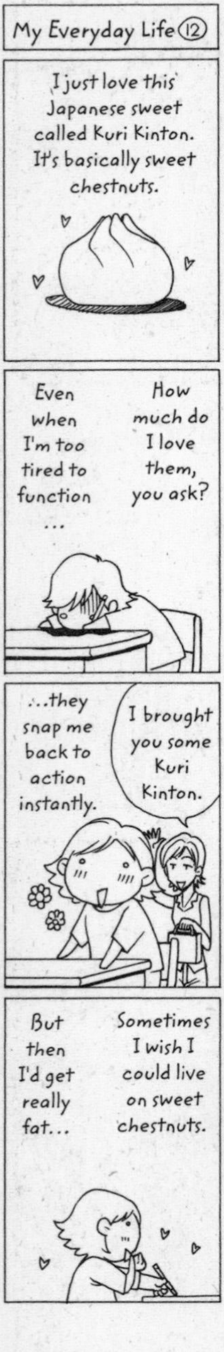
My Everyday Life ⑫
I just love this Japanese sweet called Kuri Kinton. It's basically sweet chestnuts.
How much do I love them, you ask?
Even when I'm too tired to function...
I brought you some Kuri Kinton.
...they snap me back to action instantly.
Sometimes I wish I could live on sweet chestnuts.
But then I'd get really fat...

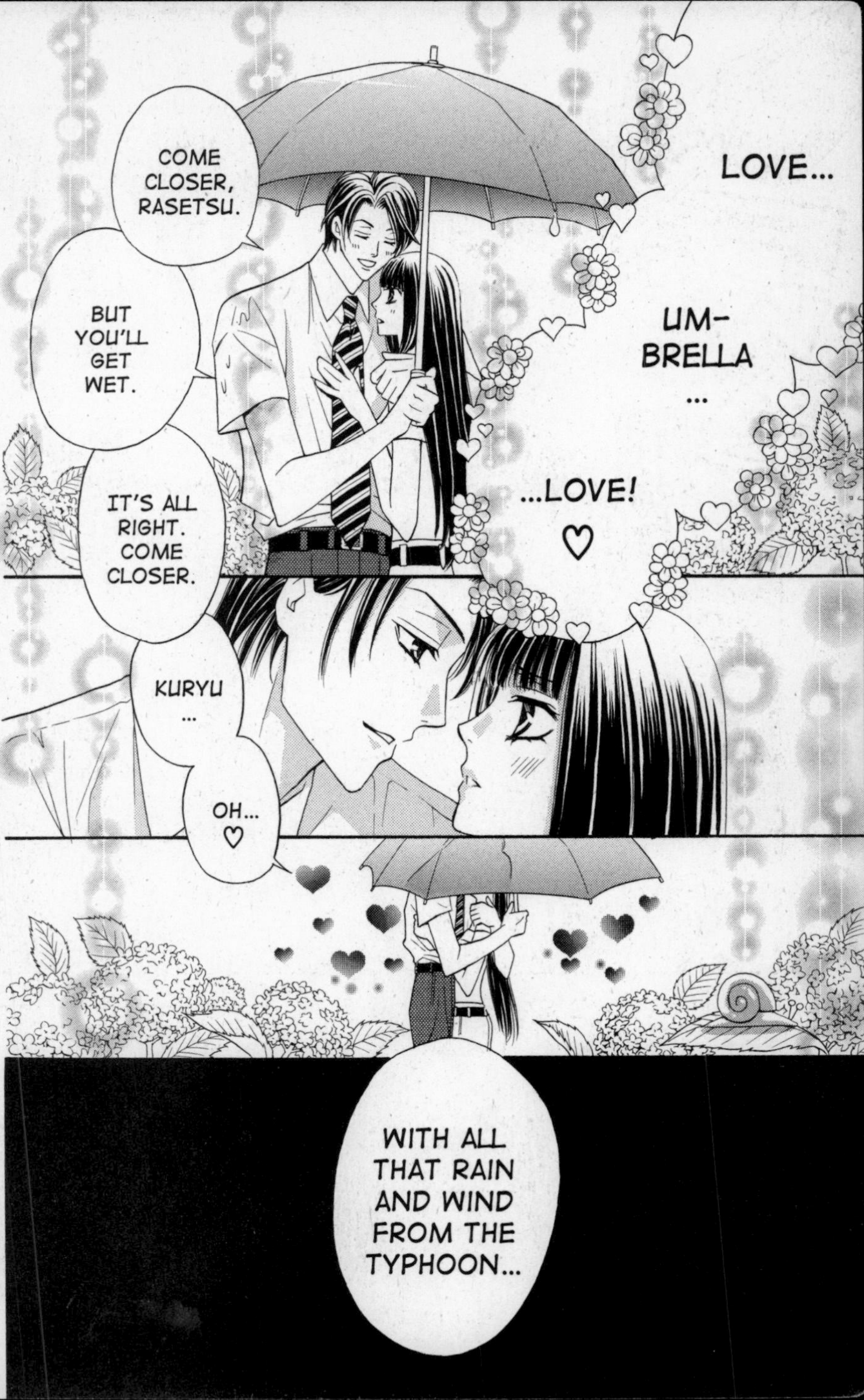
LOVE...
UM-BRELLA...
...LOVE! ♡
COME CLOSER, RASETSU.
BUT YOU'LL GET WET.
IT'S ALL RIGHT. COME CLOSER.
KURYU...
OH... ♡
WITH ALL THAT RAIN AND WIND FROM THE TYPHOON...

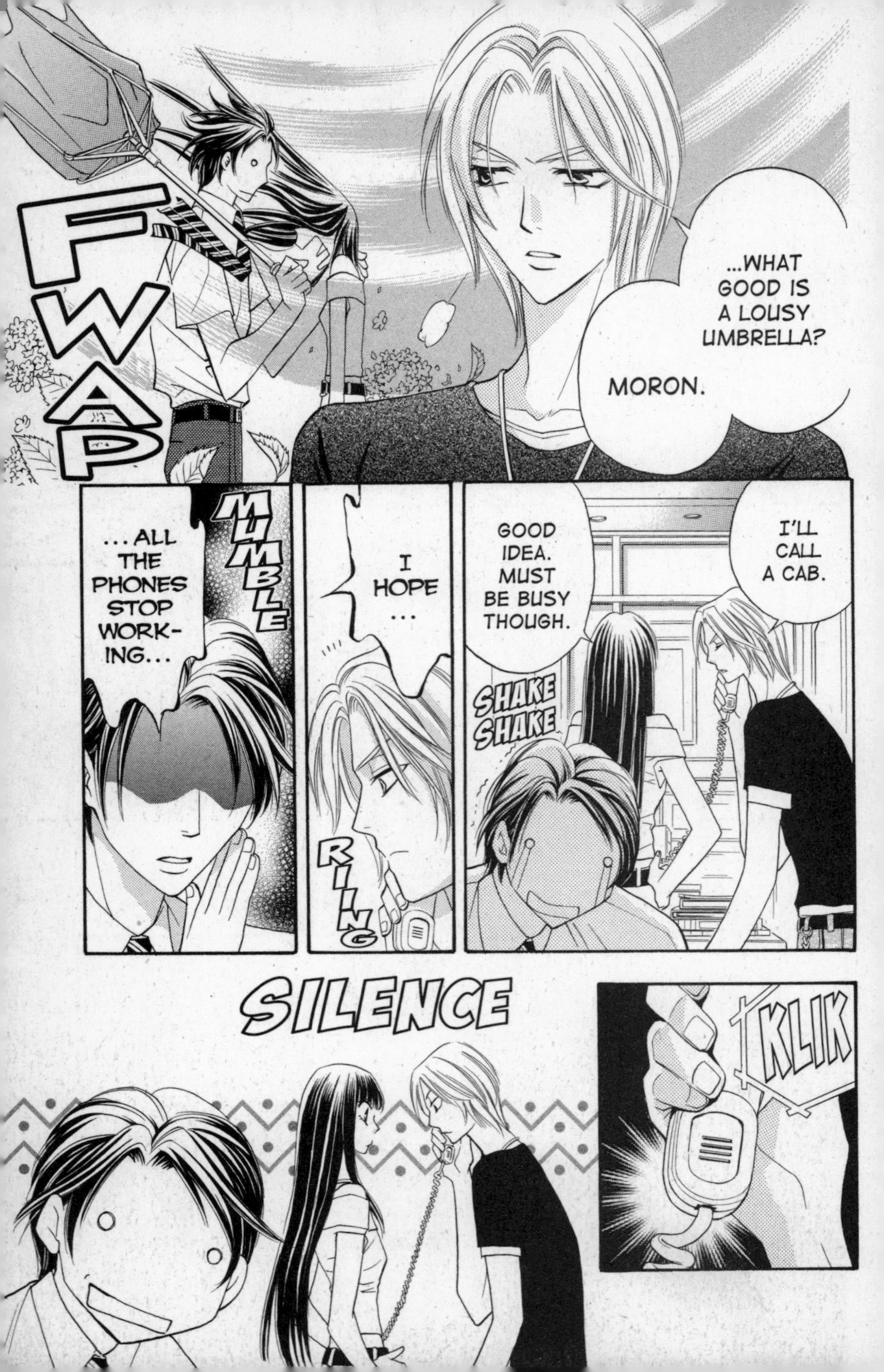
...WHAT GOOD IS A LOUSY UMBRELLA?
MORON.
FWAP
I'LL CALL A CAB.
GOOD IDEA. MUST BE BUSY THOUGH.
SHAKE SHAKE
I HOPE ...
RIING
MUMBLE
... ALL THE PHONES STOP WORK- ING...
KLIK
SILENCE

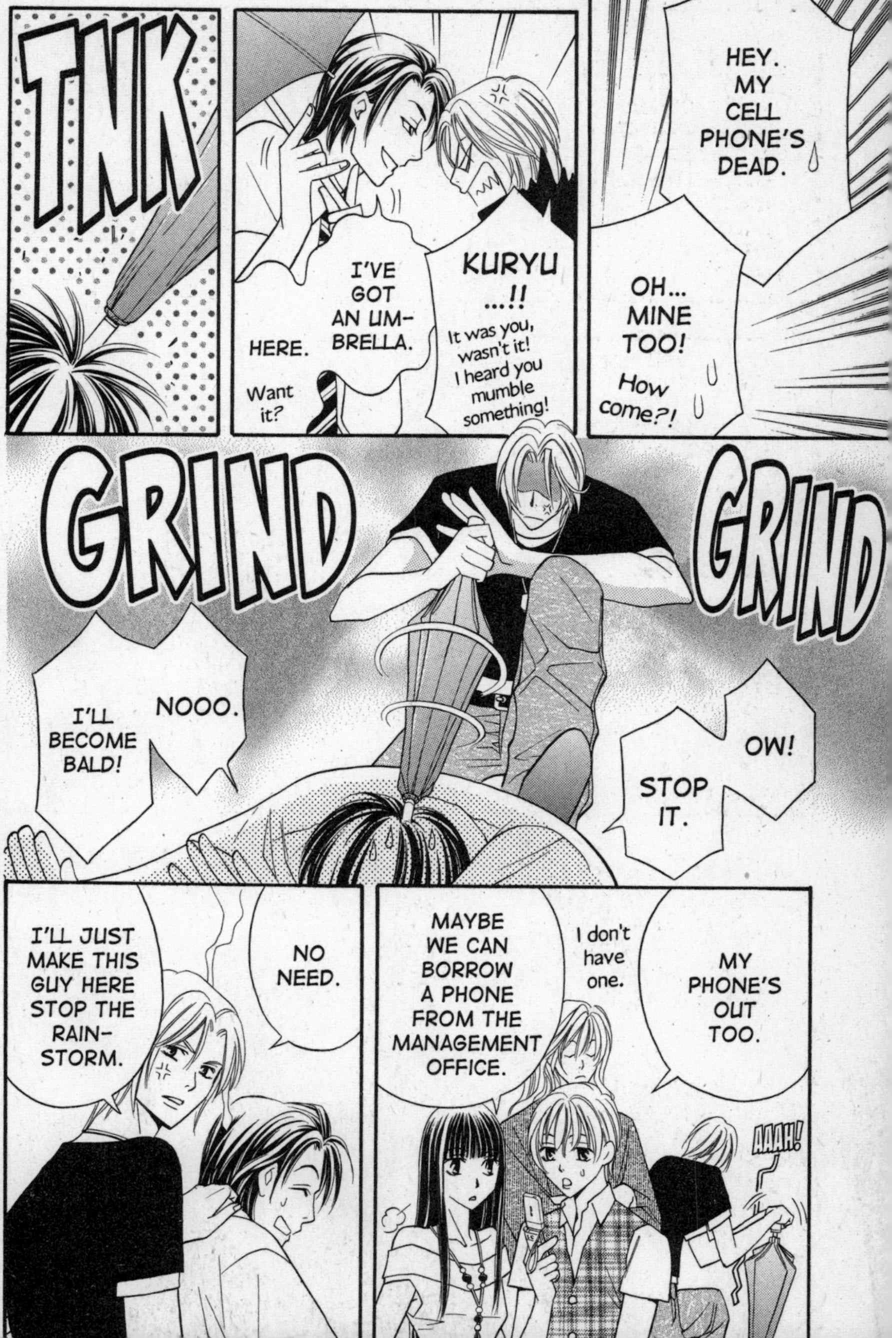
HEY. MY CELL PHONE'S DEAD.
OH... MINE TOO!
How come?!
KURYU ...!!
It was you, wasn't it! I heard you mumble something!
I'VE GOT AN UMBRELLA.
HERE.
Want it?
TNK
GRIND
GRIND
OW!
STOP IT.
NOOO.
I'LL BECOME BALD!
MY PHONE'S OUT TOO.
I don't have one.
MAYBE WE CAN BORROW A PHONE FROM THE MANAGEMENT OFFICE.
AAAH!
NO NEED.
I'LL JUST MAKE THIS GUY HERE STOP THE RAINSTORM.

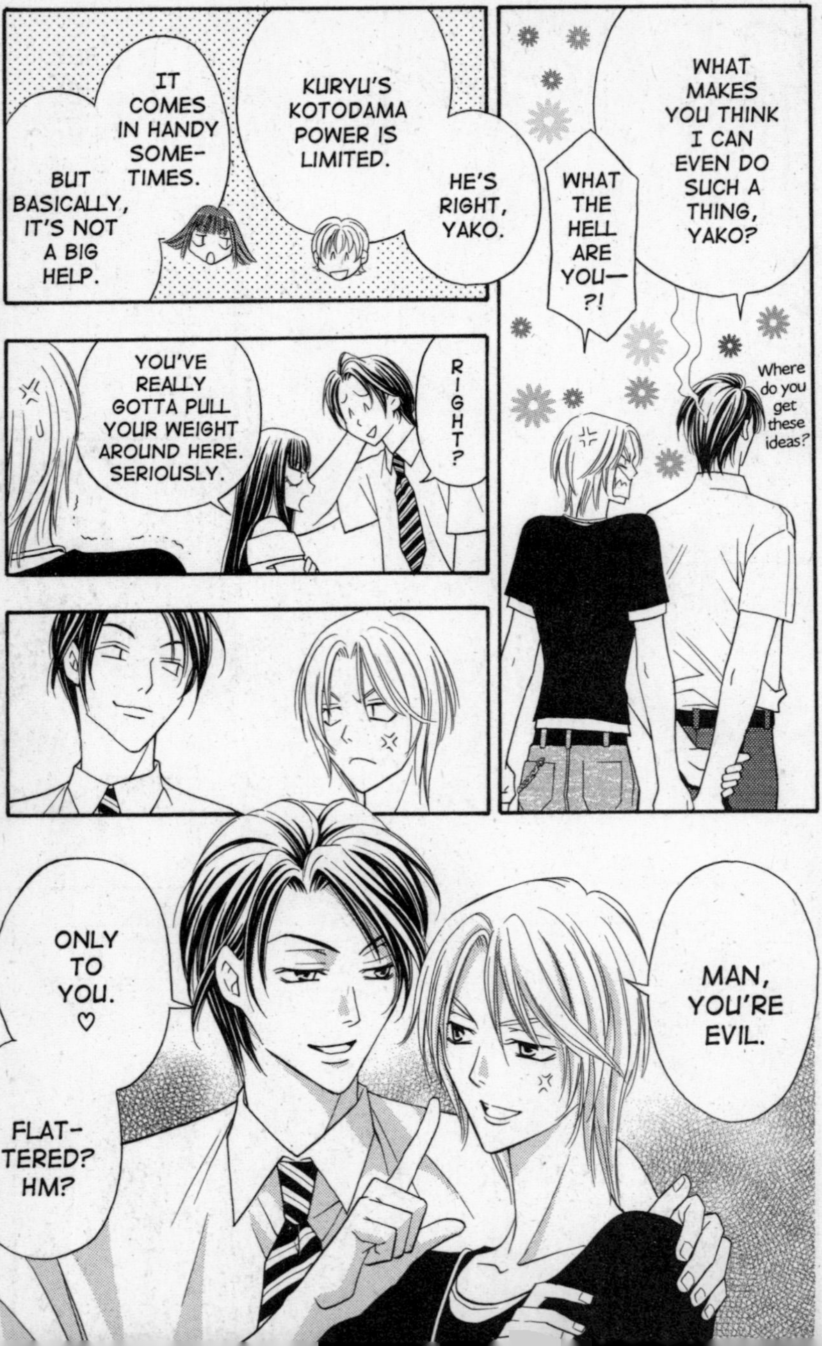
WHAT MAKES YOU THINK I CAN EVEN DO SUCH A THING, YAKO?
WHAT THE HELL ARE YOU—?!
Where do you get these ideas?
HE'S RIGHT, YAKO.
KURYU'S KOTODAMA POWER IS LIMITED.
IT COMES IN HANDY SOME-TIMES.
BUT BASICALLY, IT'S NOT A BIG HELP.
RIGHT?
YOU'VE REALLY GOTTA PULL YOUR WEIGHT AROUND HERE. SERIOUSLY.
MAN, YOU'RE EVIL.
ONLY TO YOU. ♡
FLAT-TERED? HM?

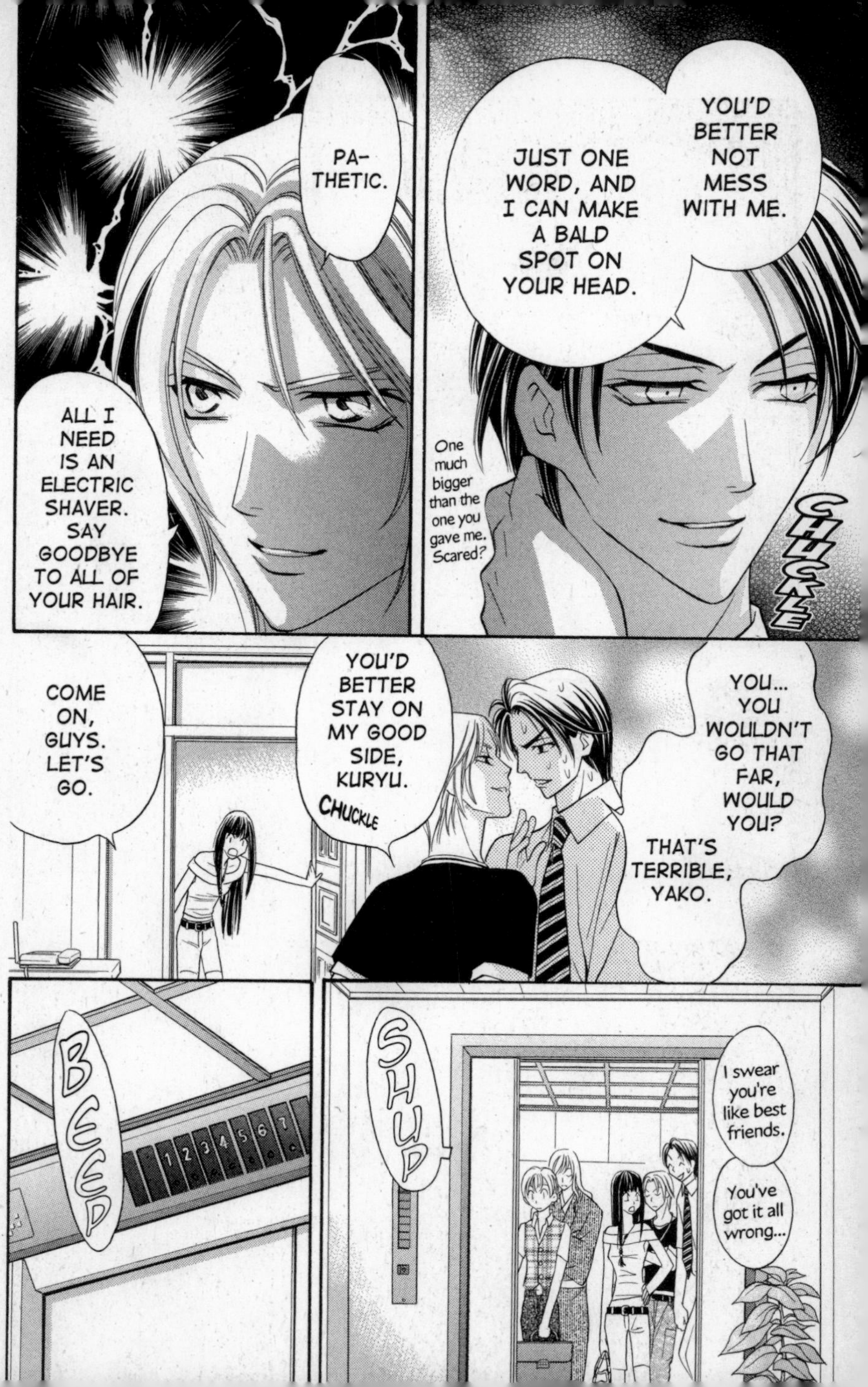
YOU'D BETTER NOT MESS WITH ME.
JUST ONE WORD, AND I CAN MAKE A BALD SPOT ON YOUR HEAD.
One much bigger than the one you gave me. Scared?
CHUCKLE
PA-THETIC.
ALL I NEED IS AN ELECTRIC SHAVER. SAY GOODBYE TO ALL OF YOUR HAIR.
YOU... YOU WOULDN'T GO THAT FAR, WOULD YOU?
THAT'S TERRIBLE, YAKO.
YOU'D BETTER STAY ON MY GOOD SIDE, KURYU.
CHUCKLE
COME ON, GUYS. LET'S GO.
SHUP
I swear you're like best friends.
You've got it all wrong...
BEEP

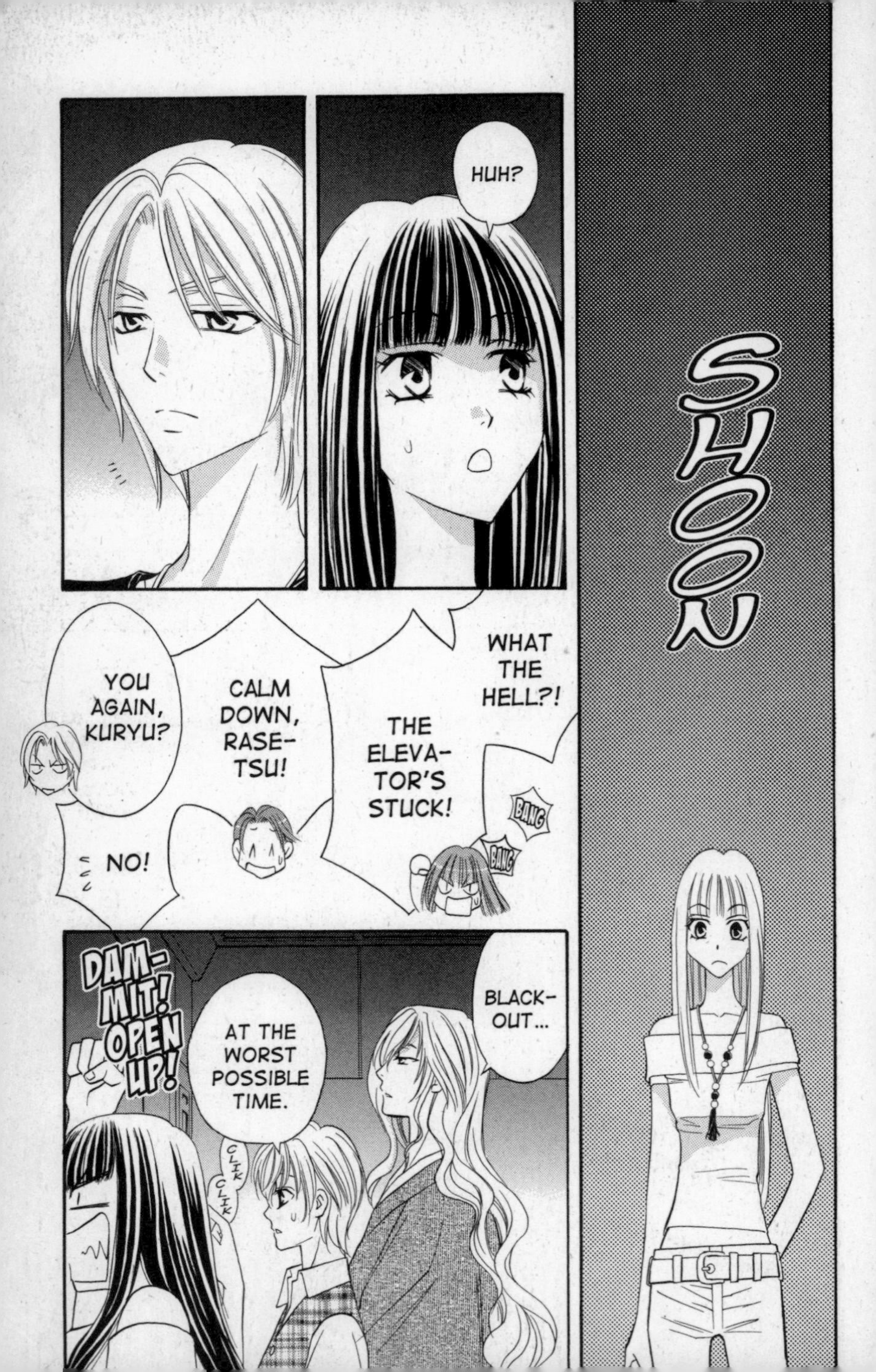
SHOON
HUH?
WHAT THE HELL?!
BANG
BANG
THE ELEVA-TOR'S STUCK!
CALM DOWN, RASE-TSU!
YOU AGAIN, KURYU?
NO!
BLACK-OUT...
AT THE WORST POSSIBLE TIME.
CLIK CLIK
DAM-MIT! OPEN UP!

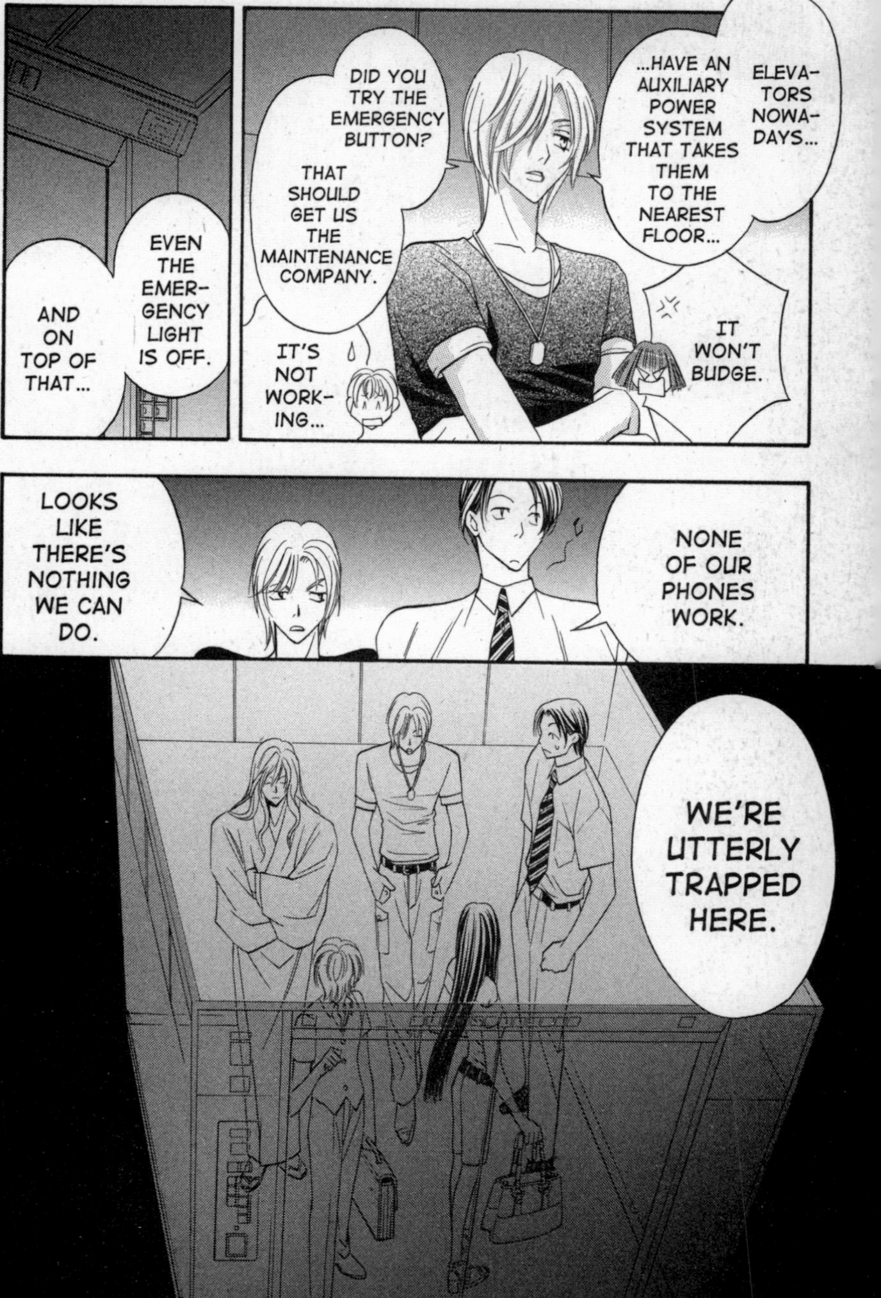
ELEVATORS NOWADAYS...
...HAVE AN AUXILIARY POWER SYSTEM THAT TAKES THEM TO THE NEAREST FLOOR...
DID YOU TRY THE EMERGENCY BUTTON?
THAT SHOULD GET US THE MAINTENANCE COMPANY.
IT WON'T BUDGE.
IT'S NOT WORKING...
EVEN THE EMERGENCY LIGHT IS OFF.
AND ON TOP OF THAT...
NONE OF OUR PHONES WORK.
LOOKS LIKE THERE'S NOTHING WE CAN DO.
WE'RE UTTERLY TRAPPED HERE.

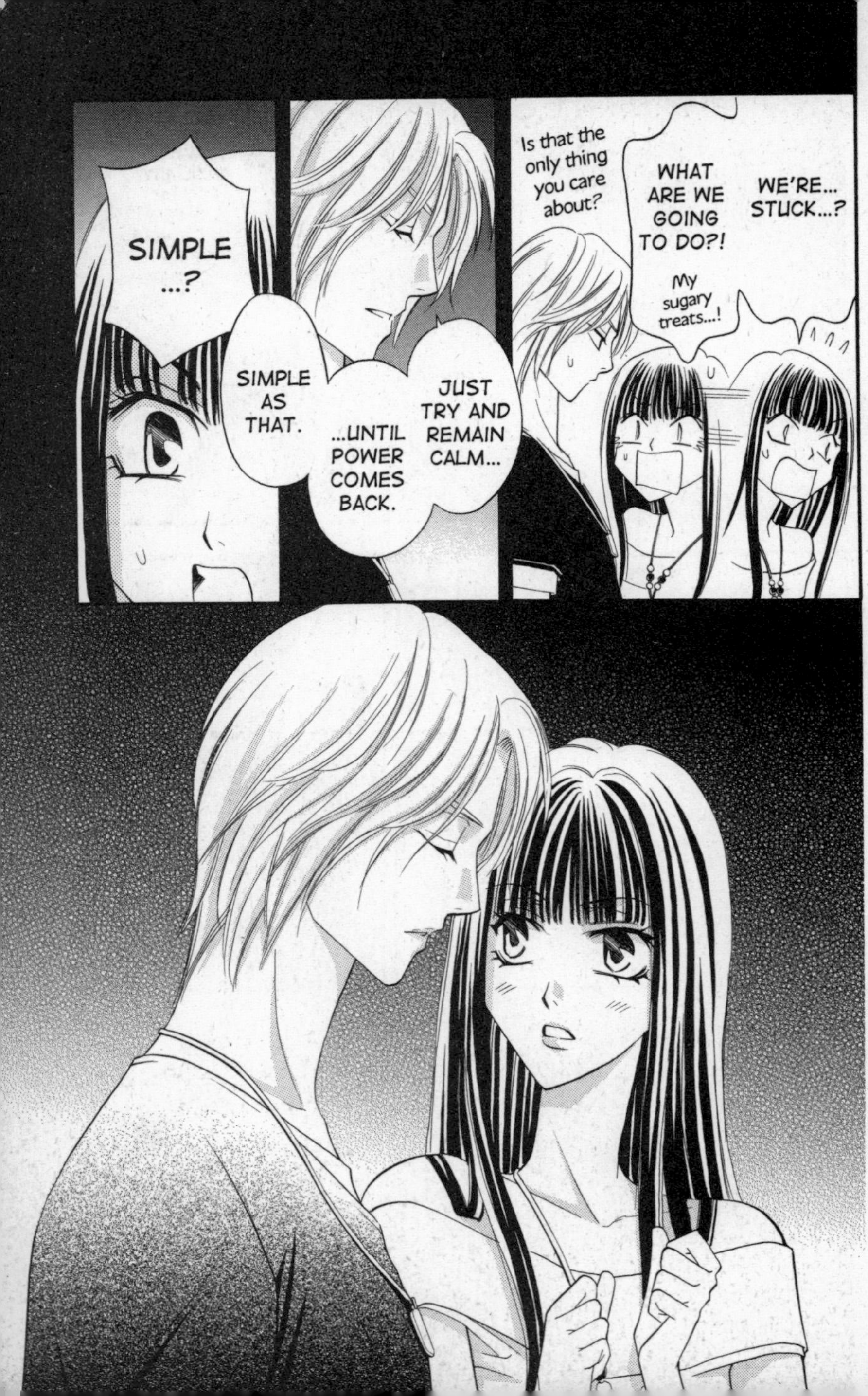
WE'RE... STUCK...?
WHAT ARE WE GOING TO DO?!
My sugary treats...!
Is that the only thing you care about?
JUST TRY AND REMAIN CALM...
...UNTIL POWER COMES BACK.
SIMPLE AS THAT.
SIMPLE ...?

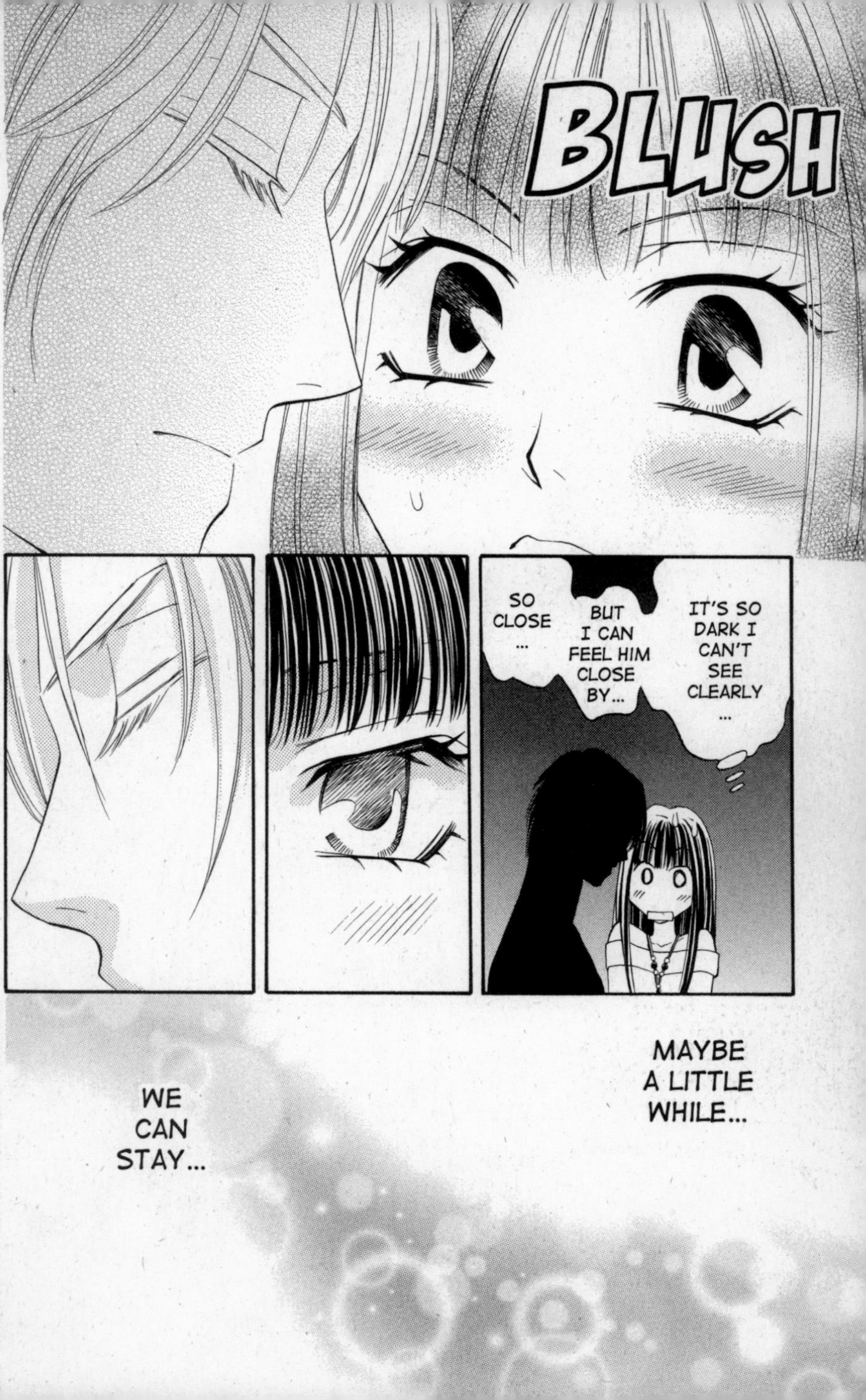
BLUSH
IT'S SO DARK I CAN'T SEE CLEARLY ...
BUT I CAN FEEL HIM CLOSE BY...
SO CLOSE ...
MAYBE A LITTLE WHILE...
WE CAN STAY...

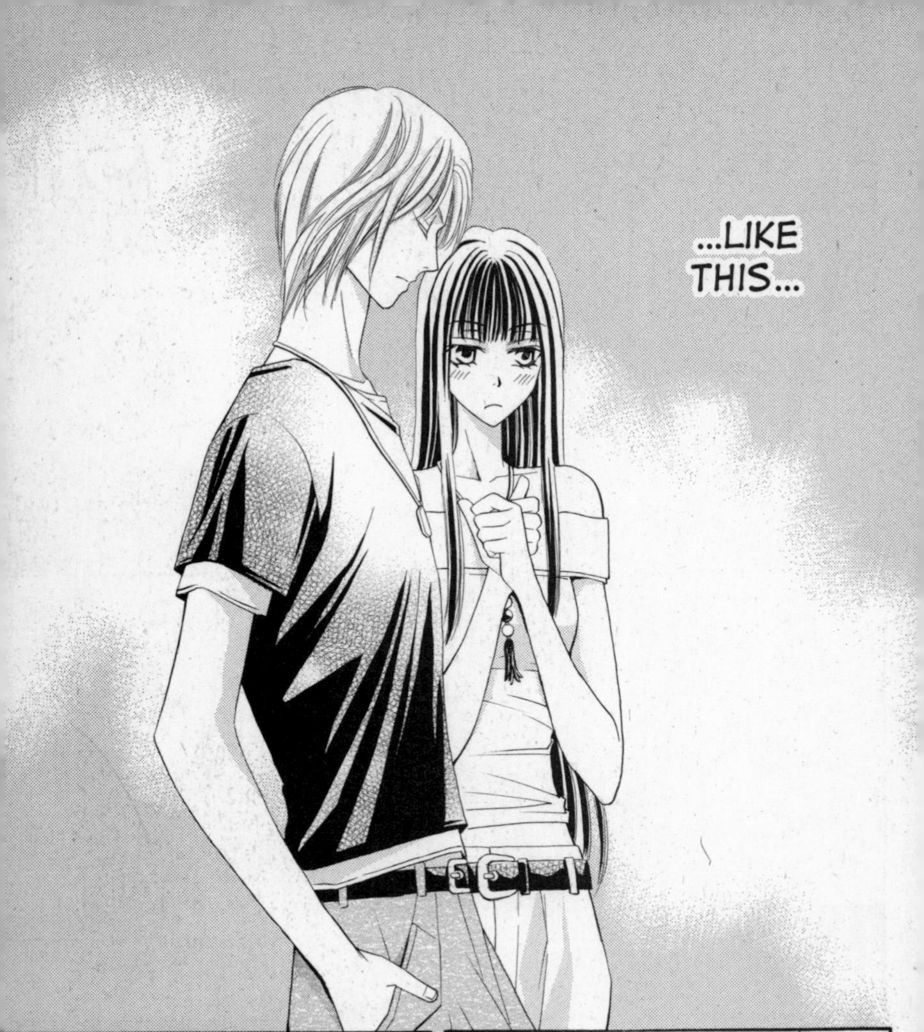
...LIKE
THIS...

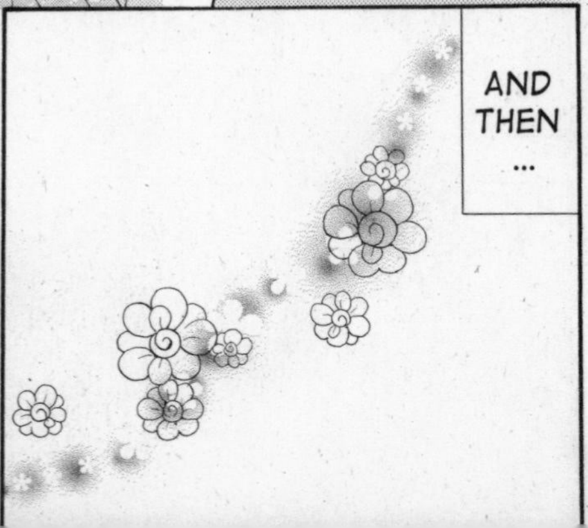
AND
THEN
...

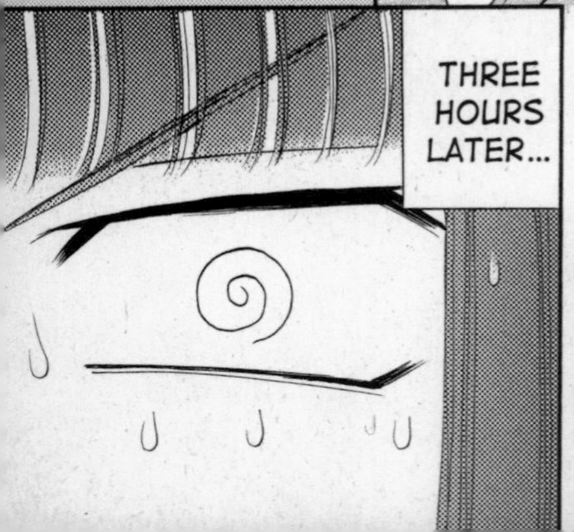
THREE
HOURS
LATER...

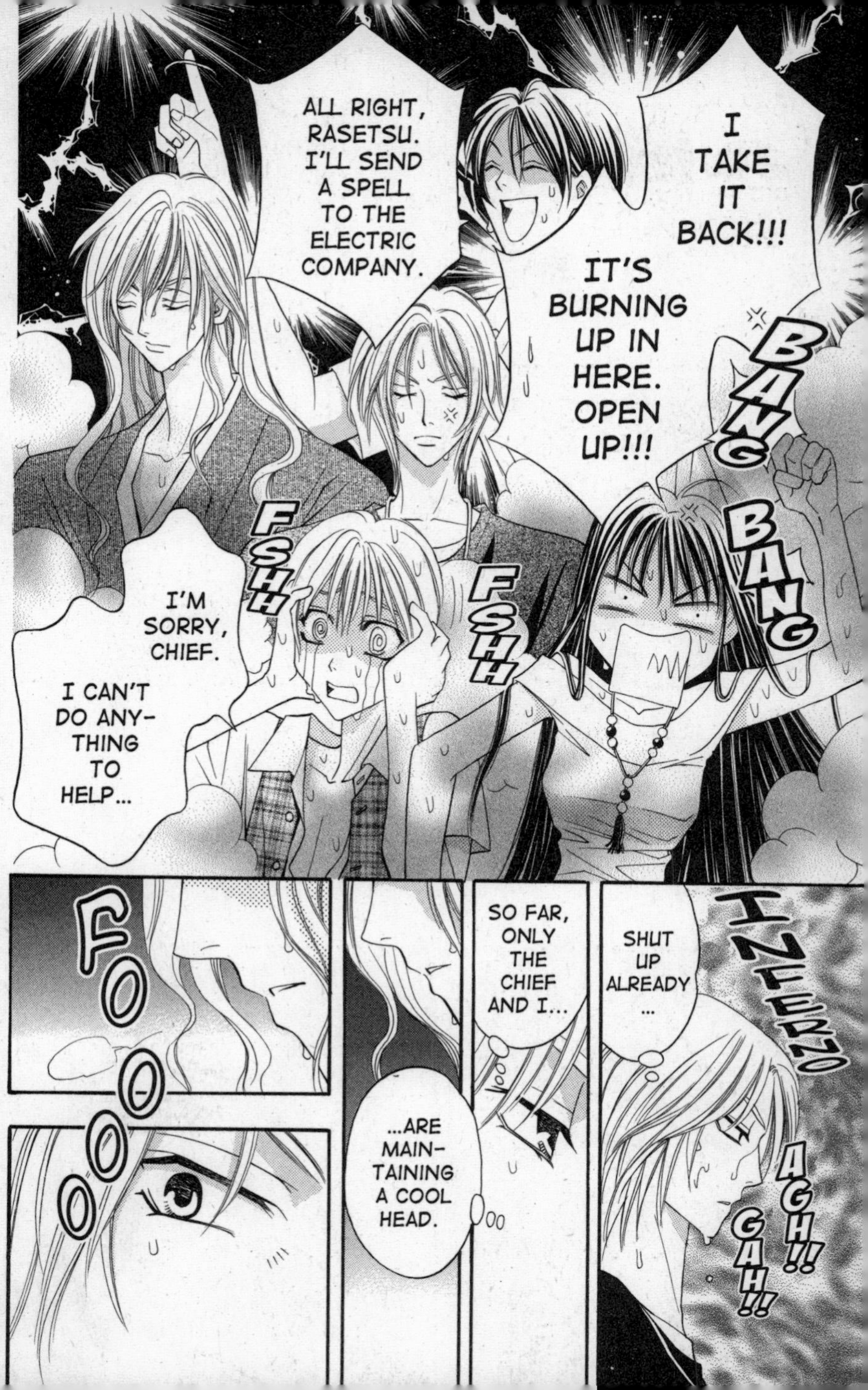
IT'S BURNING UP IN HERE. OPEN UP!!!
BANG BANG
I TAKE IT BACK!!!
ALL RIGHT, RASETSU. I'LL SEND A SPELL TO THE ELECTRIC COMPANY.
FSHH
FSHH
I'M SORRY, CHIEF.
I CAN'T DO ANY-THING TO HELP...
INFERNO
SHUT UP ALREADY ...
AGH GAH!!
SO FAR, ONLY THE CHIEF AND I...
...ARE MAIN-TAINING A COOL HEAD.
FOOOOO

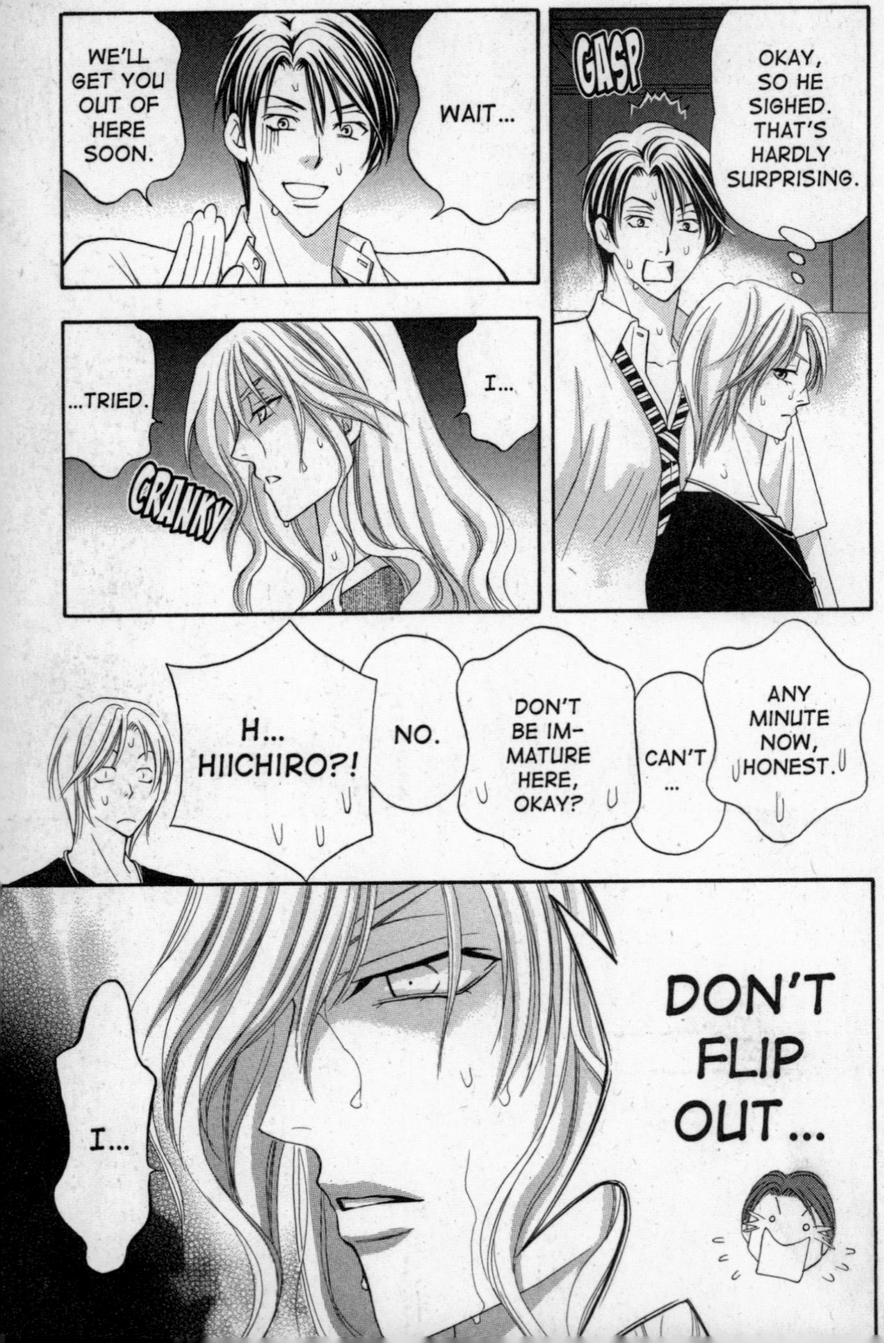
GASP
OKAY, SO HE SIGHED. THAT'S HARDLY SURPRISING.
WAIT...
WE'LL GET YOU OUT OF HERE SOON.
I...
CRANKY
...TRIED.
ANY MINUTE NOW, HONEST.
CAN'T...
DON'T BE IM-MATURE HERE, OKAY?
NO.
H... HIICHIRO?!
DON'T FLIP OUT...
I...

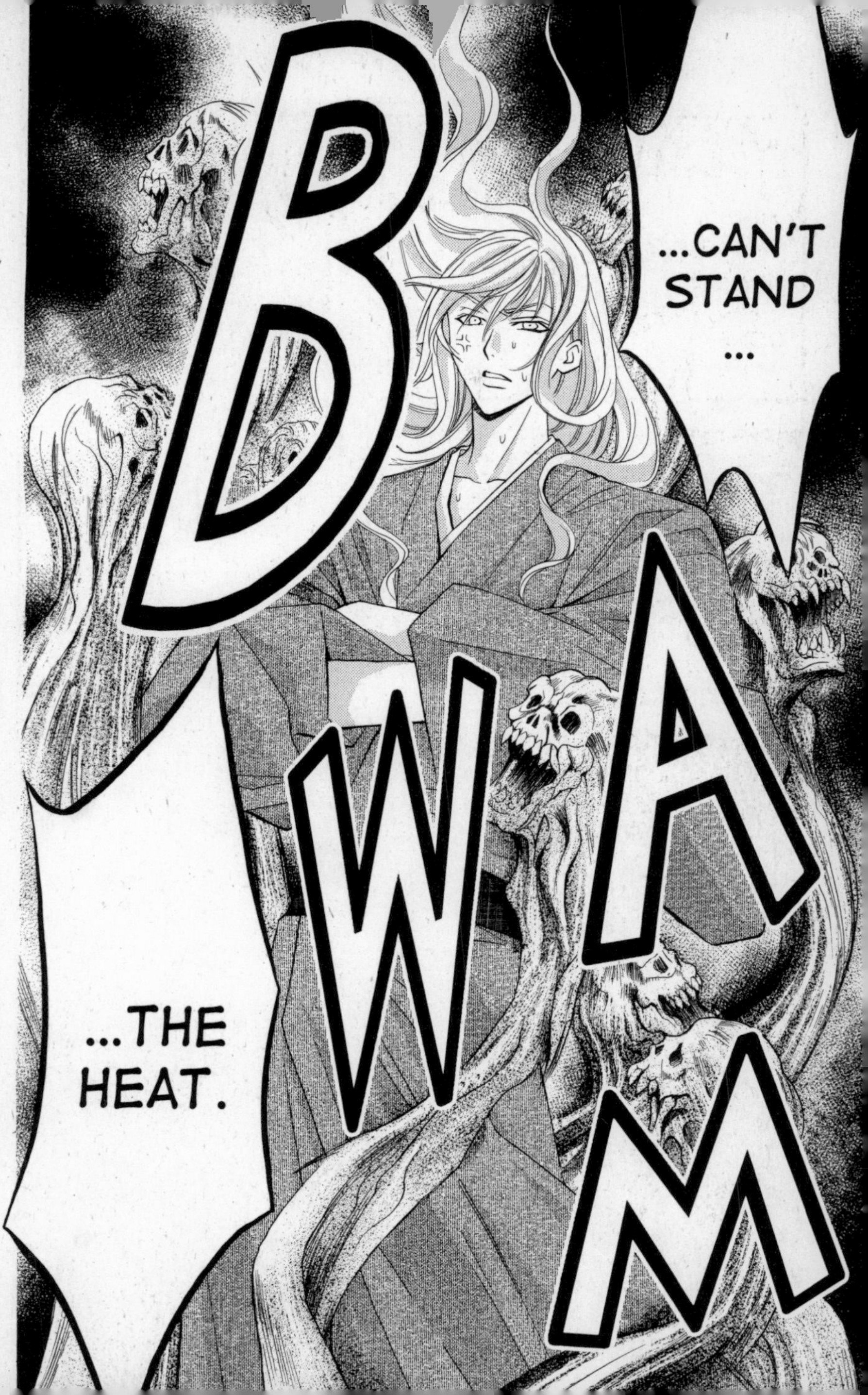
...CAN'T STAND ...
BWAM
...THE HEAT.

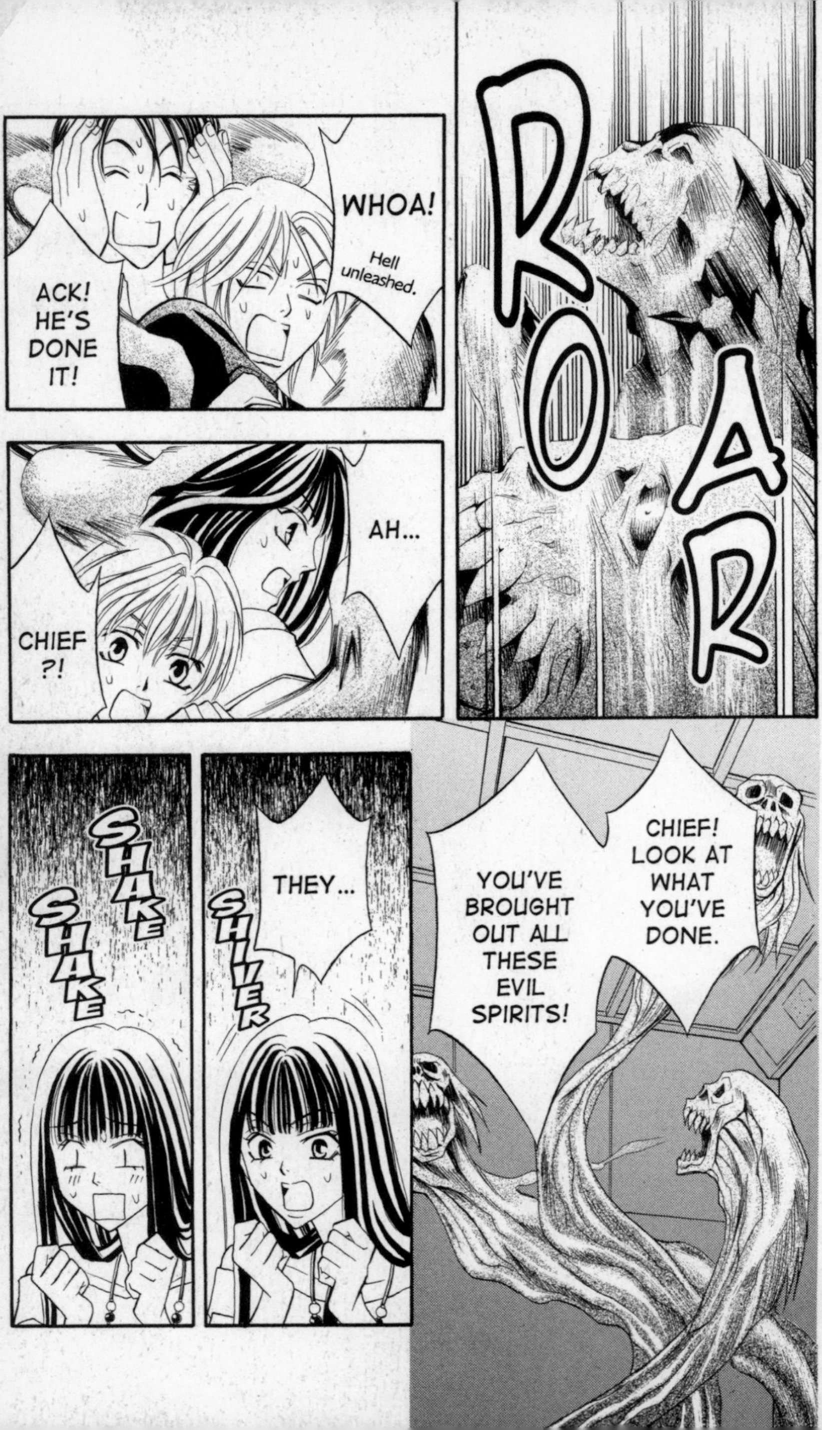
ROAR
WHOA!
Hell unleashed.
ACK! HE'S DONE IT!
AH...
CHIEF?!
CHIEF! LOOK AT WHAT YOU'VE DONE.
YOU'VE BROUGHT OUT ALL THESE EVIL SPIRITS!
THEY...
SHIVER
SHAKE
SHAKE

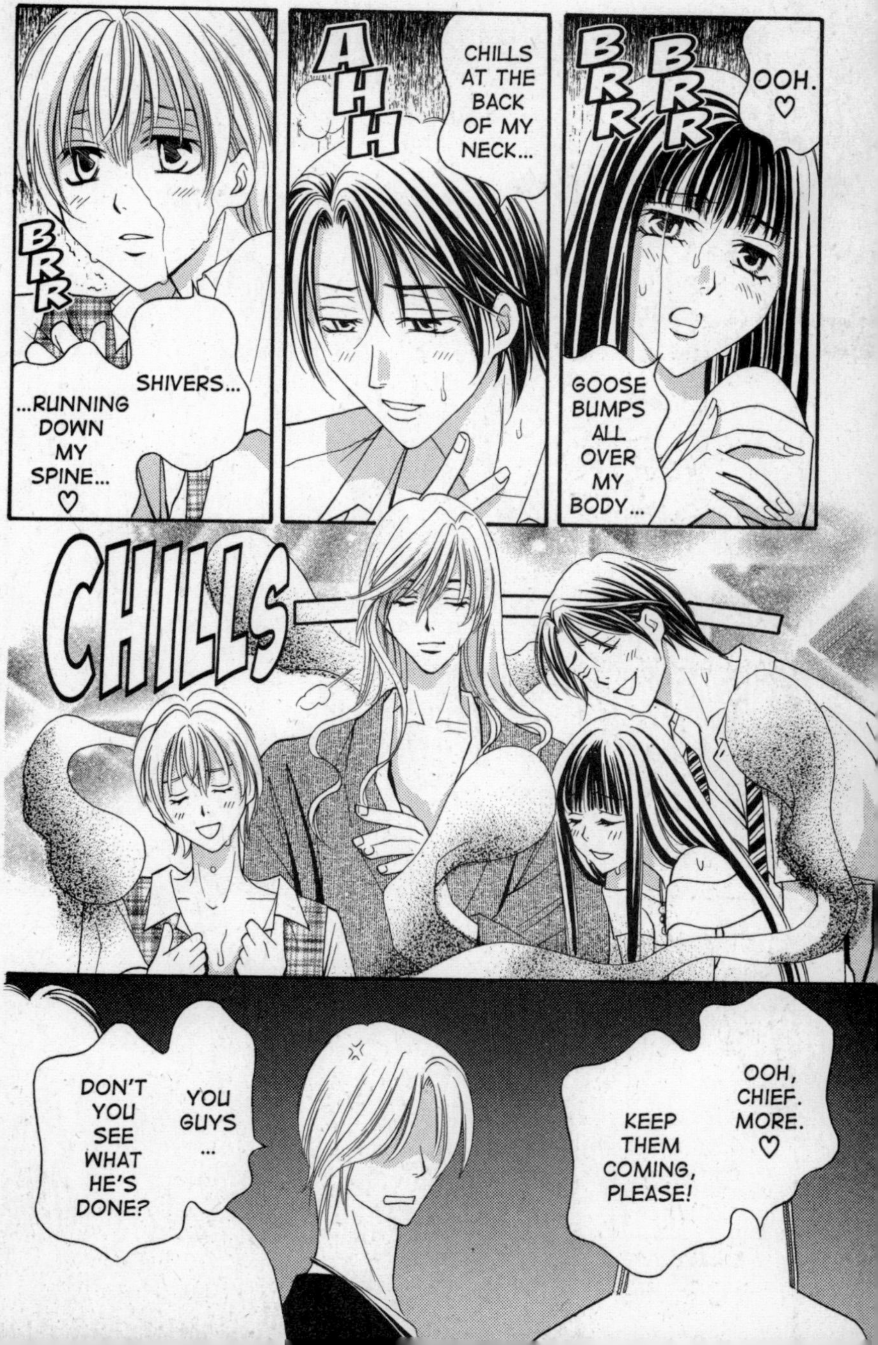
BRR BRR
OOH. ♡
GOOSE BUMPS ALL OVER MY BODY...
AHH
CHILLS AT THE BACK OF MY NECK...
BRR
SHIVERS...
...RUNNING DOWN MY SPINE... ♡
CHILLS
OOH, CHIEF. MORE. ♡
KEEP THEM COMING, PLEASE!
YOU GUYS...
DON'T YOU SEE WHAT HE'S DONE?

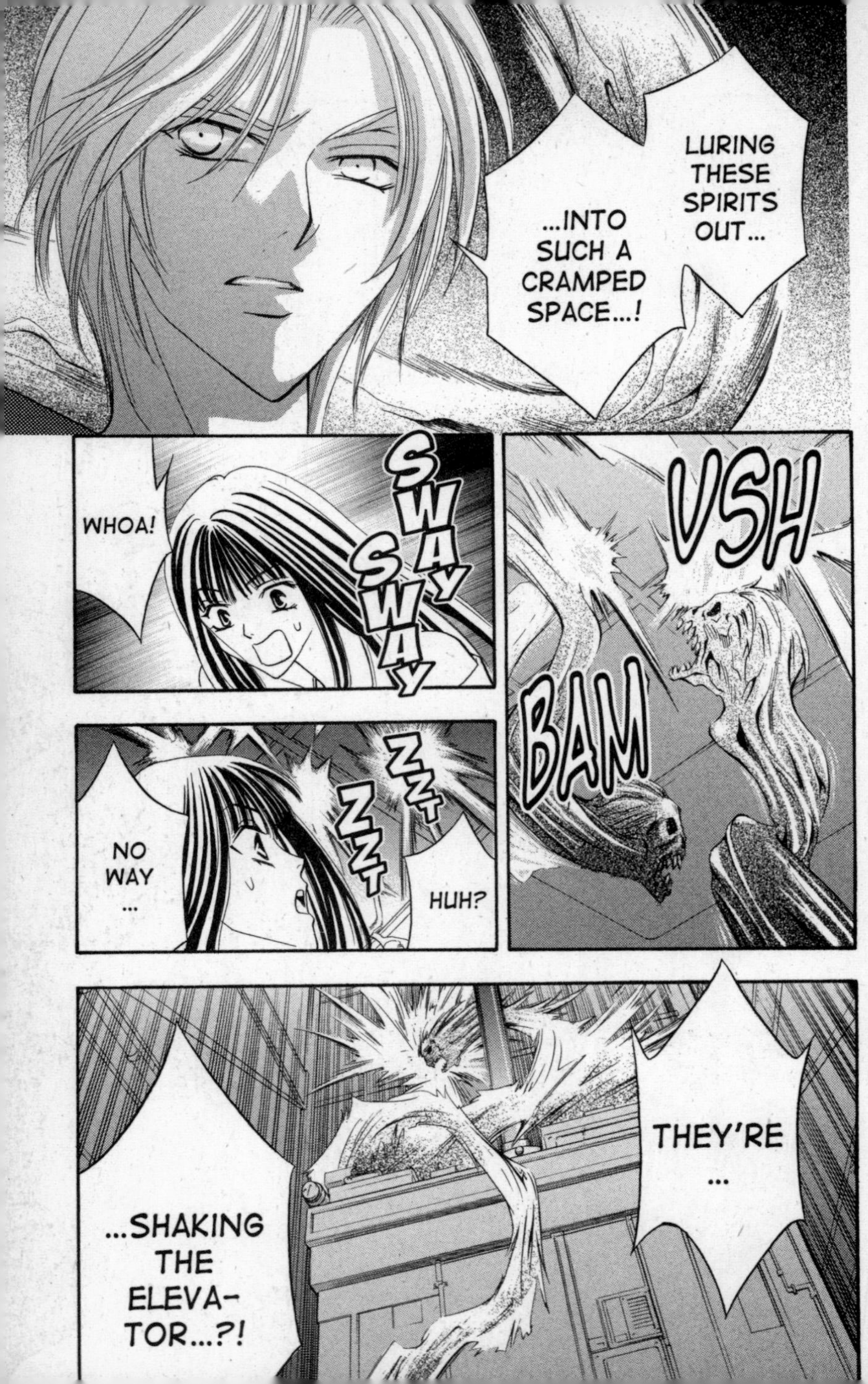
LURING THESE SPIRITS OUT...
...INTO SUCH A CRAMPED SPACE...!
VSH
BAM
SWAY
SWAY
WHOA!
ZZT
ZZT
HUH?
NO WAY ...
THEY'RE ...
...SHAKING THE ELEVA-TOR...?!

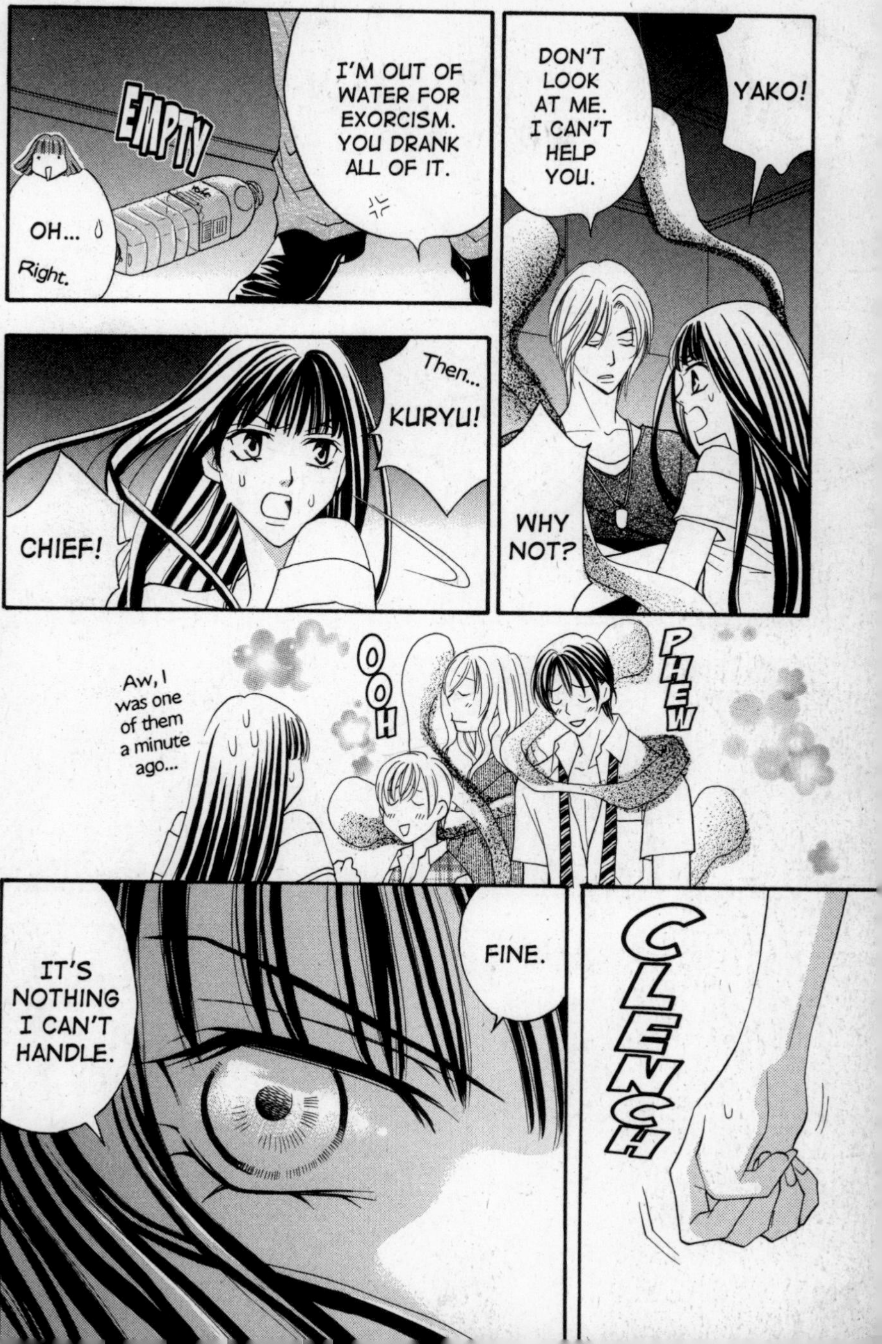
I'M OUT OF WATER FOR EXORCISM. YOU DRANK ALL OF IT.
EMPTY
OH... Right.
Then... KURYU!
CHIEF!
YAKO!
DON'T LOOK AT ME. I CAN'T HELP YOU.
WHY NOT?
PHEW
OOH
Aw, I was one of them a minute ago...
CLENCH
FINE.
IT'S NOTHING I CAN'T HANDLE.

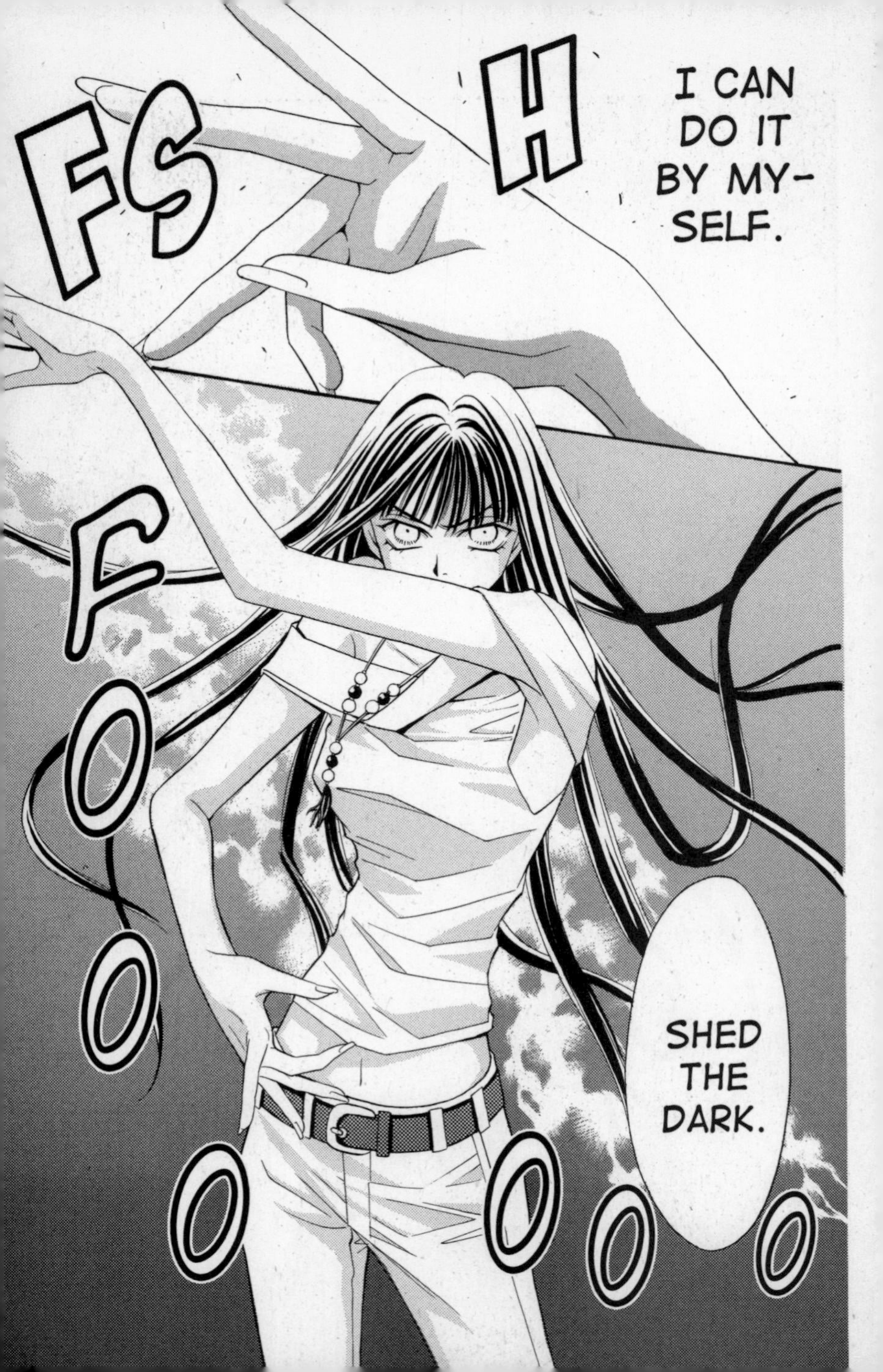
I CAN DO IT BY MY-SELF.
FSH
SHED THE DARK.
FOOOOOO

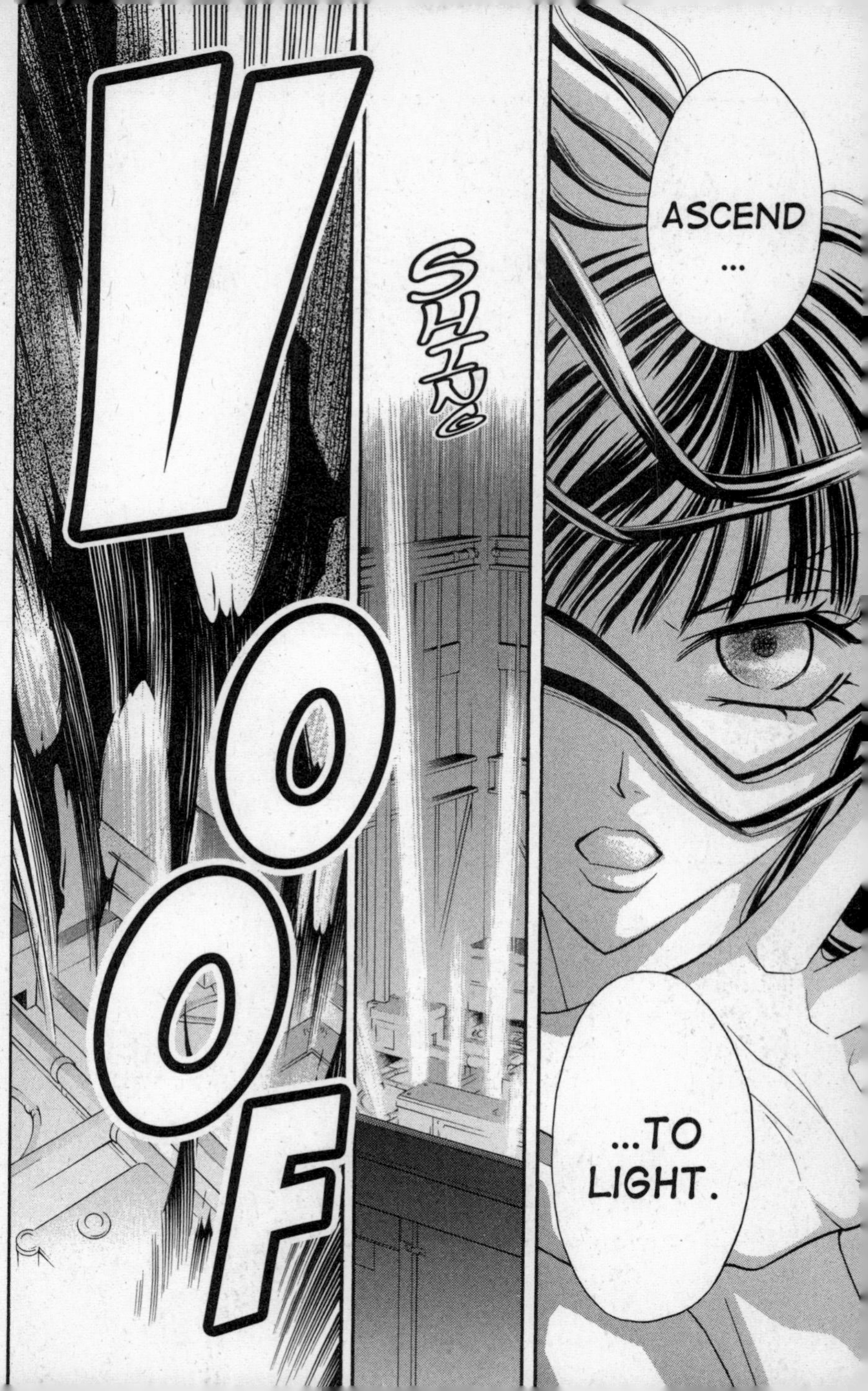
ASCEND ...
...TO LIGHT.
SHING
WOOF

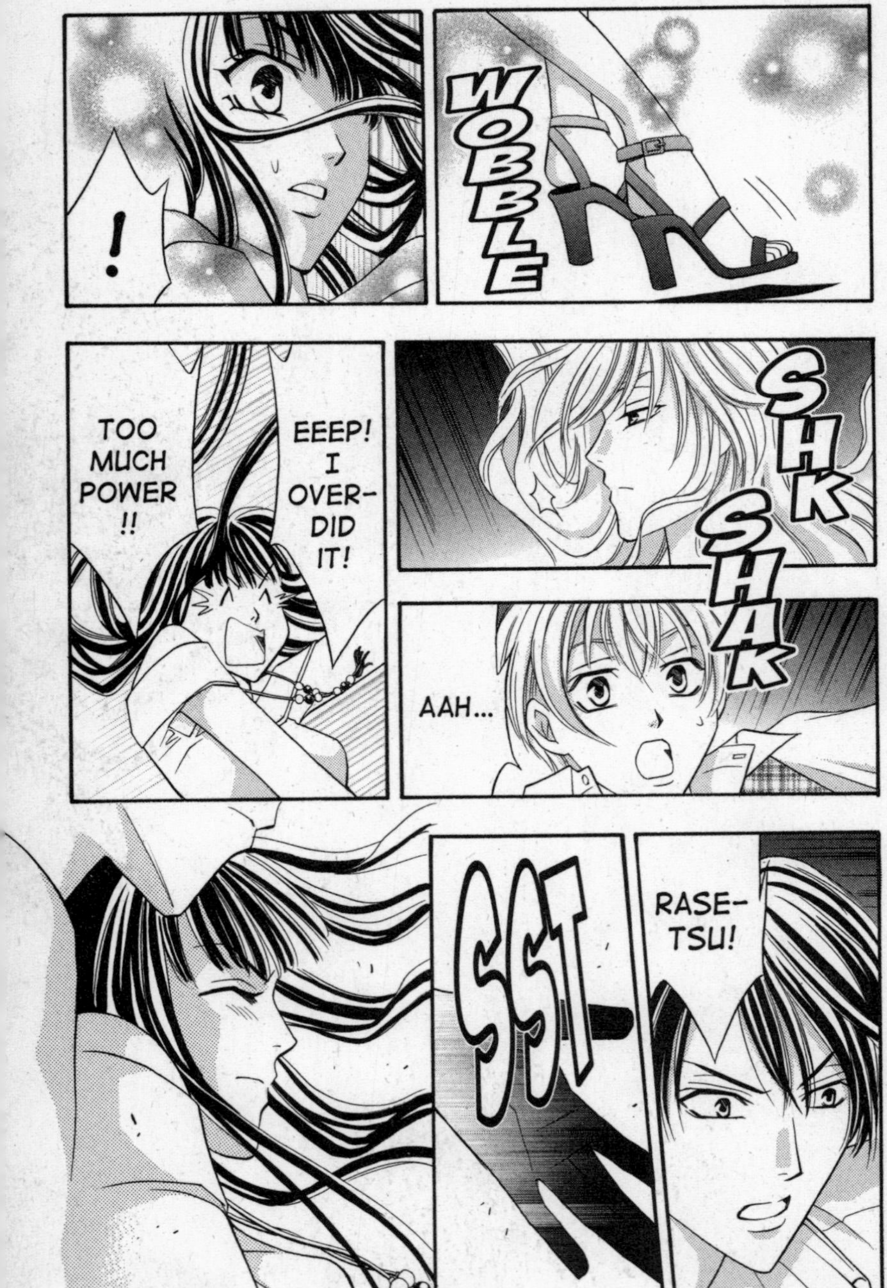
WOBBLE
!
SHK SHAK
AAH...
EEEP! I OVER-DID IT!
TOO MUCH POWER !!
RASE-TSU!
SST

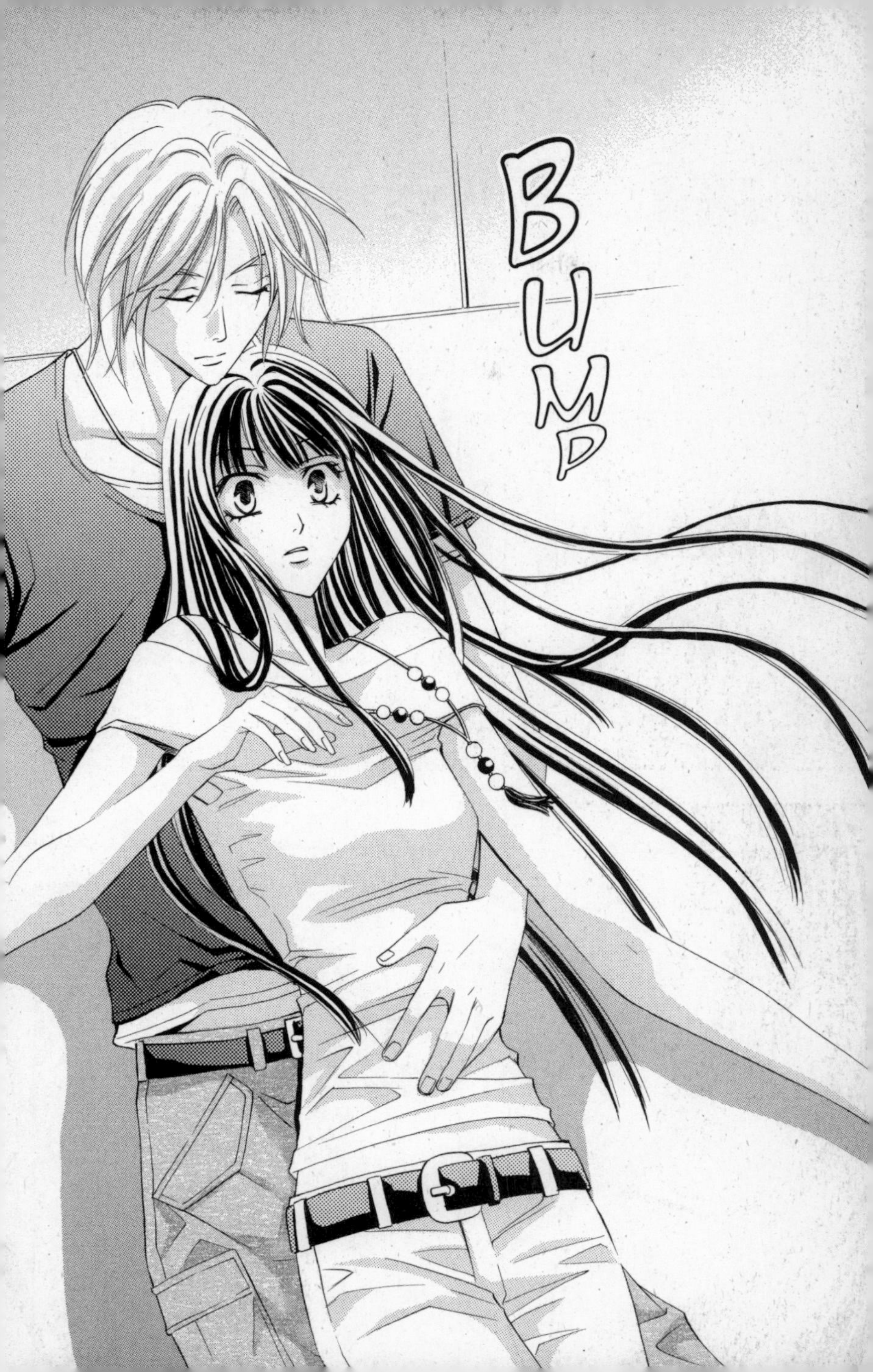
BUMP

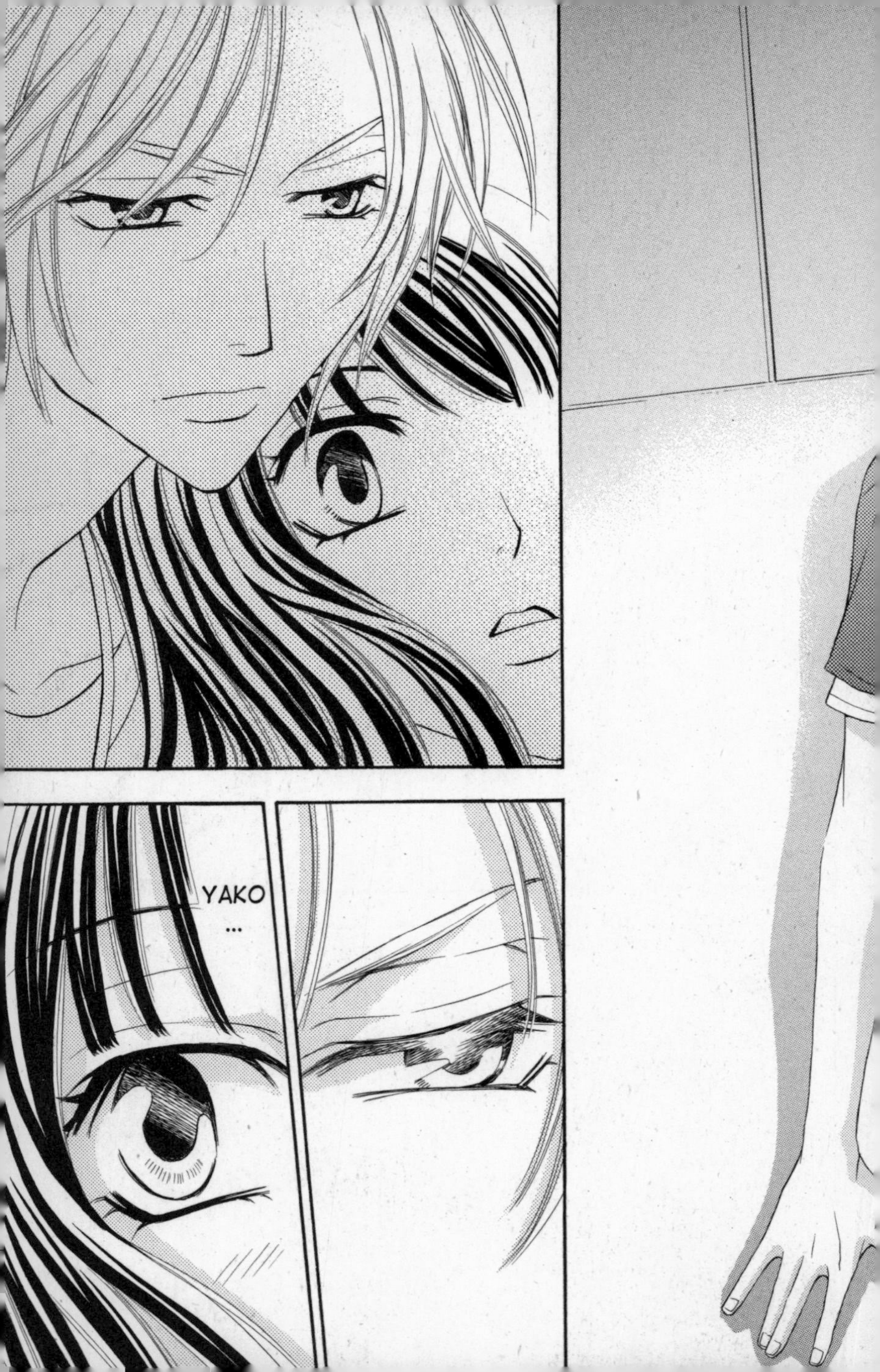
YAKO
...

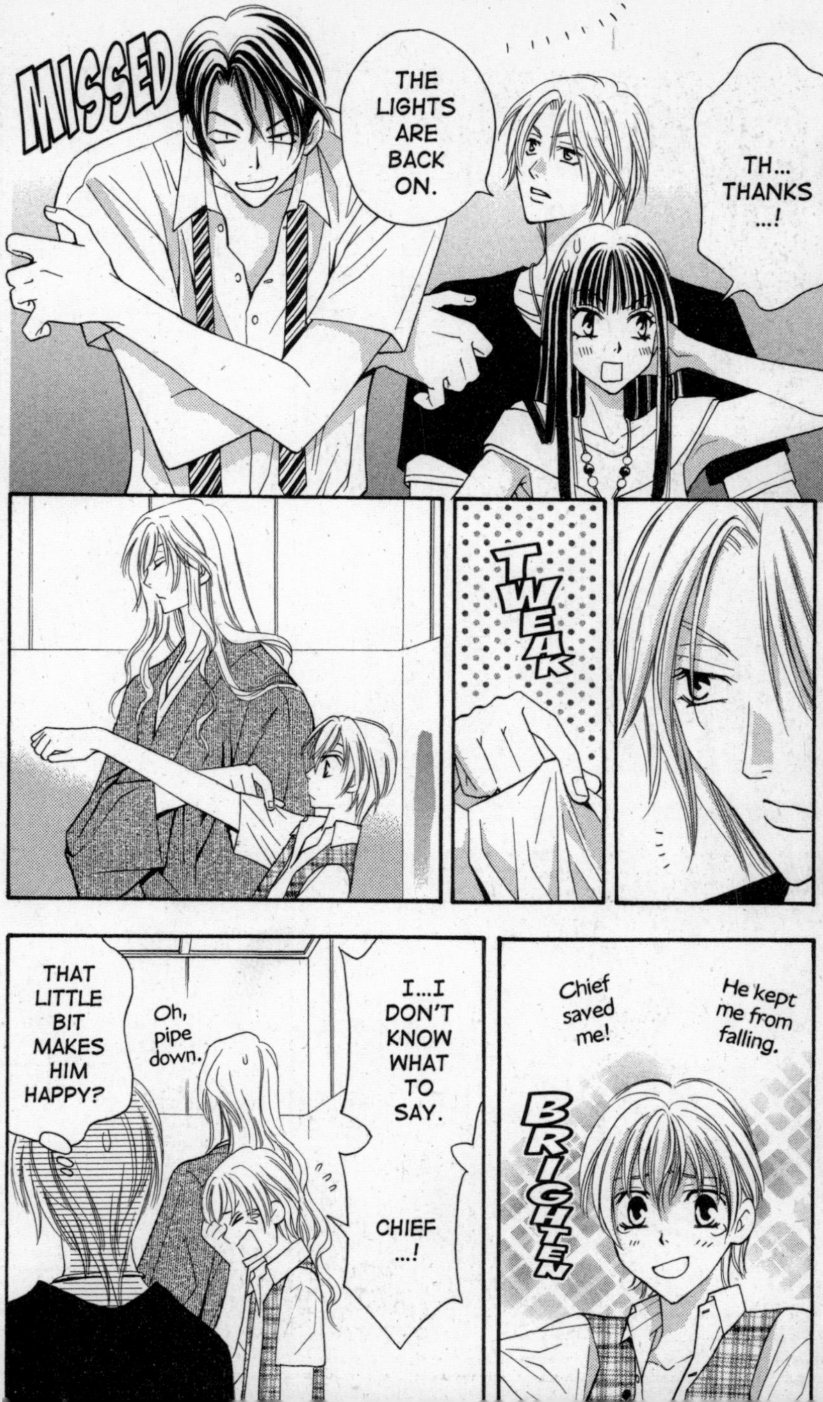
MISSED
THE LIGHTS ARE BACK ON.
TH... THANKS ...!
TWEAK
He kept me from falling.
Chief saved me!
BRIGHTEN
I...I DON'T KNOW WHAT TO SAY.
CHIEF ...!
Oh, pipe down.
THAT LITTLE BIT MAKES HIM HAPPY?

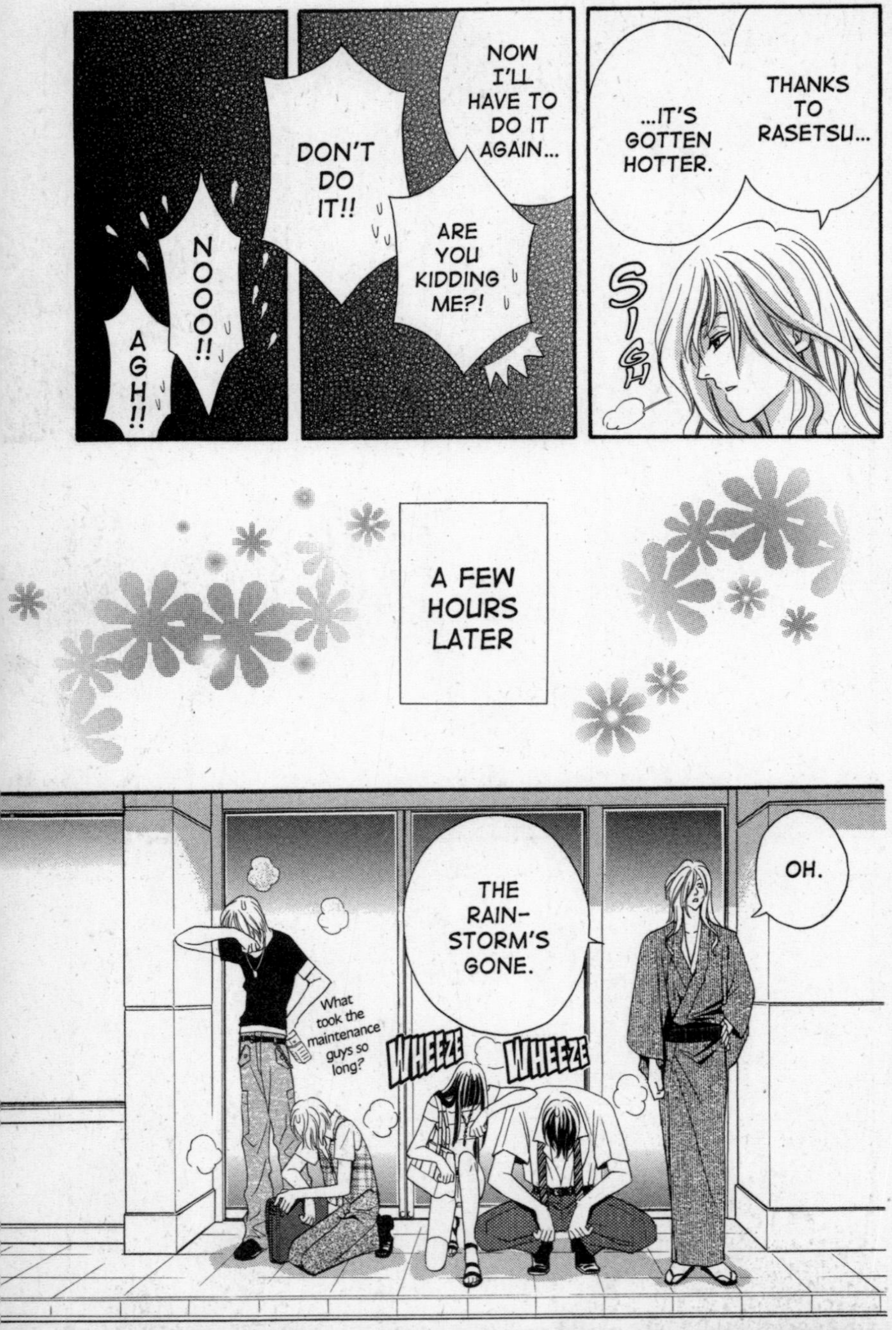
THANKS TO RASETSU...
...IT'S GOTTEN HOTTER.
SIGH
NOW I'LL HAVE TO DO IT AGAIN...
ARE YOU KIDDING ME?!
DON'T DO IT!!
NOOO!!
AGH!!
A FEW HOURS LATER
OH.
THE RAIN-STORM'S GONE.
WHEEZE
WHEEZE
What took the maintenance guys so long?

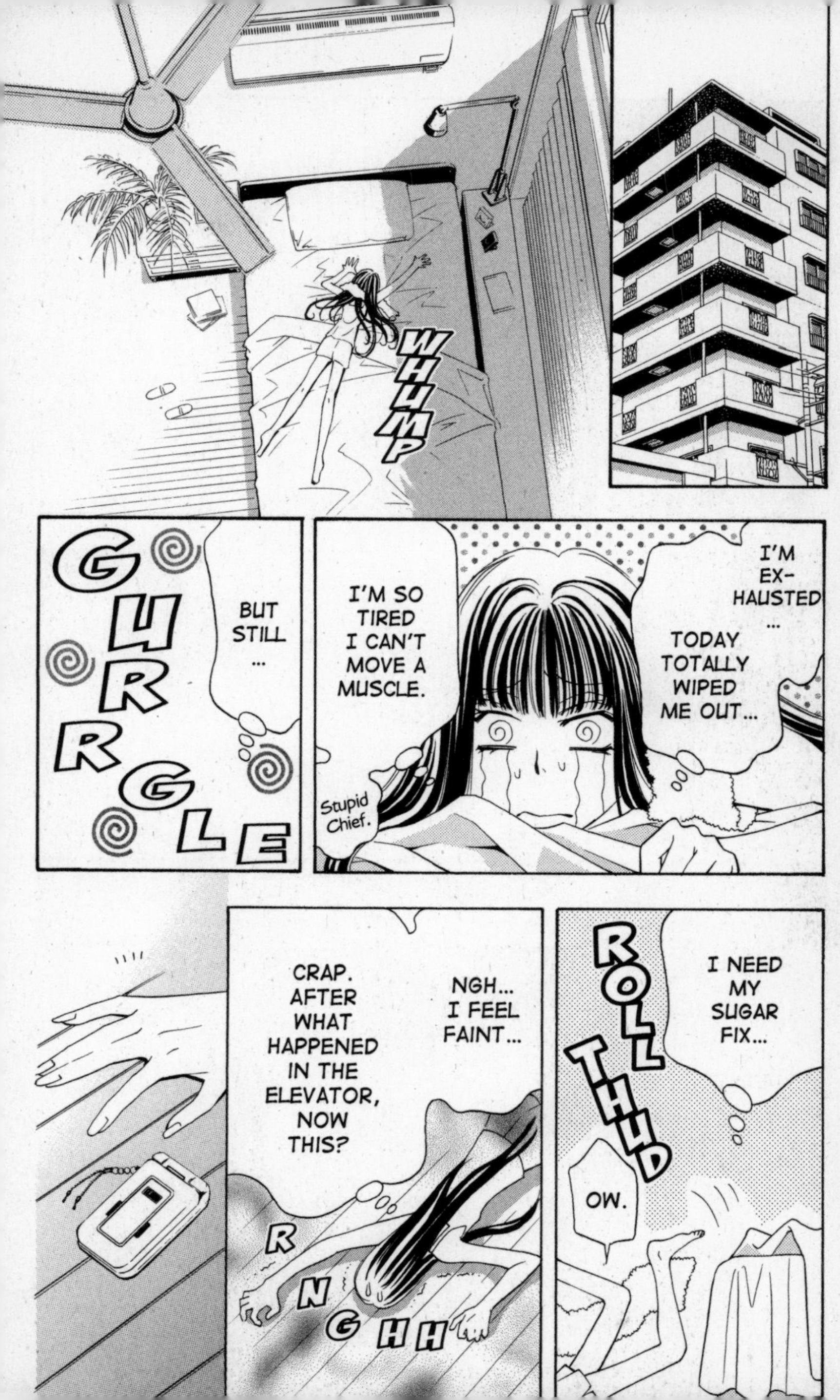
WHUMP
I'M EX-HAUSTED...
TODAY TOTALLY WIPED ME OUT...
I'M SO TIRED I CAN'T MOVE A MUSCLE.
Stupid Chief.
BUT STILL...
GURRGLE
I NEED MY SUGAR FIX...
ROLL
THUD
OW.
NGH... I FEEL FAINT...
CRAP. AFTER WHAT HAPPENED IN THE ELEVATOR, NOW THIS?
RNGHH

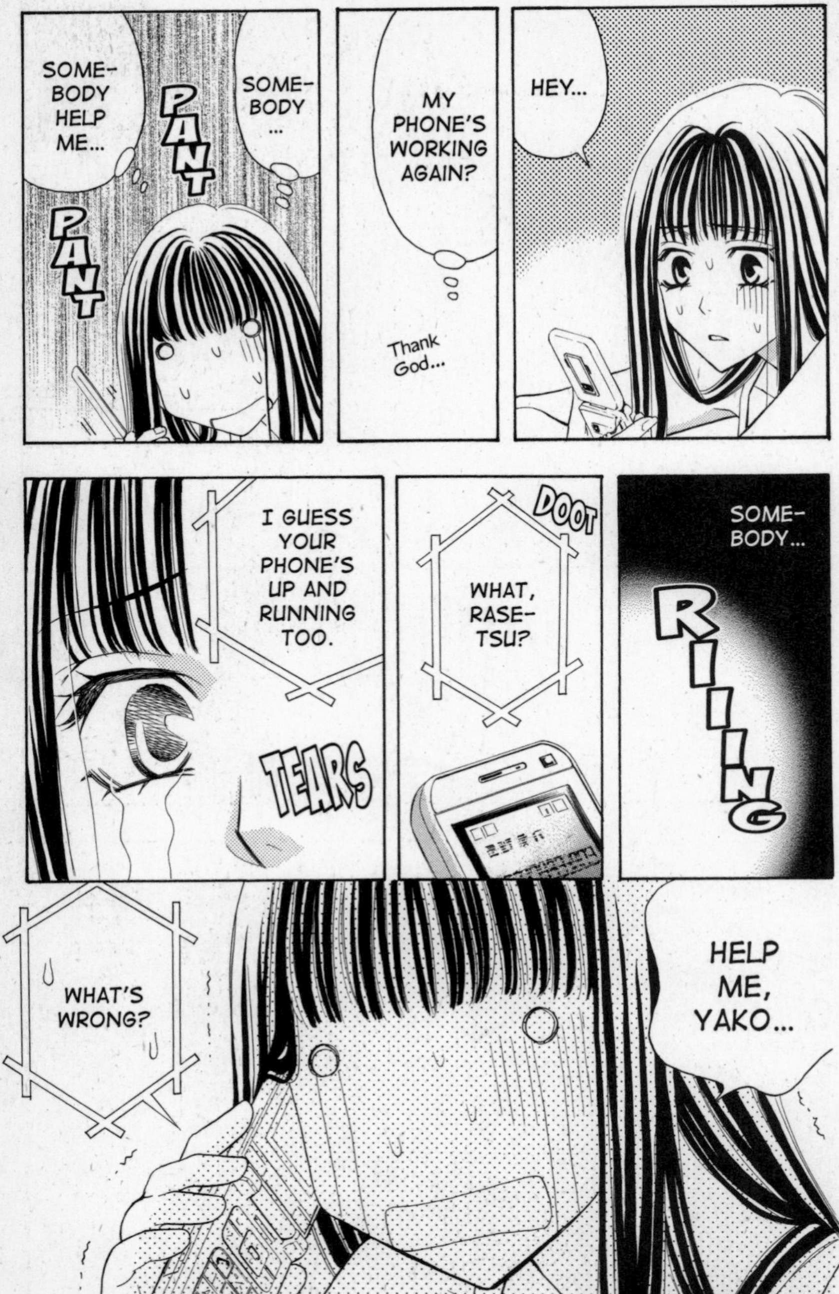
HEY...
MY PHONE'S WORKING AGAIN?
Thank God...
SOME-BODY ...
PANT
SOME-BODY HELP ME...
PANT
SOME-BODY...
RIIING
DOOT
WHAT, RASE-TSU?
I GUESS YOUR PHONE'S UP AND RUNNING TOO.
TEARS
HELP ME, YAKO...
WHAT'S WRONG?

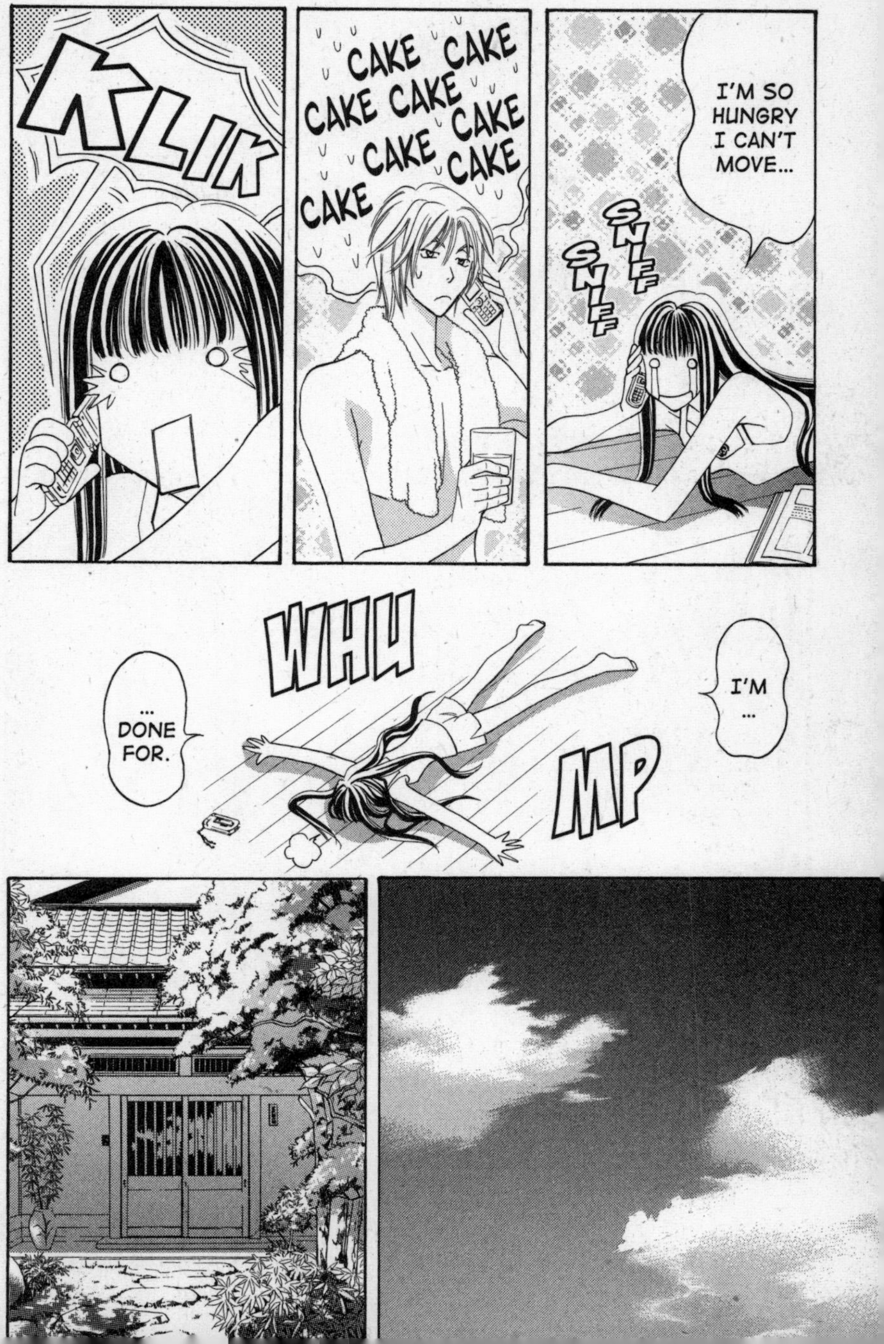
I'M SO HUNGRY I CAN'T MOVE...
SNIFF SNIFF
CAKE CAKE CAKE CAKE CAKE CAKE CAKE CAKE
KLIK
I'M ...
WHUMP
... DONE FOR.

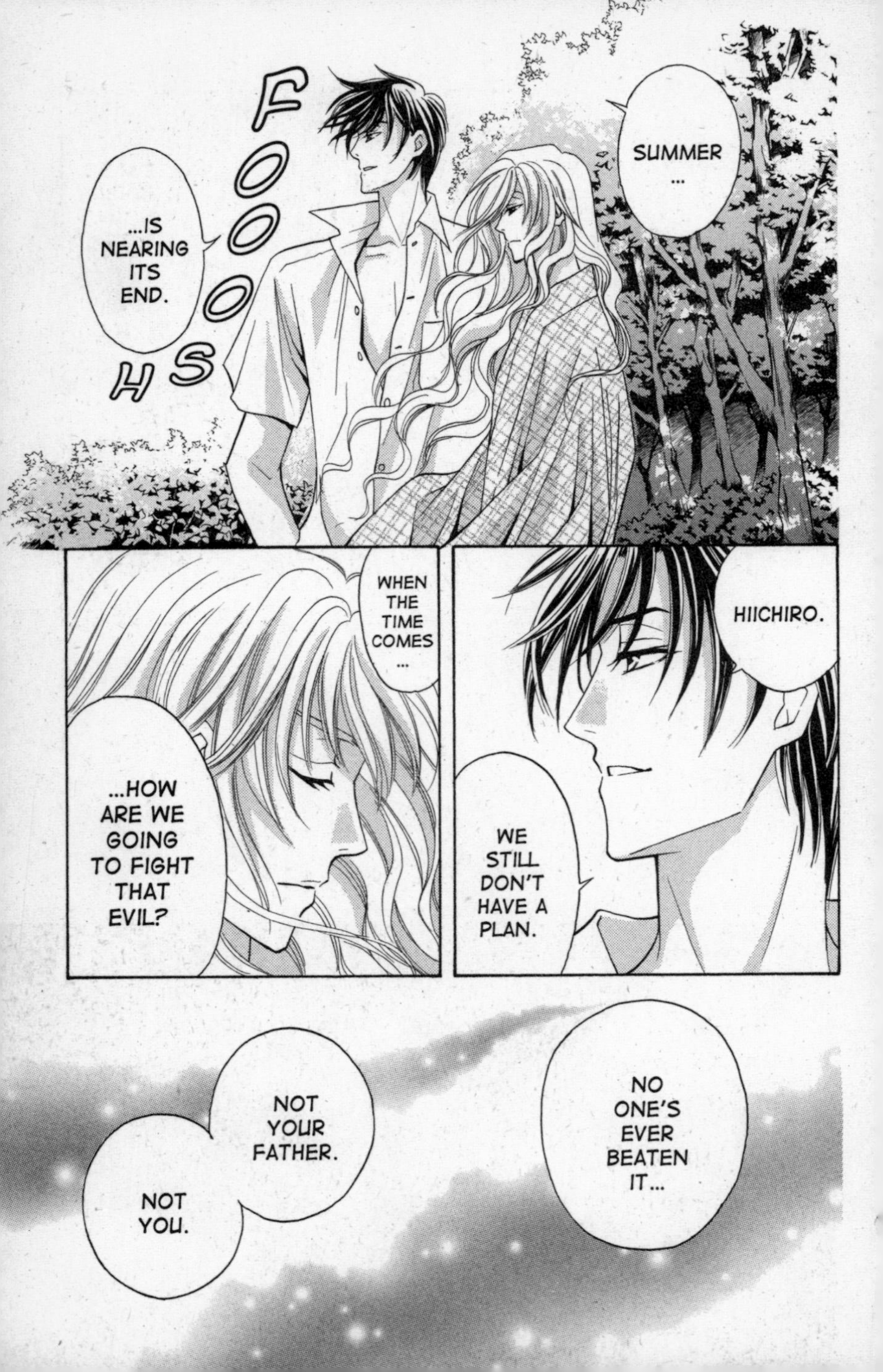
SUMMER ...
...IS NEARING ITS END.
FOOOOSH
HIICHIRO.
WE STILL DON'T HAVE A PLAN.
WHEN THE TIME COMES ...
...HOW ARE WE GOING TO FIGHT THAT EVIL?
NO ONE'S EVER BEATEN IT...
NOT YOUR FATHER.
NOT YOU.

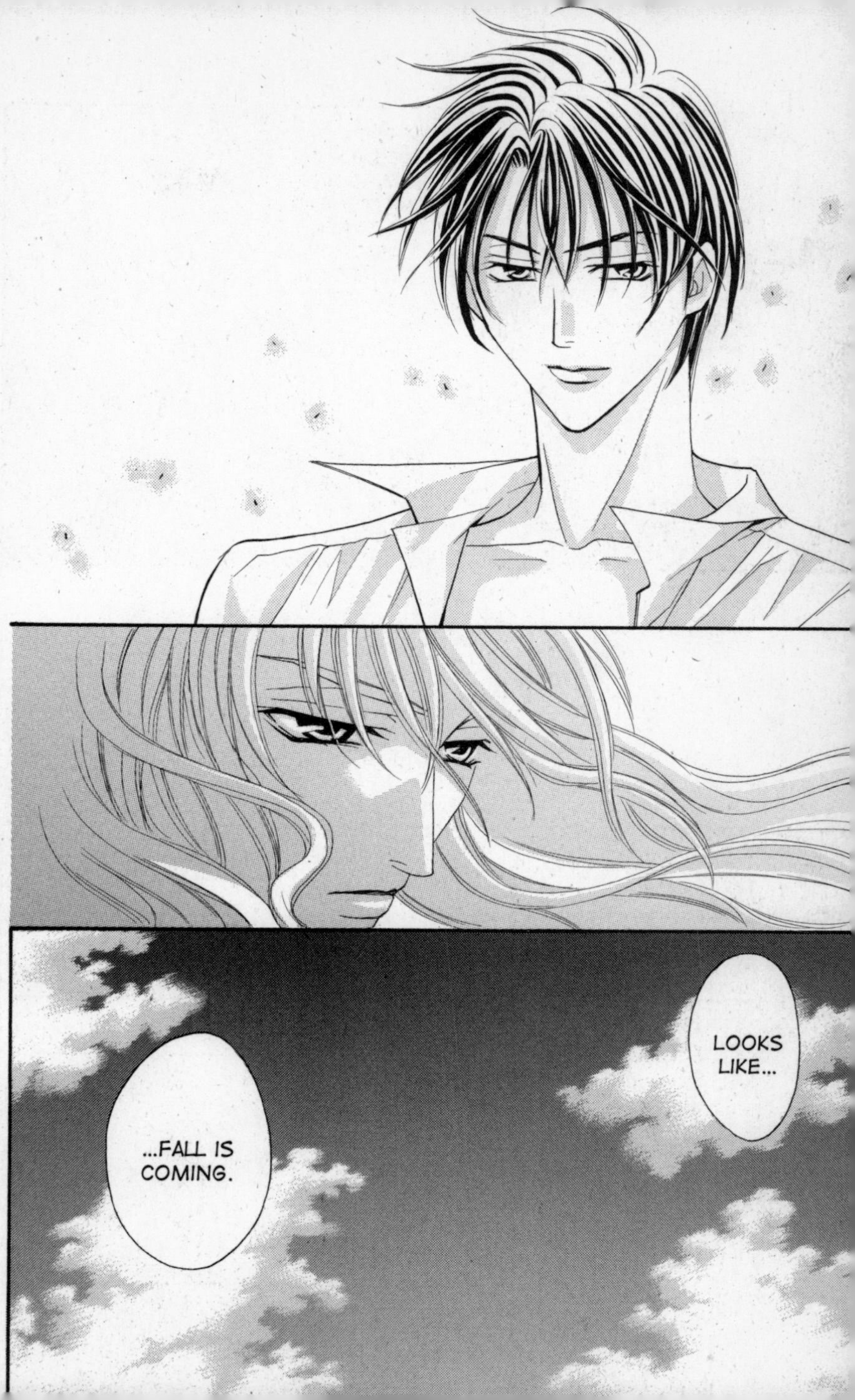
LOOKS LIKE...
...FALL IS COMING.

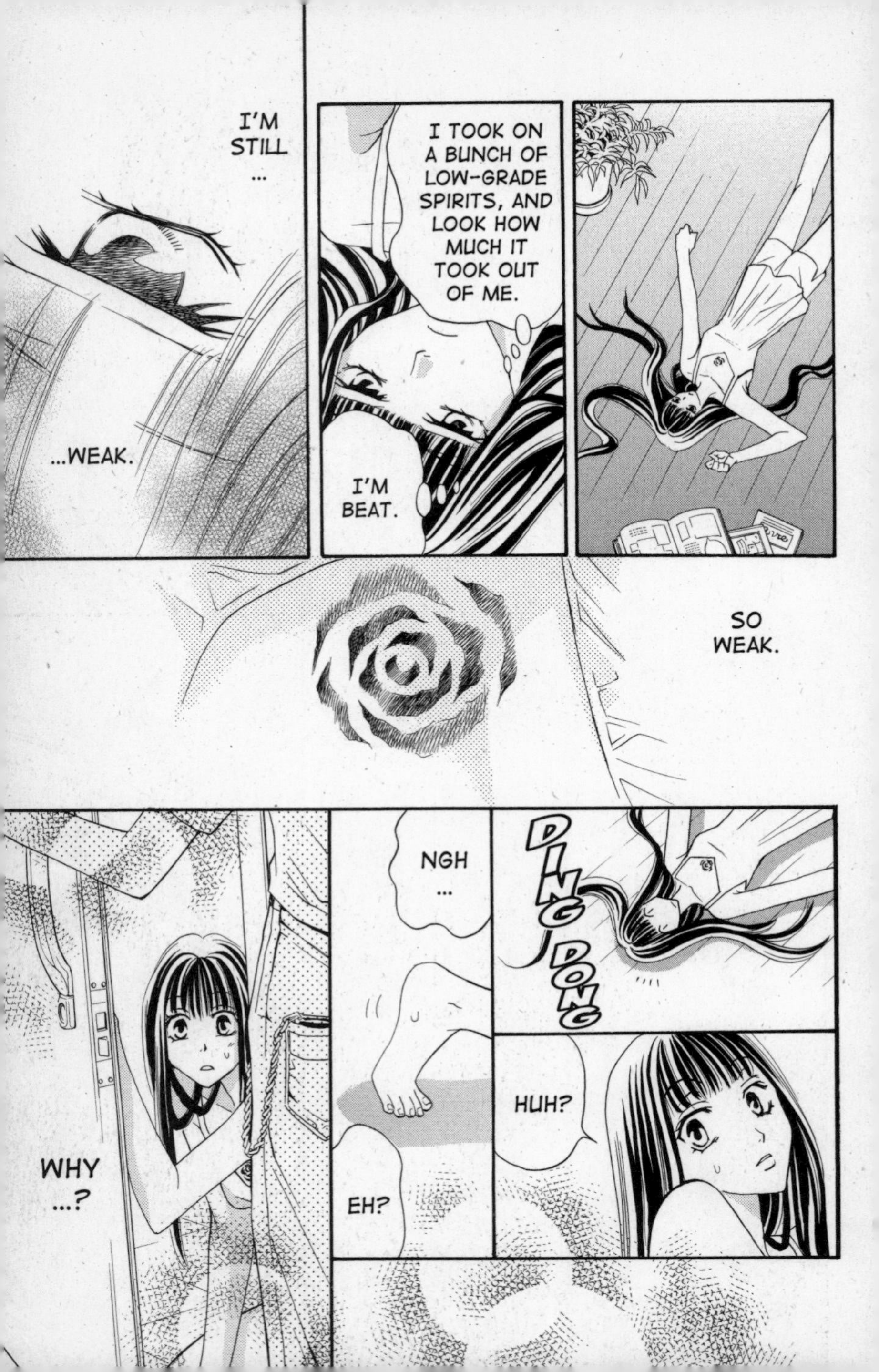
I TOOK ON A BUNCH OF LOW-GRADE SPIRITS, AND LOOK HOW MUCH IT TOOK OUT OF ME.
I'M BEAT.
I'M STILL ...
...WEAK.
SO WEAK.
DING DONG
HUH?
NGH ...
EH?
WHY ...?

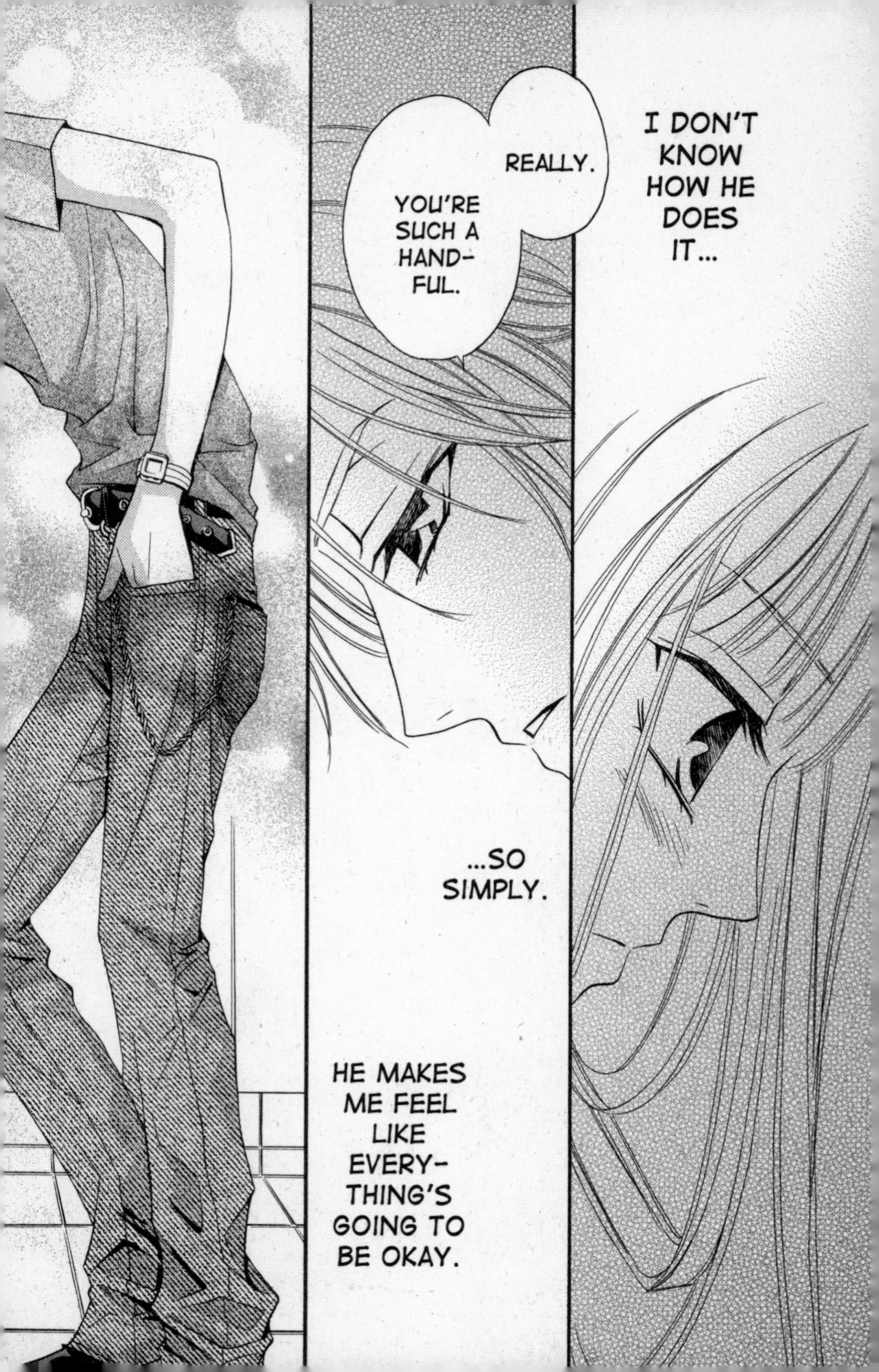
I DON'T KNOW HOW HE DOES IT...
REALLY.
YOU'RE SUCH A HAND-FUL.
...SO SIMPLY.
HE MAKES ME FEEL LIKE EVERY-THING'S GOING TO BE OKAY.

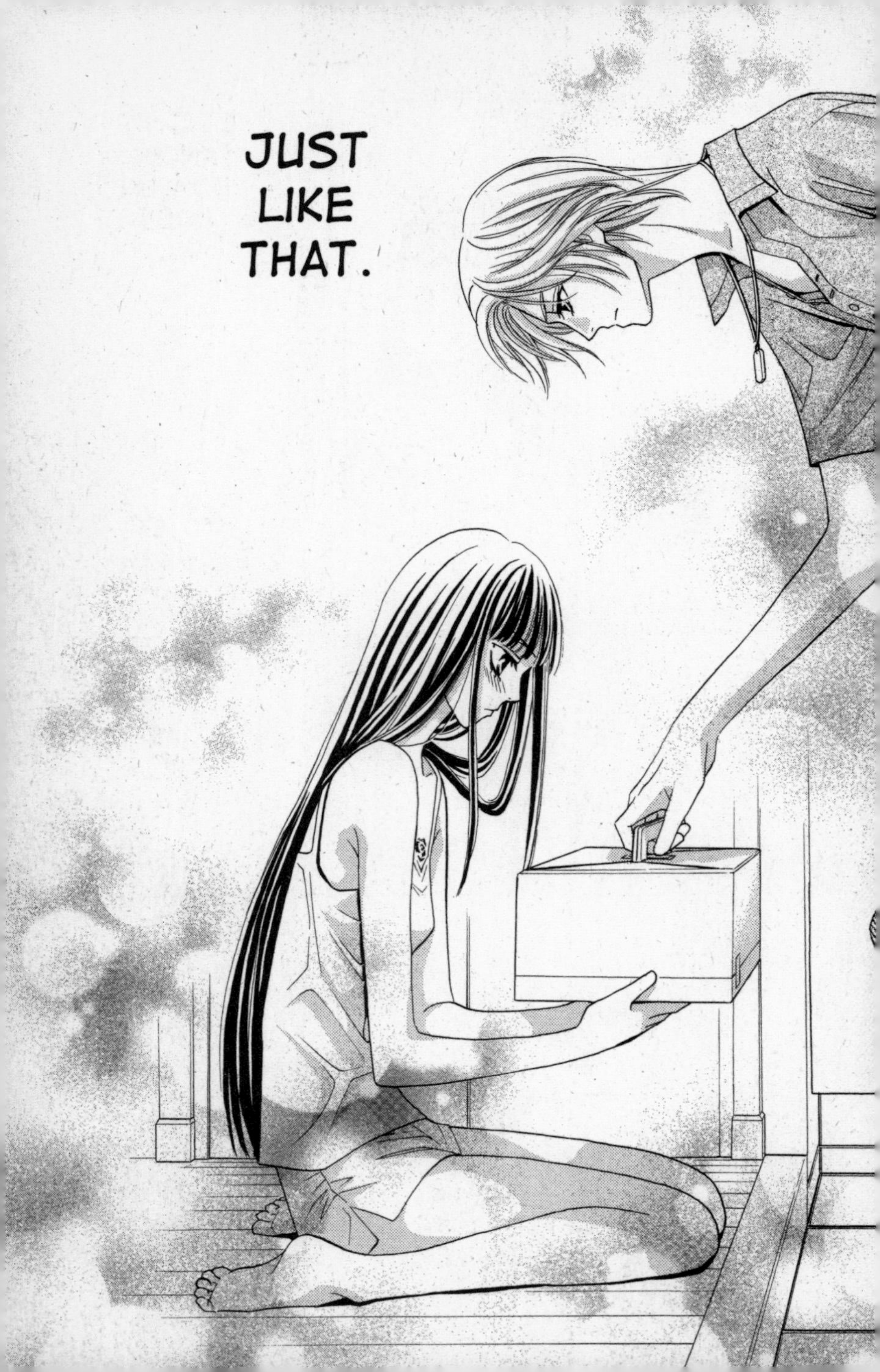
JUST LIKE THAT.

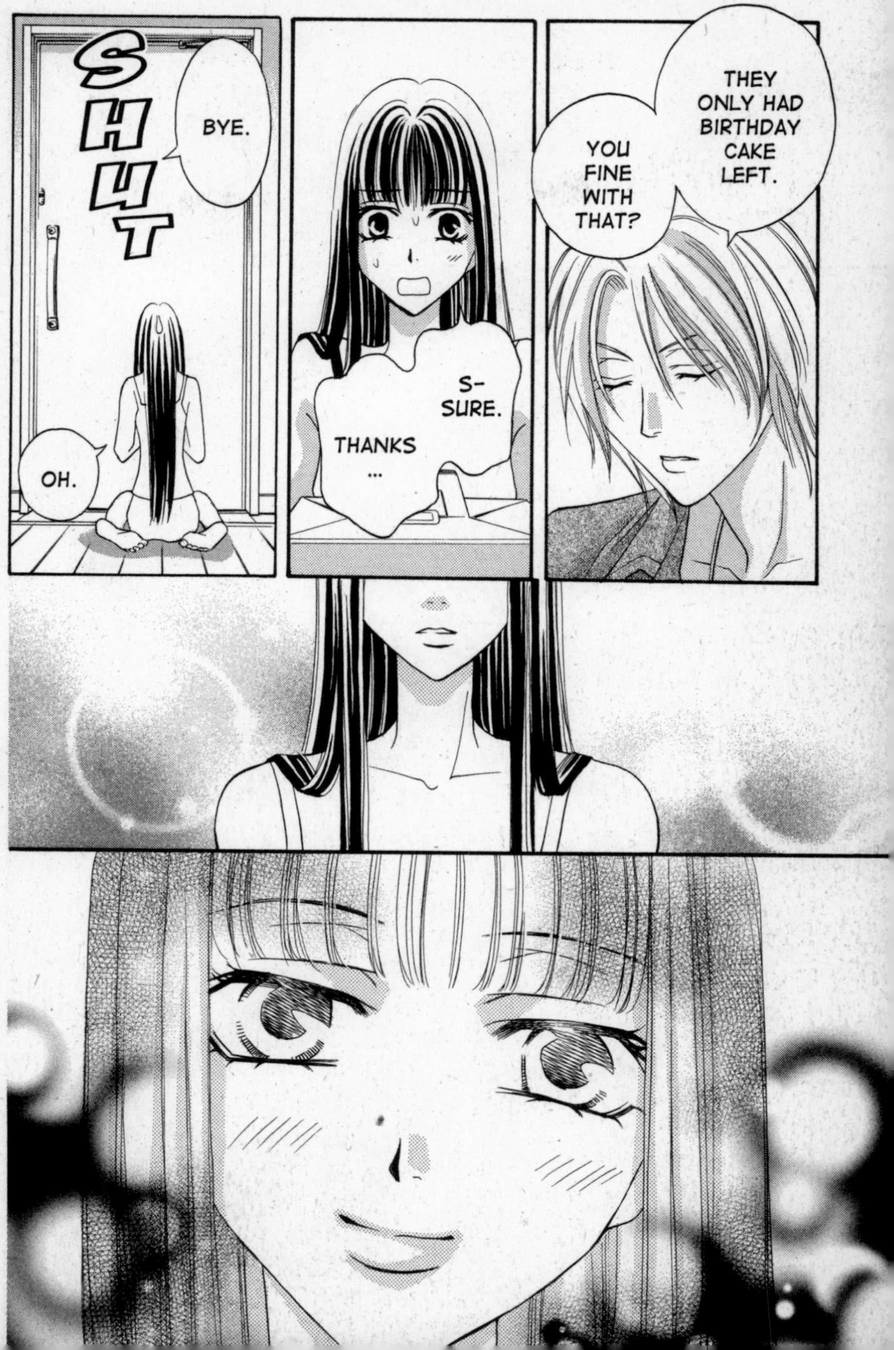
THEY ONLY HAD BIRTHDAY CAKE LEFT.
YOU FINE WITH THAT?
S- SURE.
THANKS ...
BYE.
SHUT
OH.

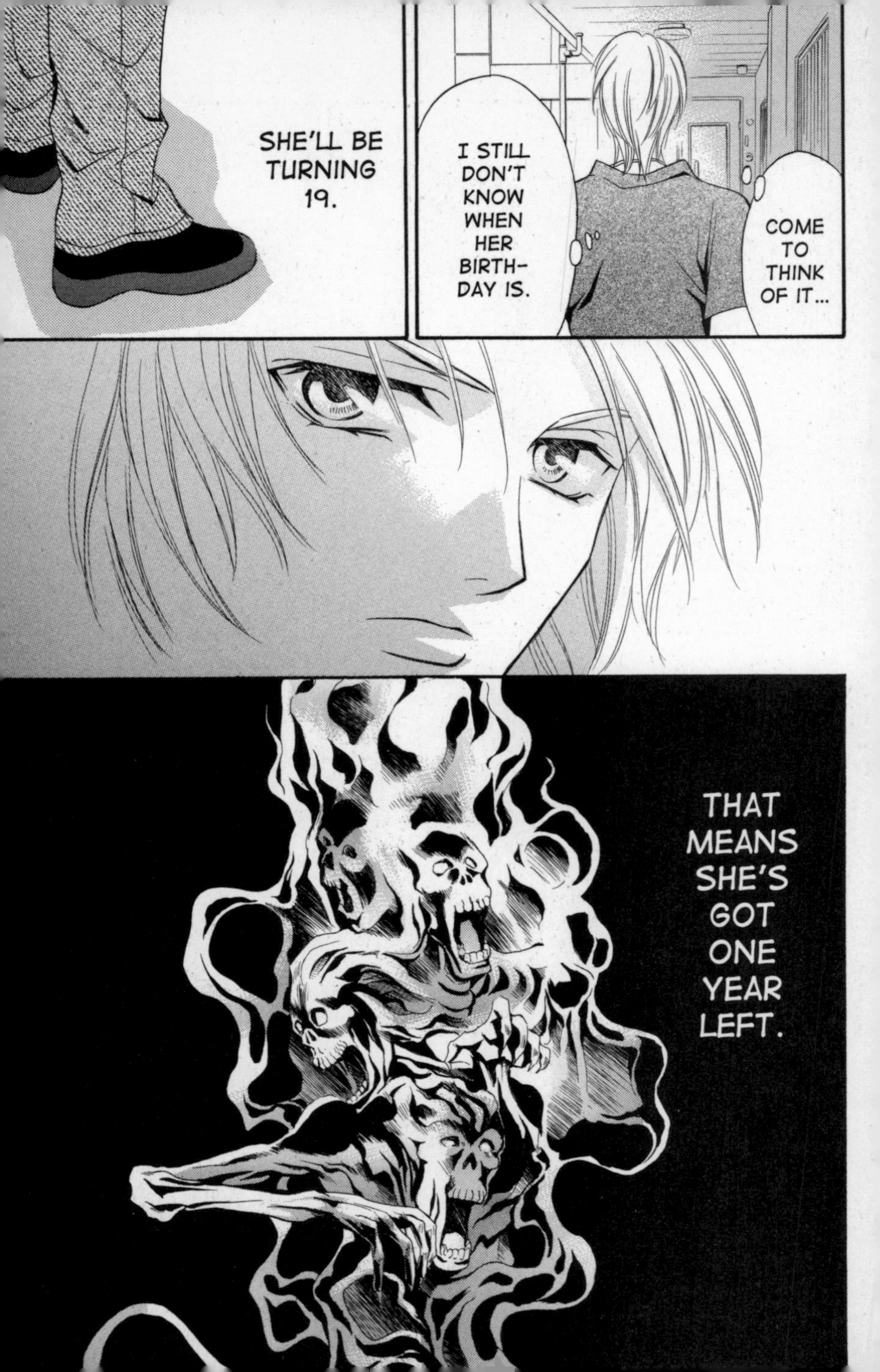
COME TO THINK OF IT...
I STILL DON'T KNOW WHEN HER BIRTH-DAY IS.
SHE'LL BE TURNING 19.
THAT MEANS SHE'S GOT ONE YEAR LEFT.

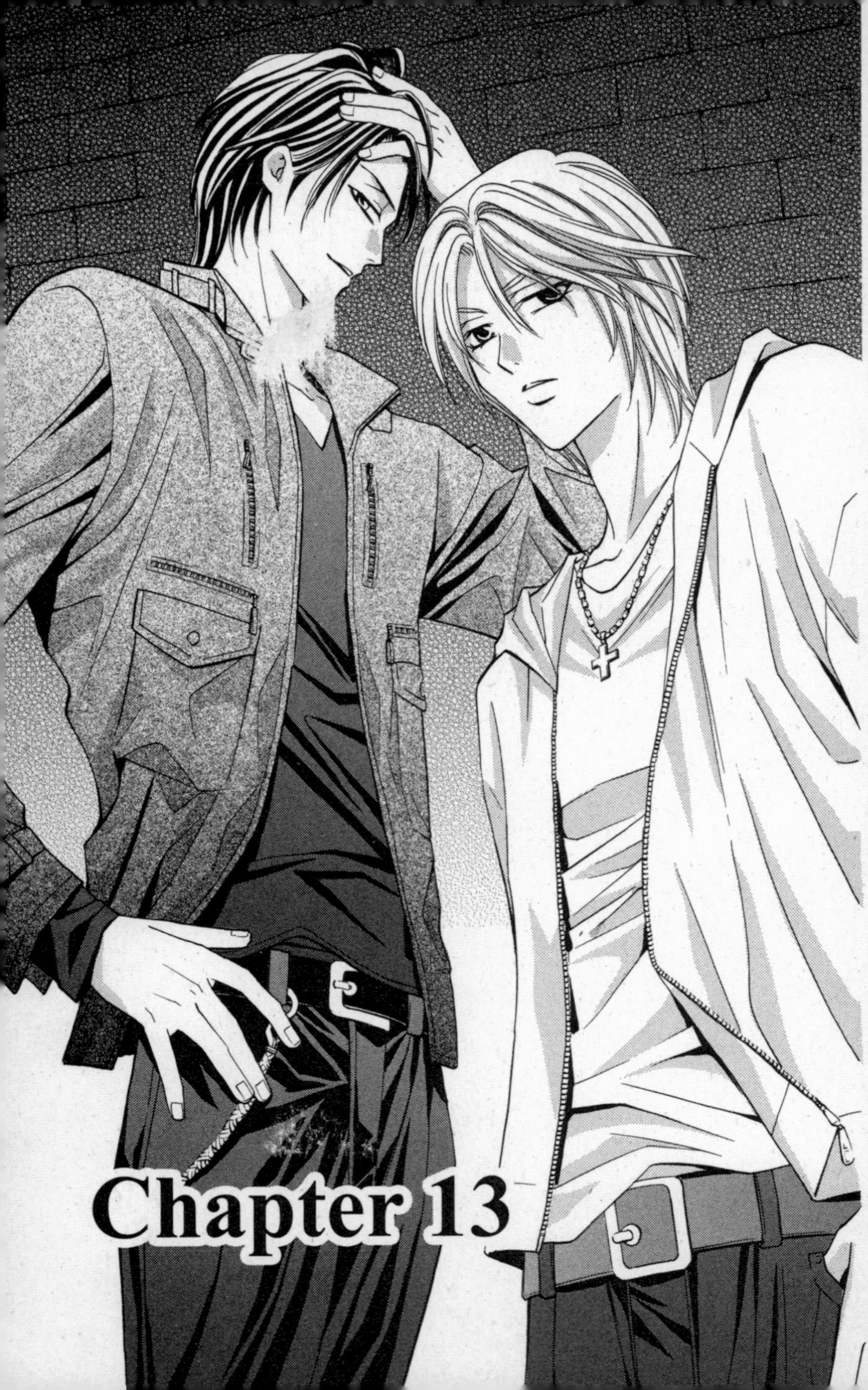
Chapter 13

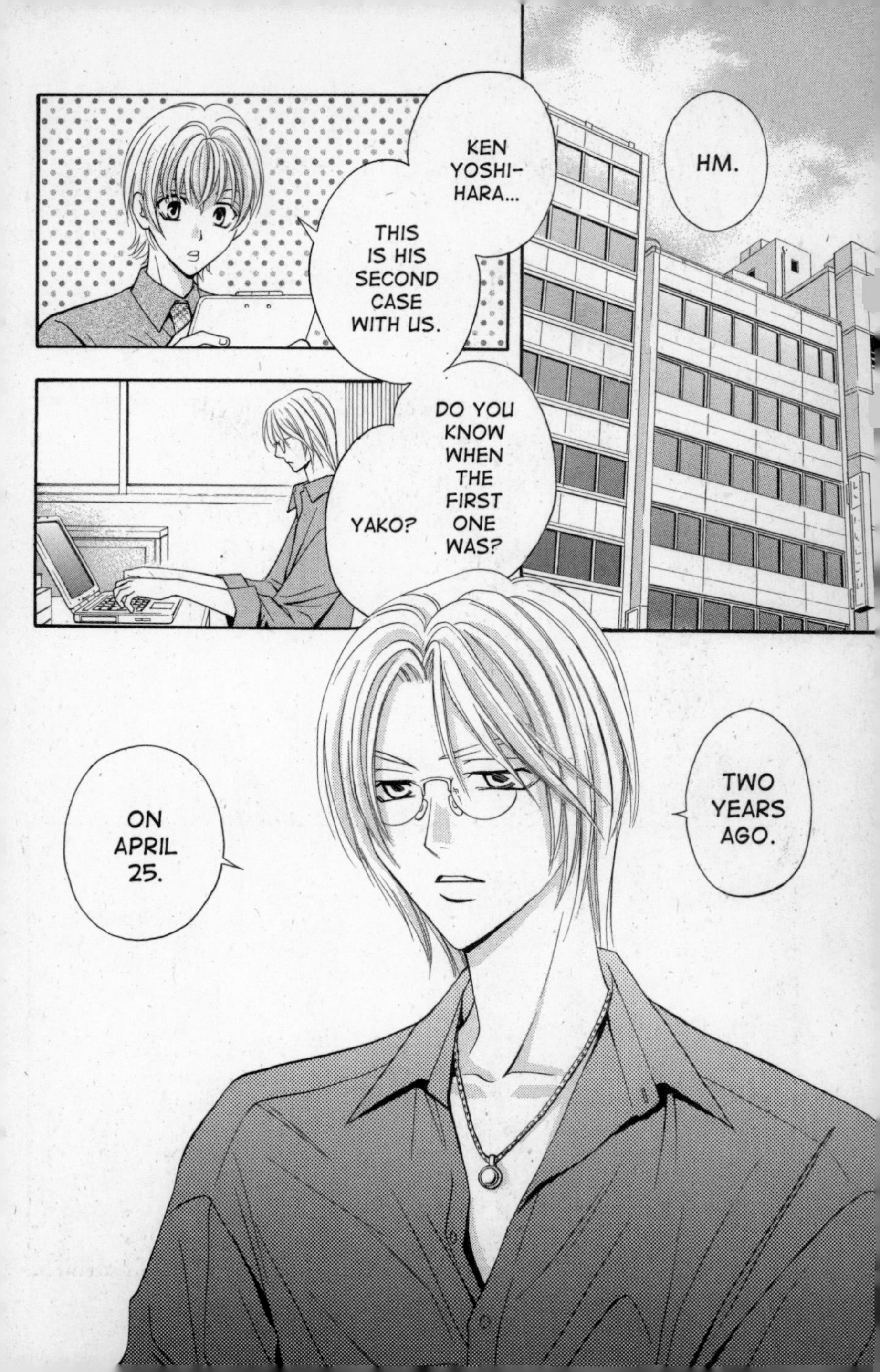
HM.
KEN YOSHI-HARA...
THIS IS HIS SECOND CASE WITH US.
DO YOU KNOW WHEN THE FIRST ONE WAS?
YAKO?
TWO YEARS AGO.
ON APRIL 25.

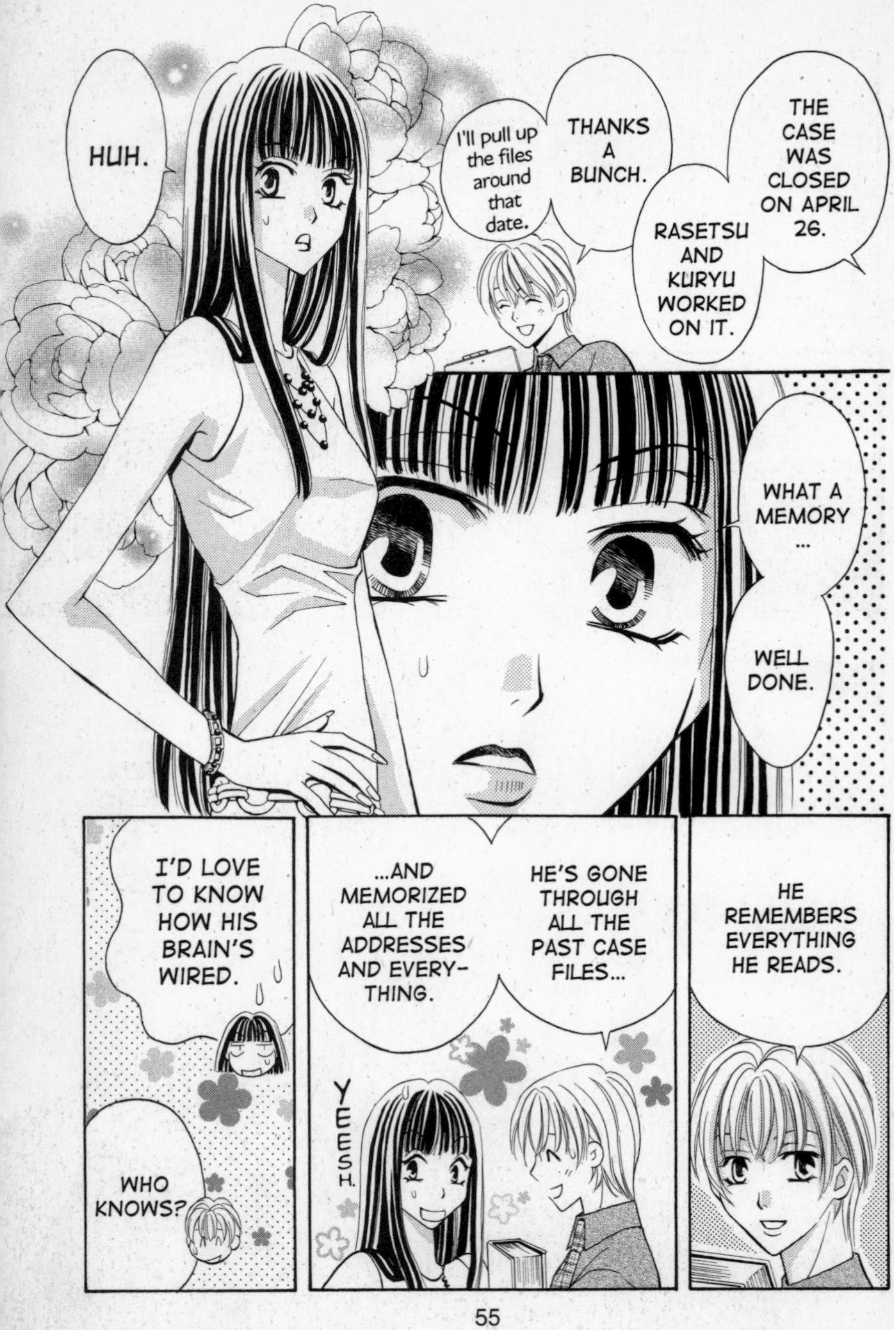
THE CASE WAS CLOSED ON APRIL 26.
RASETSU AND KURYU WORKED ON IT.
THANKS A BUNCH.
I'll pull up the files around that date.
HUH.
WHAT A MEMORY ...
WELL DONE.
HE REMEMBERS EVERYTHING HE READS.
HE'S GONE THROUGH ALL THE PAST CASE FILES...
...AND MEMORIZED ALL THE ADDRESSES AND EVERY-THING.
YEESH.
I'D LOVE TO KNOW HOW HIS BRAIN'S WIRED.
WHO KNOWS?

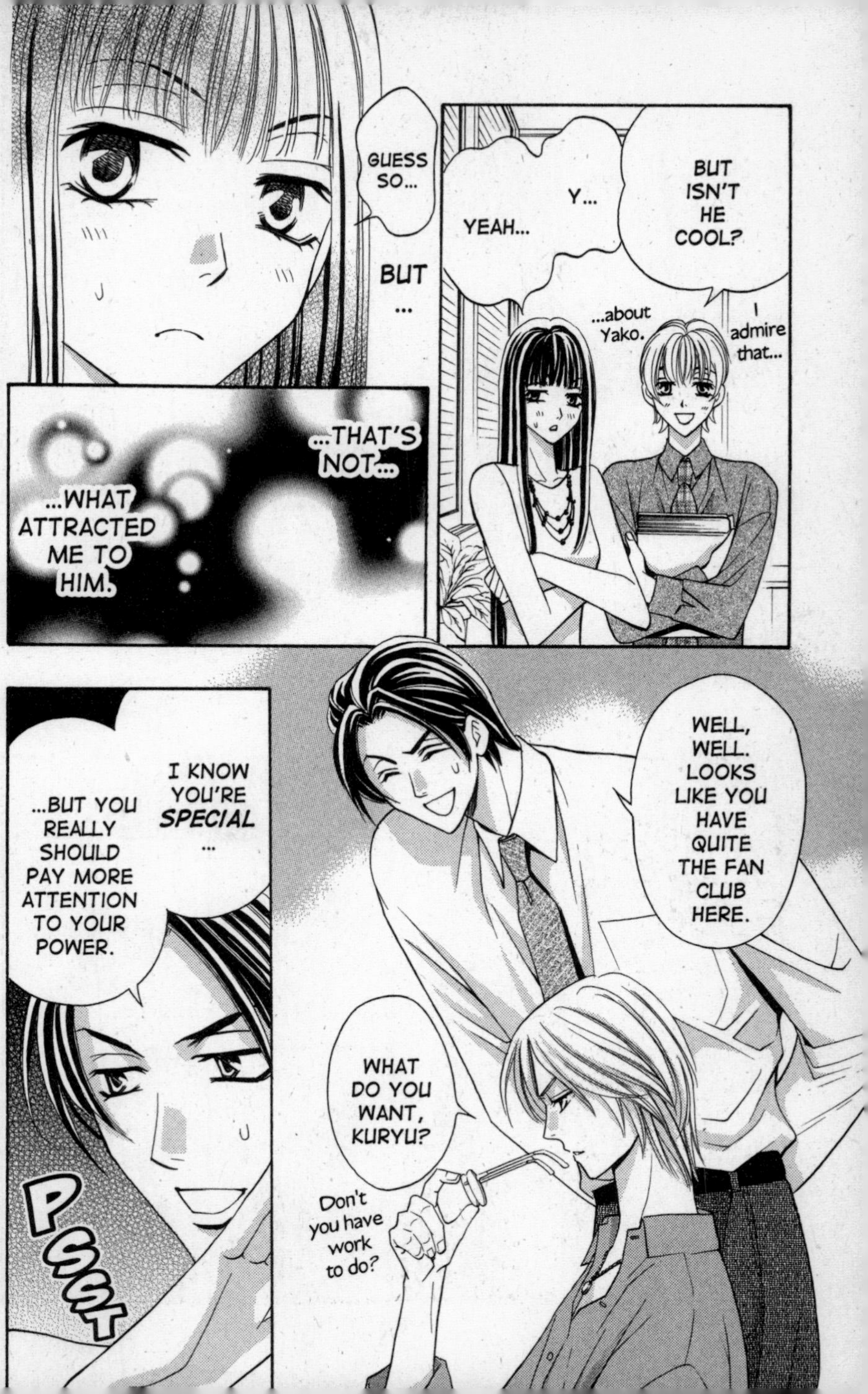
BUT ISN'T HE COOL?
I admire that...
Y... YEAH...
...about Yako.
GUESS SO...
BUT ...
...THAT'S NOT...
...WHAT ATTRACTED ME TO HIM.
WELL, WELL. LOOKS LIKE YOU HAVE QUITE THE FAN CLUB HERE.
WHAT DO YOU WANT, KURYU?
Don't you have work to do?
I KNOW YOU'RE *SPECIAL* ...
...BUT YOU REALLY SHOULD PAY MORE ATTENTION TO YOUR POWER.
PSST

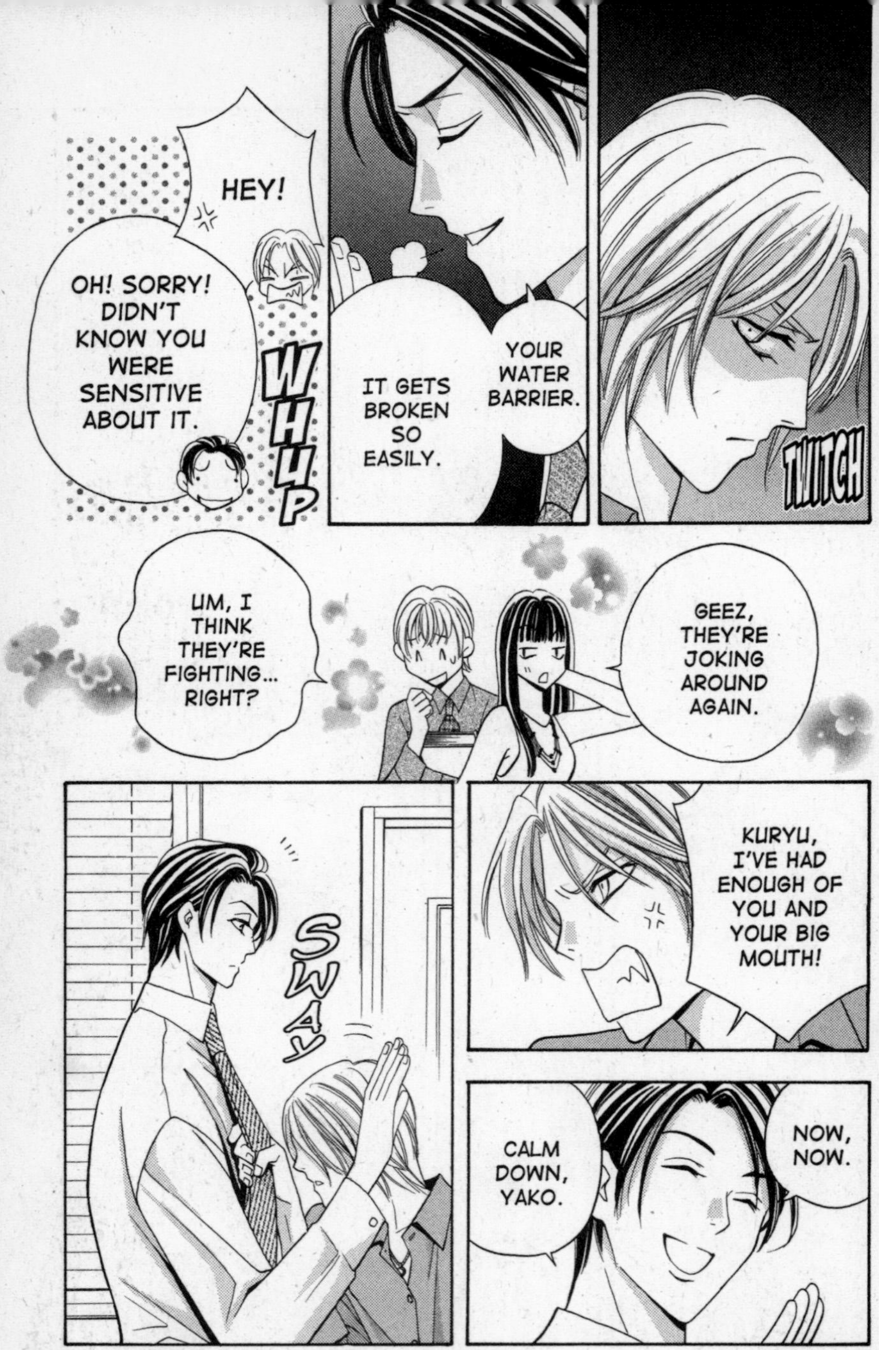
TWITCH
YOUR WATER BARRIER.
IT GETS BROKEN SO EASILY.
HEY!
OH! SORRY! DIDN'T KNOW YOU WERE SENSITIVE ABOUT IT.
WHUP
GEEZ, THEY'RE JOKING AROUND AGAIN.
UM, I THINK THEY'RE FIGHTING... RIGHT?
KURYU, I'VE HAD ENOUGH OF YOU AND YOUR BIG MOUTH!
NOW, NOW.
CALM DOWN, YAKO.
SWAY

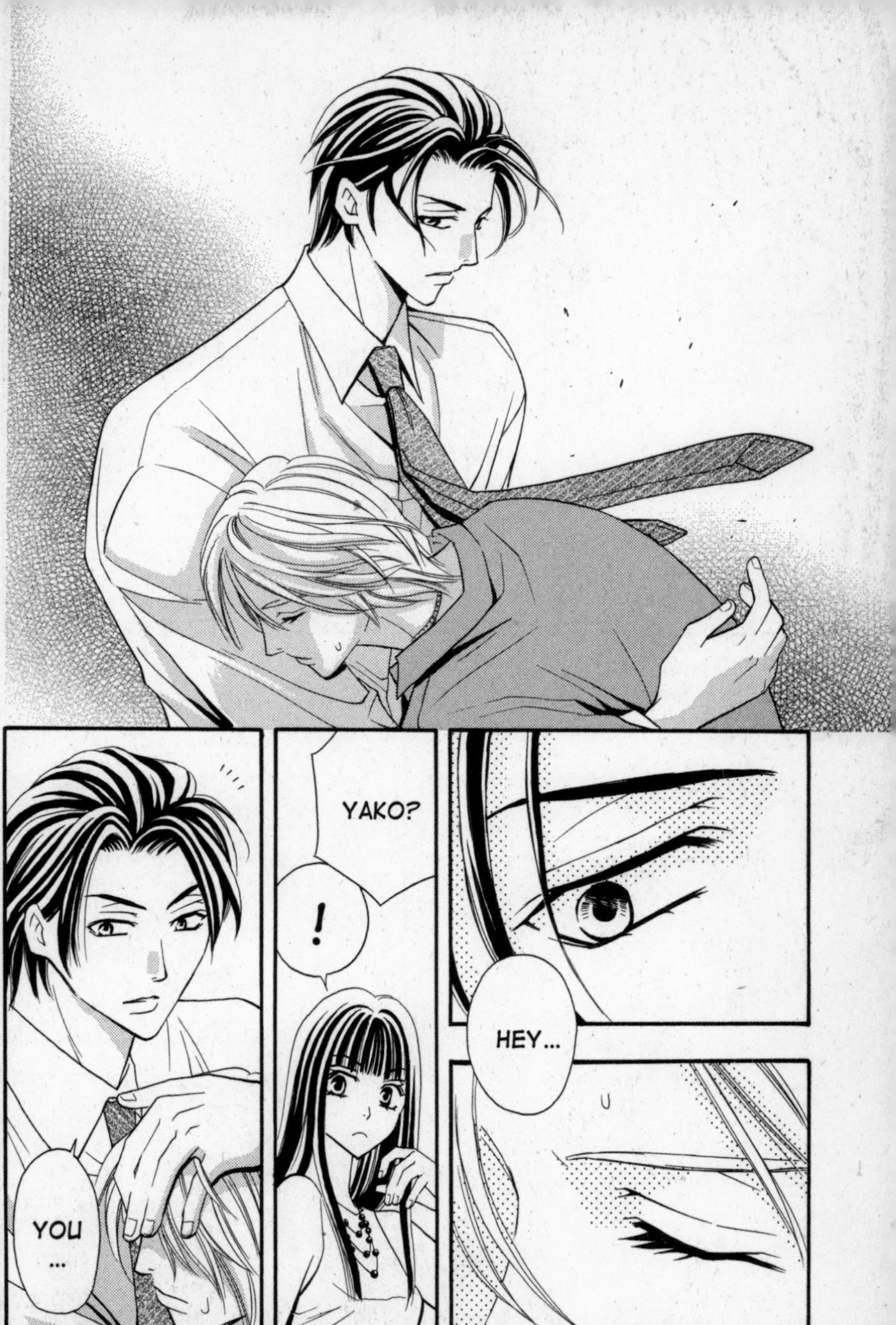
HEY...
YAKO?
!
YOU ...

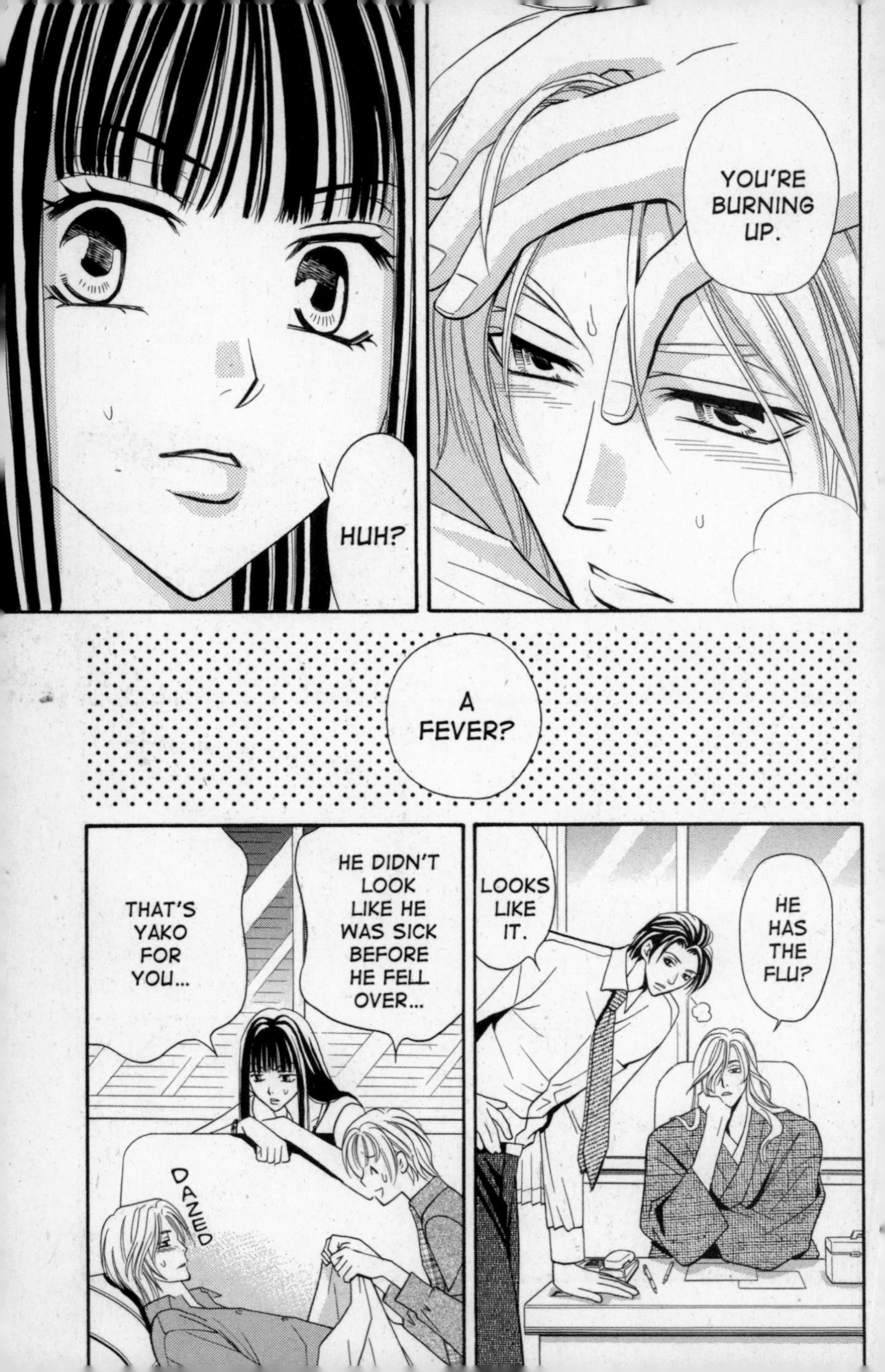
YOU'RE BURNING UP.
HUH?
A FEVER?
HE HAS THE FLU?
LOOKS LIKE IT.
HE DIDN'T LOOK LIKE HE WAS SICK BEFORE HE FELL OVER...
THAT'S YAKO FOR YOU...
DAZED

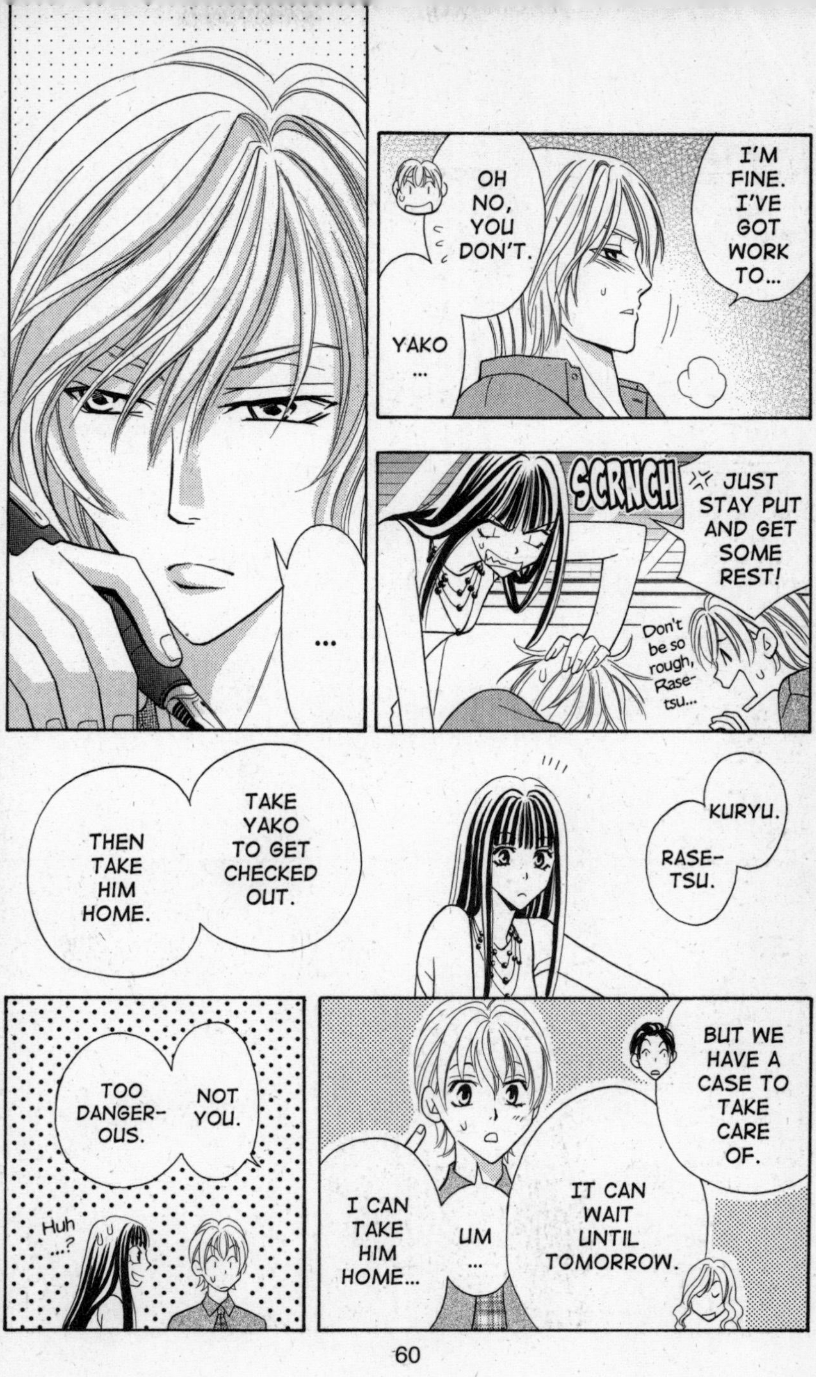
I'M FINE. I'VE GOT WORK TO...
OH NO, YOU DON'T.
YAKO...
SCRNCH
JUST STAY PUT AND GET SOME REST!
Don't be so rough, Rasetsu...
...
KURYU.
RASETSU.
TAKE YAKO TO GET CHECKED OUT.
THEN TAKE HIM HOME.
BUT WE HAVE A CASE TO TAKE CARE OF.
IT CAN WAIT UNTIL TOMORROW.
UM...
I CAN TAKE HIM HOME...
NOT YOU.
TOO DANGEROUS.
Huh...?

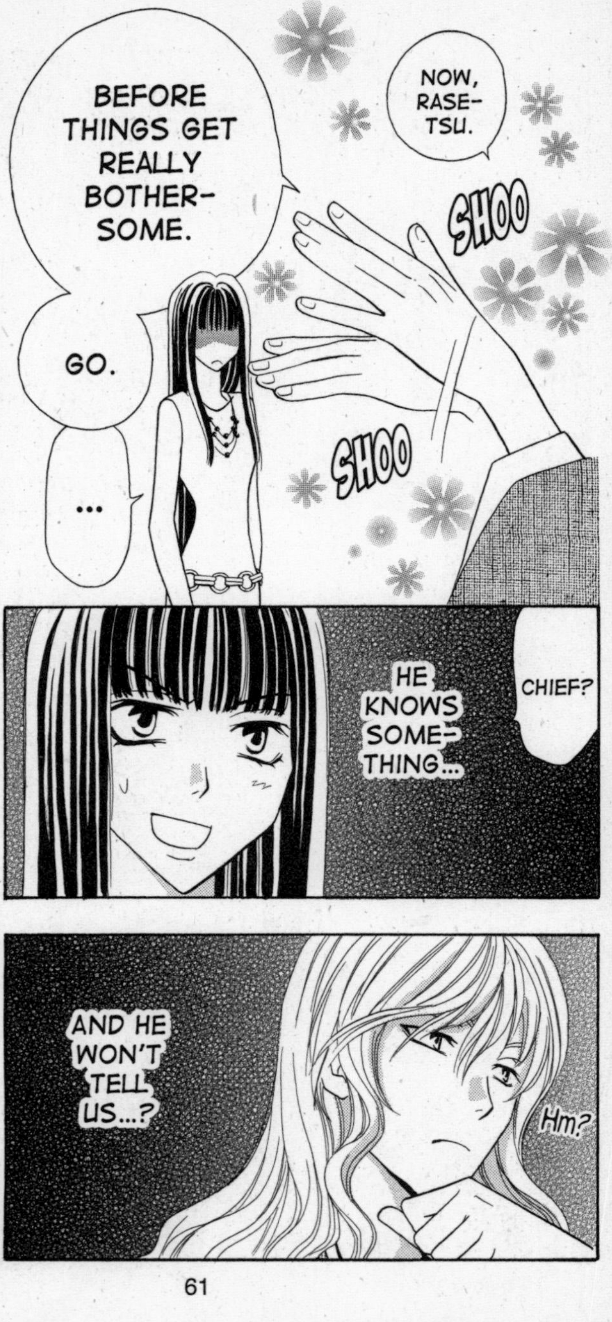
NOW, RASE-TSU.
BEFORE THINGS GET REALLY BOTHER-SOME.
GO.
...
SHOO
SHOO
CHIEF?
HE KNOWS SOME-THING...
Hm?
AND HE WON'T TELL US...?

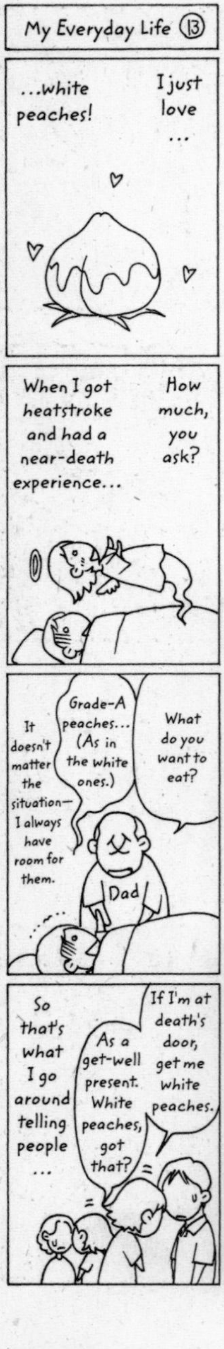
My Everyday Life ⑬
I just love...
...white peaches!
How much, you ask?
When I got heatstroke and had a near-death experience...
What do you want to eat?
Grade-A peaches... (As in the white ones.)
It doesn't matter the situation—I always have room for them.
Dad
If I'm at death's door, get me white peaches.
As a get-well present. White peaches, got that?
So that's what I go around telling people...

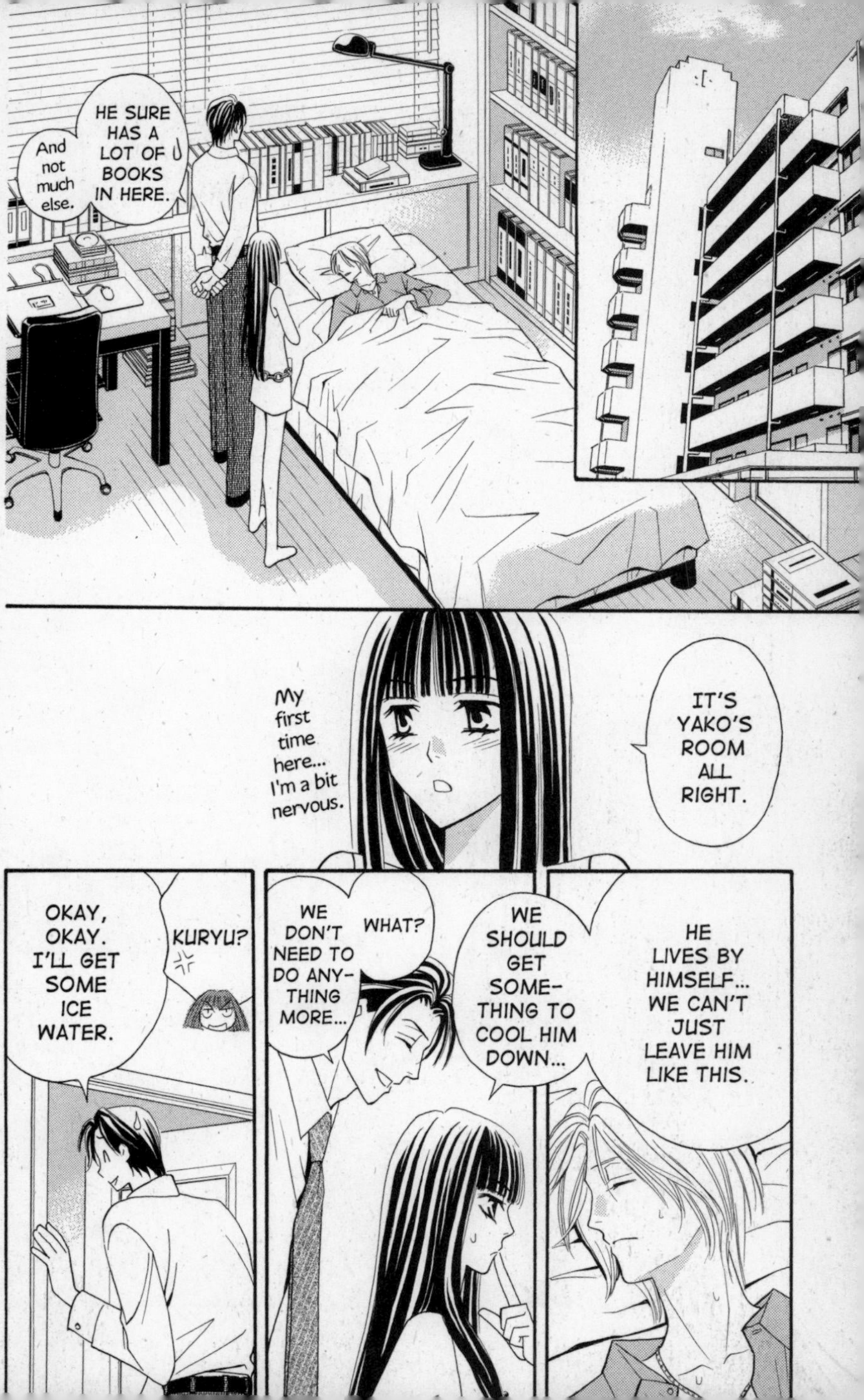
HE SURE HAS A LOT OF BOOKS IN HERE.
And not much else.
IT'S YAKO'S ROOM ALL RIGHT.
My first time here... I'm a bit nervous.
HE LIVES BY HIMSELF... WE CAN'T JUST LEAVE HIM LIKE THIS.
WE SHOULD GET SOME-THING TO COOL HIM DOWN...
WHAT?
WE DON'T NEED TO DO ANY-THING MORE...
KURYU?
OKAY, OKAY. I'LL GET SOME ICE WATER.

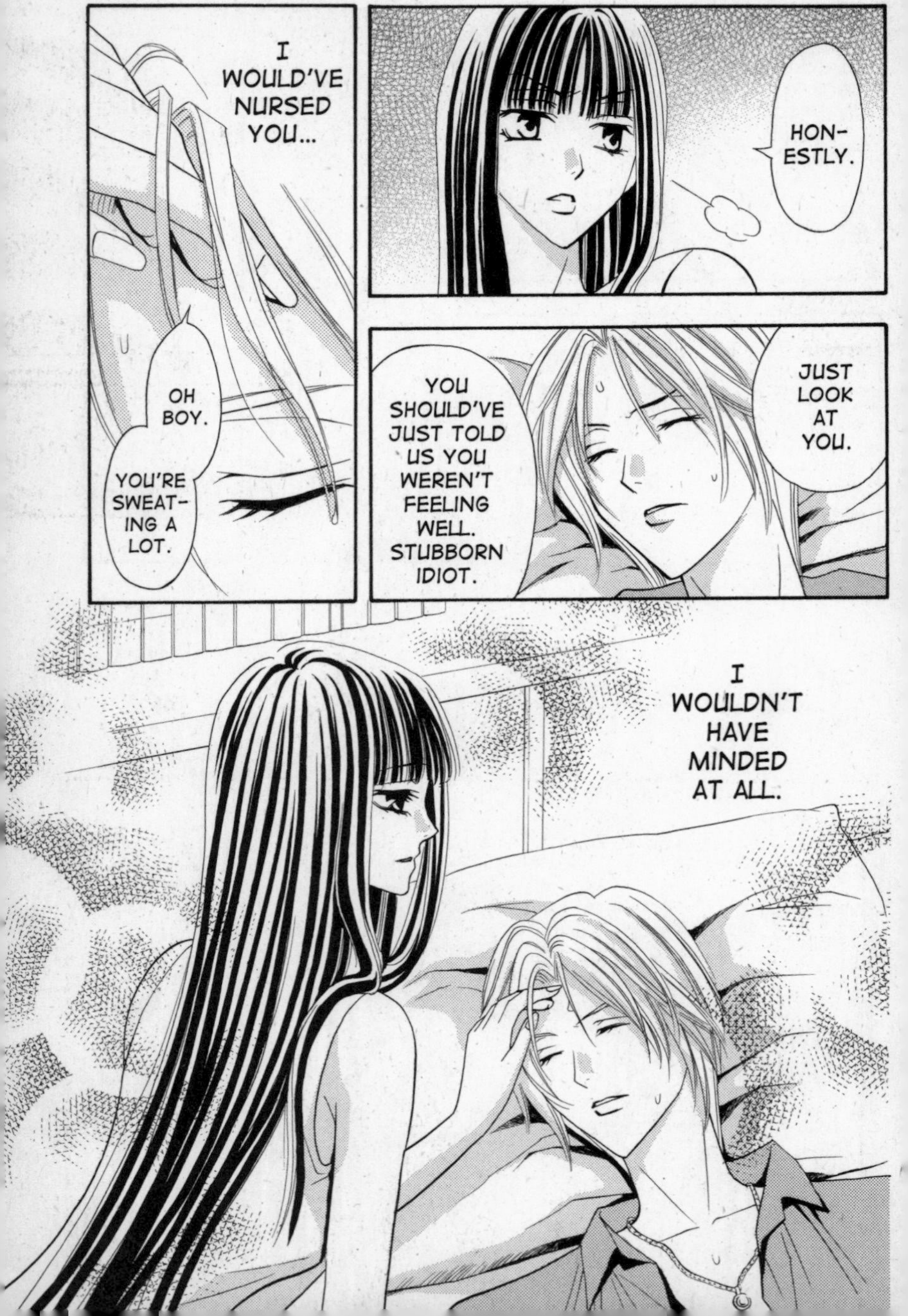
HON-ESTLY.
JUST LOOK AT YOU.
YOU SHOULD'VE JUST TOLD US YOU WEREN'T FEELING WELL. STUBBORN IDIOT.
I WOULD'VE NURSED YOU...
OH BOY.
YOU'RE SWEATING A LOT.
I WOULDN'T HAVE MINDED AT ALL.

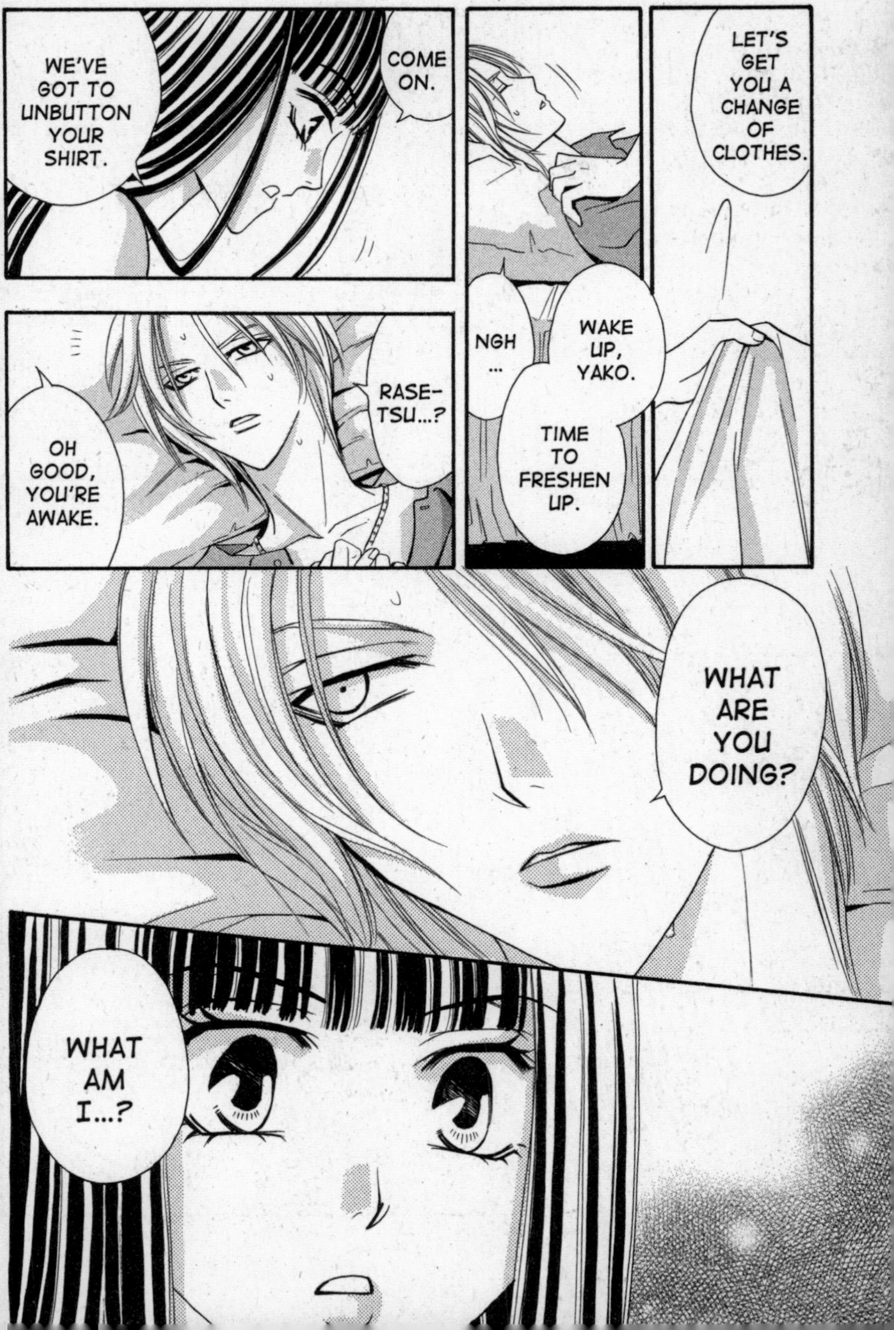
LET'S GET YOU A CHANGE OF CLOTHES.
WAKE UP, YAKO.
NGH ...
TIME TO FRESHEN UP.
COME ON.
WE'VE GOT TO UNBUTTON YOUR SHIRT.
RASE-TSU...?
OH GOOD, YOU'RE AWAKE.
WHAT ARE YOU DOING?
WHAT AM I...?

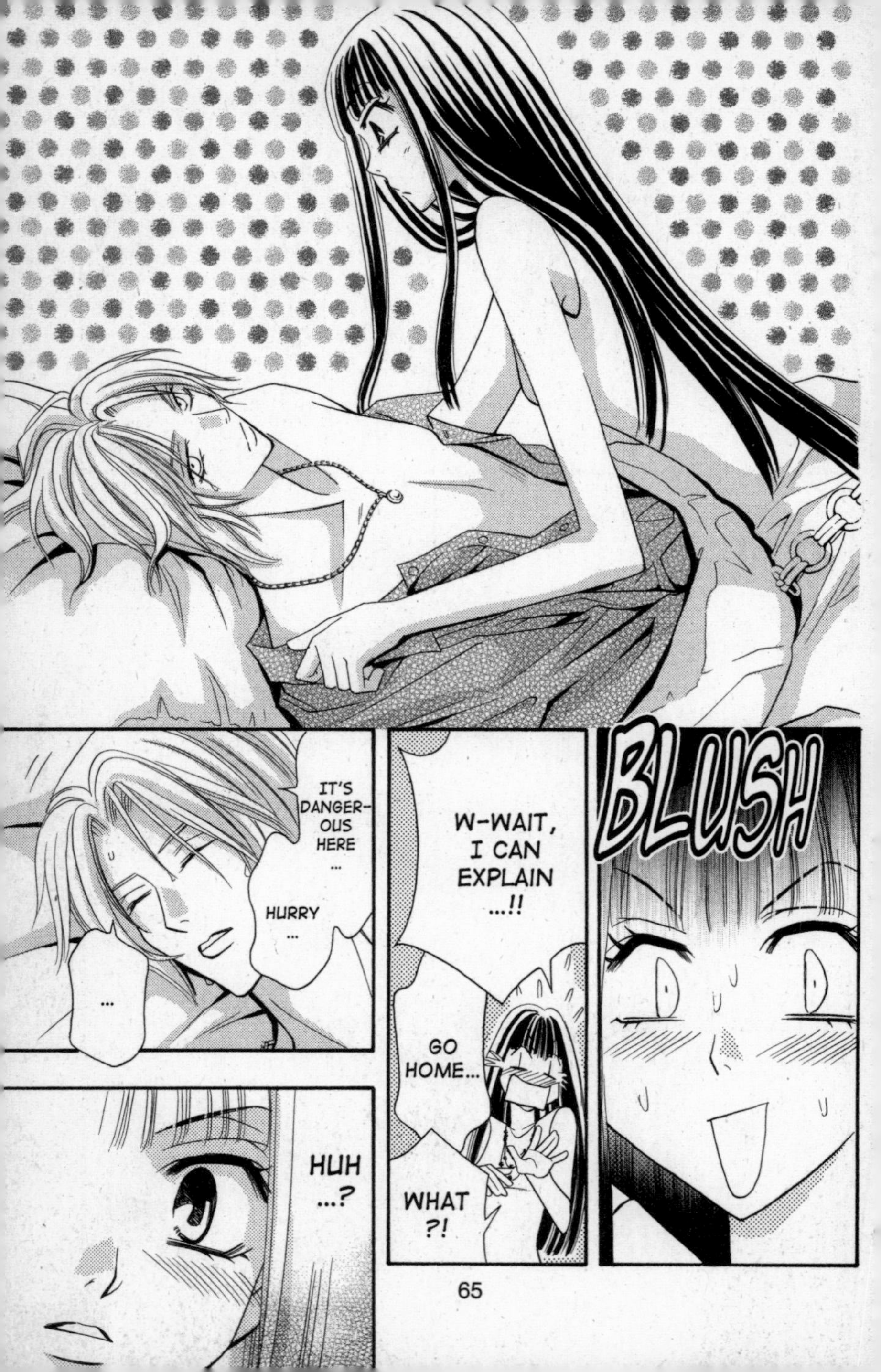
BLUSH
W-WAIT, I CAN EXPLAIN ...!!
GO HOME...
WHAT ?!
IT'S DANGER-OUS HERE ...
HURRY ...
...
HUH ...?

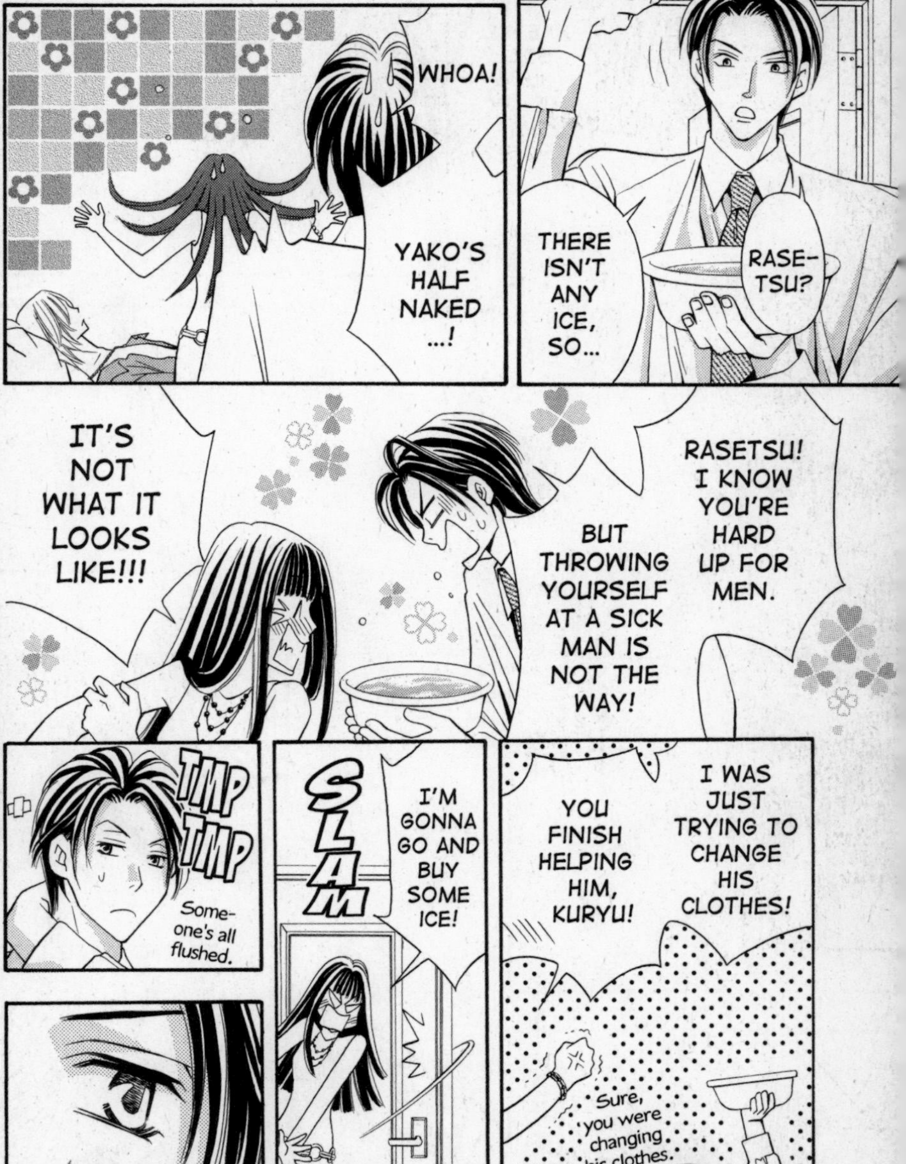
RASE-TSU?
THERE ISN'T ANY ICE, SO...
WHOA!
YAKO'S HALF NAKED ...!
RASETSU! I KNOW YOU'RE HARD UP FOR MEN.
BUT THROWING YOURSELF AT A SICK MAN IS NOT THE WAY!
IT'S NOT WHAT IT LOOKS LIKE!!!
I WAS JUST TRYING TO CHANGE HIS CLOTHES!
YOU FINISH HELPING HIM, KURYU!
Sure, you were changing his clothes.
SLAM
I'M GONNA GO AND BUY SOME ICE!
TMP TMP
Some-one's all flushed.

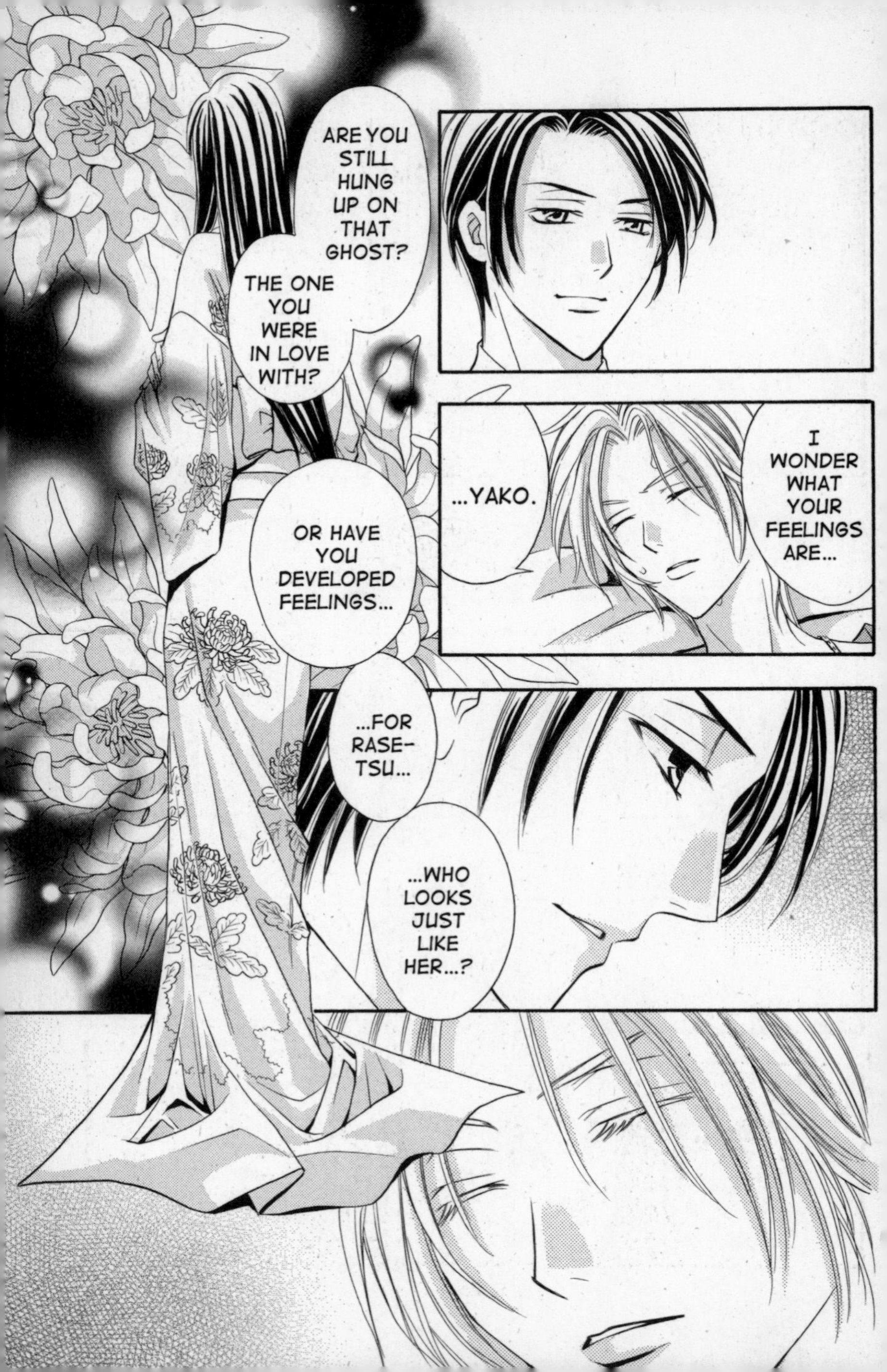
I WONDER WHAT YOUR FEELINGS ARE...
...YAKO.
ARE YOU STILL HUNG UP ON THAT GHOST?
THE ONE YOU WERE IN LOVE WITH?
OR HAVE YOU DEVELOPED FEELINGS...
...FOR RASE-TSU...
...WHO LOOKS JUST LIKE HER...?

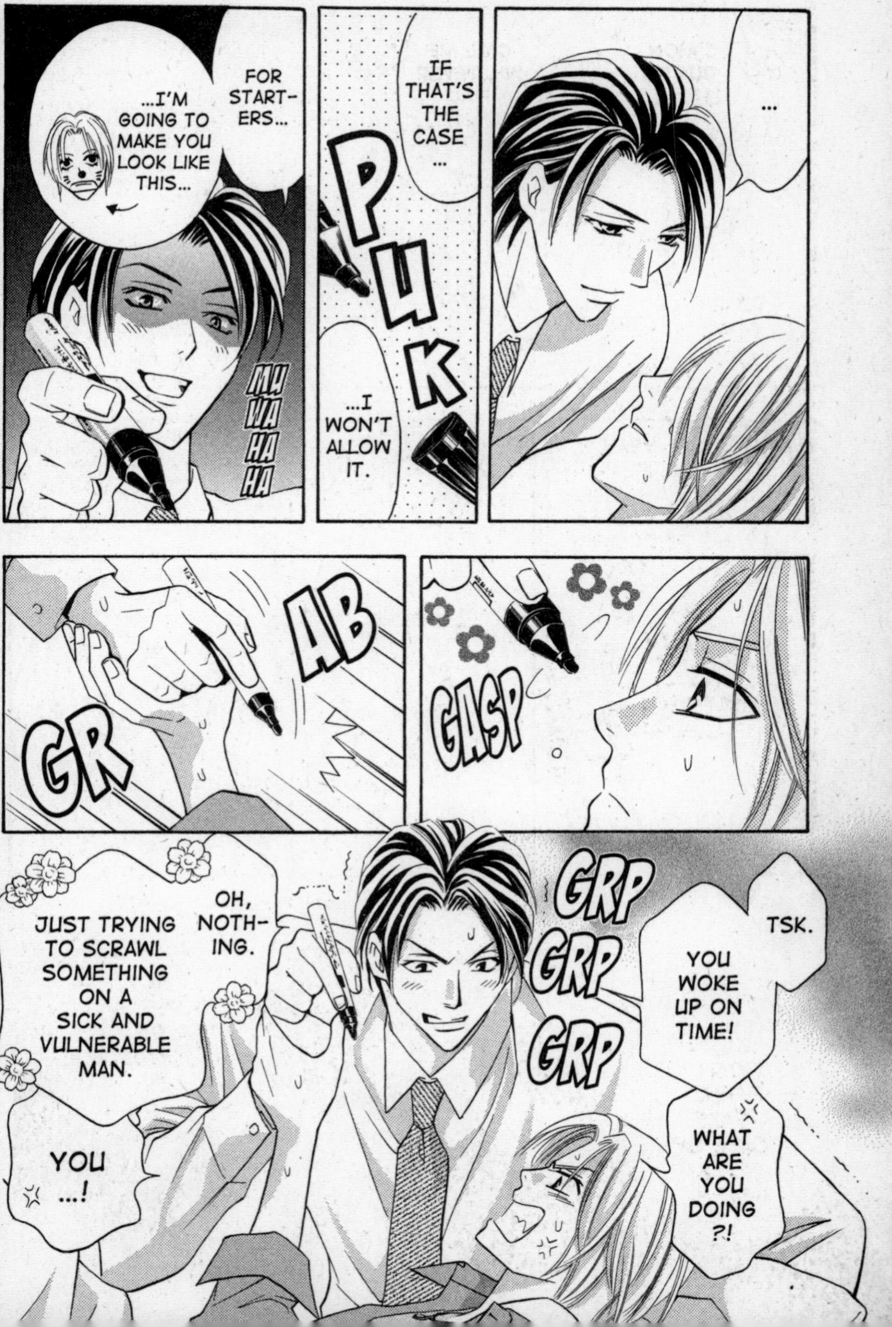
...
IF THAT'S THE CASE ...
PUK
...I WON'T ALLOW IT.
FOR STARTERS...
...I'M GOING TO MAKE YOU LOOK LIKE THIS...
MUWAHAHAHA
GASP
GR
AB
GRP GRP GRP
TSK.
YOU WOKE UP ON TIME!
WHAT ARE YOU DOING?!
OH, NOTHING.
JUST TRYING TO SCRAWL SOMETHING ON A SICK AND VULNERABLE MAN.
YOU ...!

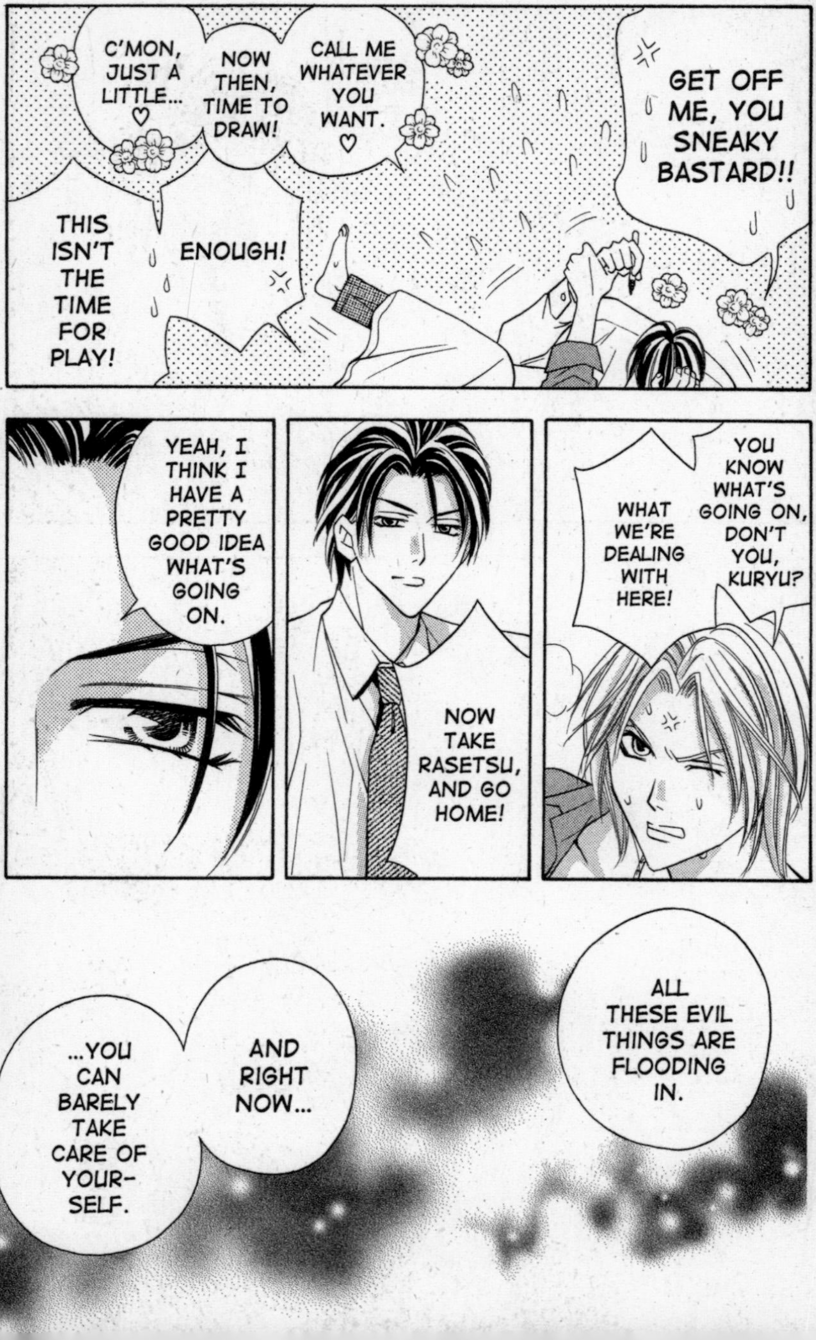
GET OFF ME, YOU SNEAKY BASTARD!!
CALL ME WHATEVER YOU WANT. ♡
NOW THEN, TIME TO DRAW!
C'MON, JUST A LITTLE... ♡
ENOUGH!
THIS ISN'T THE TIME FOR PLAY!
YOU KNOW WHAT'S GOING ON, DON'T YOU, KURYU?
WHAT WE'RE DEALING WITH HERE!
NOW TAKE RASETSU, AND GO HOME!
YEAH, I THINK I HAVE A PRETTY GOOD IDEA WHAT'S GOING ON.
ALL THESE EVIL THINGS ARE FLOODING IN.
AND RIGHT NOW...
...YOU CAN BARELY TAKE CARE OF YOURSELF.

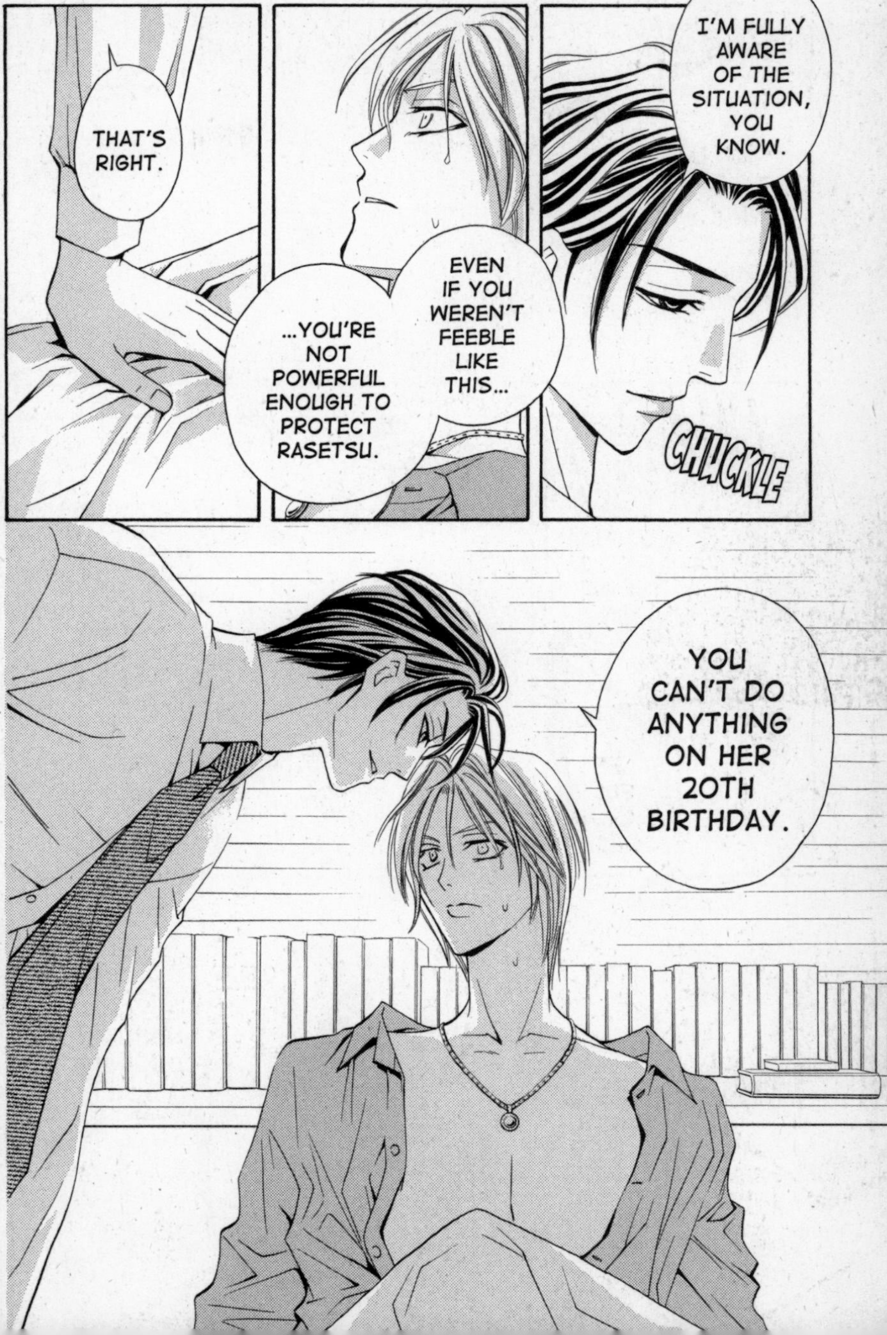
I'M FULLY AWARE OF THE SITUATION, YOU KNOW.
CHUCKLE
EVEN IF YOU WEREN'T FEEBLE LIKE THIS...
...YOU'RE NOT POWERFUL ENOUGH TO PROTECT RASETSU.
THAT'S RIGHT.
YOU CAN'T DO ANYTHING ON HER 20TH BIRTHDAY.

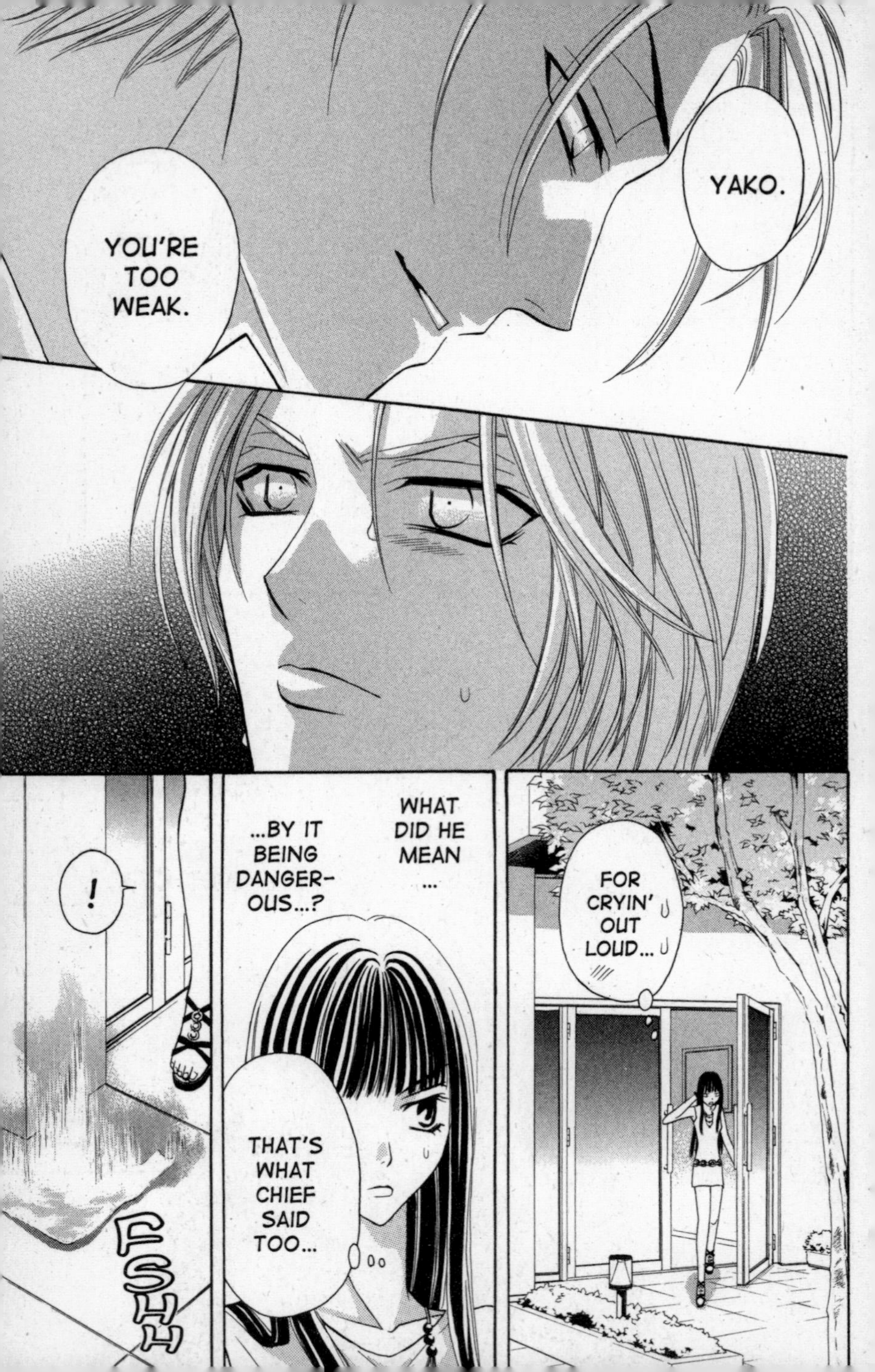
YAKO.
YOU'RE TOO WEAK.
FOR CRYIN' OUT LOUD...
WHAT DID HE MEAN ...
...BY IT BEING DANGER-OUS...?
THAT'S WHAT CHIEF SAID TOO...
!
FSHH

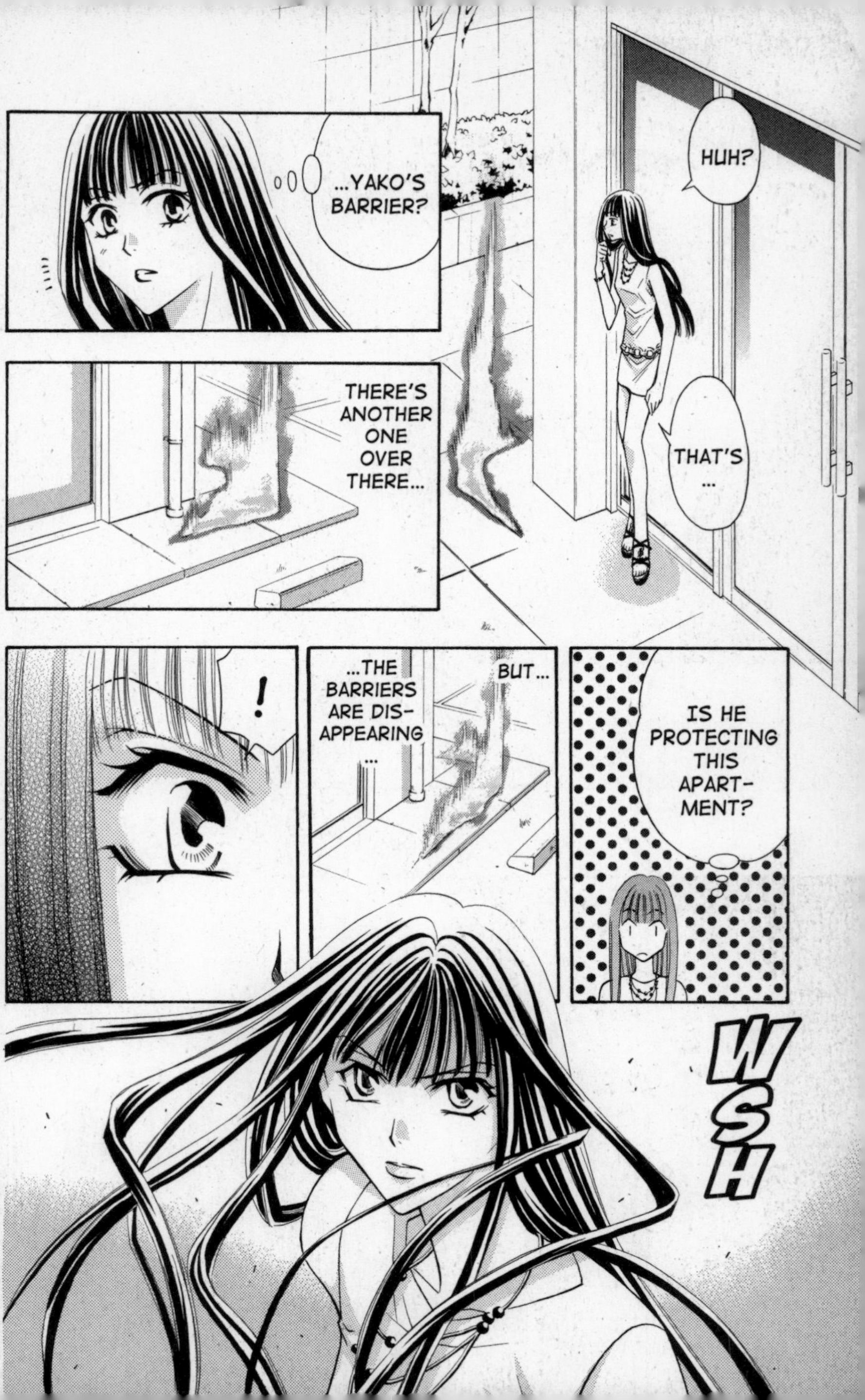
HUH?
THAT'S ...
...YAKO'S BARRIER?
THERE'S ANOTHER ONE OVER THERE...
IS HE PROTECTING THIS APARTMENT?
BUT...
...THE BARRIERS ARE DISAPPEARING ...
!
WSH

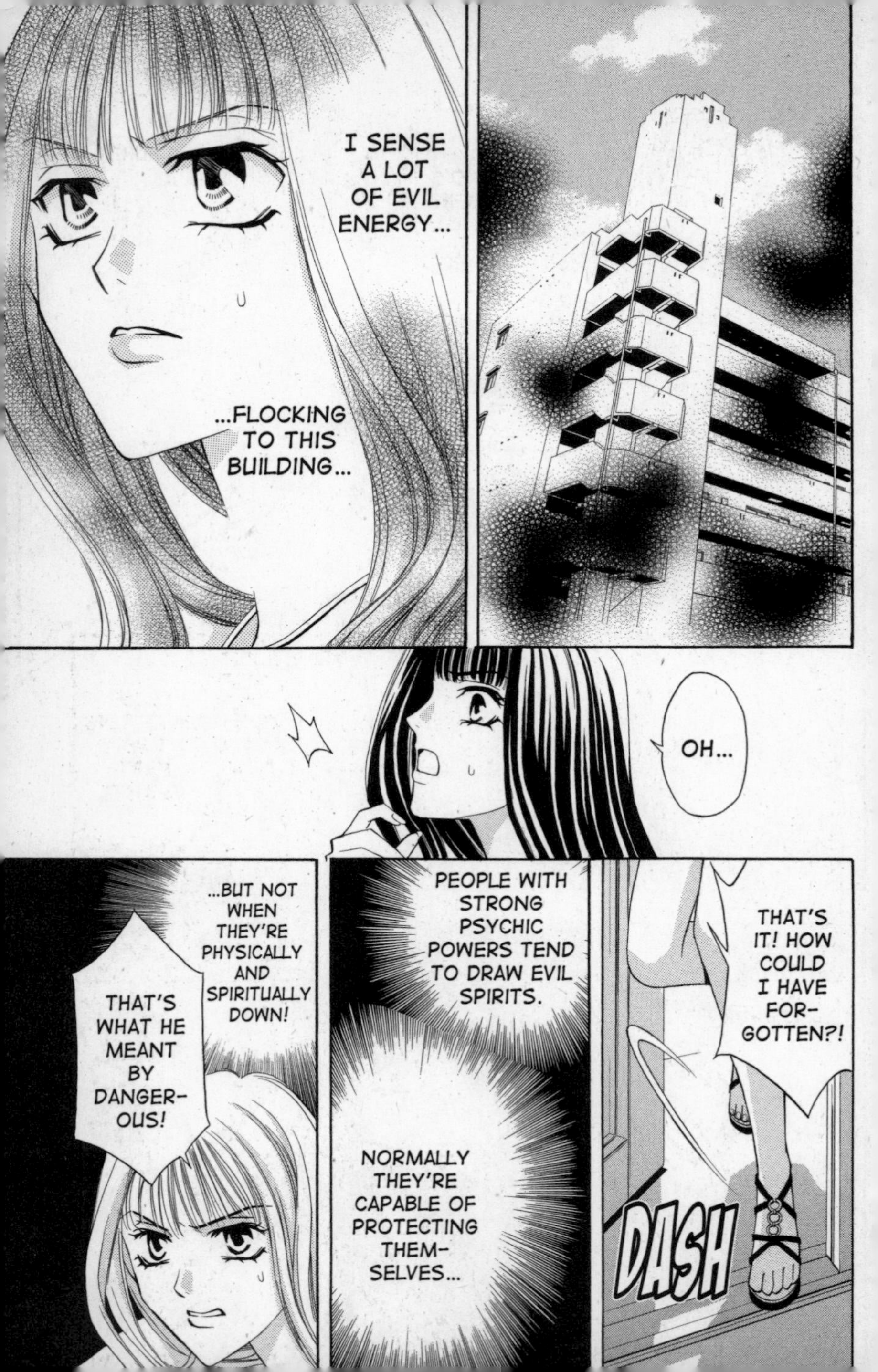
I SENSE A LOT OF EVIL ENERGY...
...FLOCKING TO THIS BUILDING...
OH...
THAT'S IT! HOW COULD I HAVE FOR-GOTTEN?!
DASH
PEOPLE WITH STRONG PSYCHIC POWERS TEND TO DRAW EVIL SPIRITS.
NORMALLY THEY'RE CAPABLE OF PROTECTING THEM-SELVES...
...BUT NOT WHEN THEY'RE PHYSICALLY AND SPIRITUALLY DOWN!
THAT'S WHAT HE MEANT BY DANGER-OUS!

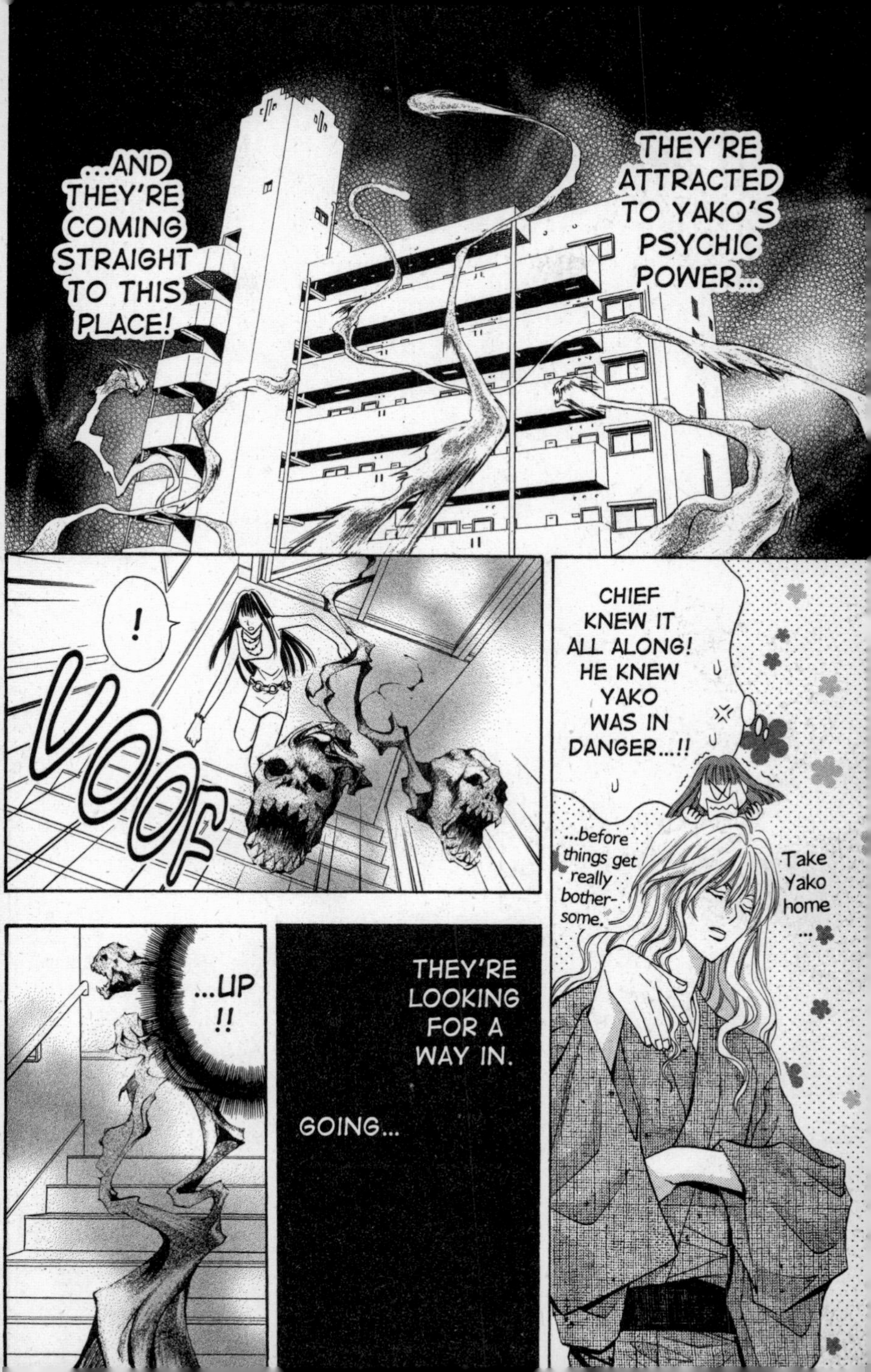
THEY'RE ATTRACTED TO YAKO'S PSYCHIC POWER...
...AND THEY'RE COMING STRAIGHT TO THIS PLACE!
CHIEF KNEW IT ALL ALONG! HE KNEW YAKO WAS IN DANGER...!!
Take Yako home...
...before things get really bother-some.
!
VOOF
THEY'RE LOOKING FOR A WAY IN.
GOING...
...UP !!

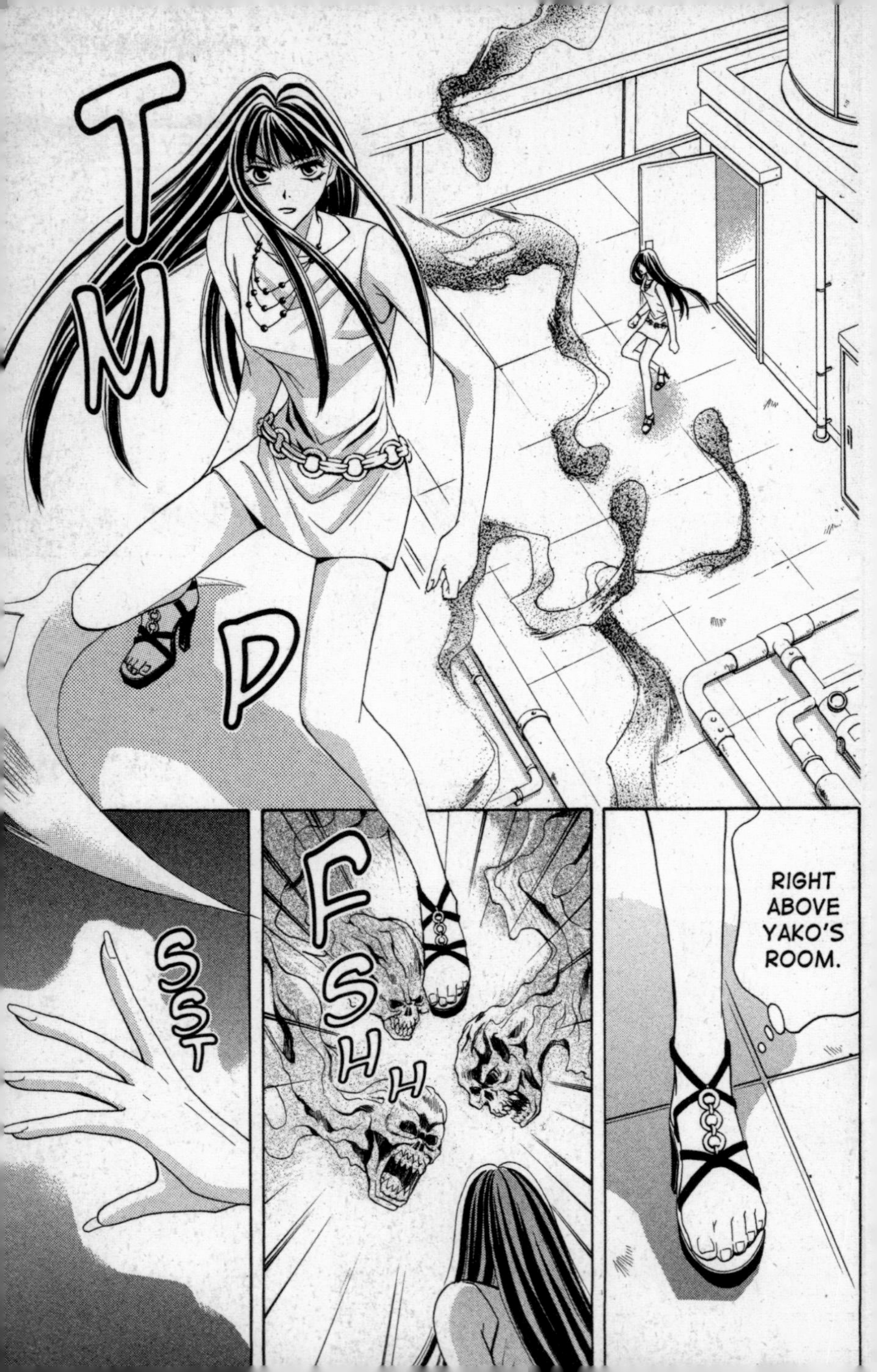
TMP
RIGHT ABOVE YAKO'S ROOM.
FSHH
SSST

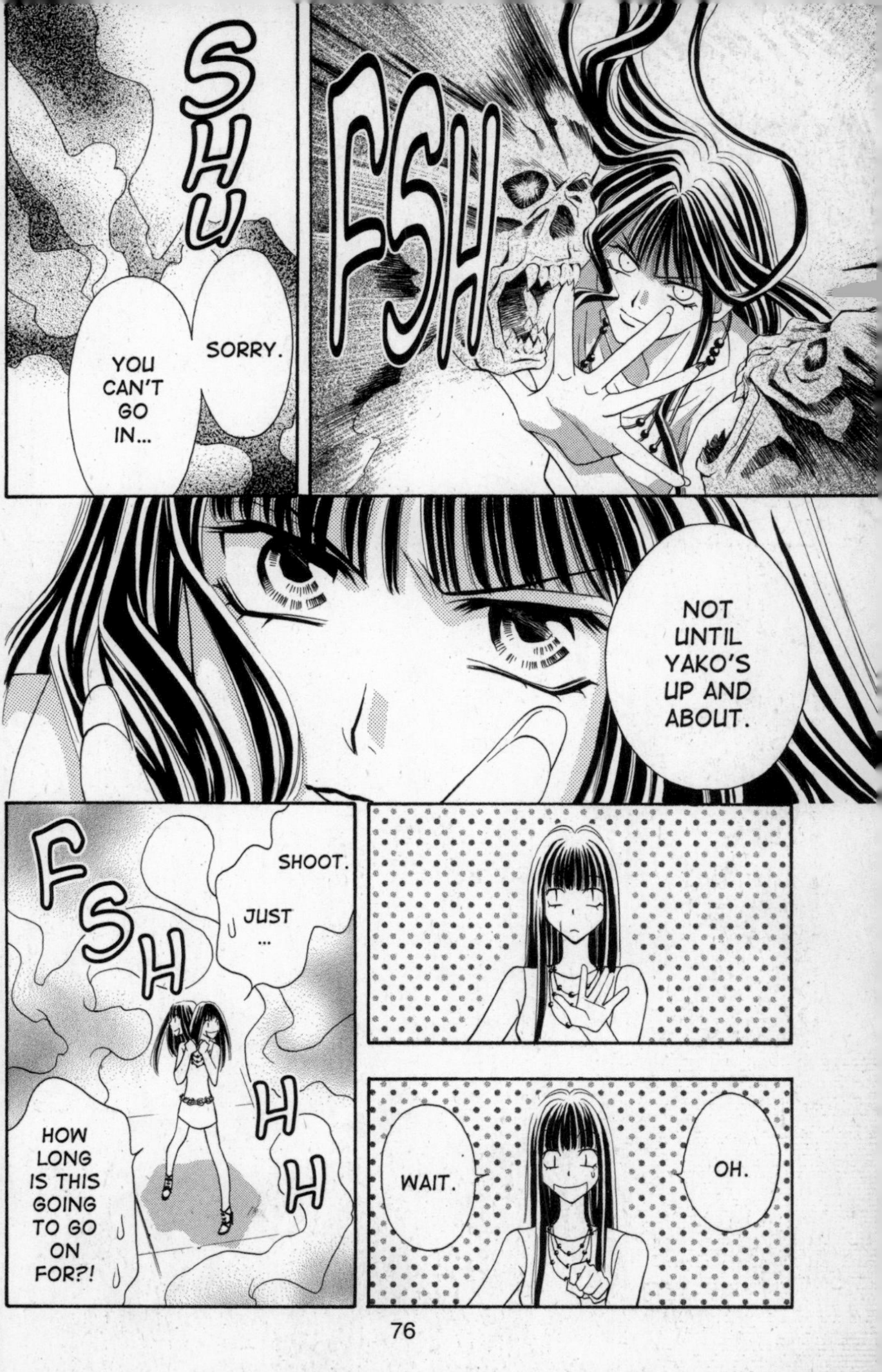
FSH
SHU
SORRY.
YOU CAN'T GO IN...
NOT UNTIL YAKO'S UP AND ABOUT.
OH.
WAIT.
SHOOT.
JUST ...
FSH
HH
HOW LONG IS THIS GOING TO GO ON FOR?!

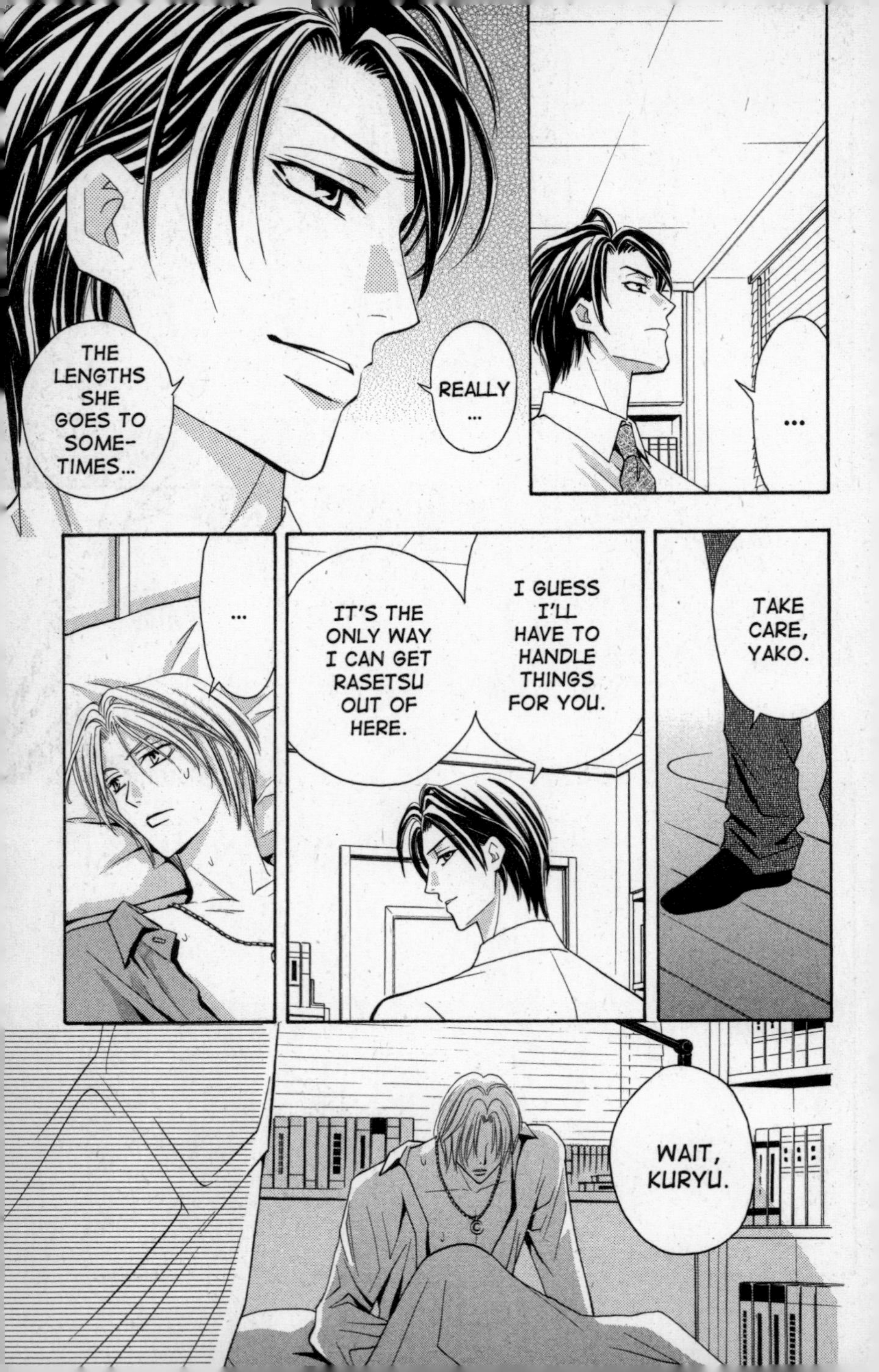
...
REALLY...
THE LENGTHS SHE GOES TO SOME-TIMES...
TAKE CARE, YAKO.
I GUESS I'LL HAVE TO HANDLE THINGS FOR YOU.
IT'S THE ONLY WAY I CAN GET RASETSU OUT OF HERE.
...
WAIT, KURYU.

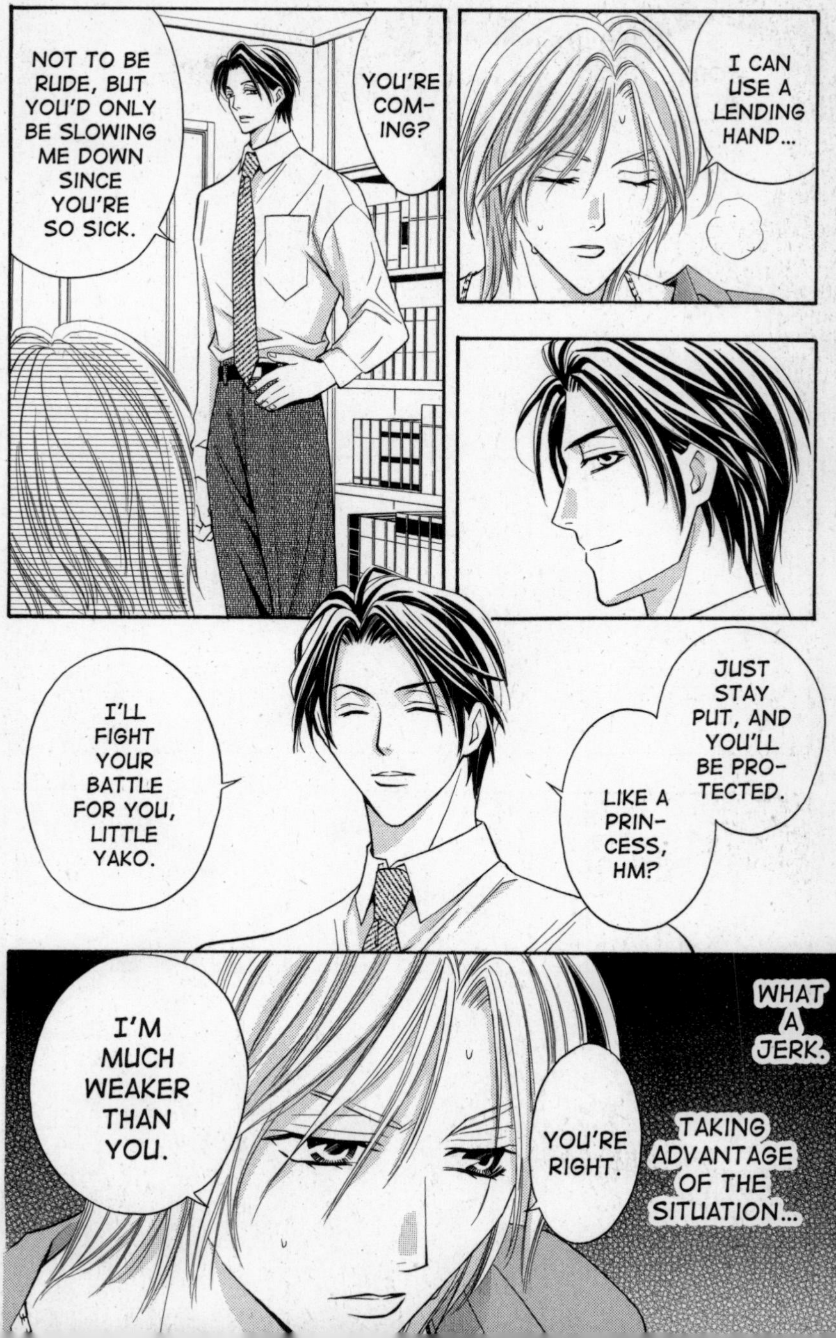
I CAN USE A LENDING HAND...
YOU'RE COMING?
NOT TO BE RUDE, BUT YOU'D ONLY BE SLOWING ME DOWN SINCE YOU'RE SO SICK.
JUST STAY PUT, AND YOU'LL BE PROTECTED.
LIKE A PRINCESS, HM?
I'LL FIGHT YOUR BATTLE FOR YOU, LITTLE YAKO.
WHAT A JERK.
TAKING ADVANTAGE OF THE SITUATION...
YOU'RE RIGHT.
I'M MUCH WEAKER THAN YOU.

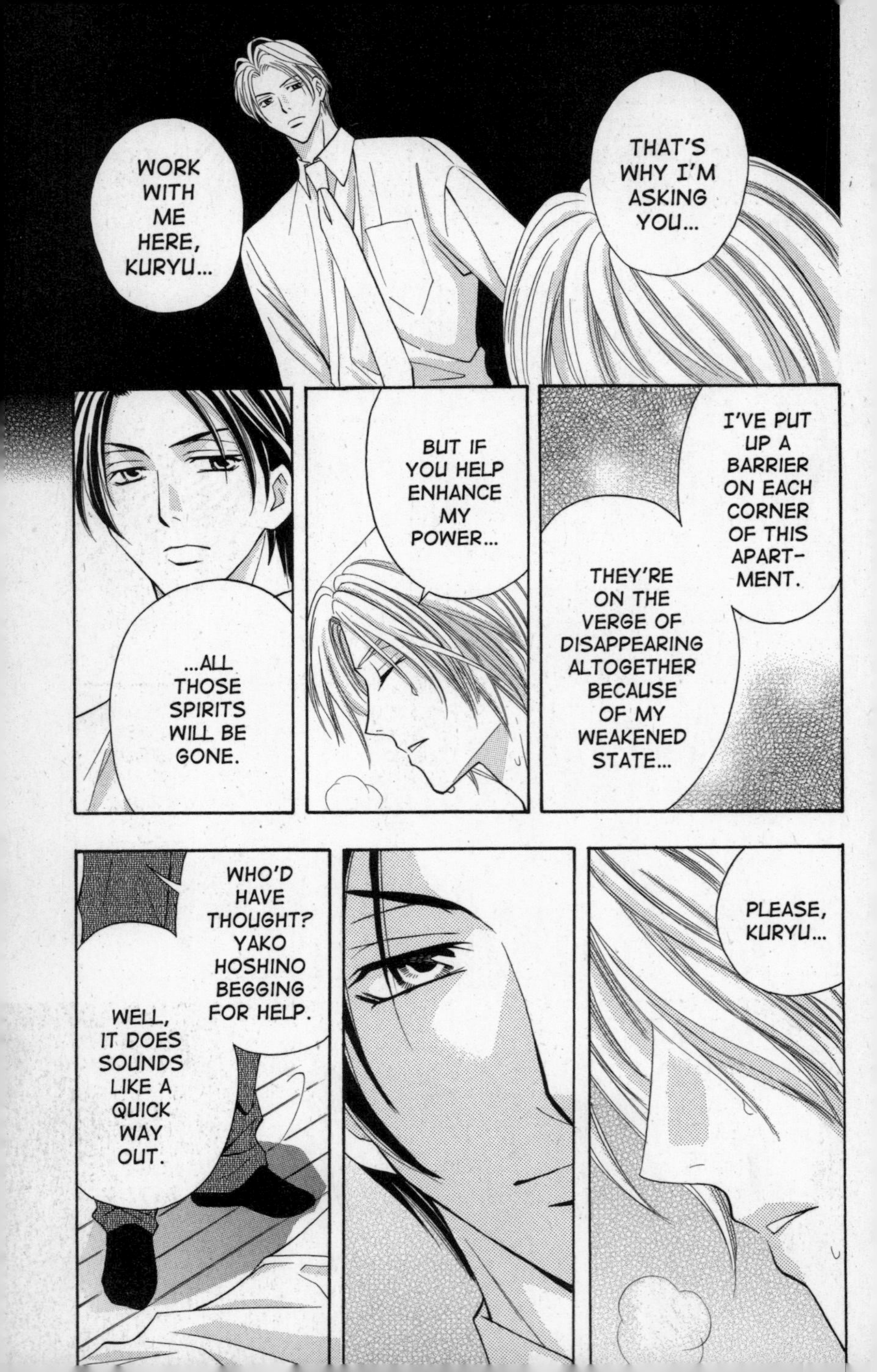
THAT'S WHY I'M ASKING YOU...
WORK WITH ME HERE, KURYU...
I'VE PUT UP A BARRIER ON EACH CORNER OF THIS APART-MENT.
THEY'RE ON THE VERGE OF DISAPPEARING ALTOGETHER BECAUSE OF MY WEAKENED STATE...
BUT IF YOU HELP ENHANCE MY POWER...
...ALL THOSE SPIRITS WILL BE GONE.
PLEASE, KURYU...
WHO'D HAVE THOUGHT? YAKO HOSHINO BEGGING FOR HELP.
WELL, IT DOES SOUNDS LIKE A QUICK WAY OUT.

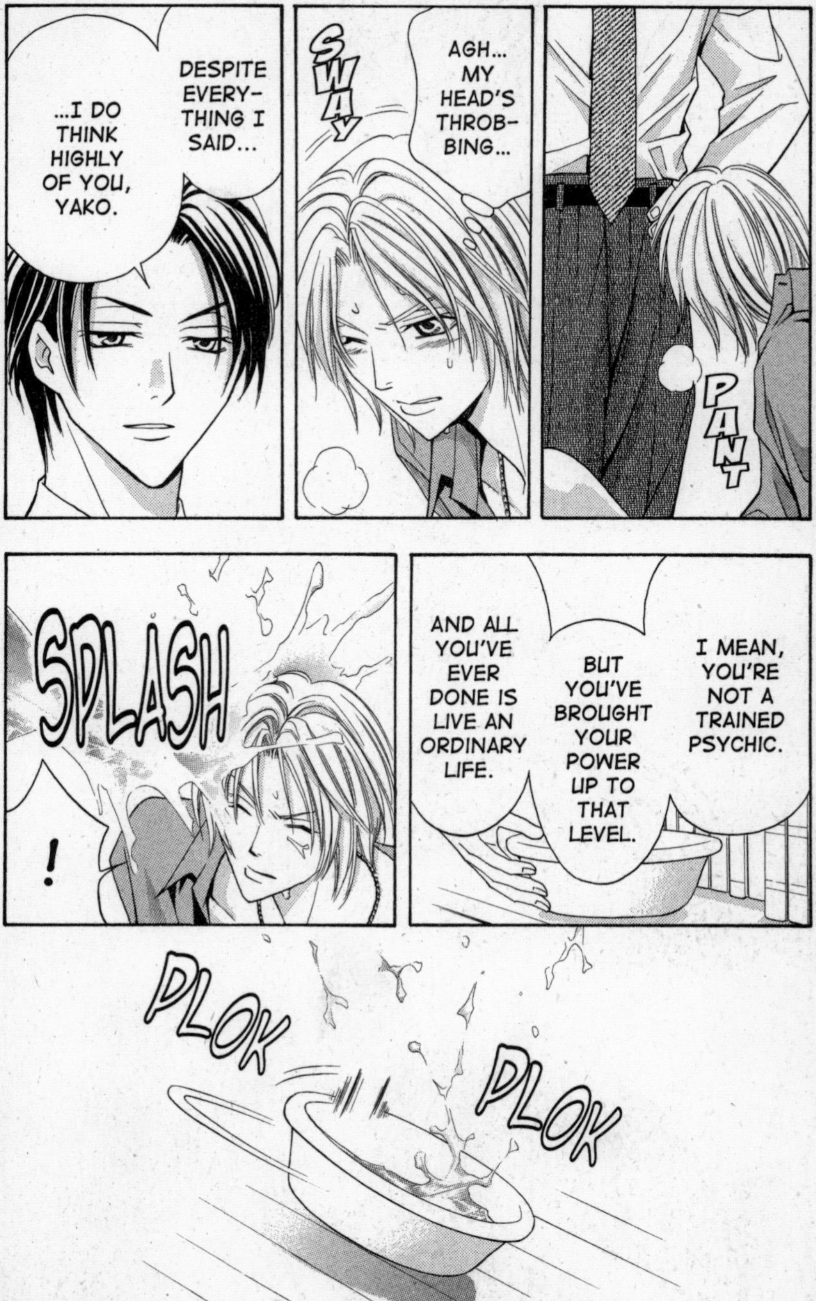
PANT
AGH... MY HEAD'S THROBBING...
SWAY
DESPITE EVERYTHING I SAID...
...I DO THINK HIGHLY OF YOU, YAKO.
I MEAN, YOU'RE NOT A TRAINED PSYCHIC.
BUT YOU'VE BROUGHT YOUR POWER UP TO THAT LEVEL.
AND ALL YOU'VE EVER DONE IS LIVE AN ORDINARY LIFE.
SPLASH
!
PLOK
PLOK

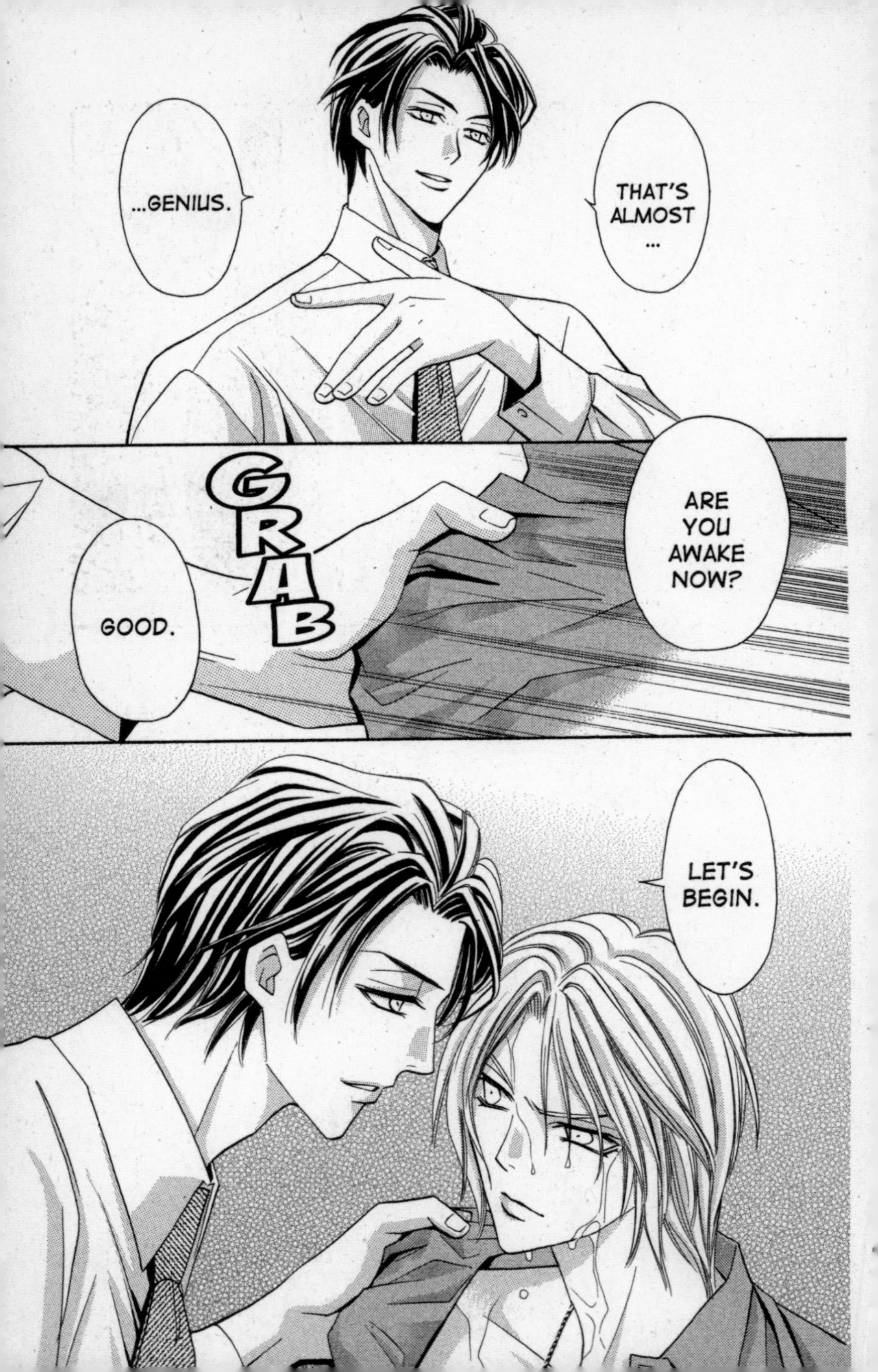
THAT'S ALMOST ...
...GENIUS.
ARE YOU AWAKE NOW?
GRAB
GOOD.
LET'S BEGIN.

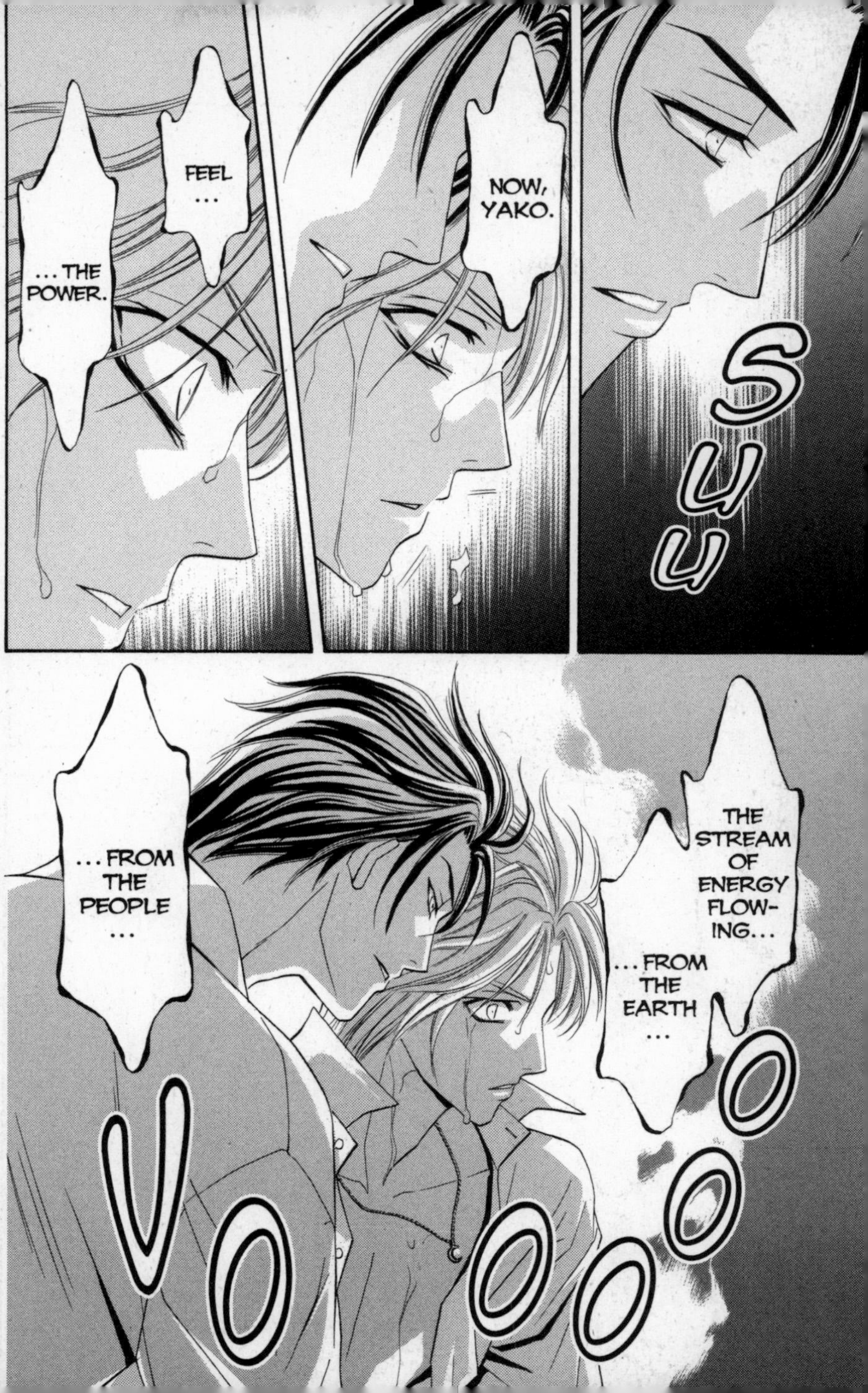
SUUU
NOW, YAKO.
FEEL...
...THE POWER.
THE STREAM OF ENERGY FLOWING...
...FROM THE EARTH...
...FROM THE PEOPLE...
VOOOOOO

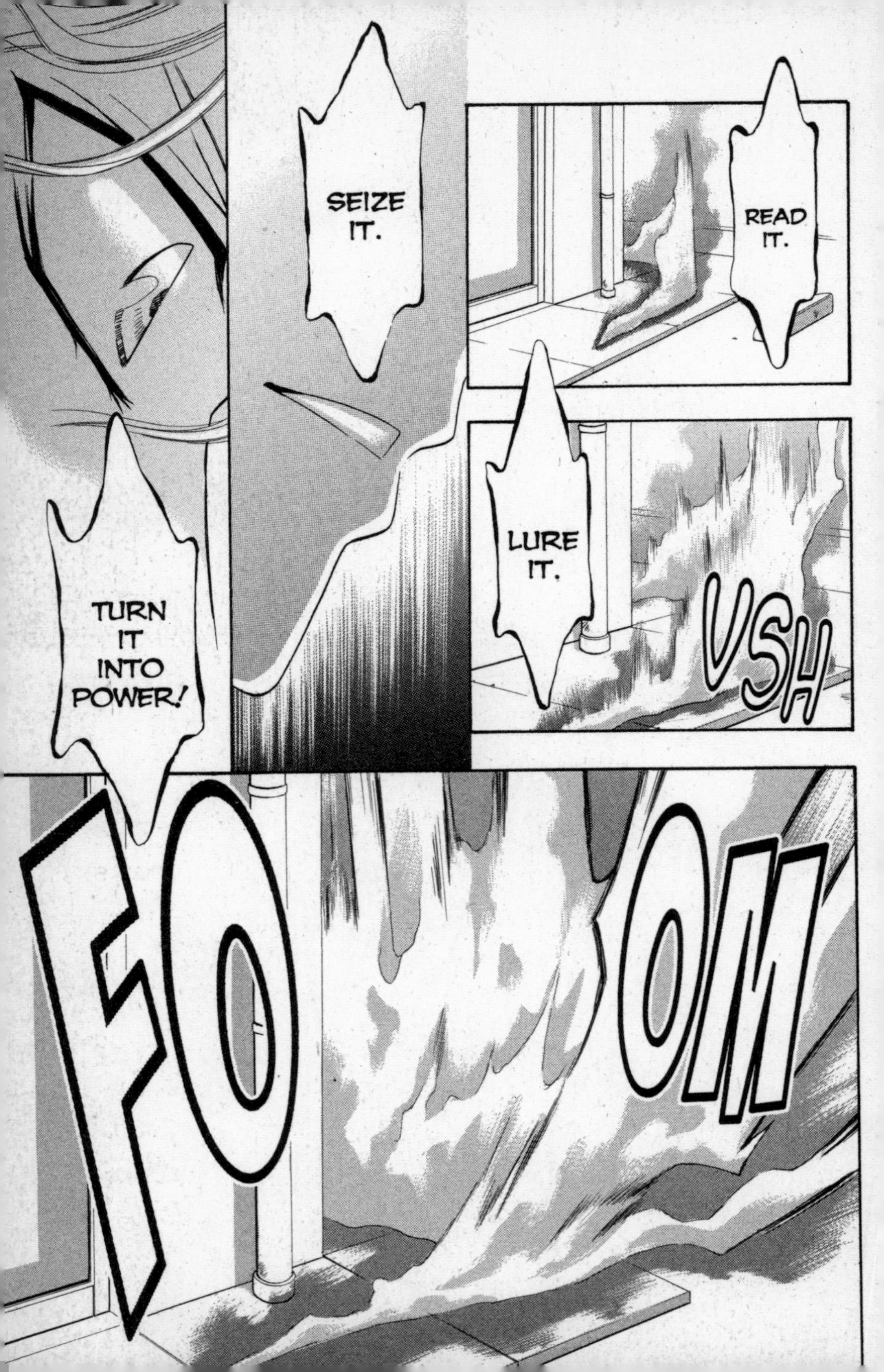
READ IT.
LURE IT.
VSH
SEIZE IT.
TURN IT INTO POWER!
FOOM

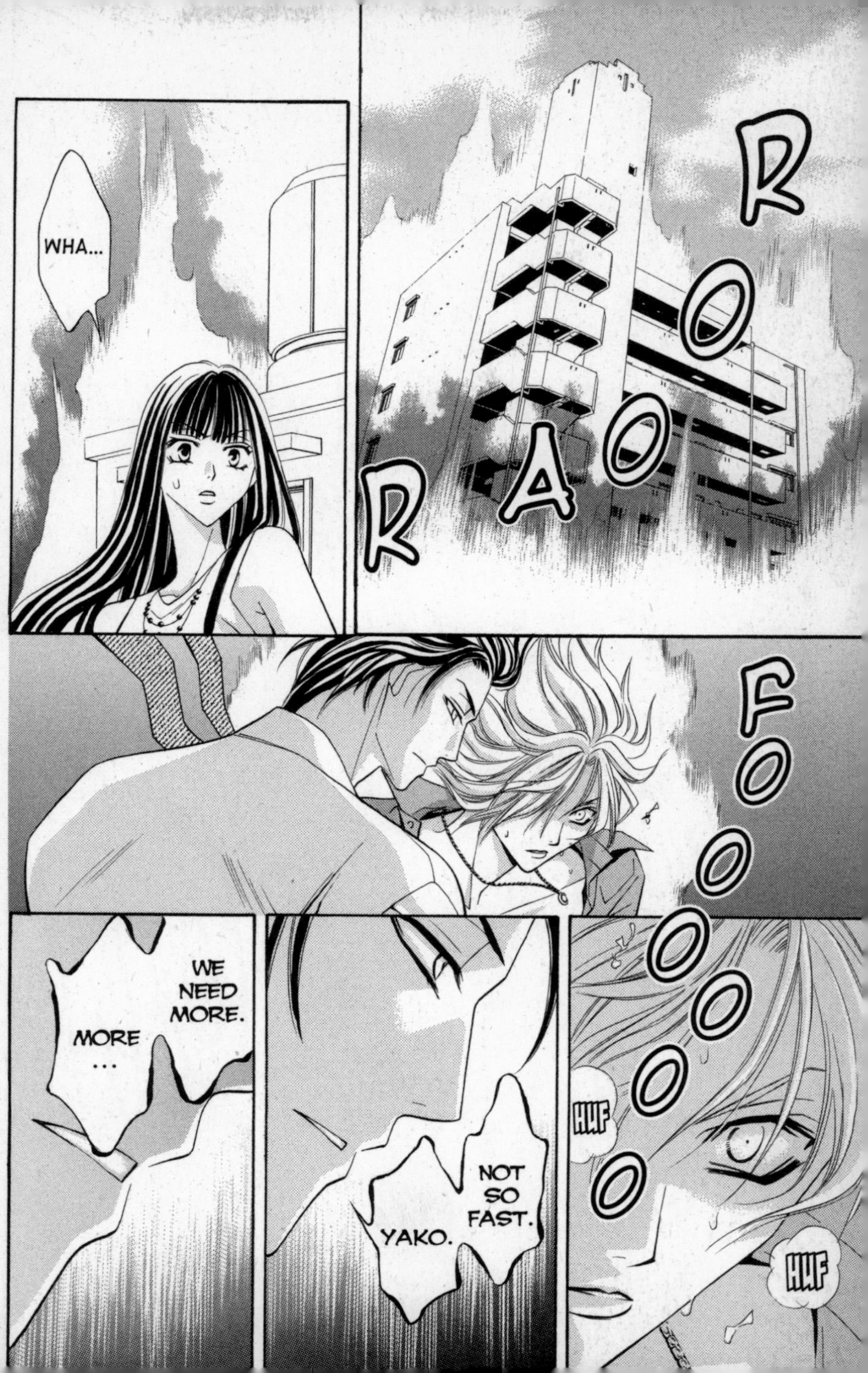
ROAR
WHA...
FOOOOOOOO
HUF
HUF
NOT SO FAST.
YAKO.
WE NEED MORE.
MORE ...

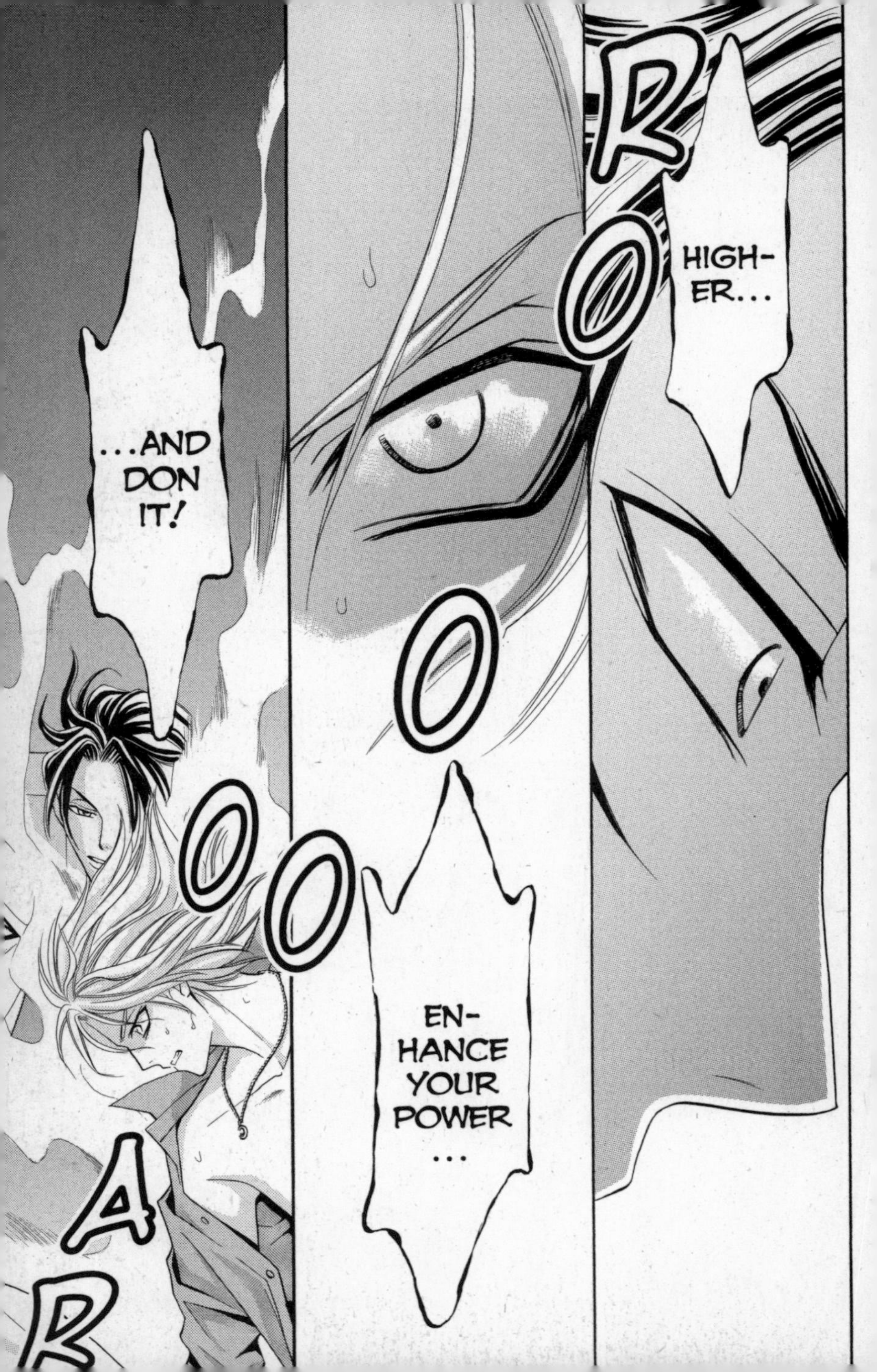
HIGH-ER...
EN-HANCE YOUR POWER...
...AND DON IT!
ROOOOOAR

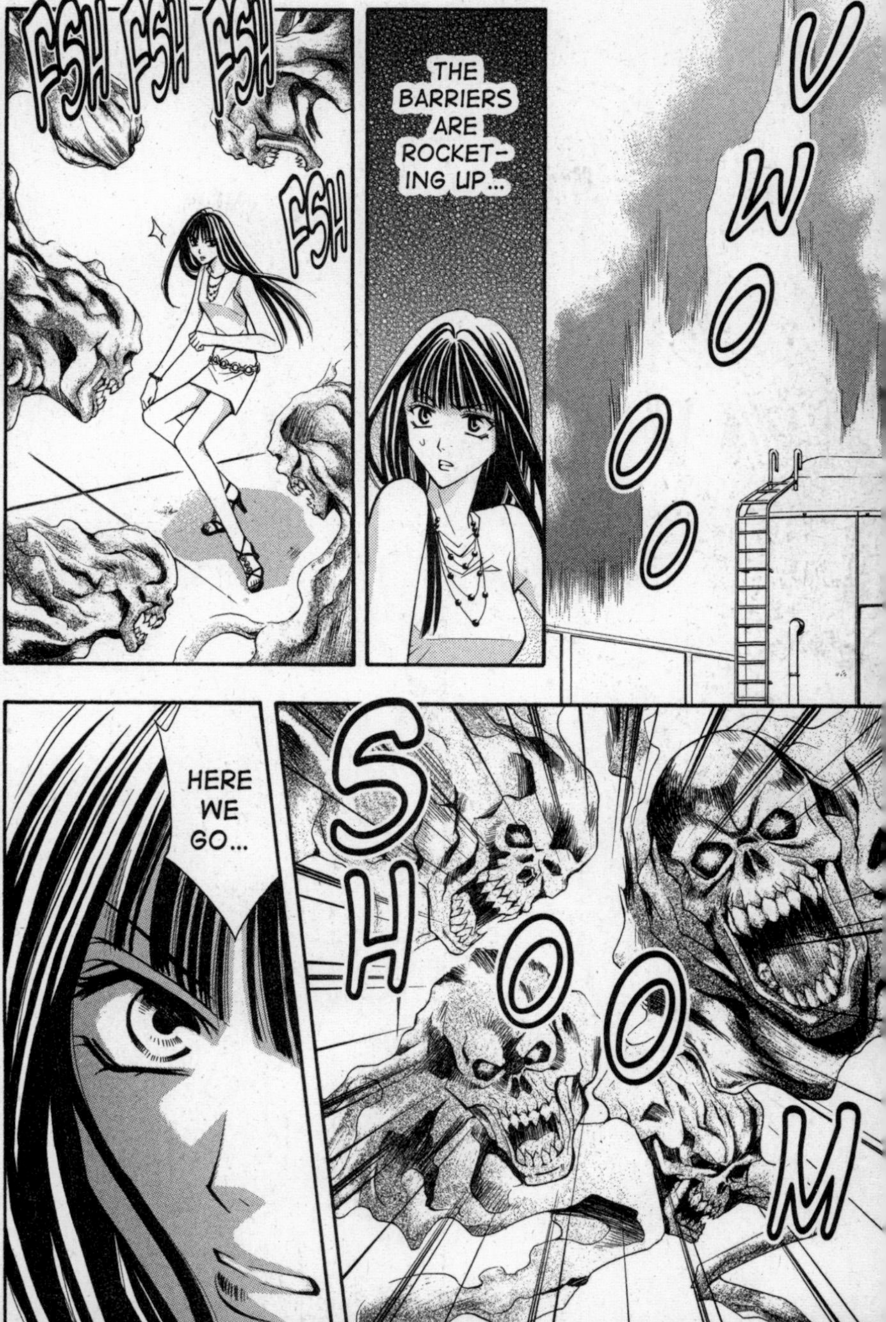
VWOOOOO
THE BARRIERS ARE ROCKET-ING UP...
FSH FSH FSH
FSH
SHOOOOM
HERE WE GO...

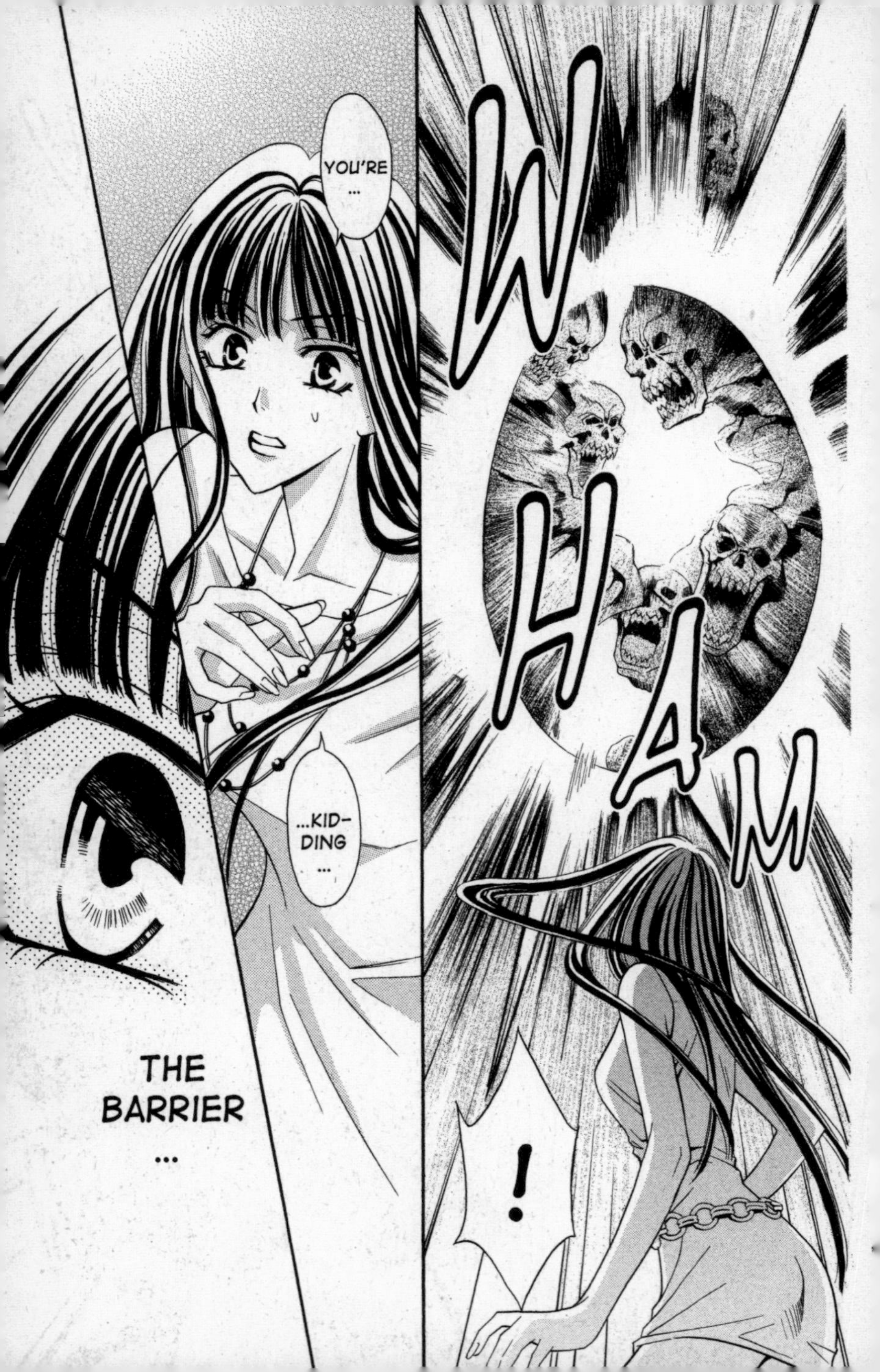
WHAM
!
YOU'RE ...
...KID-DING ...
THE BARRIER ...

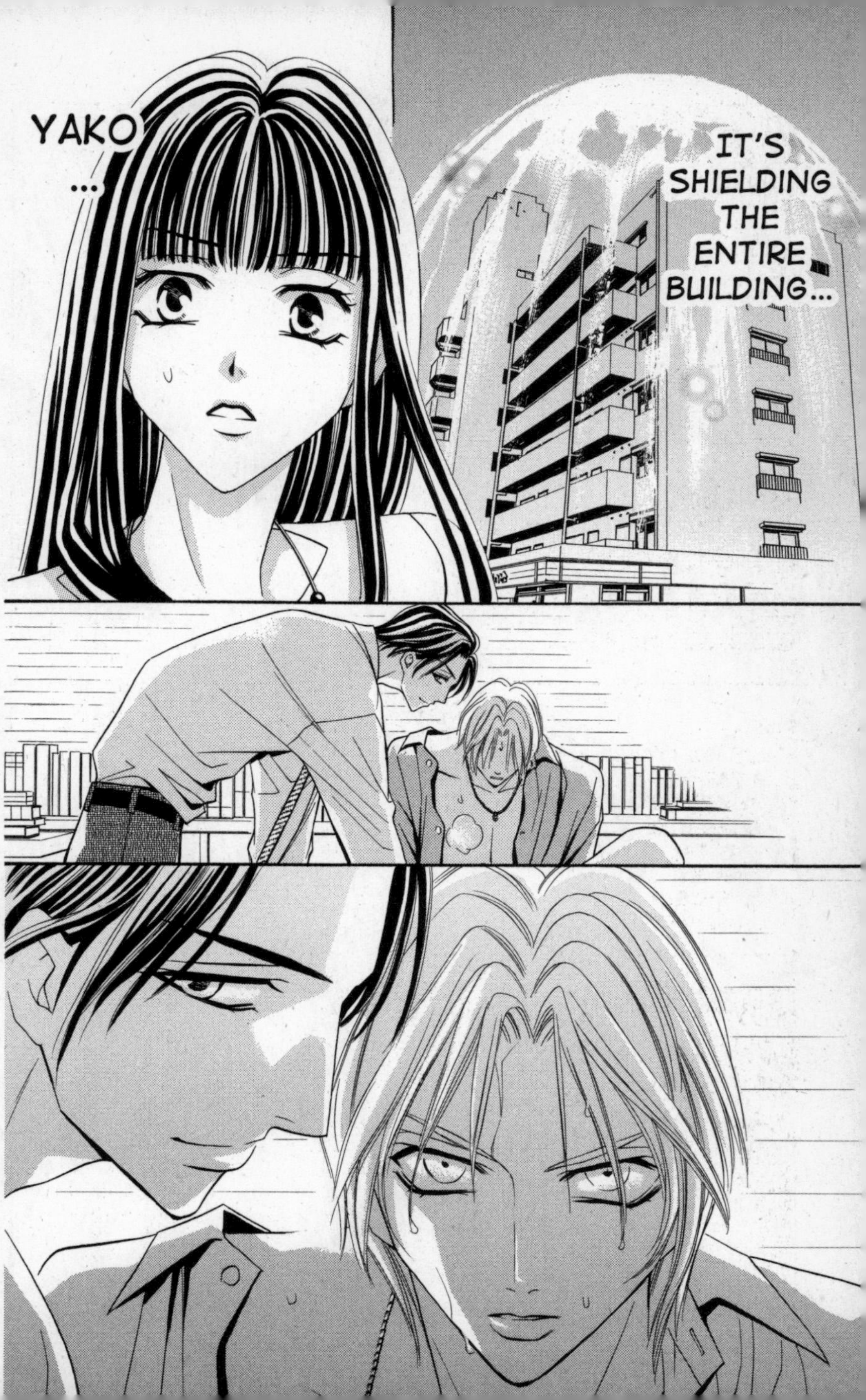
IT'S SHIELDING THE ENTIRE BUILDING...
YAKO ...

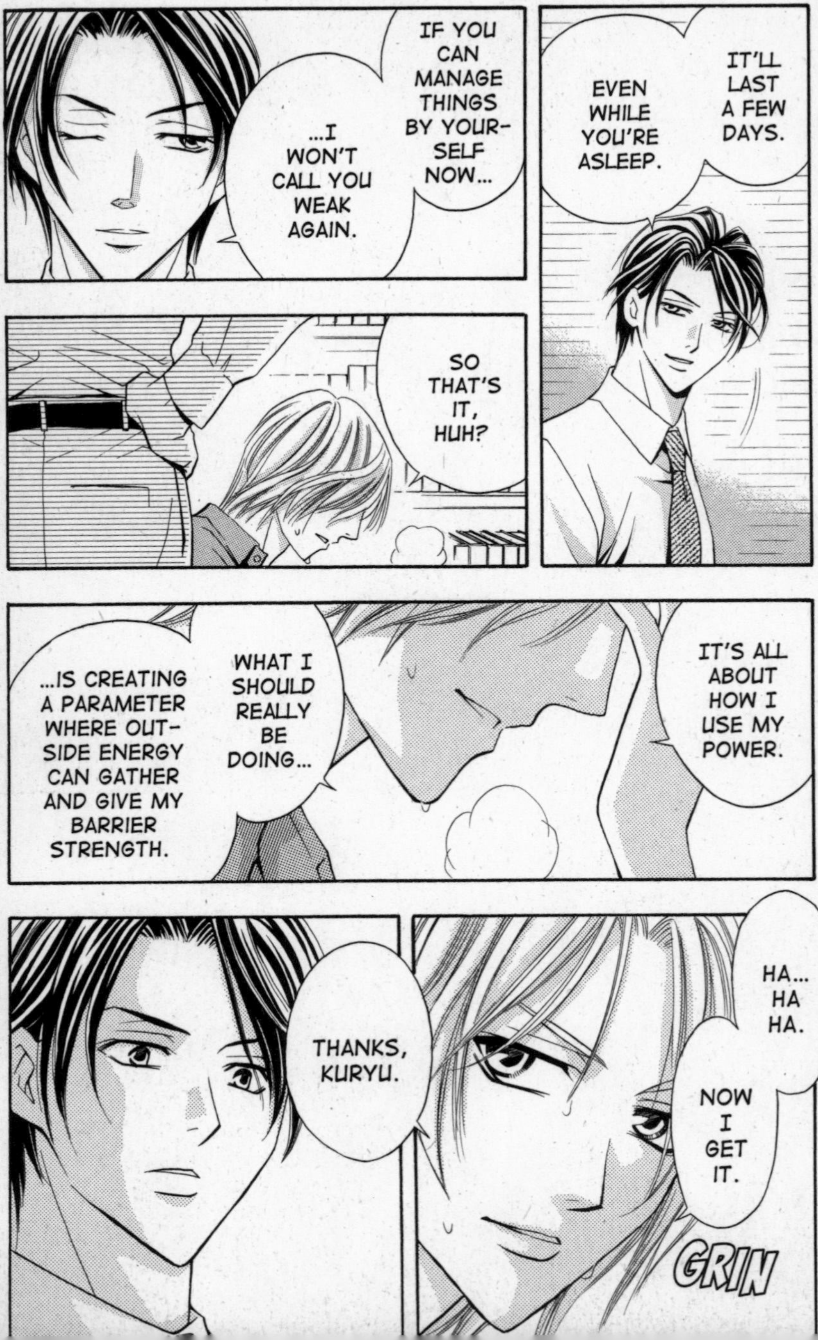
IT'LL LAST A FEW DAYS.
EVEN WHILE YOU'RE ASLEEP.
IF YOU CAN MANAGE THINGS BY YOURSELF NOW...
...I WON'T CALL YOU WEAK AGAIN.
SO THAT'S IT, HUH?
IT'S ALL ABOUT HOW I USE MY POWER.
WHAT I SHOULD REALLY BE DOING...
...IS CREATING A PARAMETER WHERE OUTSIDE ENERGY CAN GATHER AND GIVE MY BARRIER STRENGTH.
HA... HA HA.
NOW I GET IT.
GRIN
THANKS, KURYU.

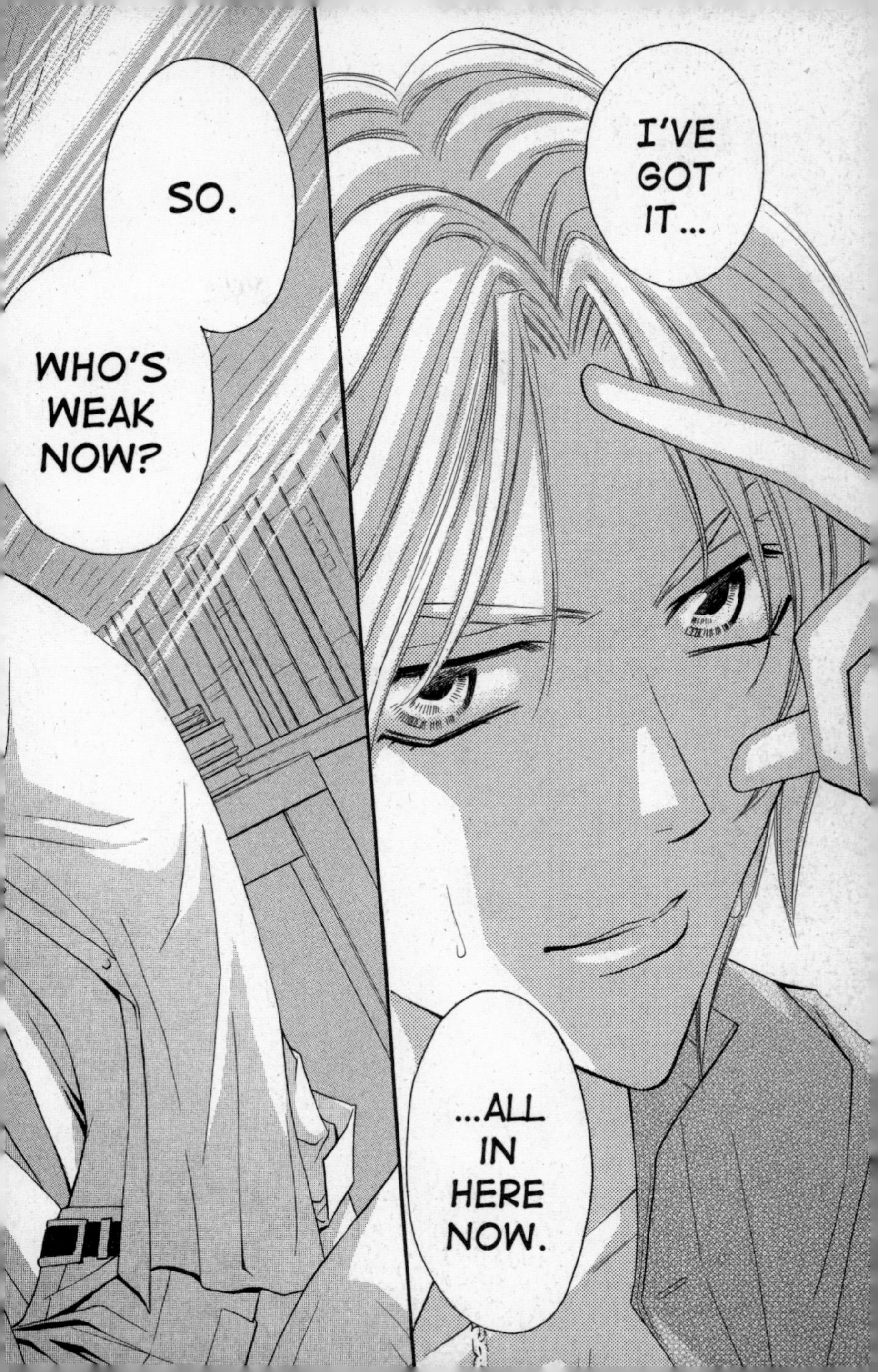
I'VE GOT IT...
...ALL IN HERE NOW.
SO.
WHO'S WEAK NOW?

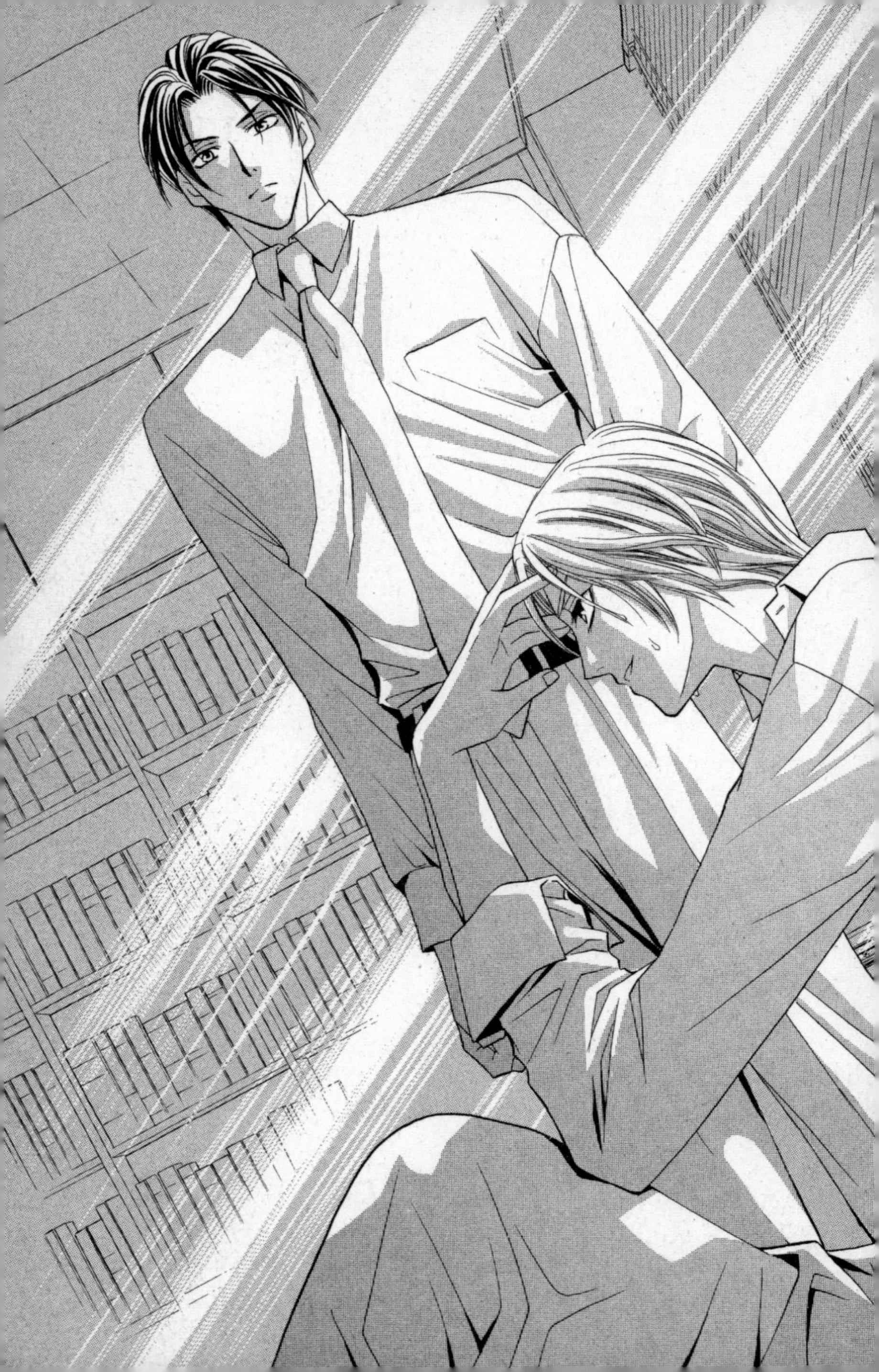

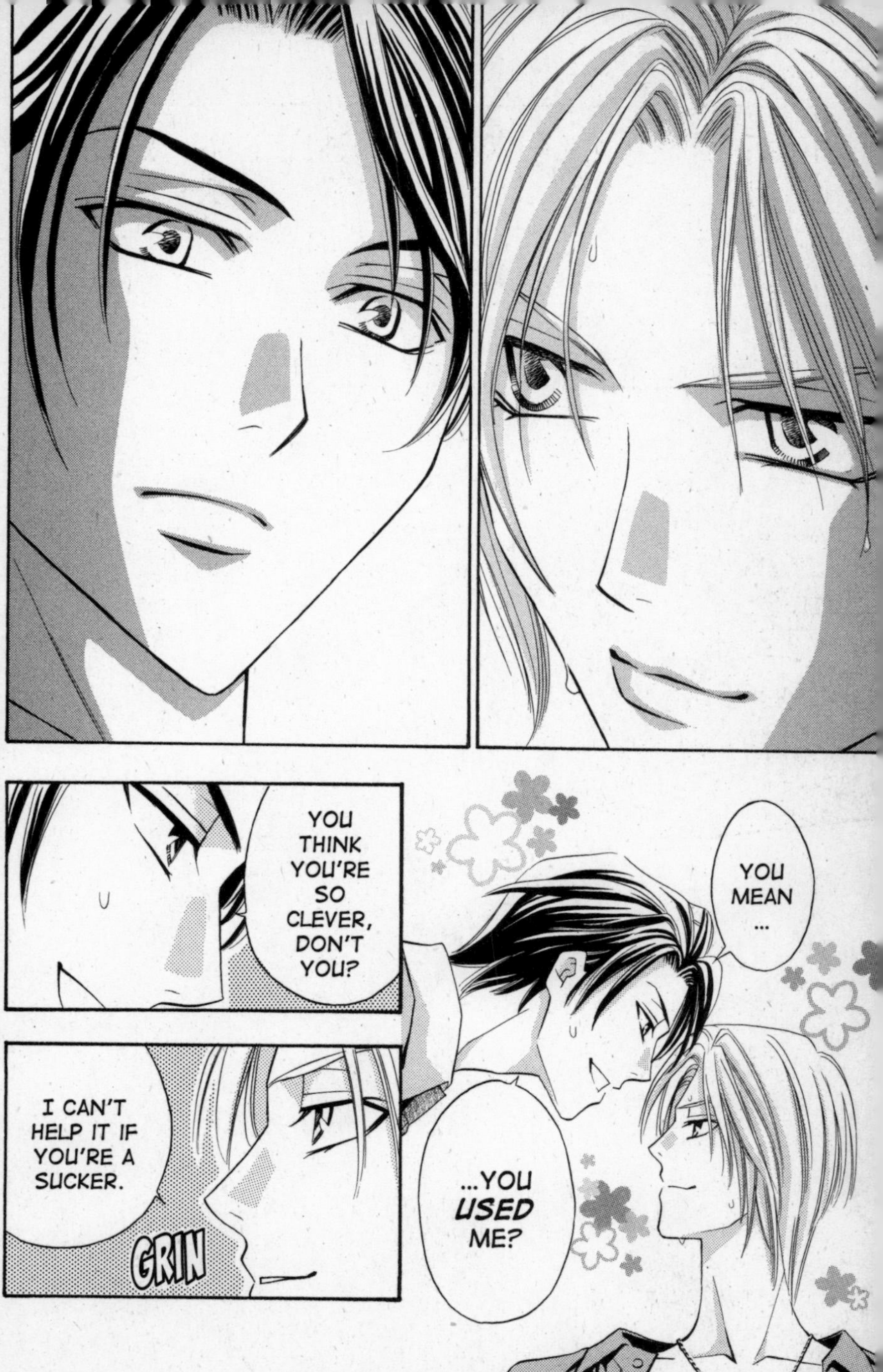
YOU MEAN ...
...YOU *USED* ME?
YOU THINK YOU'RE SO CLEVER, DON'T YOU?
I CAN'T HELP IT IF YOU'RE A SUCKER.
GRIN

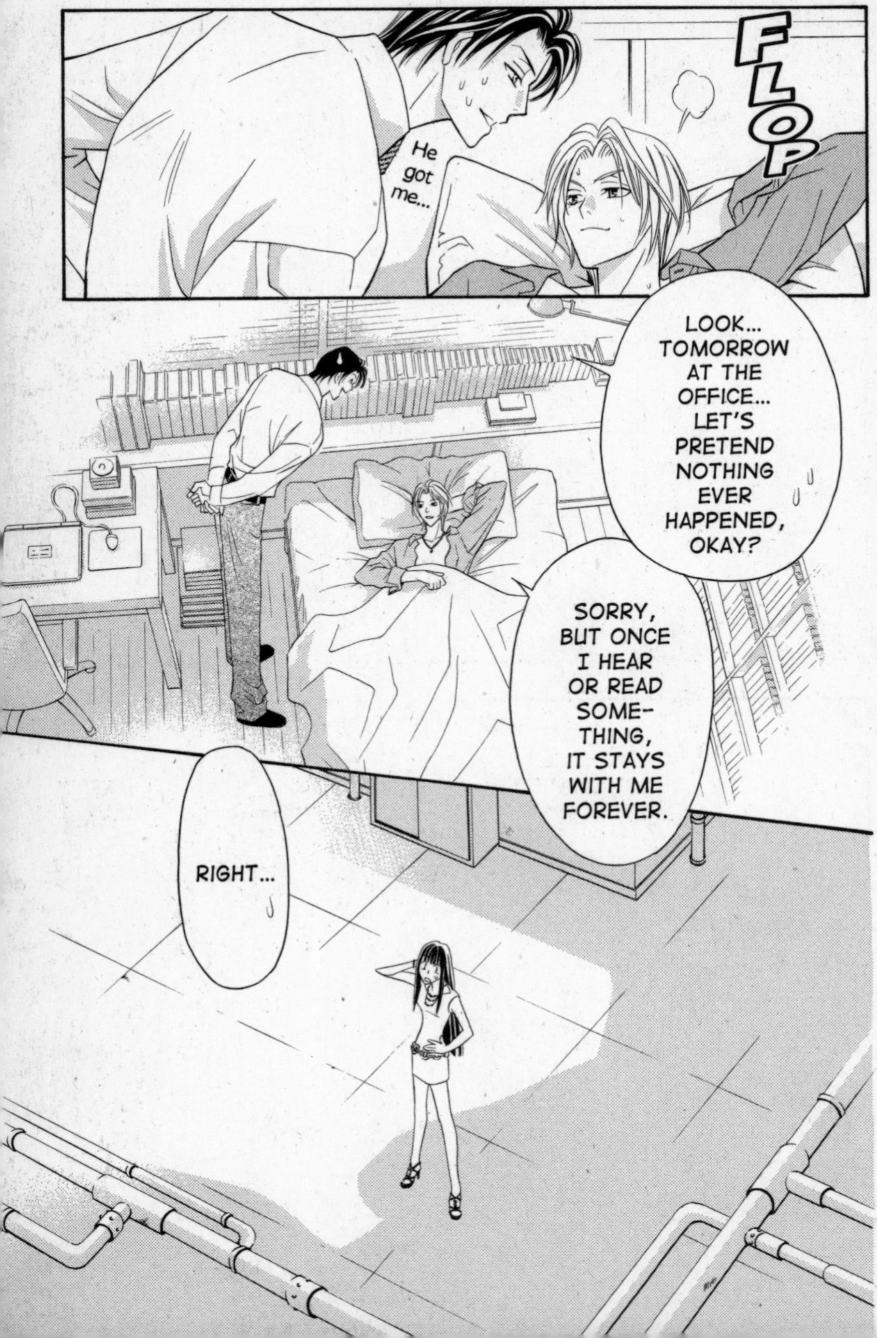
FLOP
He got me...
LOOK... TOMORROW AT THE OFFICE... LET'S PRETEND NOTHING EVER HAPPENED, OKAY?
SORRY, BUT ONCE I HEAR OR READ SOME-THING, IT STAYS WITH ME FOREVER.
RIGHT...

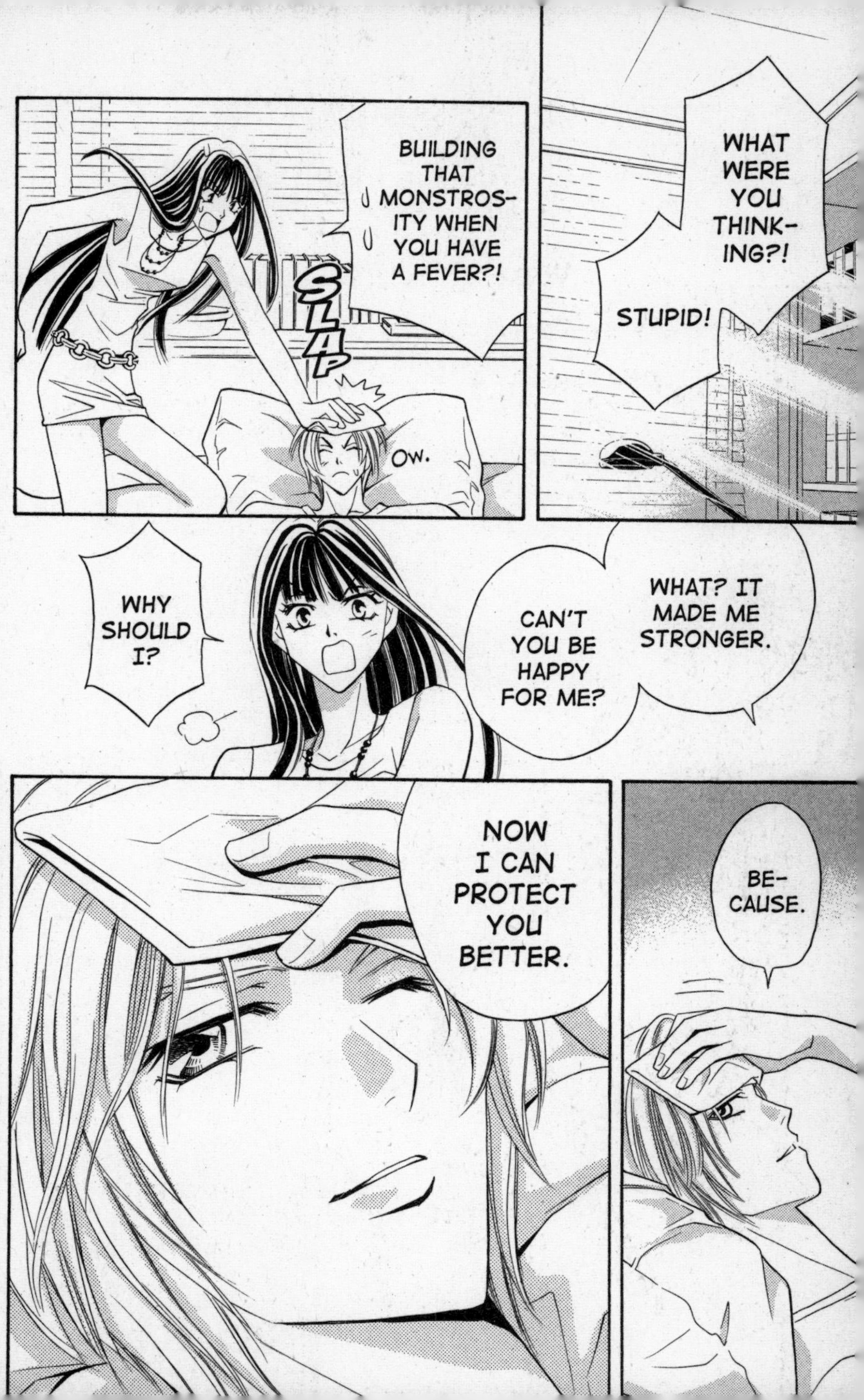
WHAT WERE YOU THINK-ING?!
STUPID!
BUILDING THAT MONSTROS-ITY WHEN YOU HAVE A FEVER?!
SLAP
OW.
WHAT? IT MADE ME STRONGER.
CAN'T YOU BE HAPPY FOR ME?
WHY SHOULD I?
BE-CAUSE.
NOW I CAN PROTECT YOU BETTER.

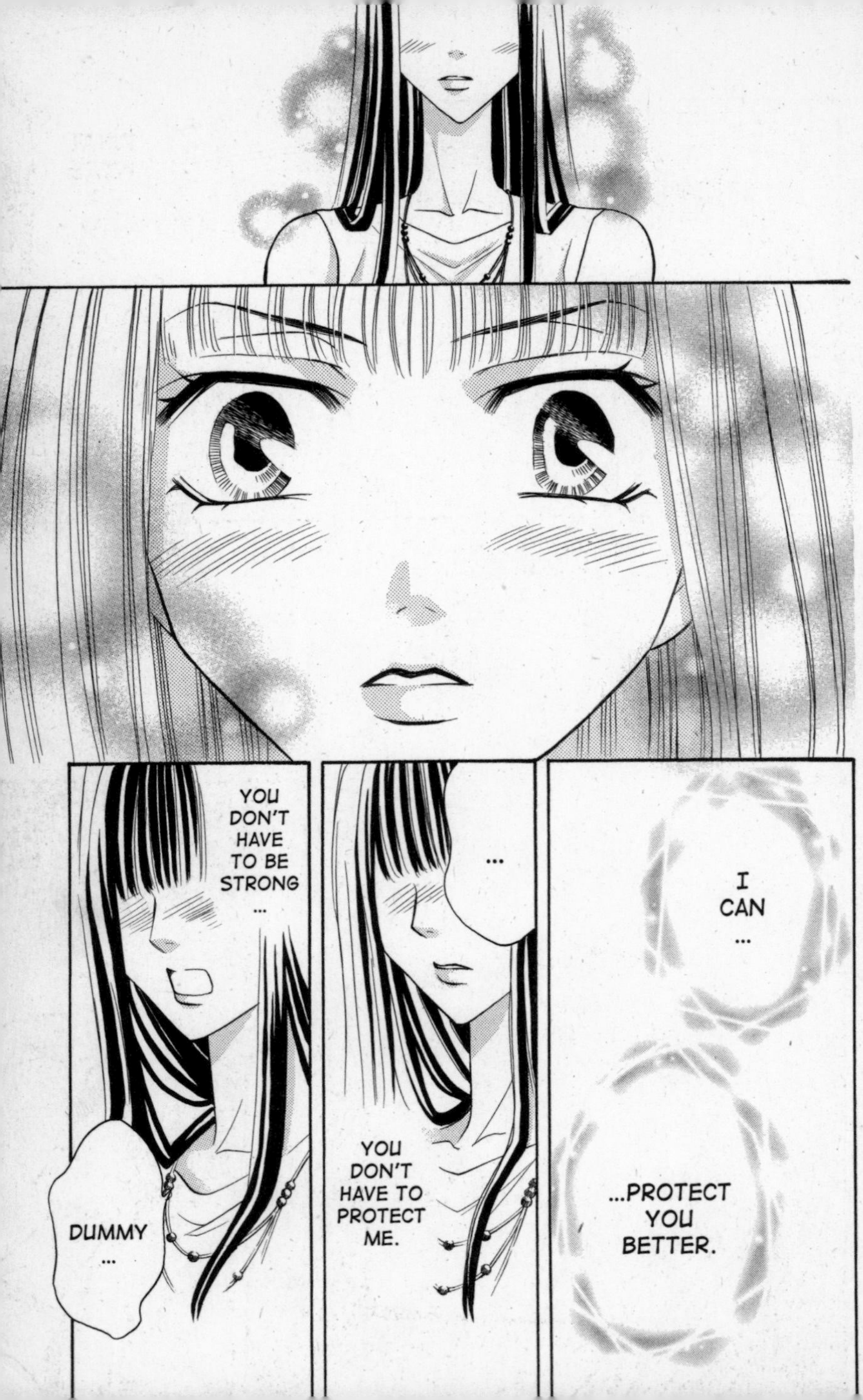
I CAN ...
...PROTECT YOU BETTER.
...
YOU DON'T HAVE TO PROTECT ME.
YOU DON'T HAVE TO BE STRONG ...
DUMMY ...

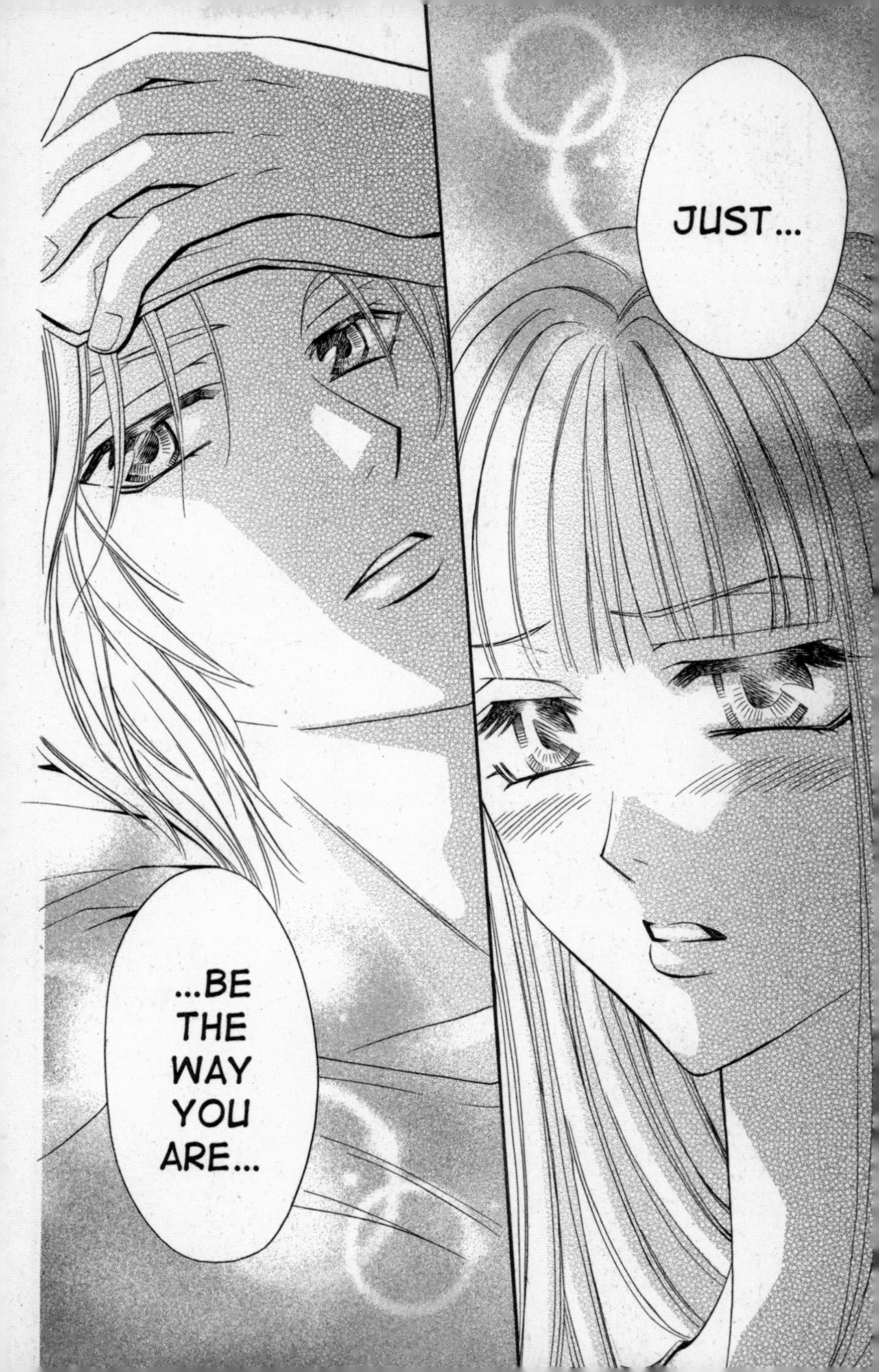
JUST...
...BE THE WAY YOU ARE...

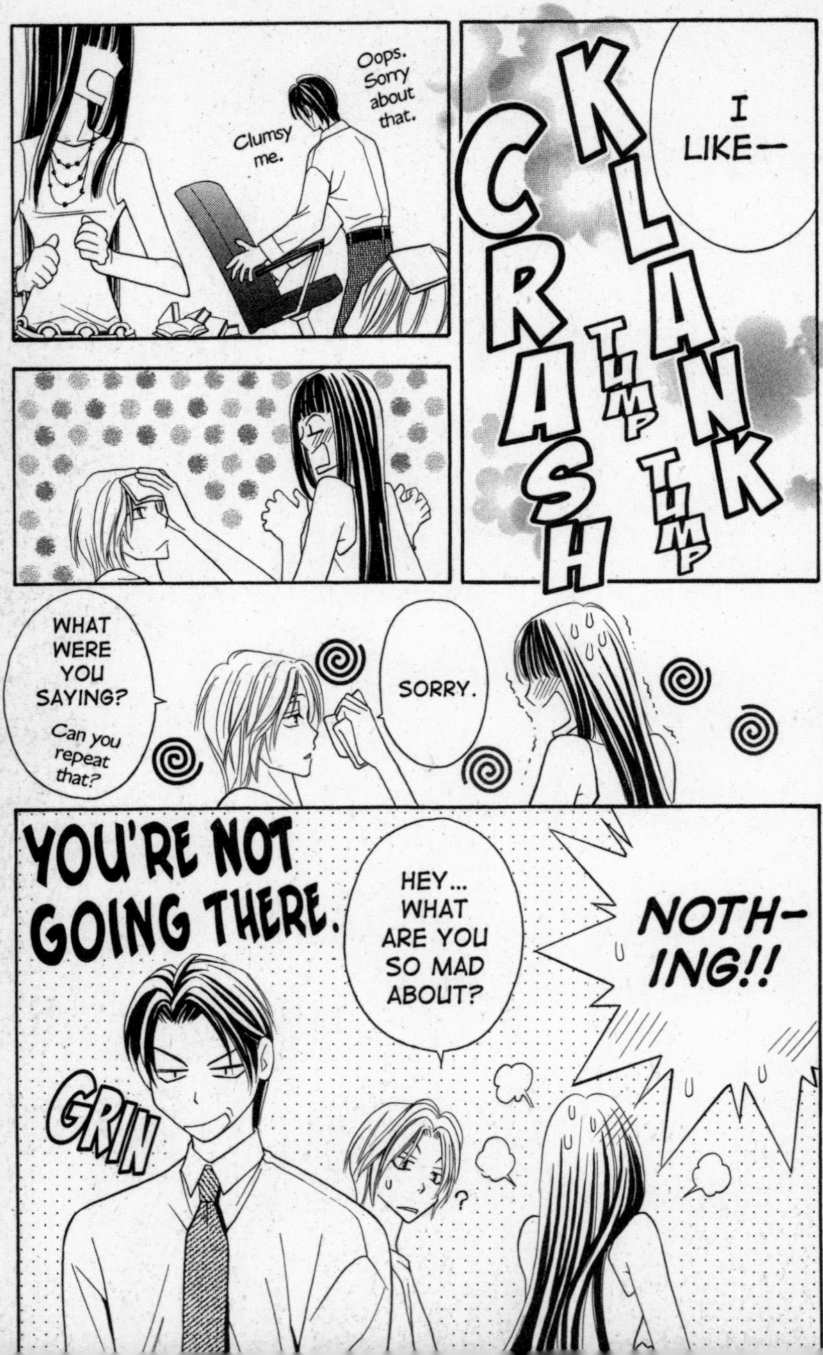
I LIKE—
CRASH
KLANK
TUMP
TUMP
Oops. Sorry about that.
Clumsy me.
SORRY.
WHAT WERE YOU SAYING?
Can you repeat that?
NOTH-ING!!
HEY... WHAT ARE YOU SO MAD ABOUT?
YOU'RE NOT GOING THERE.
GRIN

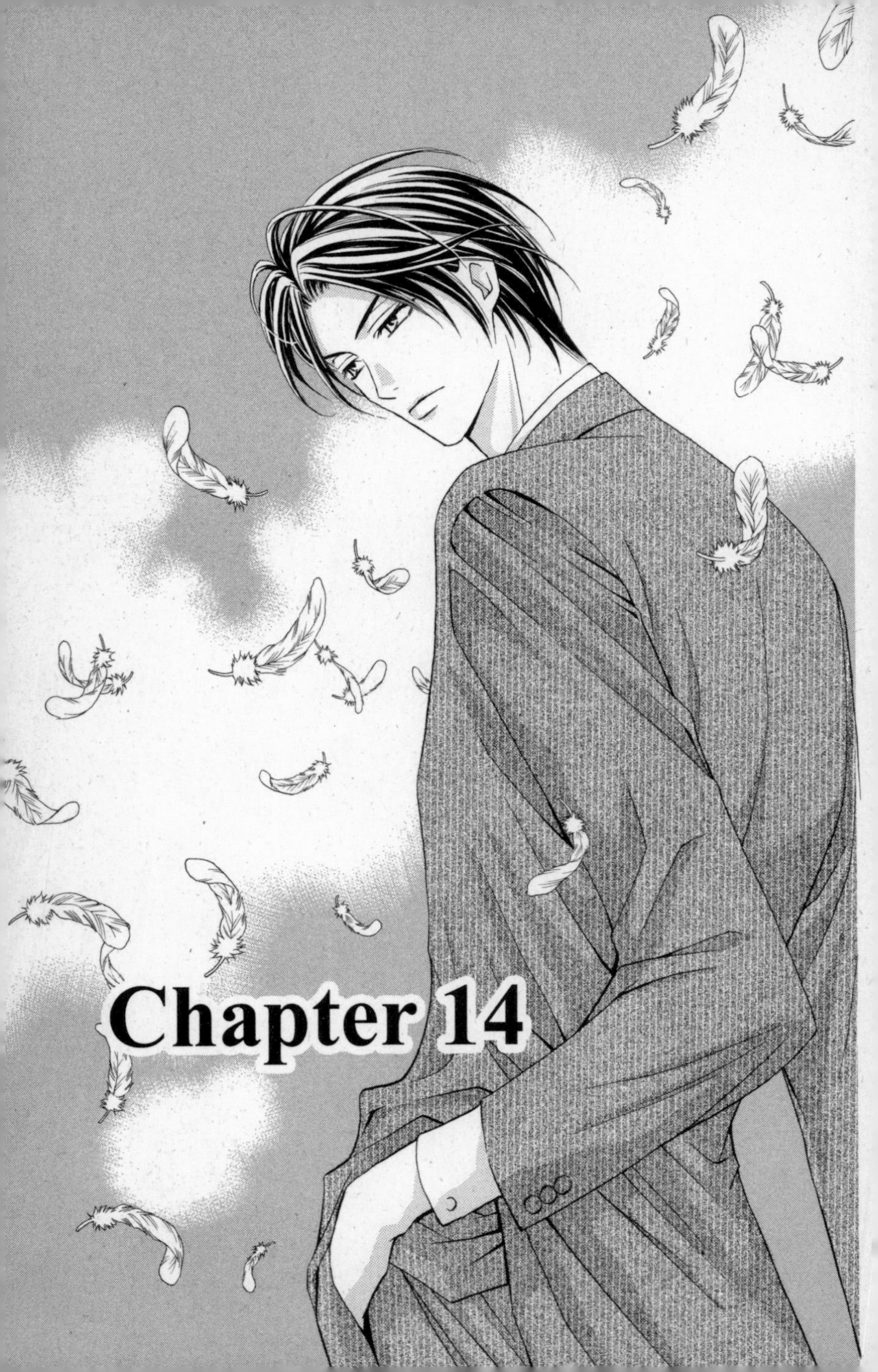
Chapter 14

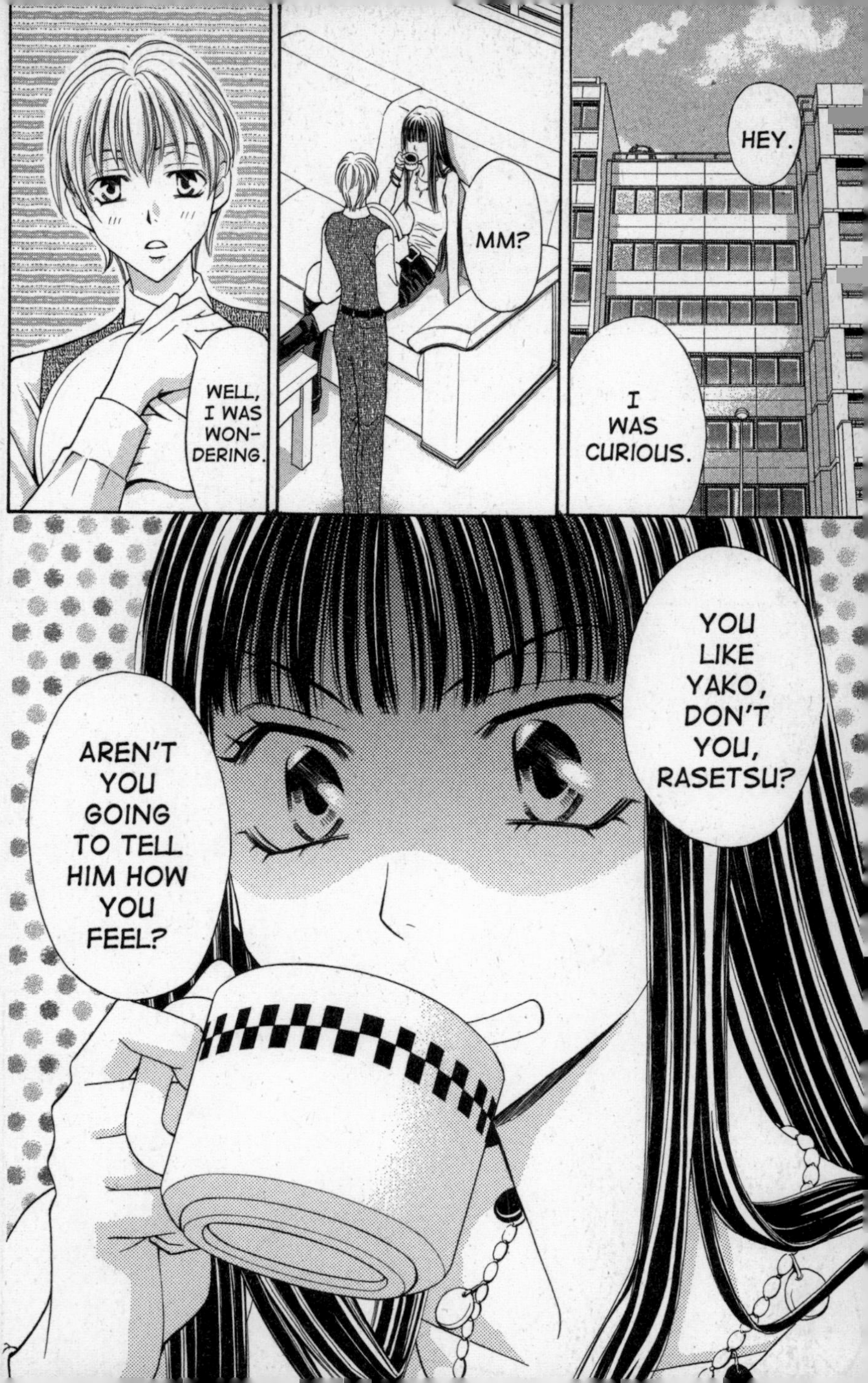
HEY.
I WAS CURIOUS.
MM?
WELL, I WAS WONDERING.
YOU LIKE YAKO, DON'T YOU, RASETSU?
AREN'T YOU GOING TO TELL HIM HOW YOU FEEL?

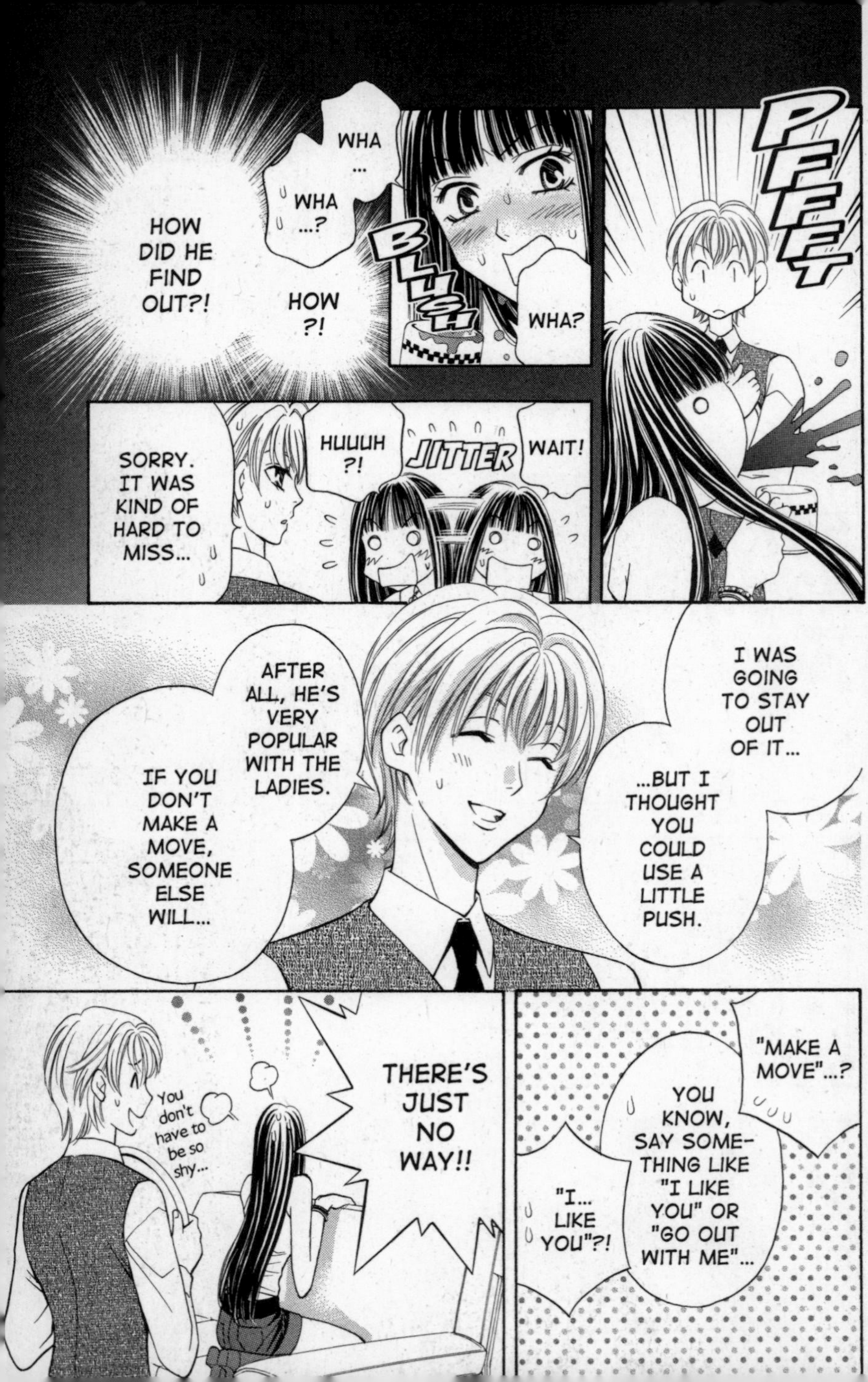
PFFFT
WHA?
WHA ... WHA ...?
BLUSH
HOW ?!
HOW DID HE FIND OUT?!
WAIT!
JITTER
HUUUH ?!
SORRY. IT WAS KIND OF HARD TO MISS...
I WAS GOING TO STAY OUT OF IT...
...BUT I THOUGHT YOU COULD USE A LITTLE PUSH.
AFTER ALL, HE'S VERY POPULAR WITH THE LADIES.
IF YOU DON'T MAKE A MOVE, SOMEONE ELSE WILL...
"MAKE A MOVE"...?
YOU KNOW, SAY SOME-THING LIKE "I LIKE YOU" OR "GO OUT WITH ME"...
"I... LIKE YOU"?!
THERE'S JUST NO WAY!!
You don't have to be so shy...

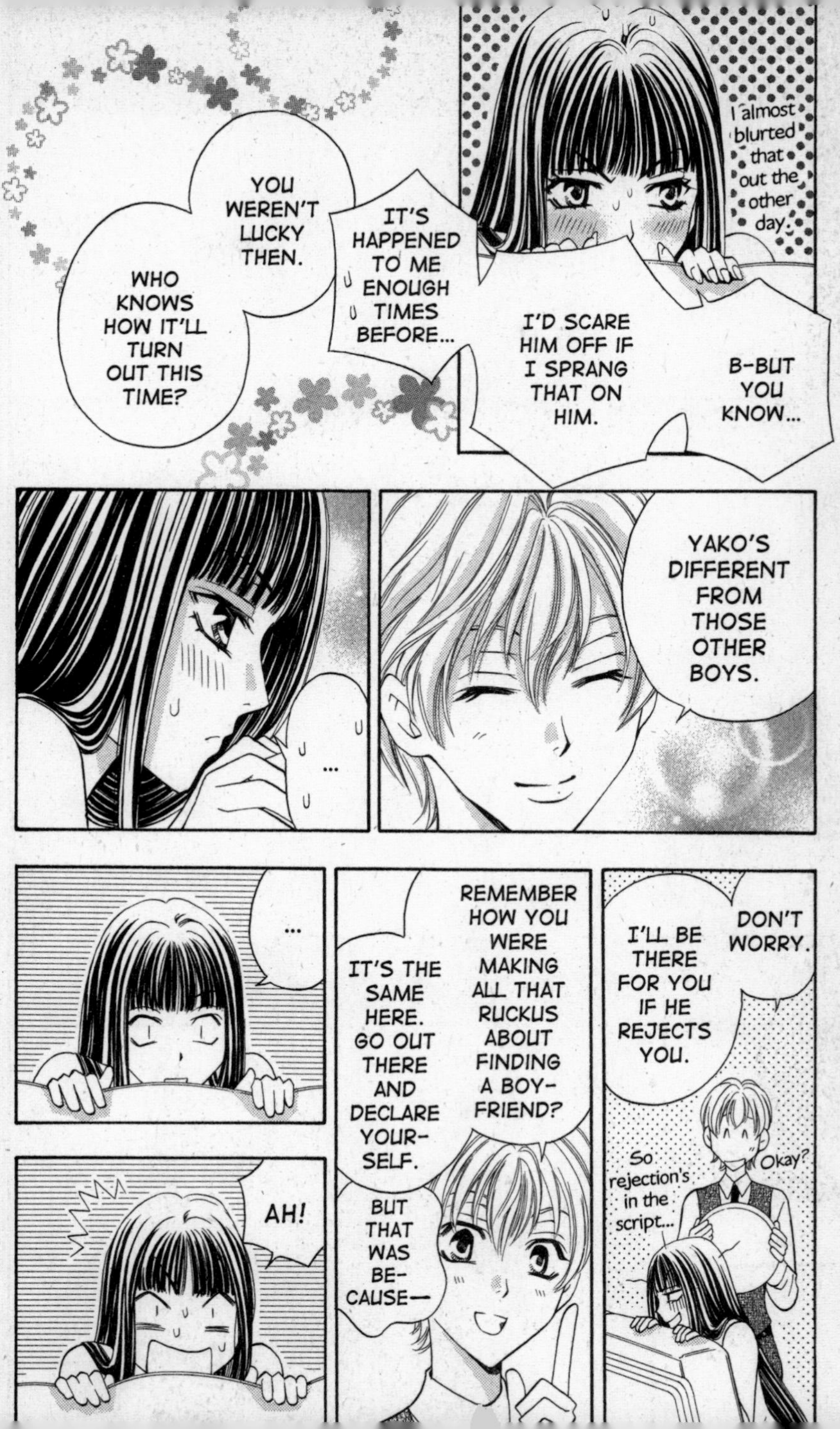
I almost blurted that out the other day.
B-BUT YOU KNOW...
I'D SCARE HIM OFF IF I SPRANG THAT ON HIM.
IT'S HAPPENED TO ME ENOUGH TIMES BEFORE...
YOU WEREN'T LUCKY THEN.
WHO KNOWS HOW IT'LL TURN OUT THIS TIME?
YAKO'S DIFFERENT FROM THOSE OTHER BOYS.
...
DON'T WORRY.
I'LL BE THERE FOR YOU IF HE REJECTS YOU.
Okay?
So rejection's in the script...
REMEMBER HOW YOU WERE MAKING ALL THAT RUCKUS ABOUT FINDING A BOY-FRIEND?
IT'S THE SAME HERE. GO OUT THERE AND DECLARE YOUR-SELF.
BUT THAT WAS BE-CAUSE—
...
AH!

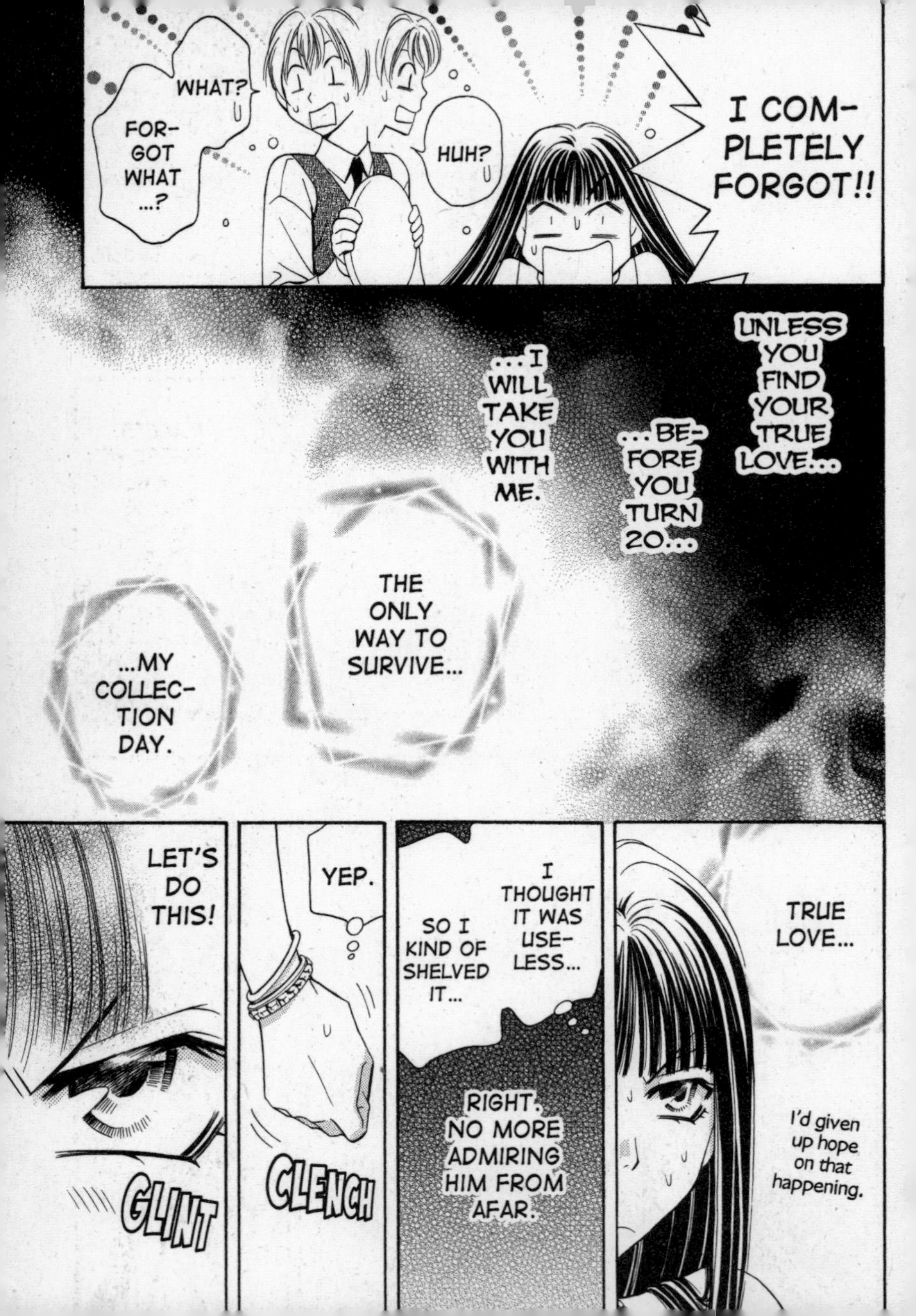
I COMPLETELY FORGOT!!
HUH?
WHAT? FORGOT WHAT ...?
UNLESS YOU FIND YOUR TRUE LOVE...
...BEFORE YOU TURN 20...
...I WILL TAKE YOU WITH ME.
THE ONLY WAY TO SURVIVE...
...MY COLLECTION DAY.
TRUE LOVE...
I'd given up hope on that happening.
I THOUGHT IT WAS USELESS...
SO I KIND OF SHELVED IT...
RIGHT. NO MORE ADMIRING HIM FROM AFAR.
YEP.
CLENCH
LET'S DO THIS!
GLINT

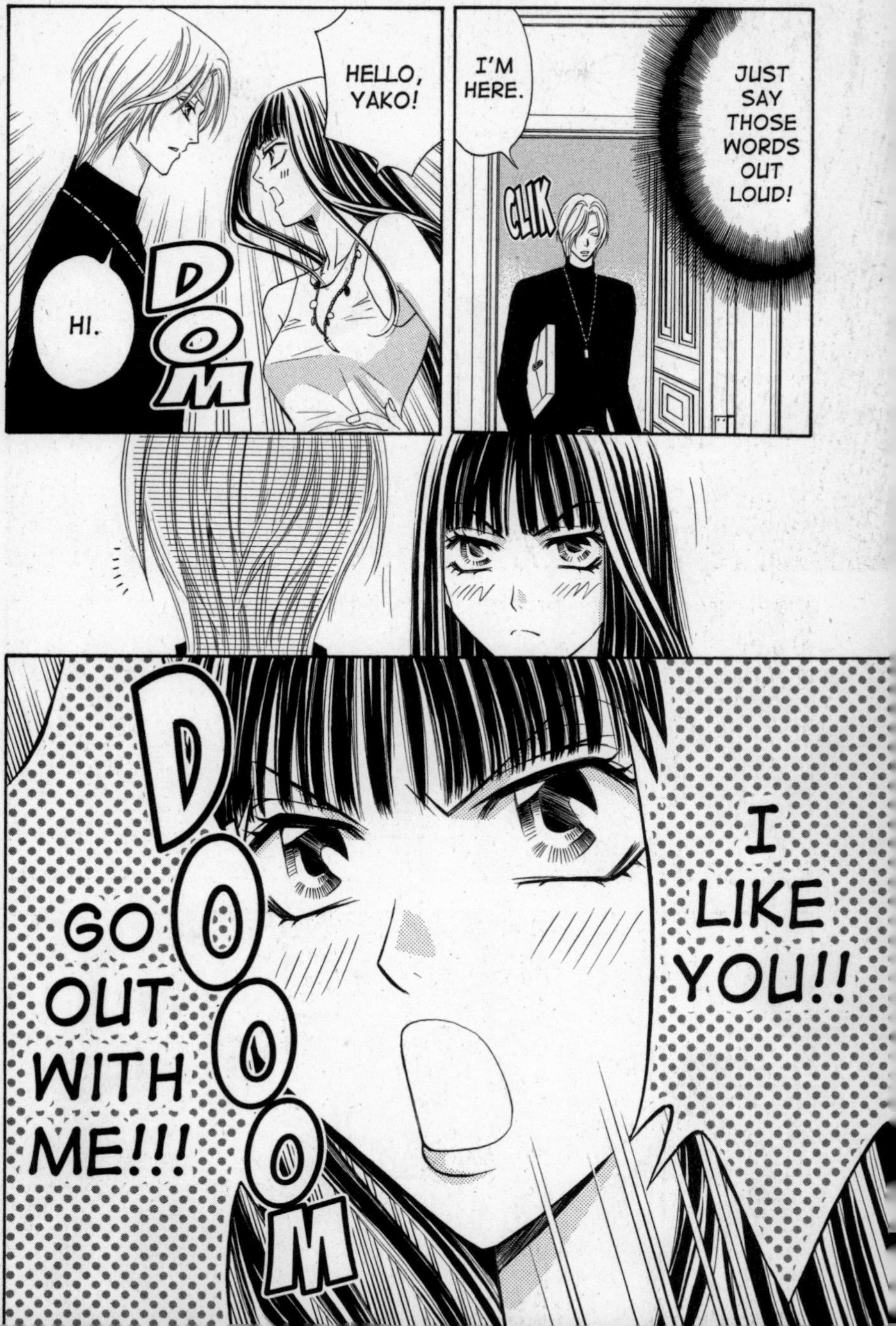
JUST SAY THOSE WORDS OUT LOUD!
I'M HERE.
CLIK
HELLO, YAKO!
DOM
HI.
I LIKE YOU!!
DOOOOOM
GO OUT WITH ME!!!

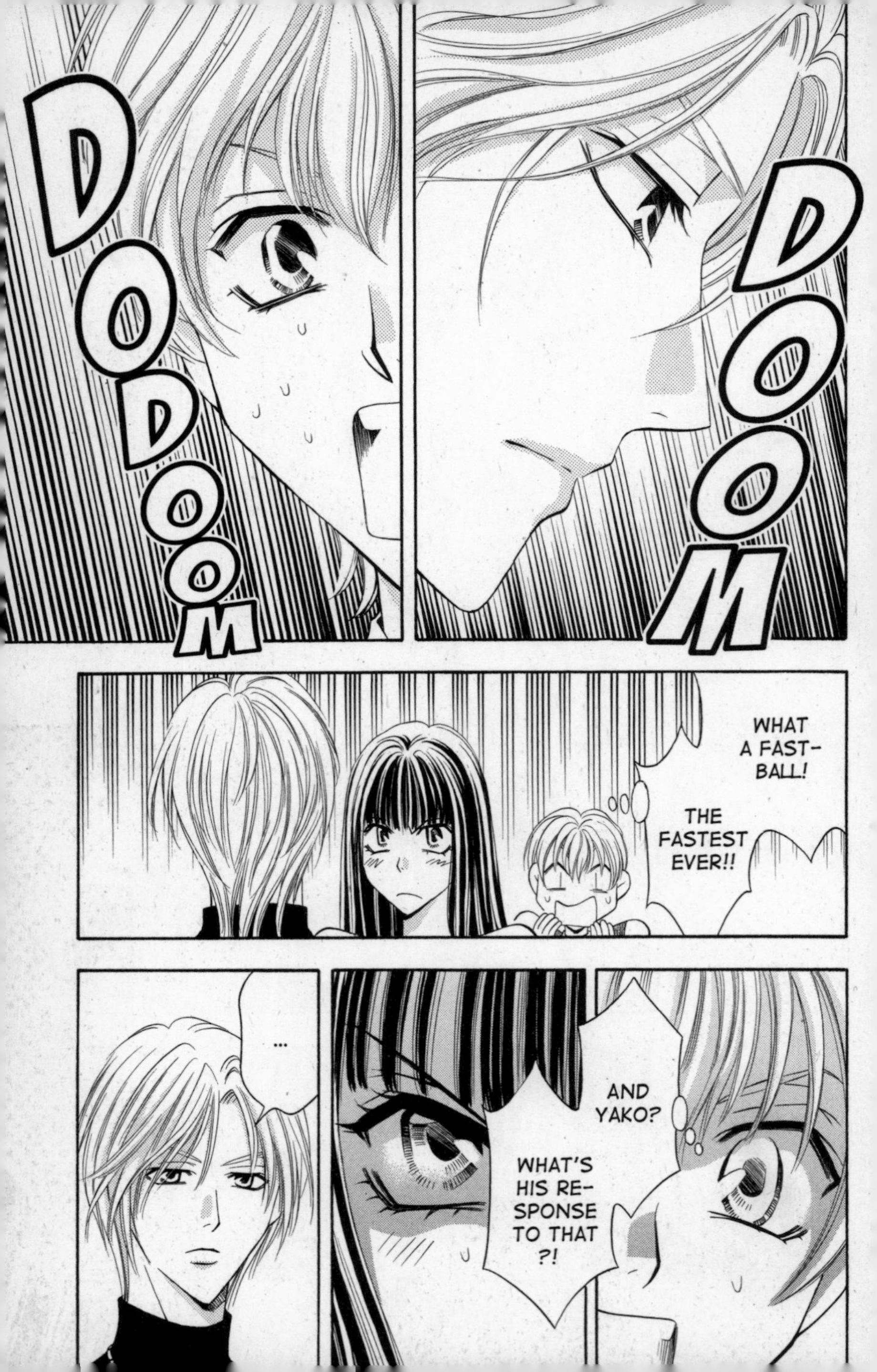
DODOOM
DODODOOM
WHAT A FAST-BALL!
THE FASTEST EVER!!
AND YAKO?
WHAT'S HIS RE-SPONSE TO THAT ?!
...

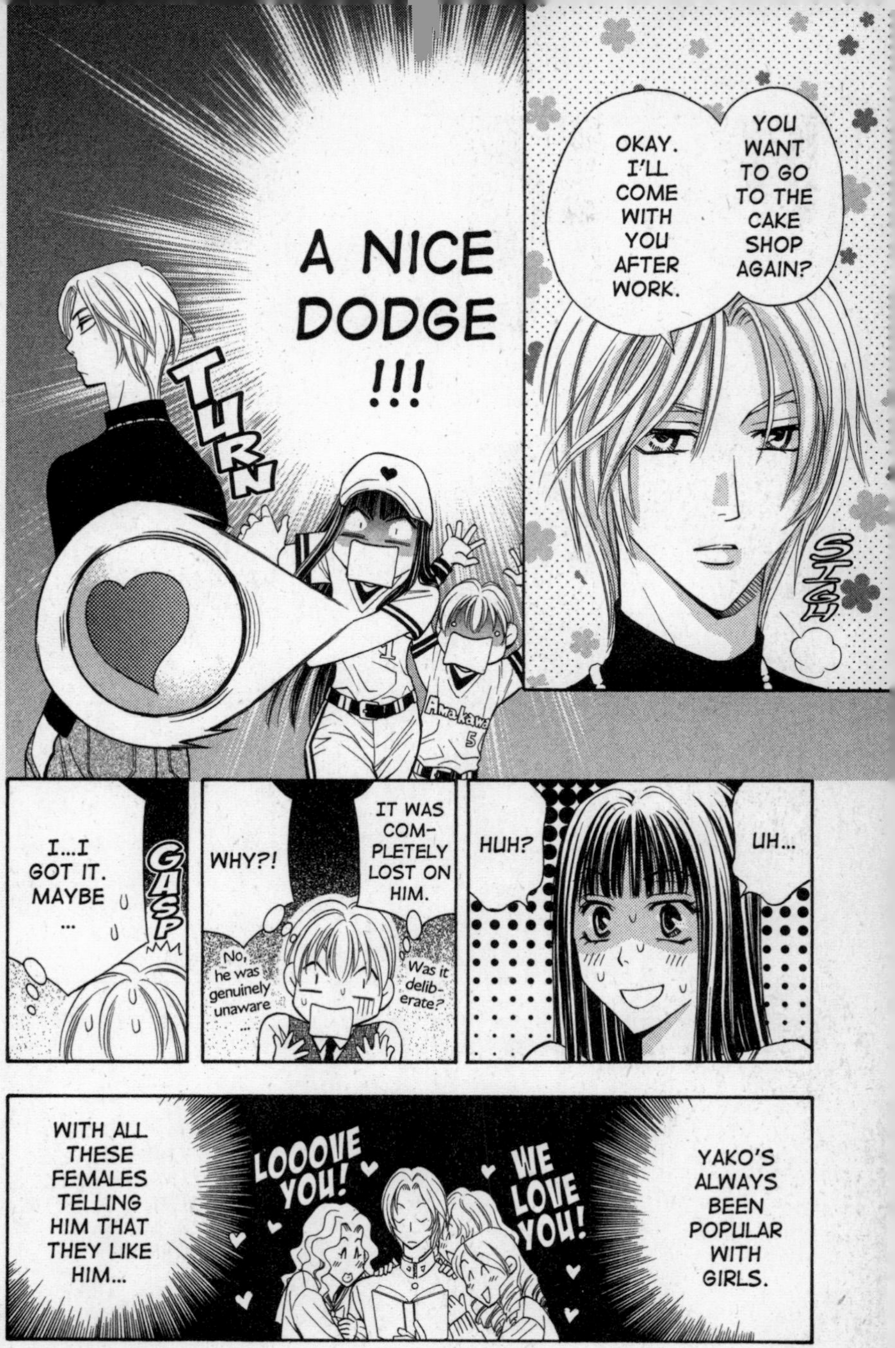
YOU WANT TO GO TO THE CAKE SHOP AGAIN?
OKAY. I'LL COME WITH YOU AFTER WORK.
SIGH
A NICE DODGE!!!
TURN
Amakawa
UH...
HUH?
IT WAS COM-PLETELY LOST ON HIM.
WHY?!
Was it delib-erate?
No, he was genuinely unaware...
GASP
I...I GOT IT. MAYBE...
YAKO'S ALWAYS BEEN POPULAR WITH GIRLS.
WE LOVE YOU!
LOOOVE YOU!
WITH ALL THESE FEMALES TELLING HIM THAT THEY LIKE HIM...

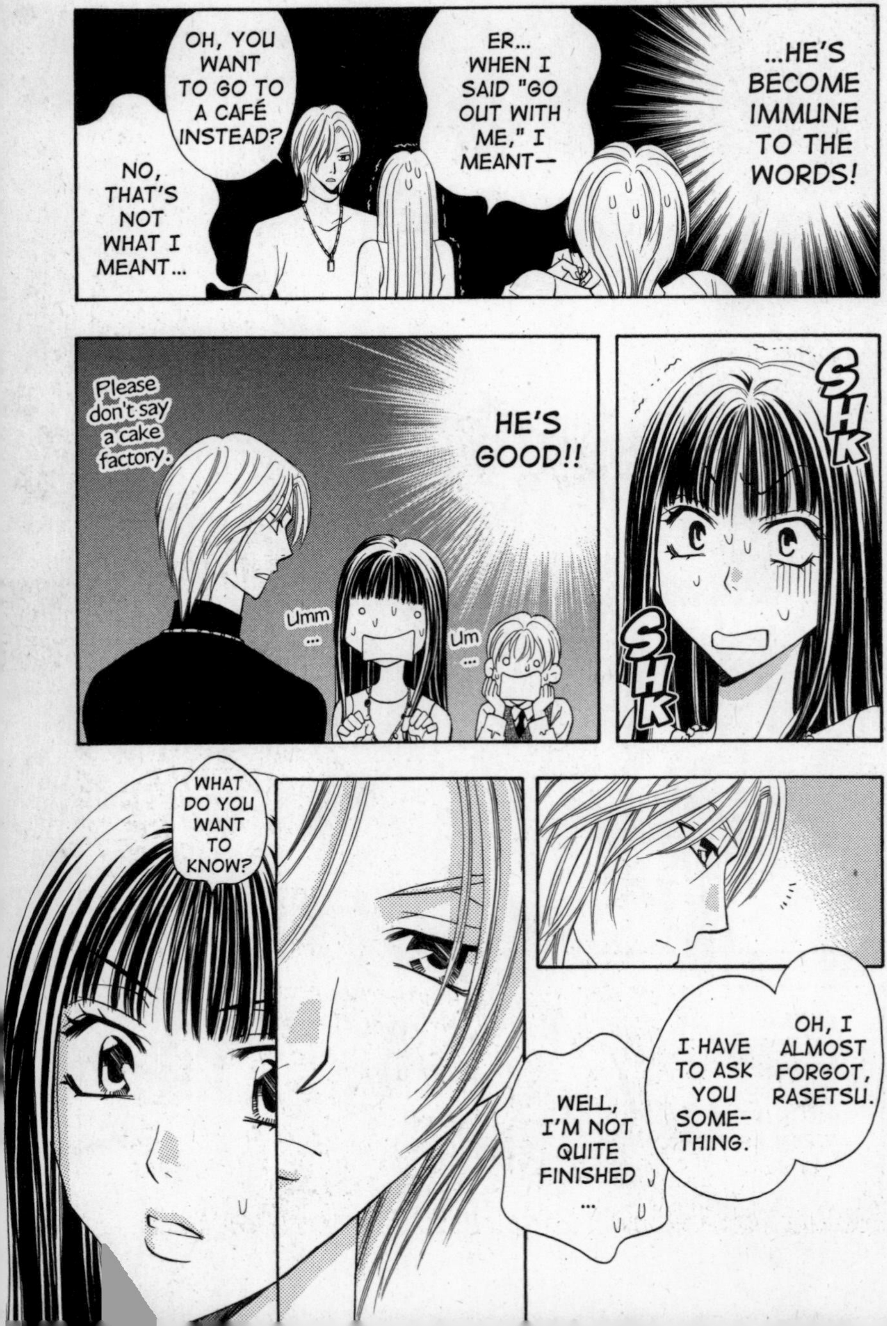
ER... WHEN I SAID "GO OUT WITH ME," I MEANT—
OH, YOU WANT TO GO TO A CAFÉ INSTEAD?
NO, THAT'S NOT WHAT I MEANT...
...HE'S BECOME IMMUNE TO THE WORDS!
SHK
SHK
HE'S GOOD!!
Please don't say a cake factory.
Umm ...
Um ...
OH, I ALMOST FORGOT, RASETSU.
I HAVE TO ASK YOU SOMETHING.
WELL, I'M NOT QUITE FINISHED ...
WHAT DO YOU WANT TO KNOW?

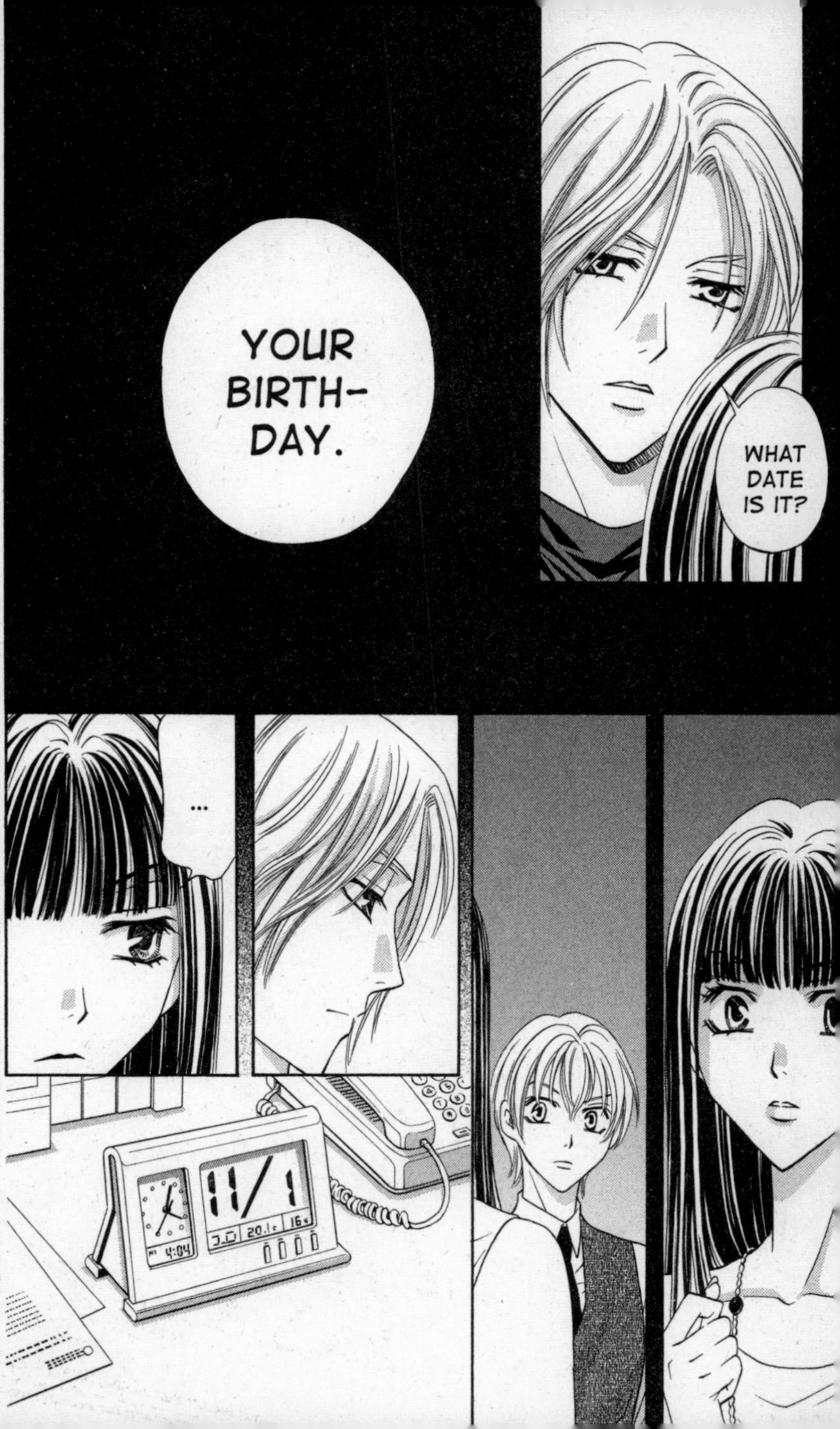
WHAT DATE IS IT?
YOUR BIRTH-DAY.
...

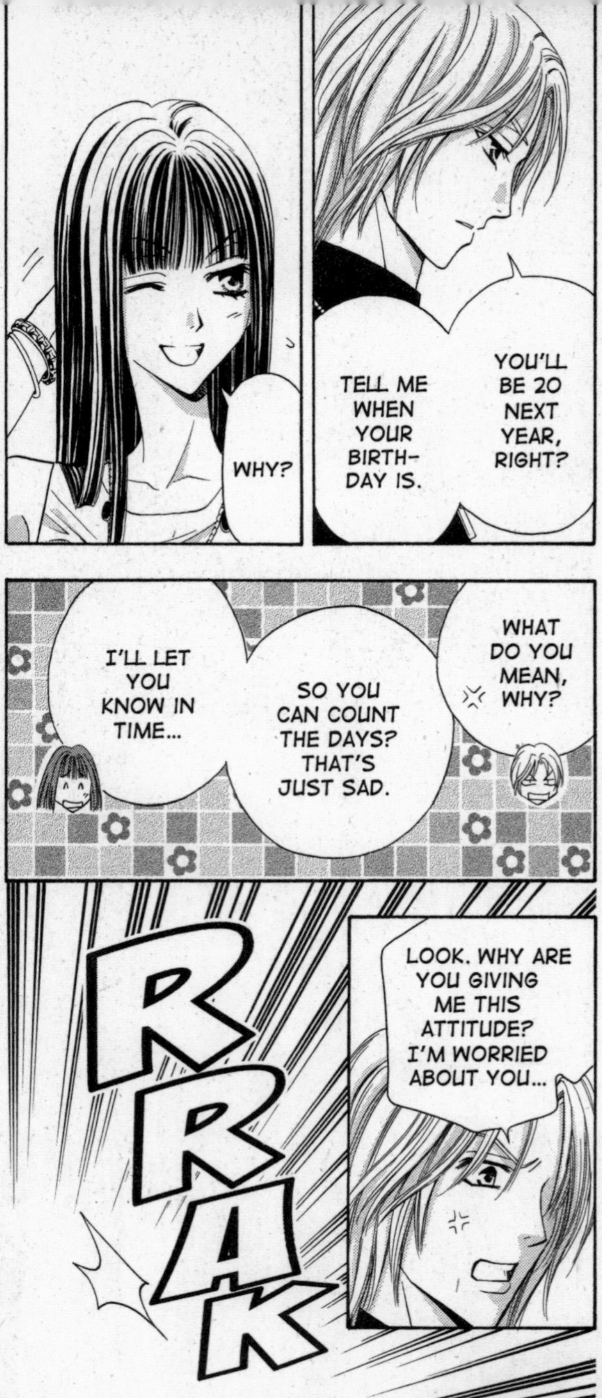
YOU'LL BE 20 NEXT YEAR, RIGHT?
TELL ME WHEN YOUR BIRTH-DAY IS.
WHY?
WHAT DO YOU MEAN, WHY?
SO YOU CAN COUNT THE DAYS? THAT'S JUST SAD.
I'LL LET YOU KNOW IN TIME...
LOOK. WHY ARE YOU GIVING ME THIS ATTITUDE? I'M WORRIED ABOUT YOU...
RRAK

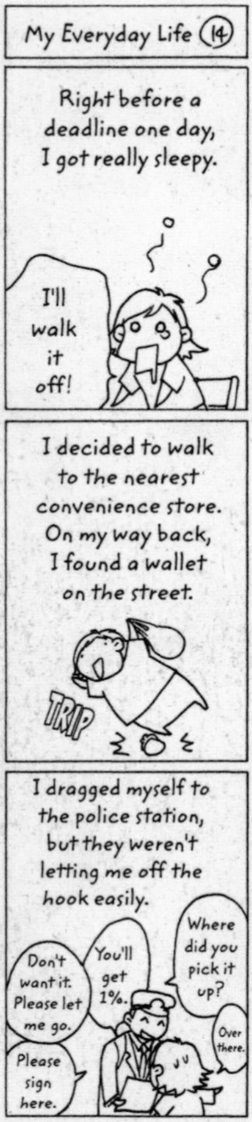
My Everyday Life 14
Right before a deadline one day, I got really sleepy.
I'll walk it off!
I decided to walk to the nearest convenience store. On my way back, I found a wallet on the street.
TRIP
I dragged myself to the police station, but they weren't letting me off the hook easily.
Where did you pick it up?
Over there.
You'll get 1%.
Don't want it. Please let me go.
Please sign here.
The wallet had 700 yen* in it...
It's all yours if the owner doesn't turn up.
I don't want it. I just want to go home.
Sign here...
Agh.

*About $7.75

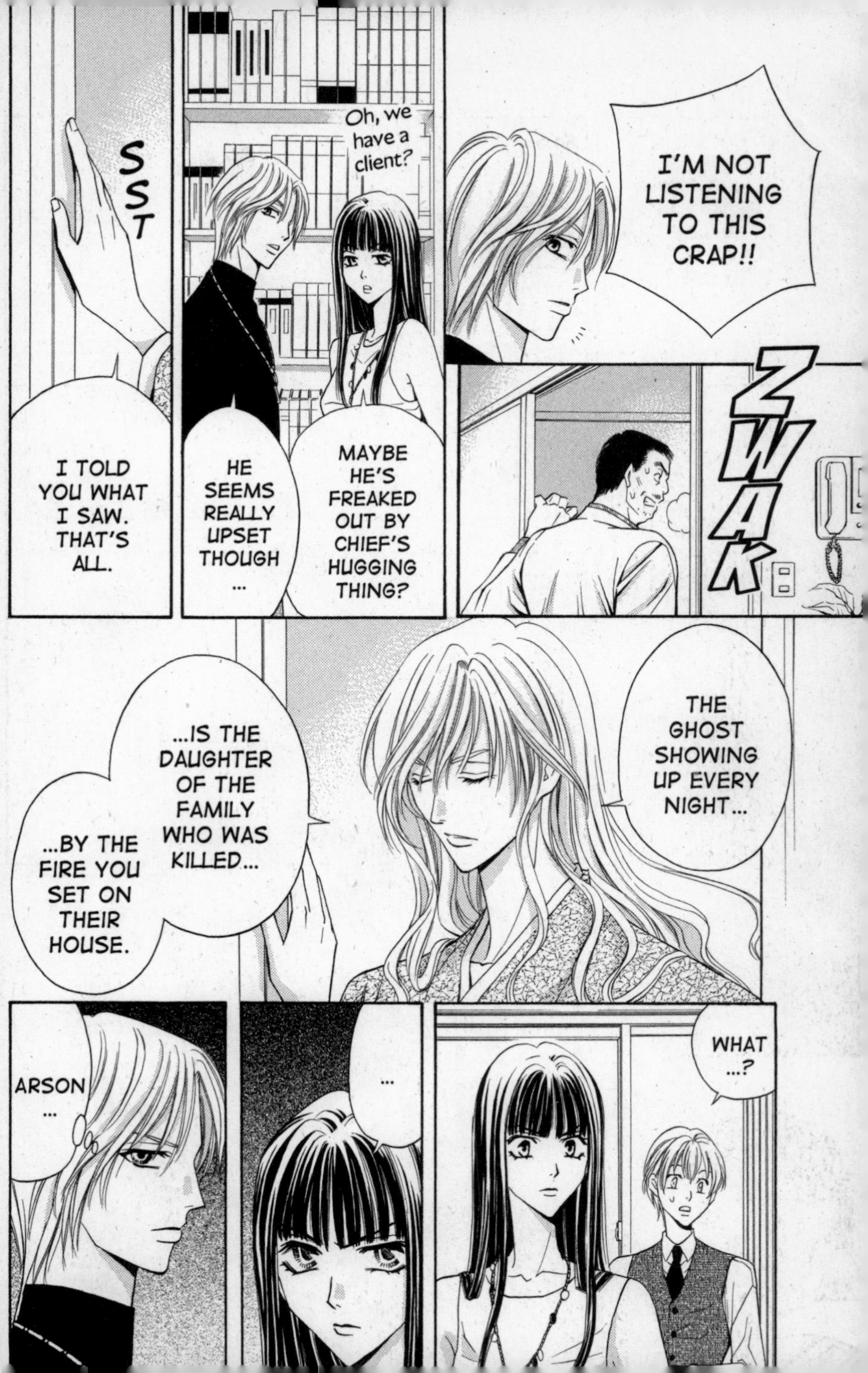
I'M NOT LISTENING TO THIS CRAP!!
ZWAK
Oh, we have a client?
MAYBE HE'S FREAKED OUT BY CHIEF'S HUGGING THING?
HE SEEMS REALLY UPSET THOUGH ...
SSST
I TOLD YOU WHAT I SAW. THAT'S ALL.
THE GHOST SHOWING UP EVERY NIGHT...
...IS THE DAUGHTER OF THE FAMILY WHO WAS KILLED...
...BY THE FIRE YOU SET ON THEIR HOUSE.
WHAT ...?
...
ARSON ...

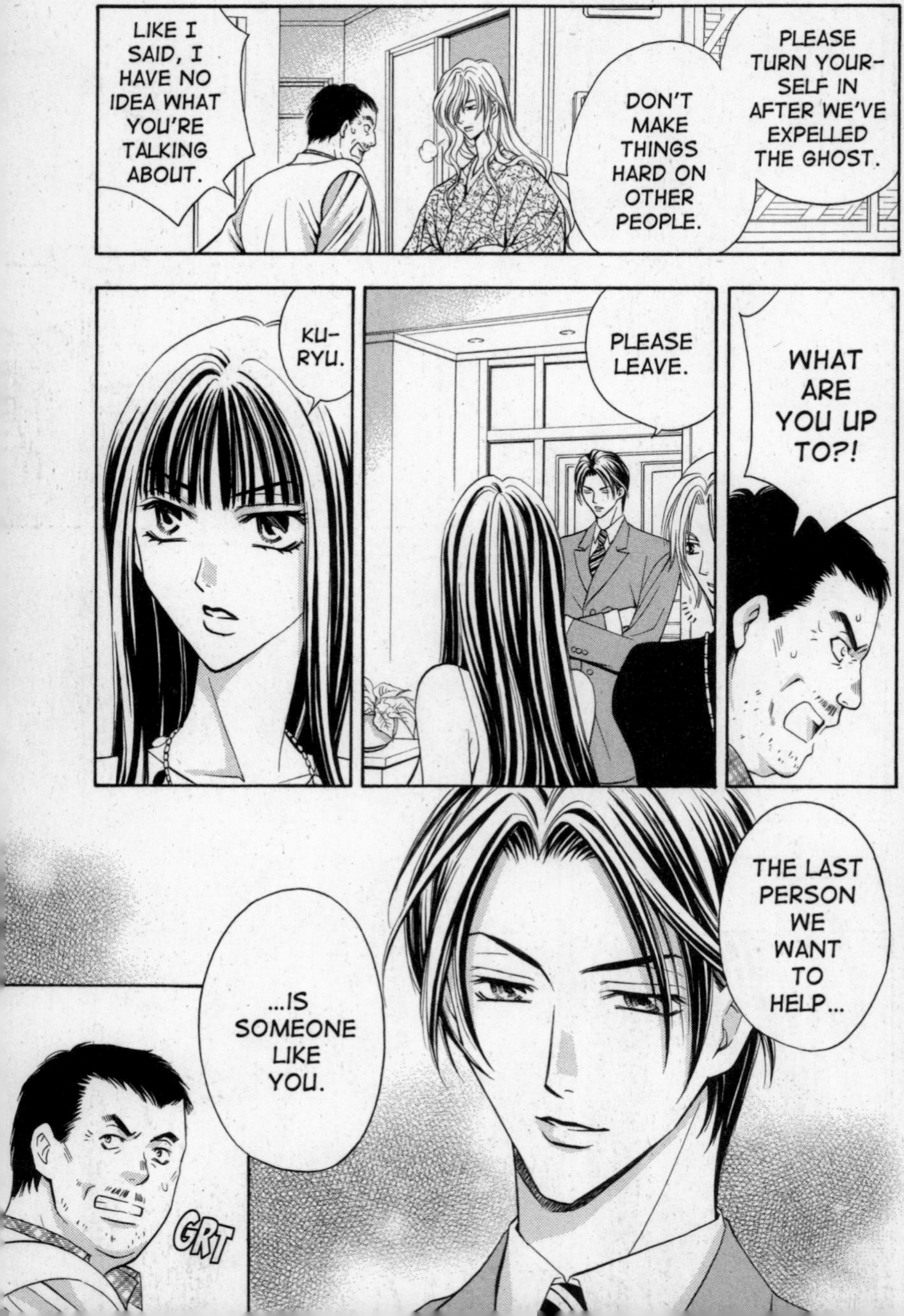
PLEASE TURN YOURSELF IN AFTER WE'VE EXPELLED THE GHOST.
DON'T MAKE THINGS HARD ON OTHER PEOPLE.
LIKE I SAID, I HAVE NO IDEA WHAT YOU'RE TALKING ABOUT.
WHAT ARE YOU UP TO?!
PLEASE LEAVE.
KU-RYU.
THE LAST PERSON WE WANT TO HELP...
...IS SOMEONE LIKE YOU.
GRT

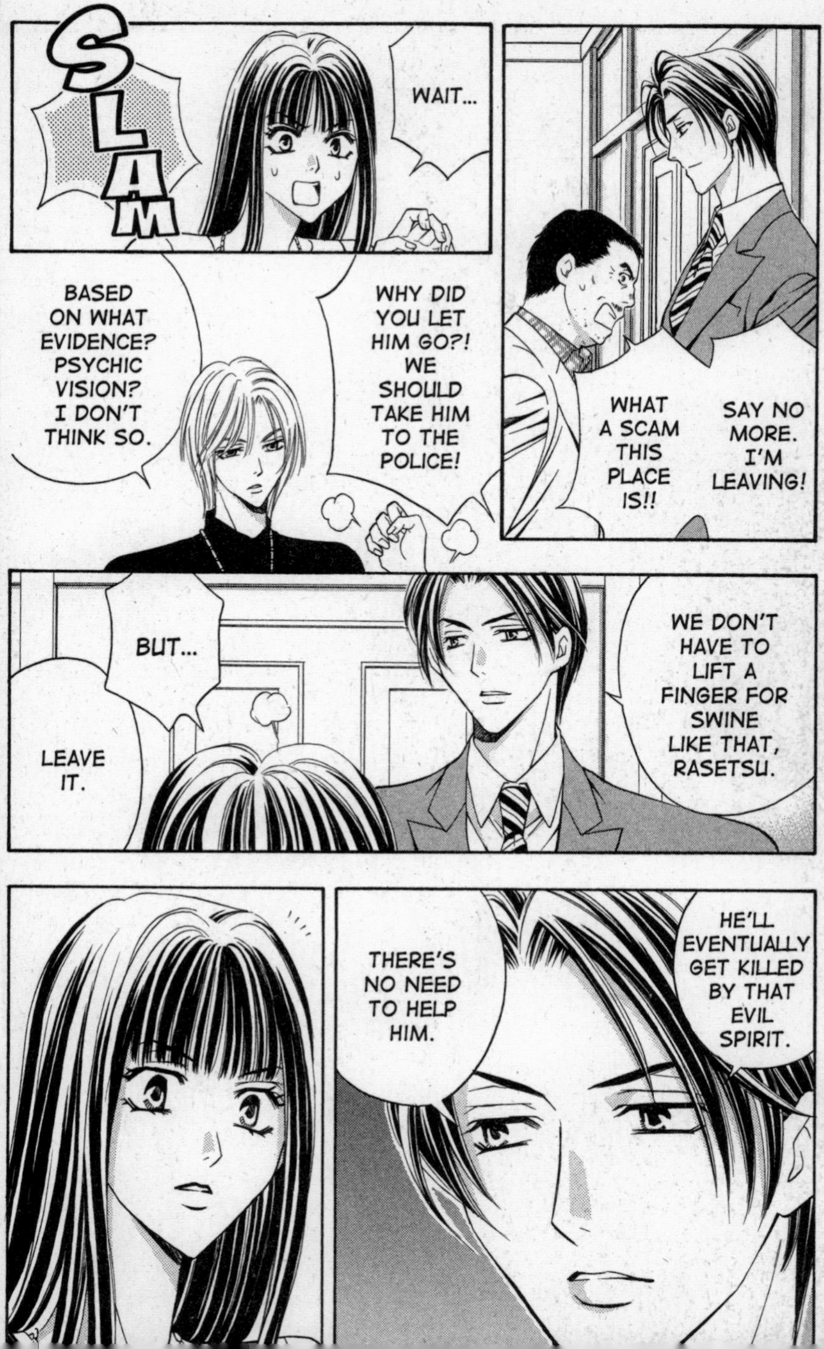
SAY NO MORE. I'M LEAVING!
WHAT A SCAM THIS PLACE IS!!
SLAM
WAIT...
WHY DID YOU LET HIM GO?! WE SHOULD TAKE HIM TO THE POLICE!
BASED ON WHAT EVIDENCE? PSYCHIC VISION? I DON'T THINK SO.
WE DON'T HAVE TO LIFT A FINGER FOR SWINE LIKE THAT, RASETSU.
BUT...
LEAVE IT.
HE'LL EVENTUALLY GET KILLED BY THAT EVIL SPIRIT.
THERE'S NO NEED TO HELP HIM.

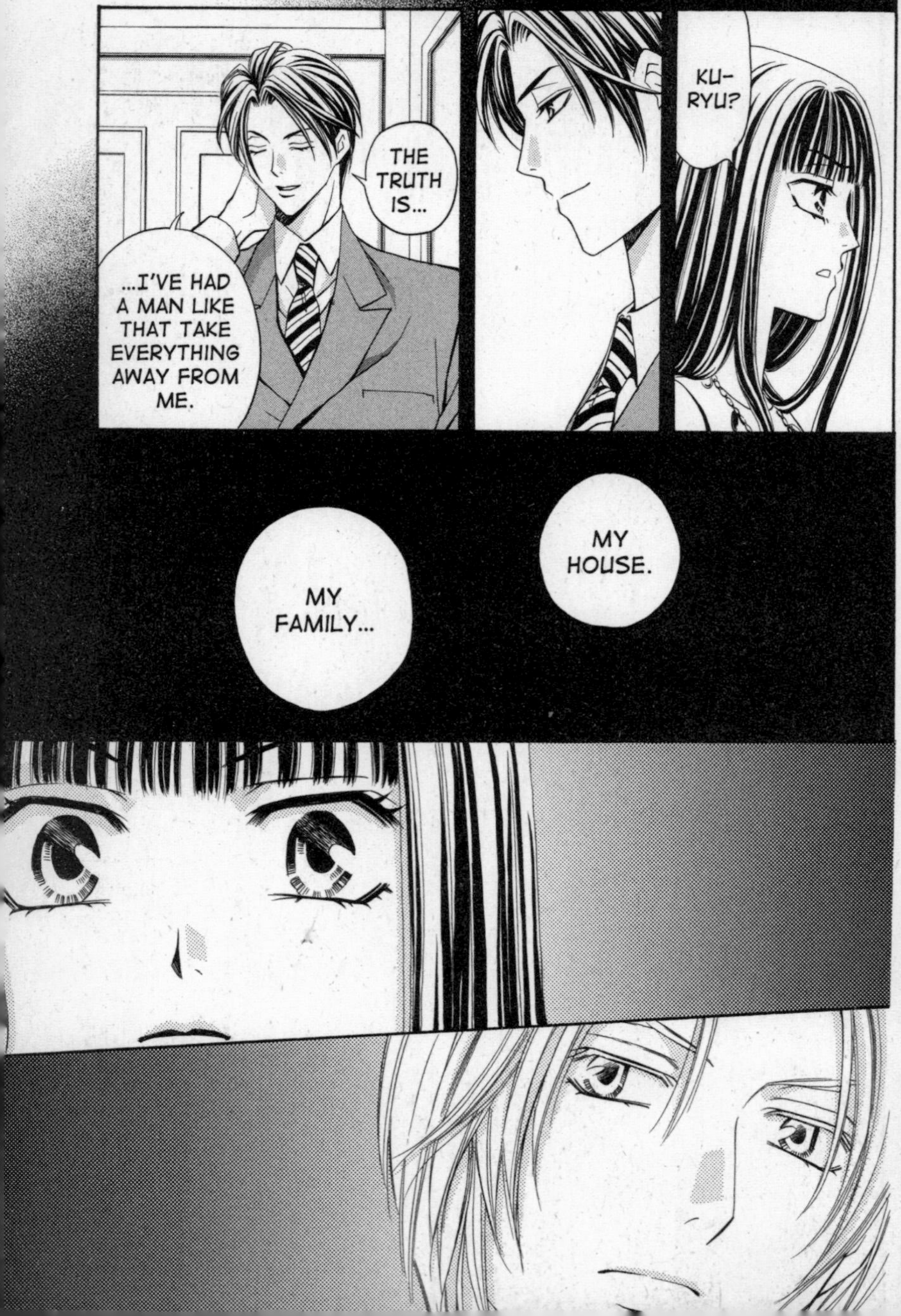
KU-RYU?
THE TRUTH IS...
...I'VE HAD A MAN LIKE THAT TAKE EVERYTHING AWAY FROM ME.
MY HOUSE.
MY FAMILY...

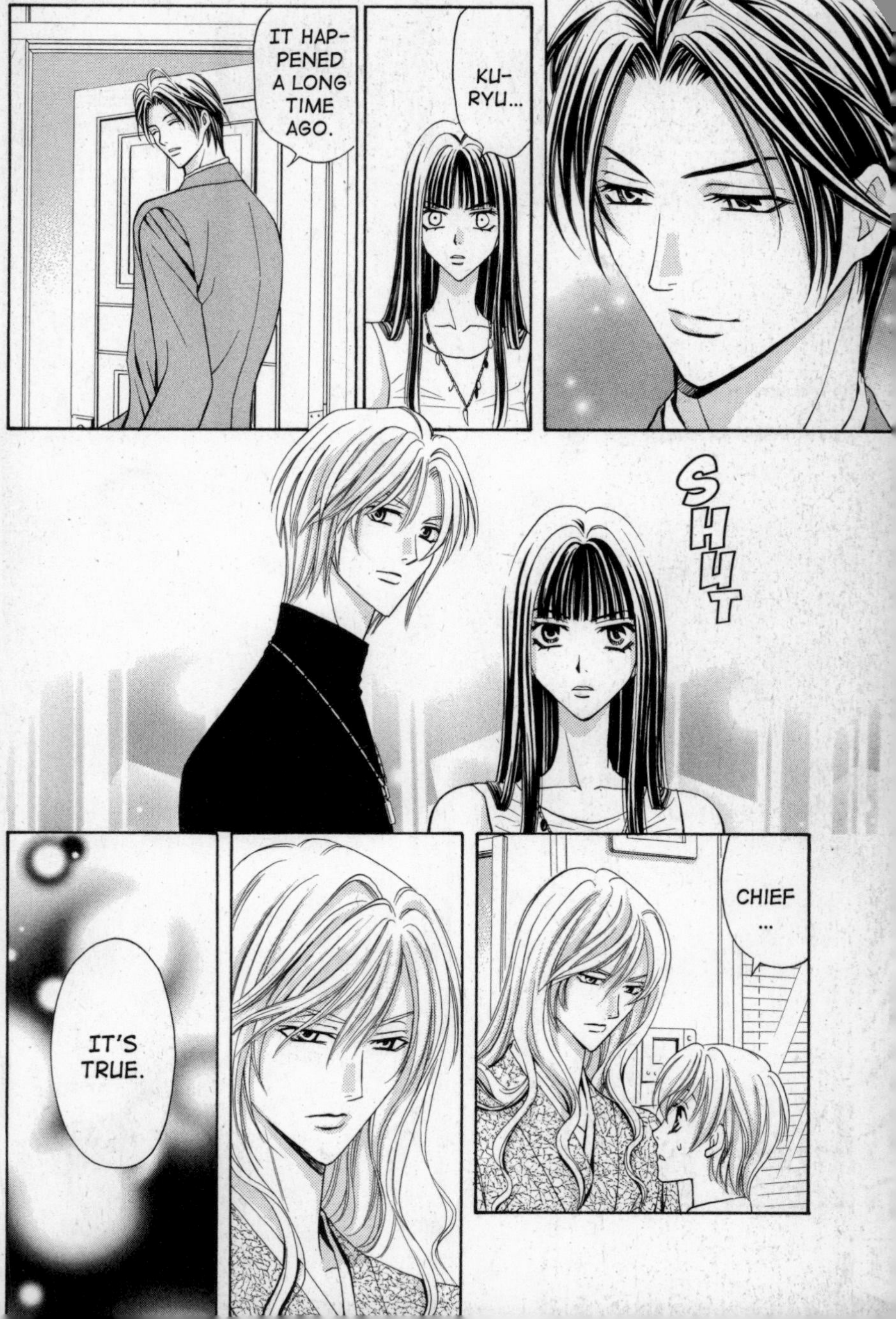
KU-
RYU...
IT HAP-
PENED
A LONG
TIME
AGO.
SHUT
CHIEF
...
IT'S
TRUE.

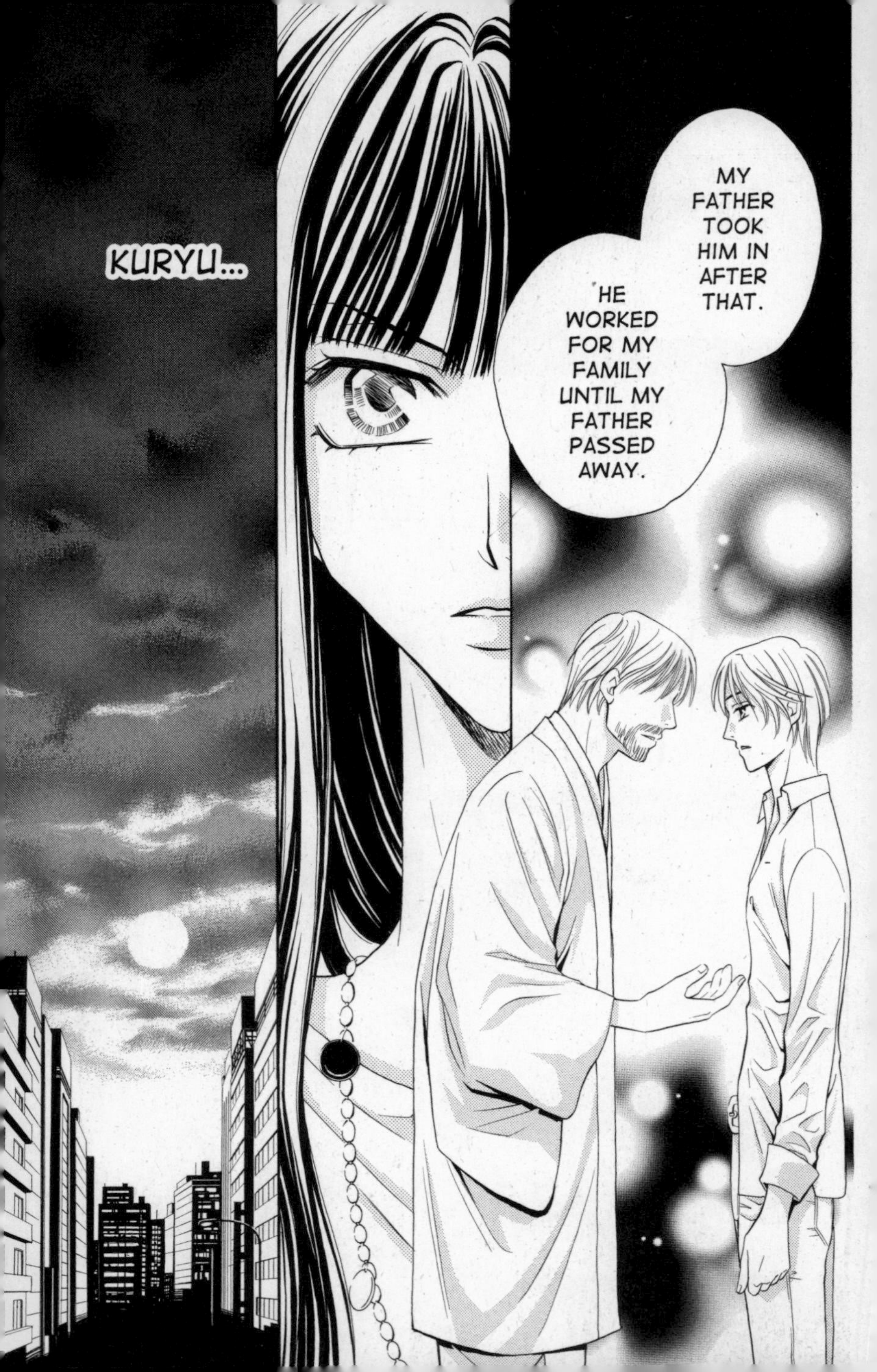
MY FATHER TOOK HIM IN AFTER THAT.
HE WORKED FOR MY FAMILY UNTIL MY FATHER PASSED AWAY.
KURYU...

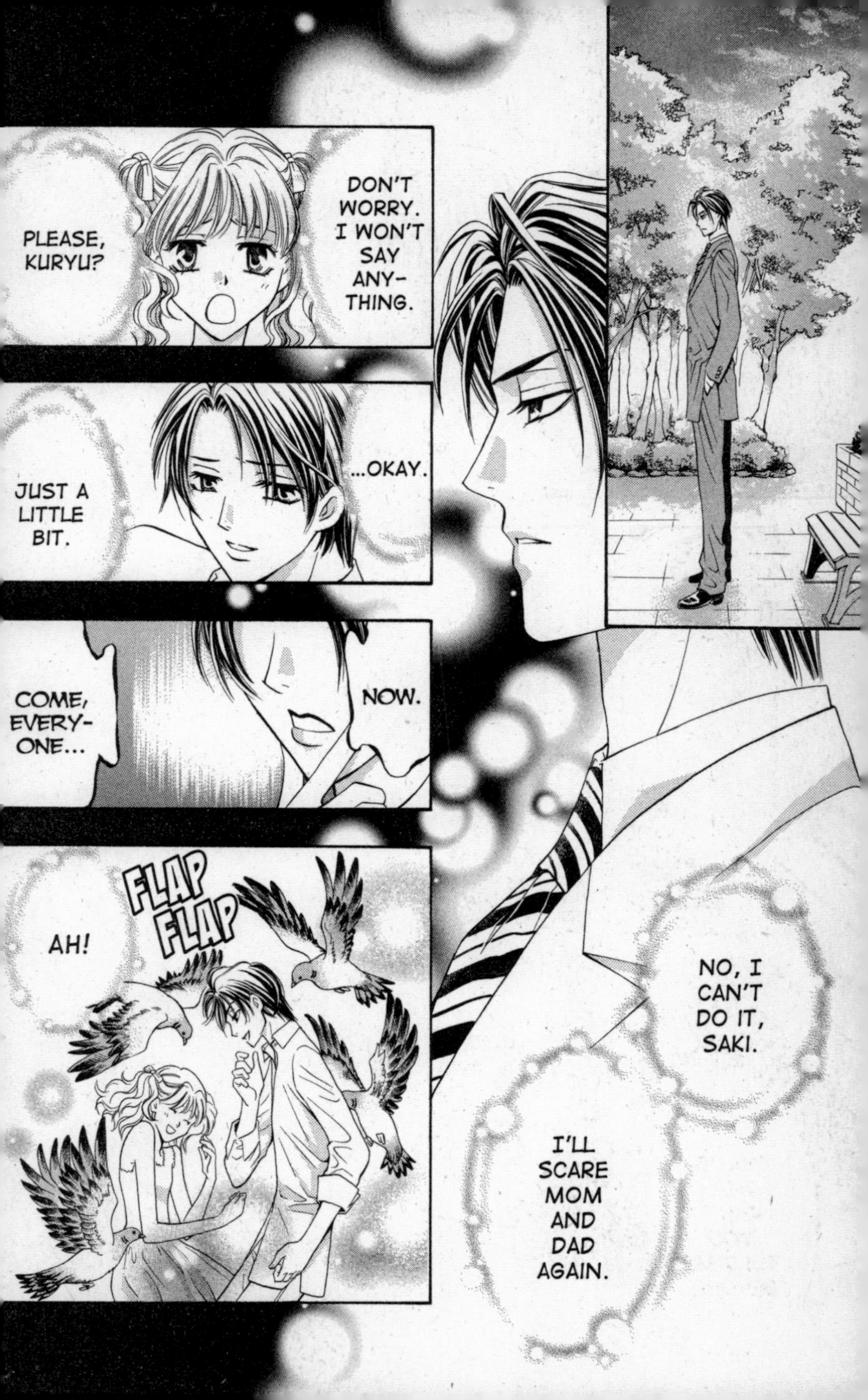
DON'T WORRY. I WON'T SAY ANY-THING.
PLEASE, KURYU?
...OKAY.
JUST A LITTLE BIT.
NOW.
COME, EVERY-ONE...
FLAP FLAP
AH!
NO, I CAN'T DO IT, SAKI.
I'LL SCARE MOM AND DAD AGAIN.

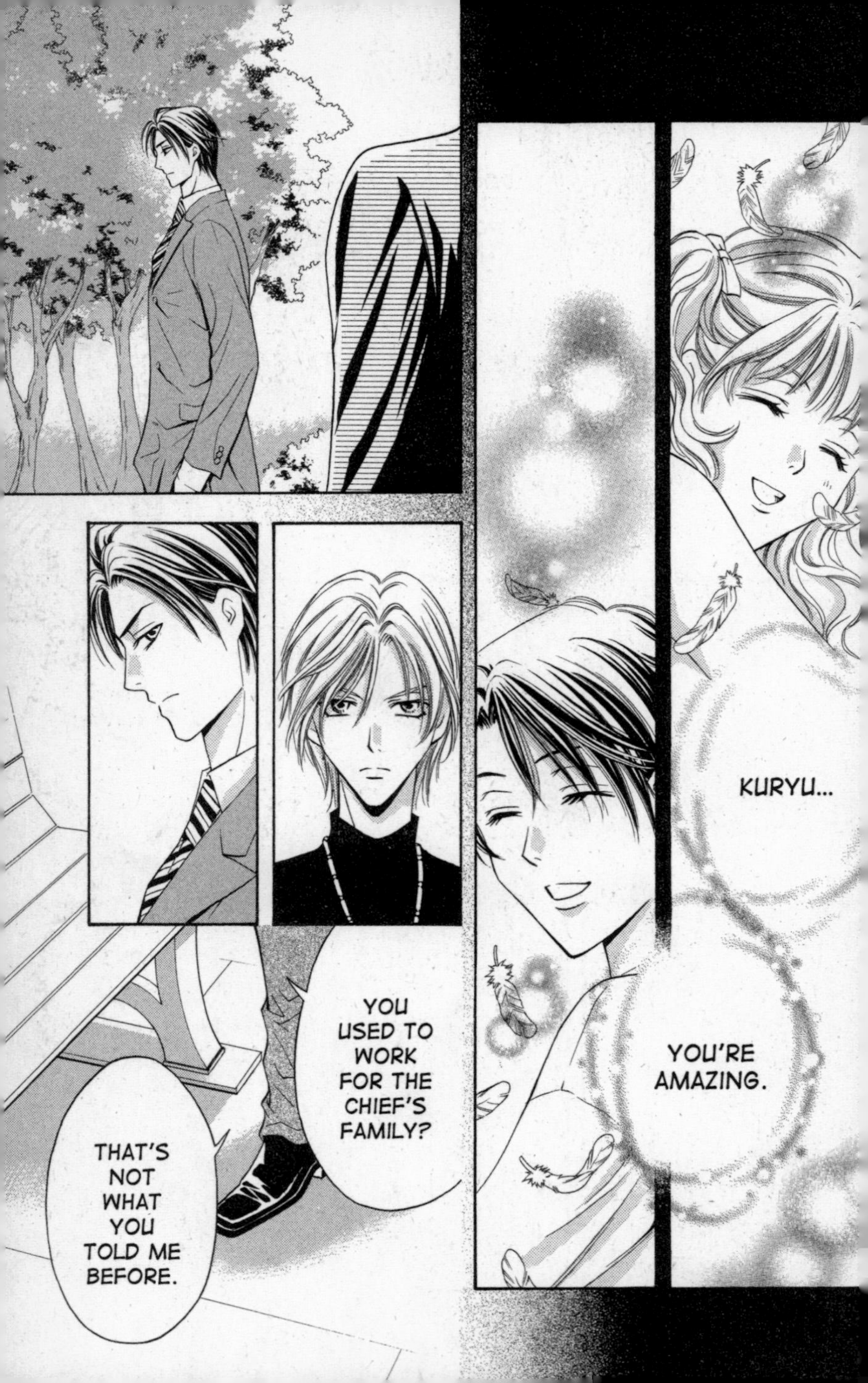
KURYU...
YOU'RE AMAZING.
YOU USED TO WORK FOR THE CHIEF'S FAMILY?
THAT'S NOT WHAT YOU TOLD ME BEFORE.

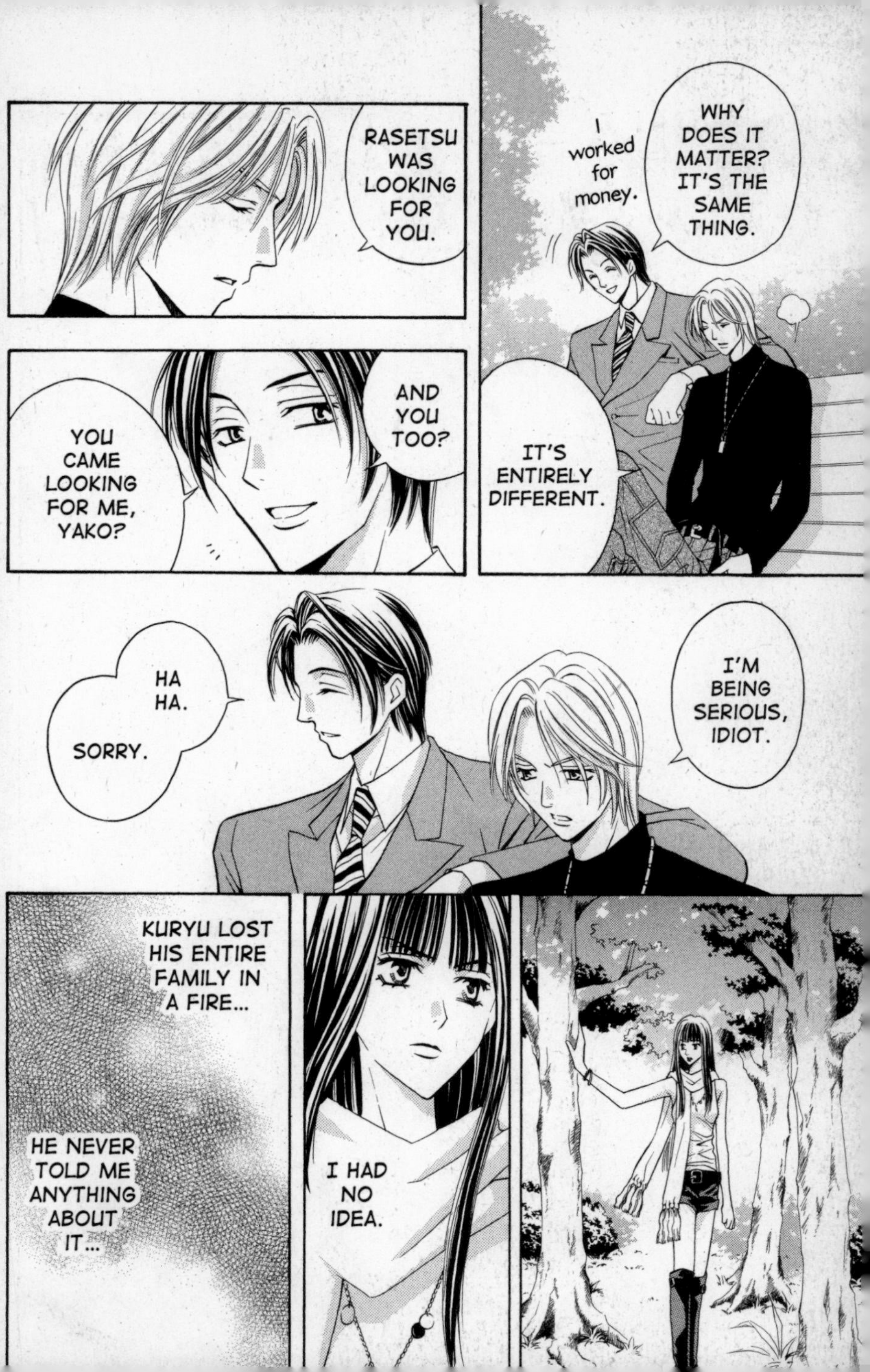
WHY DOES IT MATTER? IT'S THE SAME THING.
I worked for money.
IT'S ENTIRELY DIFFERENT.
RASETSU WAS LOOKING FOR YOU.
AND YOU TOO?
YOU CAME LOOKING FOR ME, YAKO?
I'M BEING SERIOUS, IDIOT.
HA HA.
SORRY.
I HAD NO IDEA.
KURYU LOST HIS ENTIRE FAMILY IN A FIRE...
HE NEVER TOLD ME ANYTHING ABOUT IT...

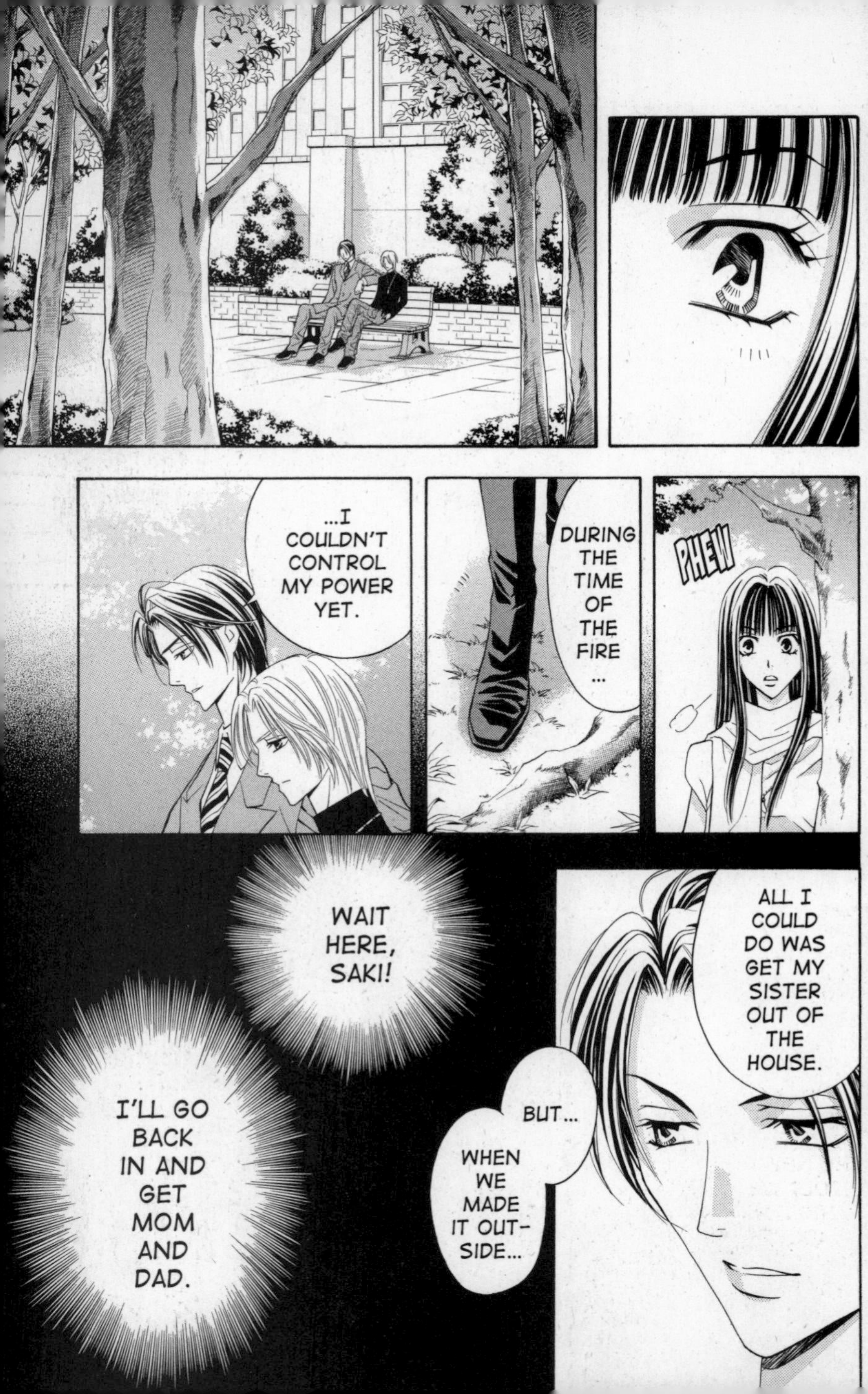
PHEW
DURING THE TIME OF THE FIRE...
...I COULDN'T CONTROL MY POWER YET.
ALL I COULD DO WAS GET MY SISTER OUT OF THE HOUSE.
BUT...
WHEN WE MADE IT OUT-SIDE...
WAIT HERE, SAKI!
I'LL GO BACK IN AND GET MOM AND DAD.

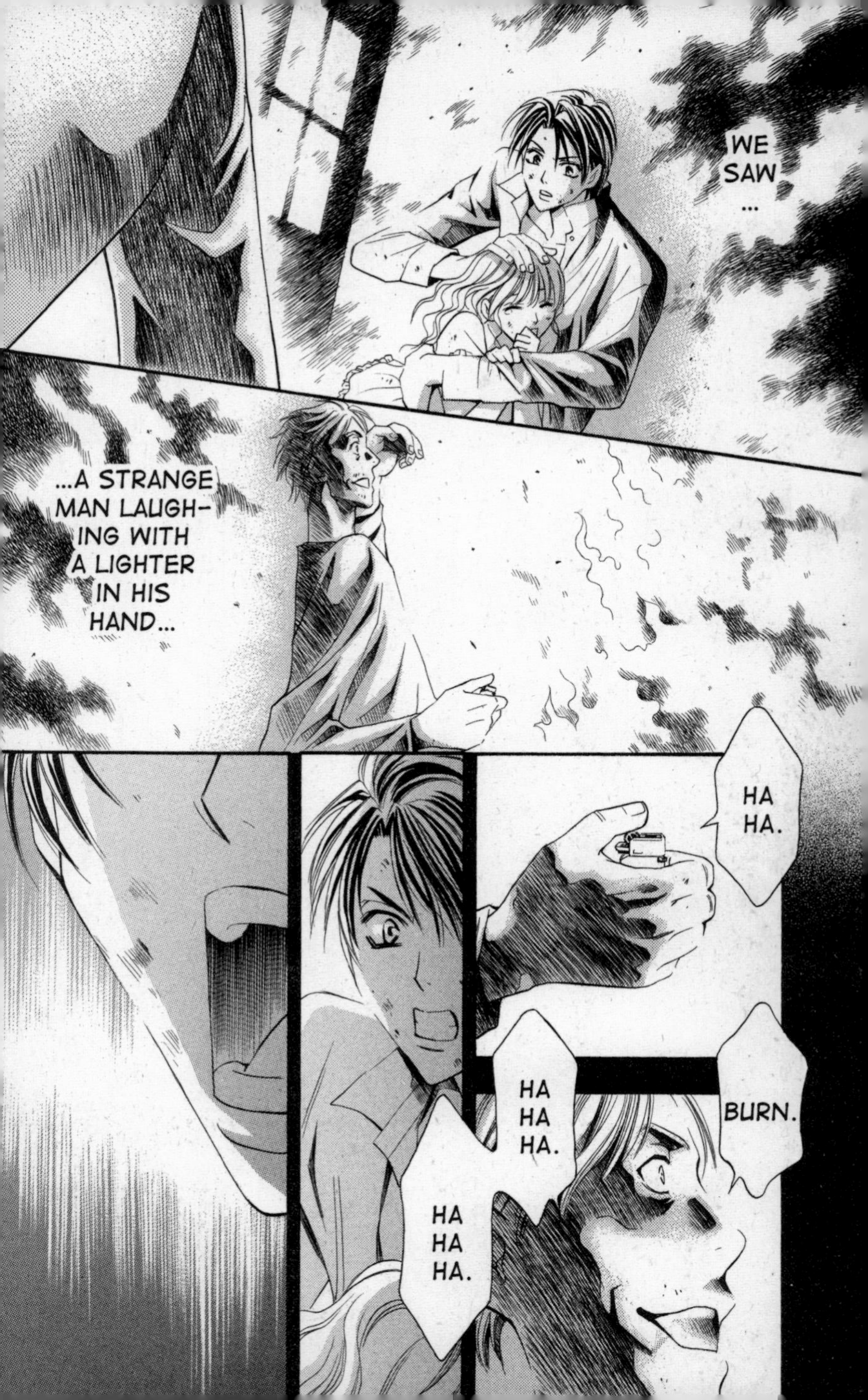
WE SAW ...
...A STRANGE MAN LAUGHING WITH A LIGHTER IN HIS HAND...
HA HA.
BURN.
HA HA HA.
HA HA HA.

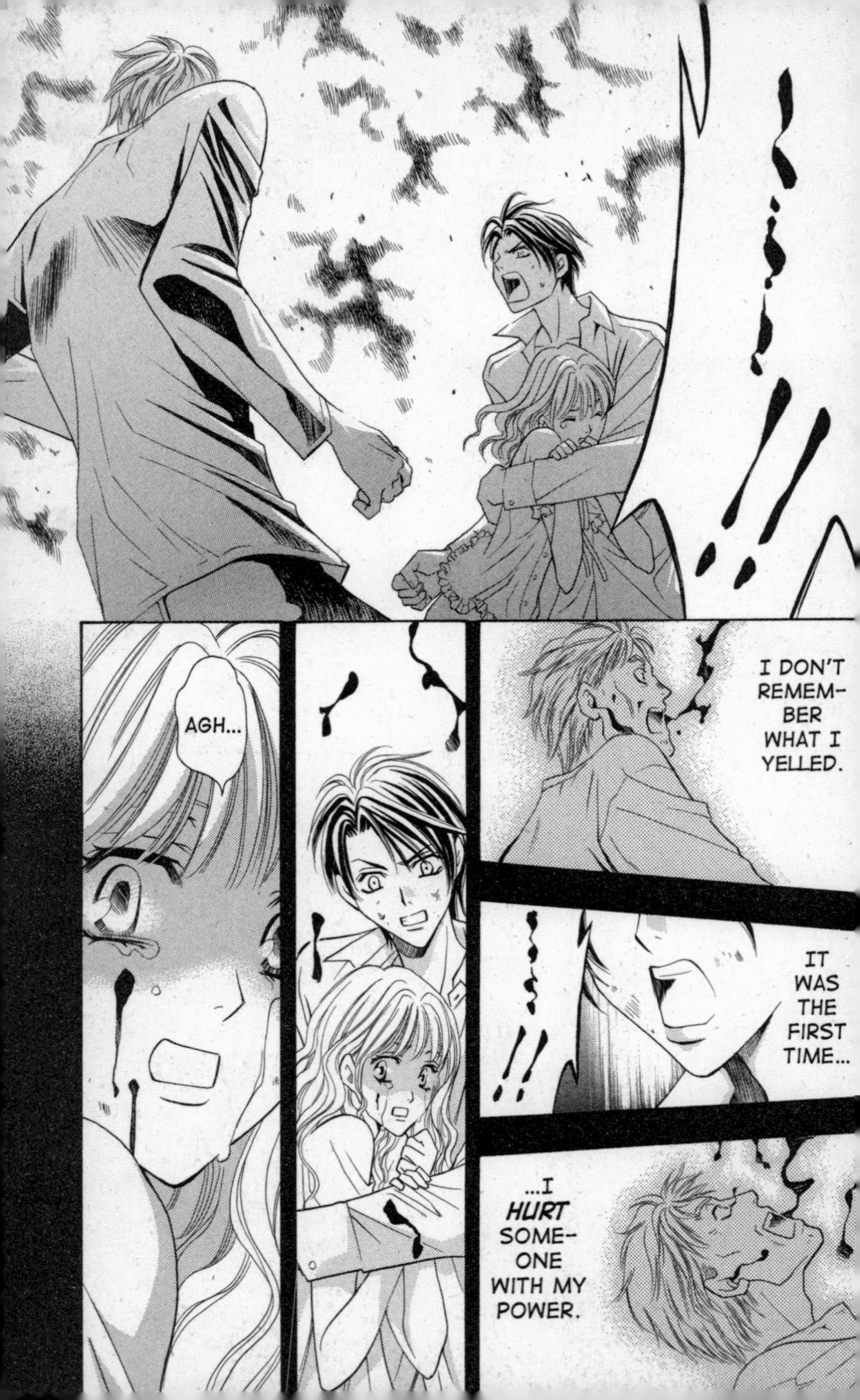
I DON'T REMEMBER WHAT I YELLED.
IT WAS THE FIRST TIME...
...I *HURT* SOMEONE WITH MY POWER.
AGH...

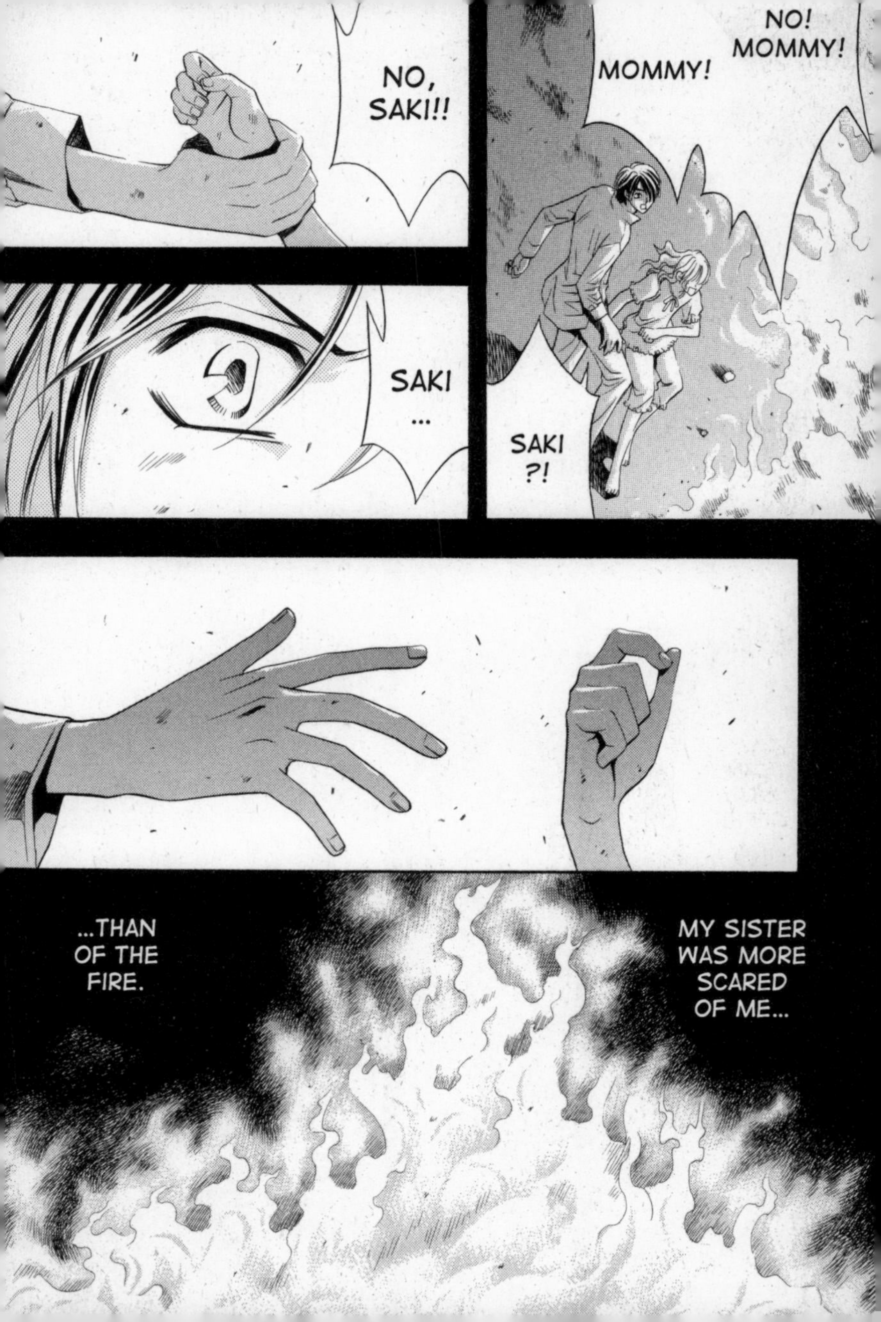
NO! MOMMY!
MOMMY!
SAKI ?!
NO, SAKI!!
SAKI ...
MY SISTER WAS MORE SCARED OF ME...
...THAN OF THE FIRE.

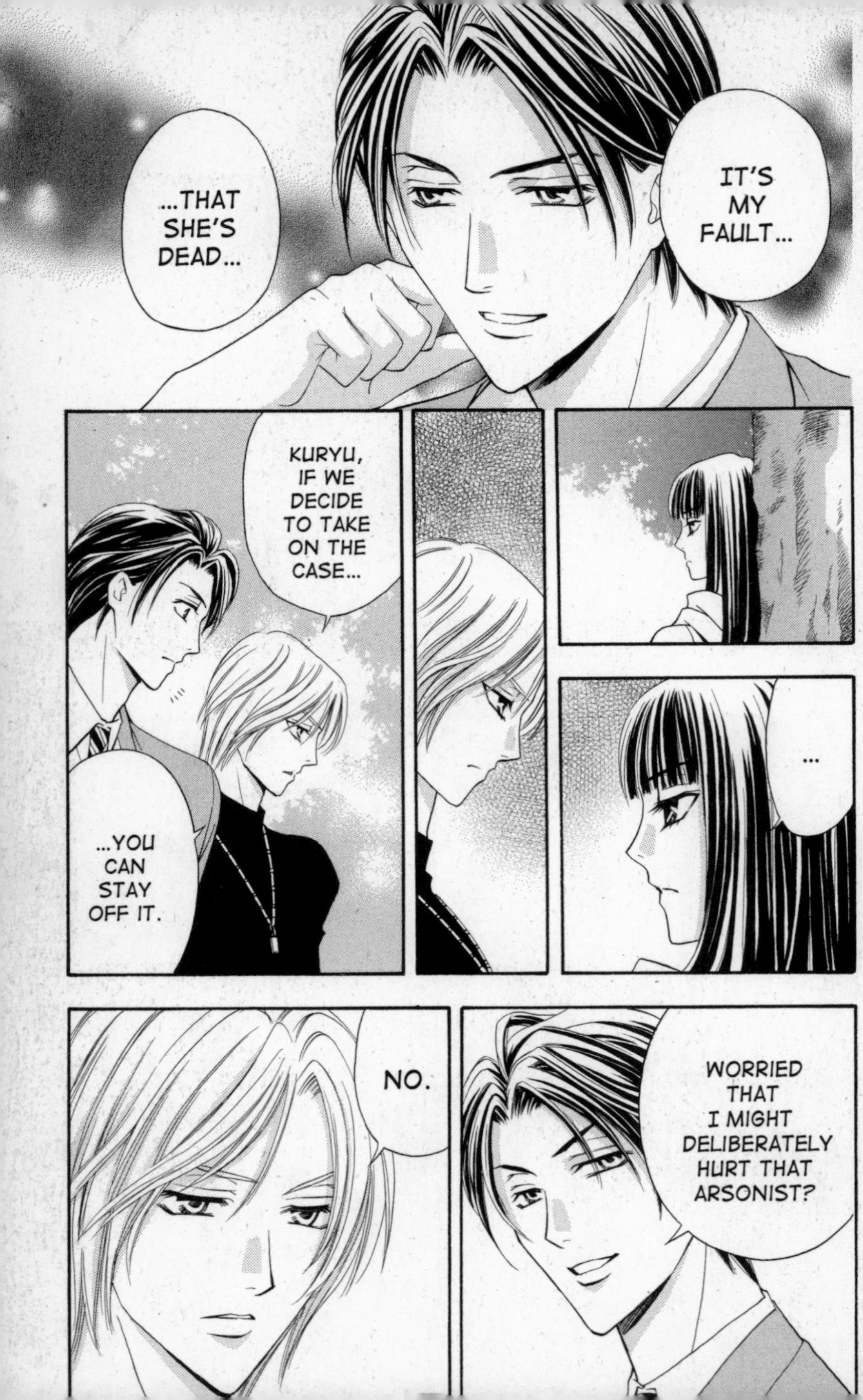
IT'S MY FAULT...
...THAT SHE'S DEAD...
...
KURYU, IF WE DECIDE TO TAKE ON THE CASE...
...YOU CAN STAY OFF IT.
WORRIED THAT I MIGHT DELIBERATELY HURT THAT ARSONIST?
NO.

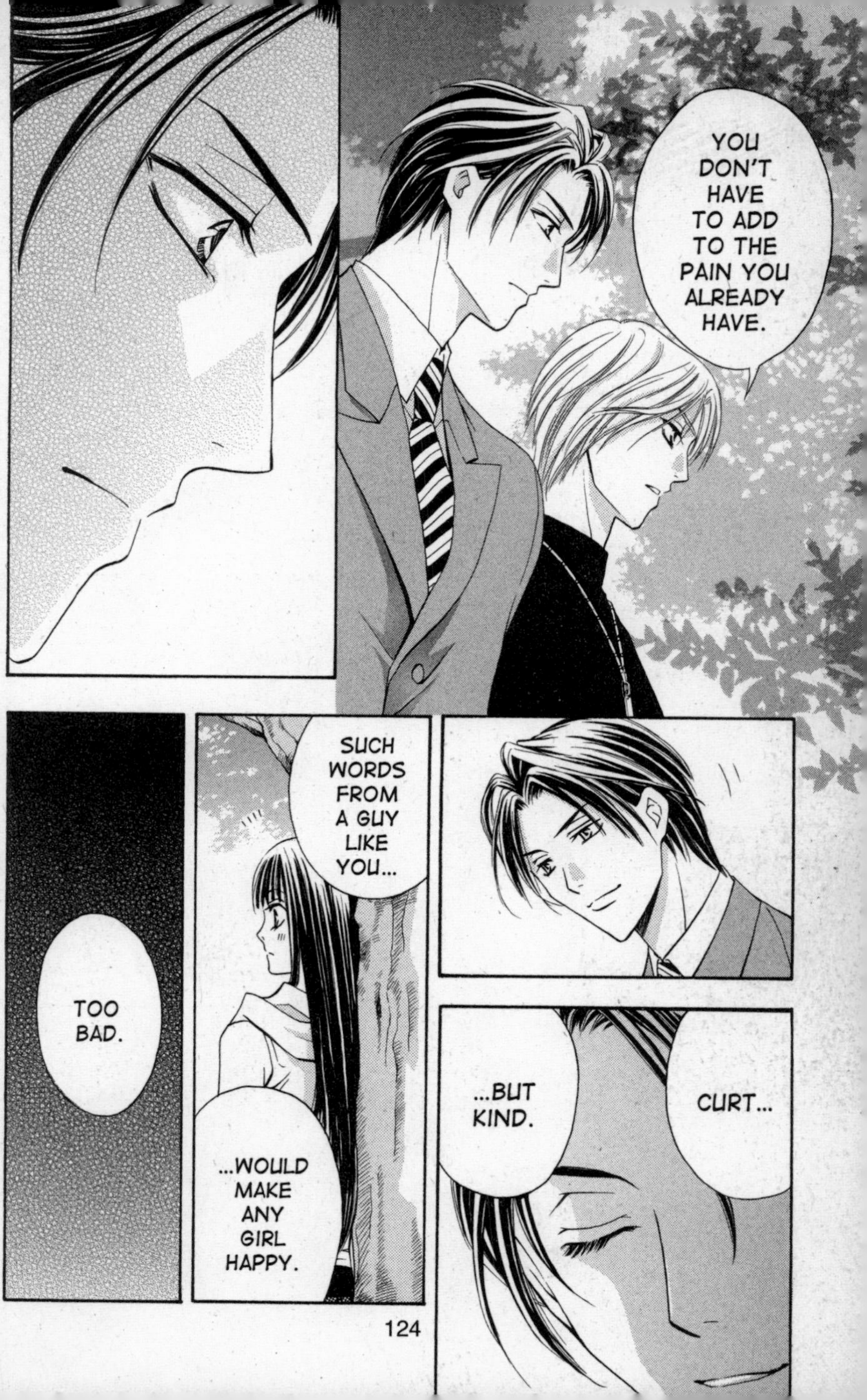
YOU DON'T HAVE TO ADD TO THE PAIN YOU ALREADY HAVE.
CURT...
...BUT KIND.
SUCH WORDS FROM A GUY LIKE YOU...
...WOULD MAKE ANY GIRL HAPPY.
TOO BAD.

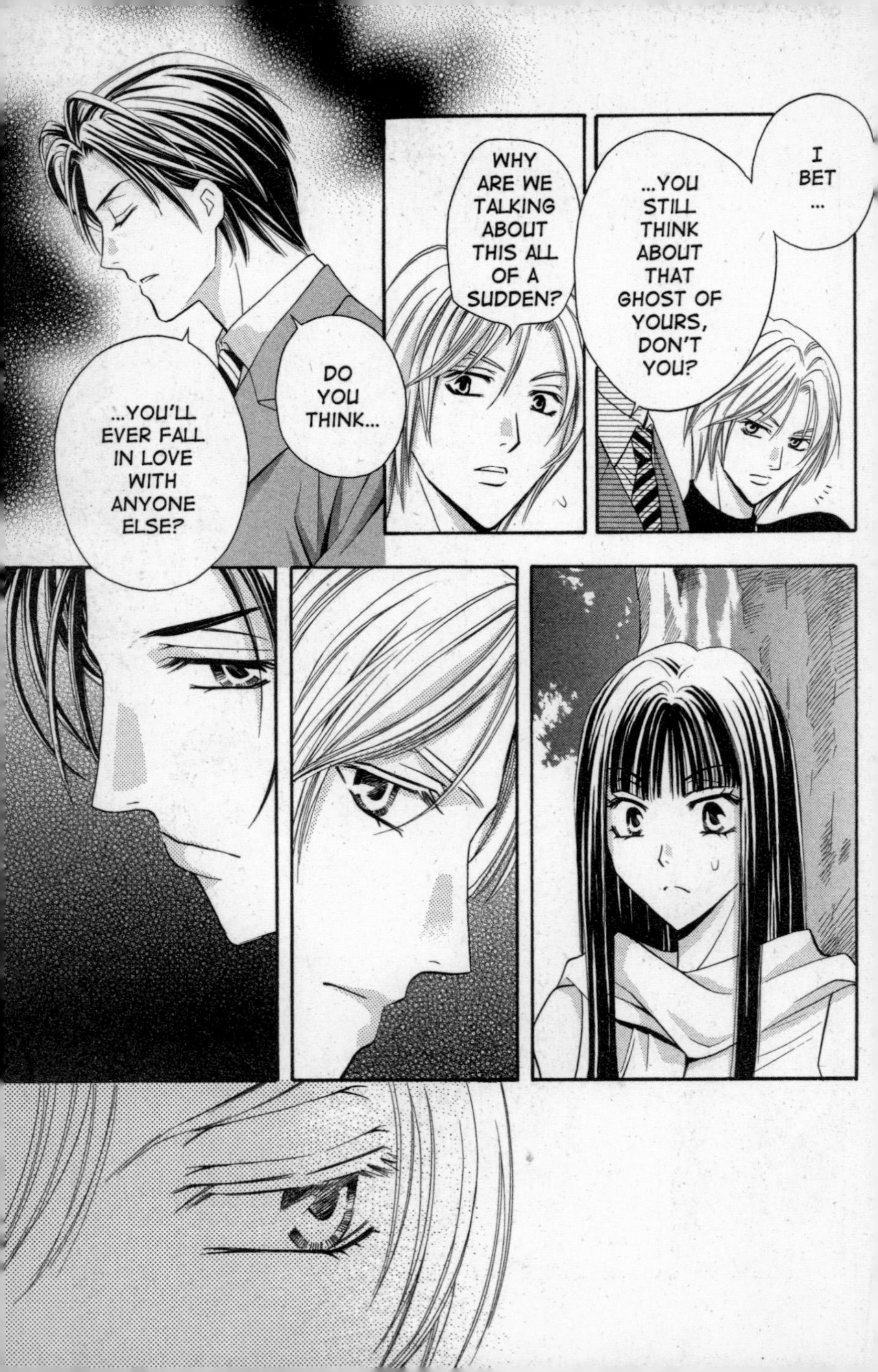
I BET ...
...YOU STILL THINK ABOUT THAT GHOST OF YOURS, DON'T YOU?
WHY ARE WE TALKING ABOUT THIS ALL OF A SUDDEN?
DO YOU THINK...
...YOU'LL EVER FALL IN LOVE WITH ANYONE ELSE?

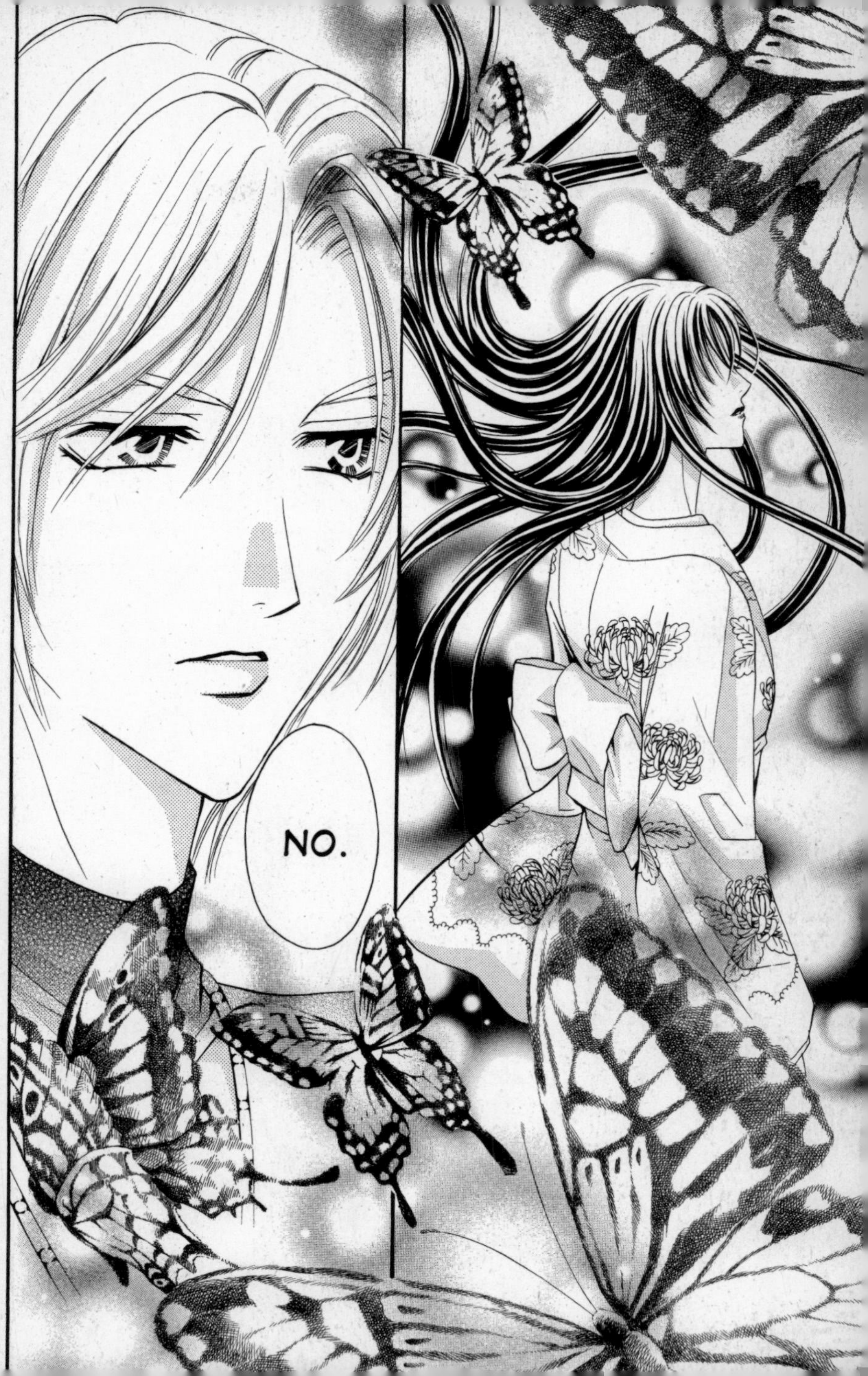
NO.

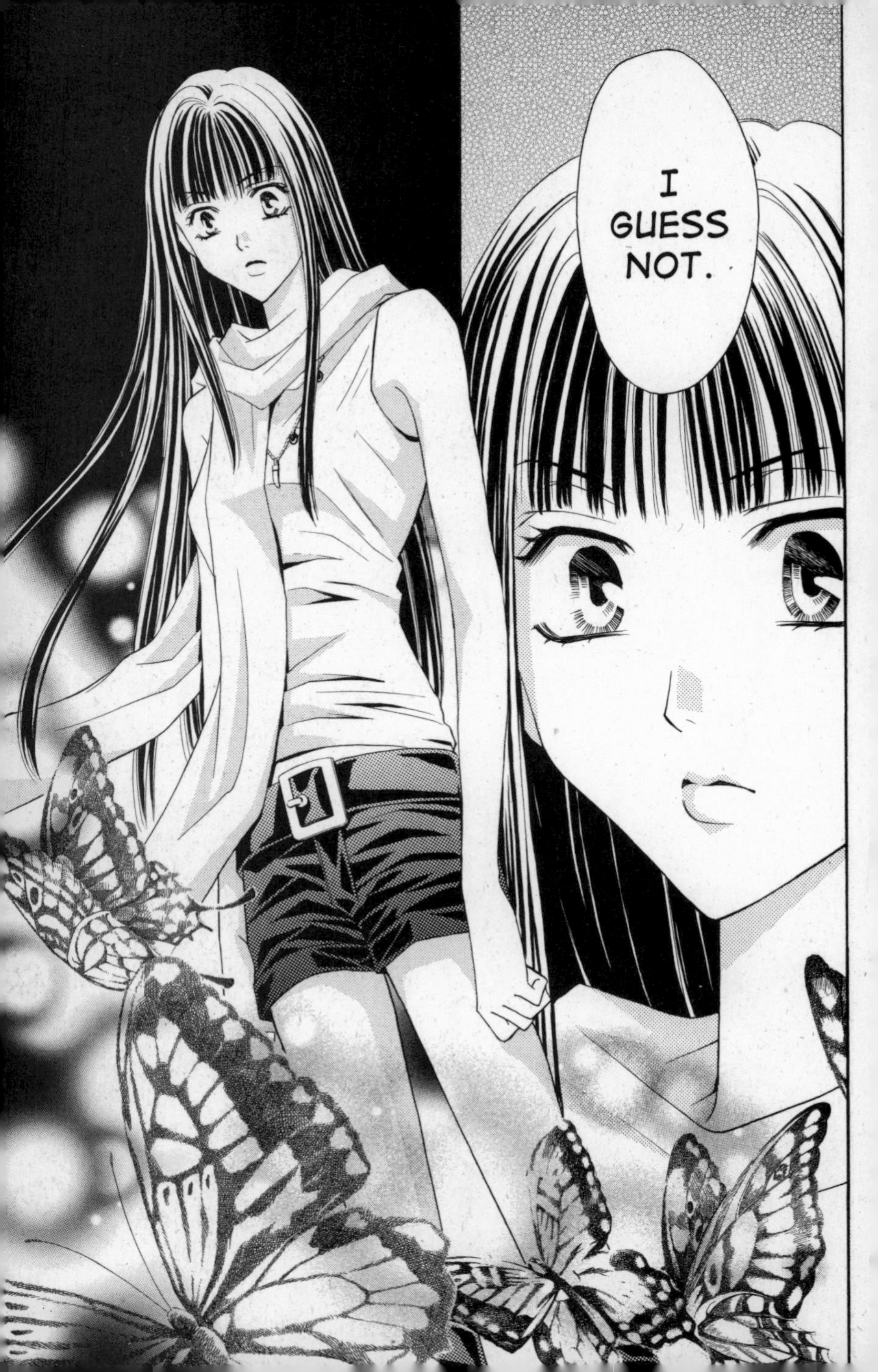
I GUESS NOT.

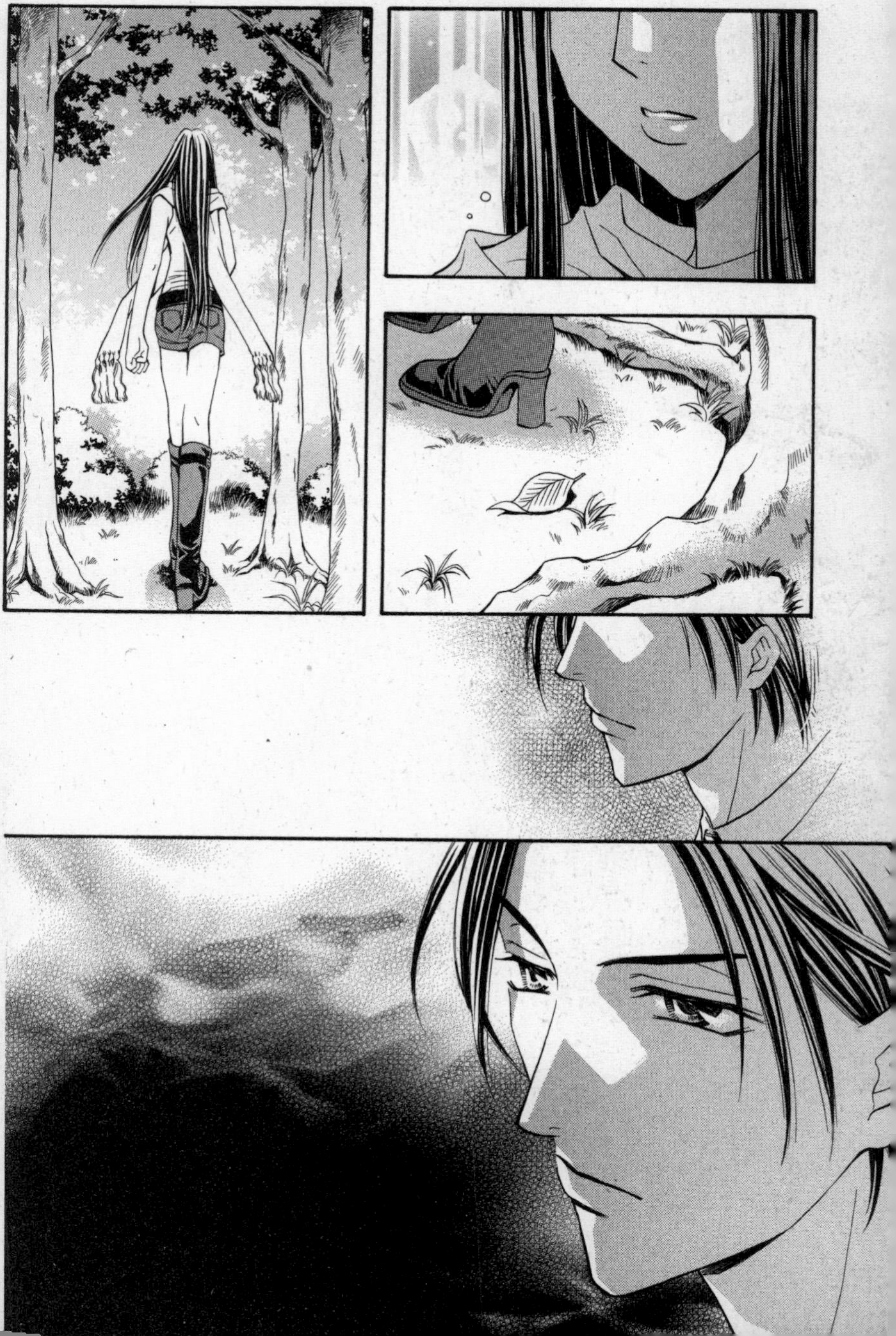

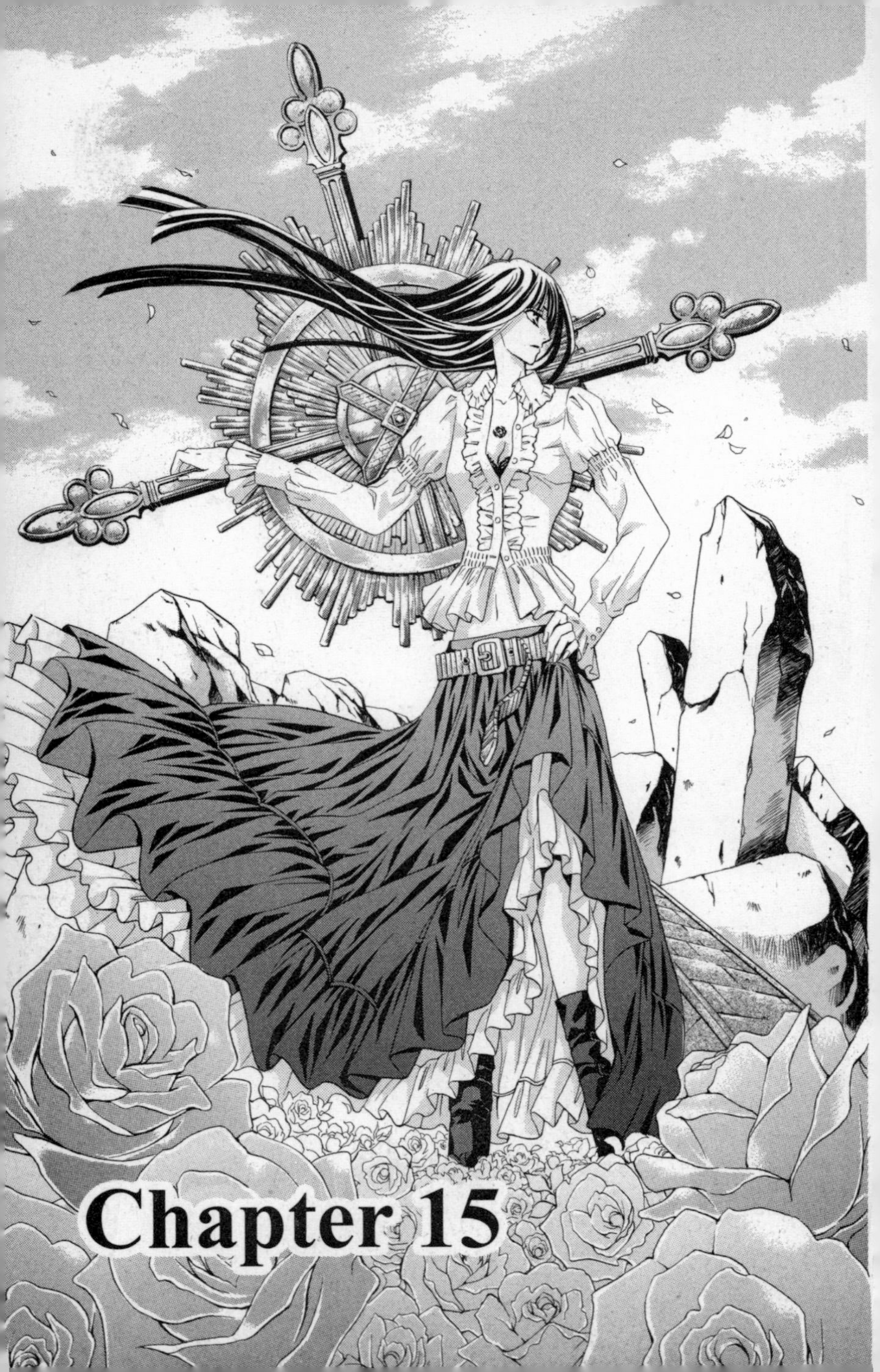
Chapter 15

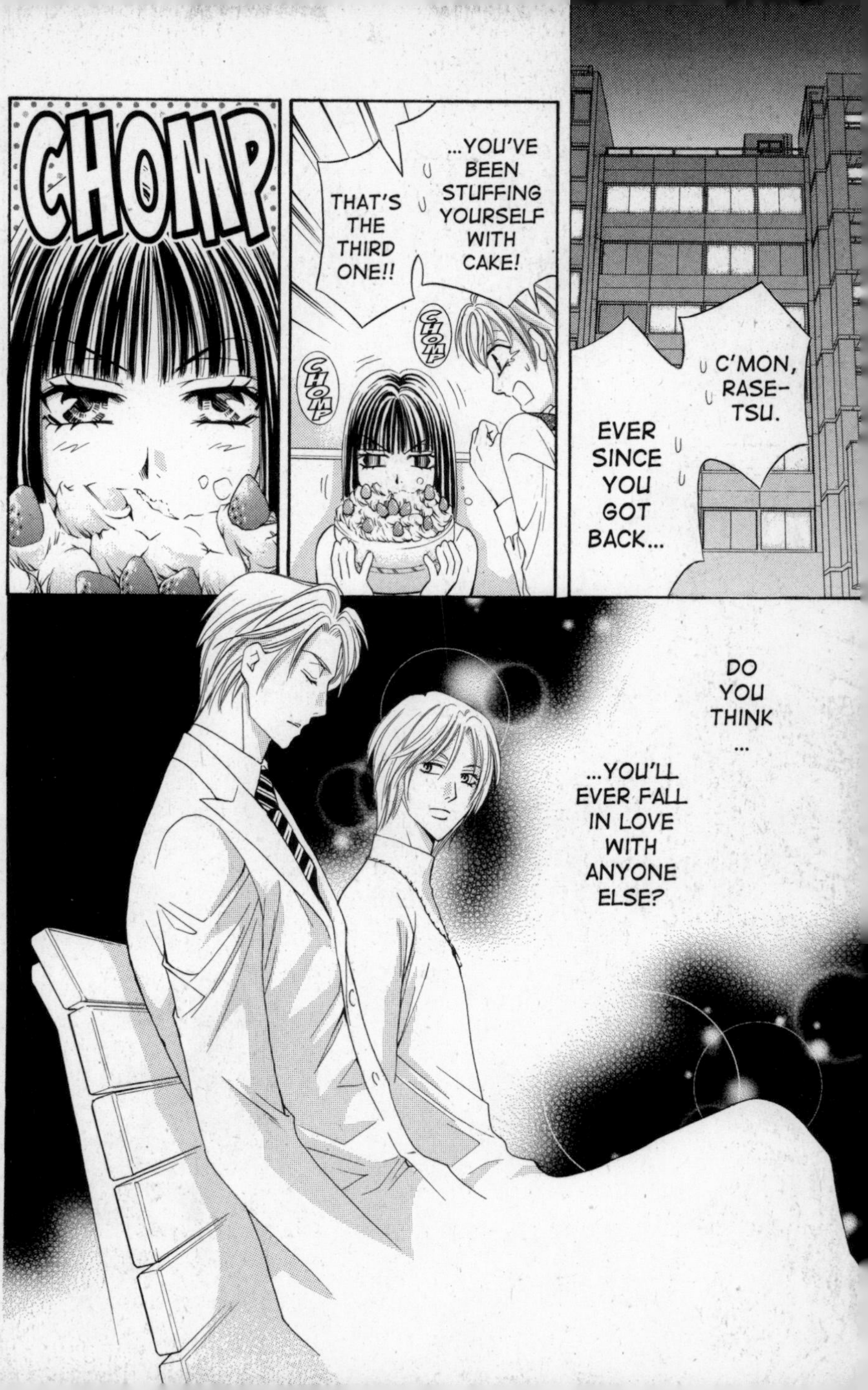
C'MON, RASE-TSU.
EVER SINCE YOU GOT BACK...
...YOU'VE BEEN STUFFING YOURSELF WITH CAKE!
THAT'S THE THIRD ONE!!
CHOMP
CHOMP
CHOMP
DO YOU THINK...
...YOU'LL EVER FALL IN LOVE WITH ANYONE ELSE?

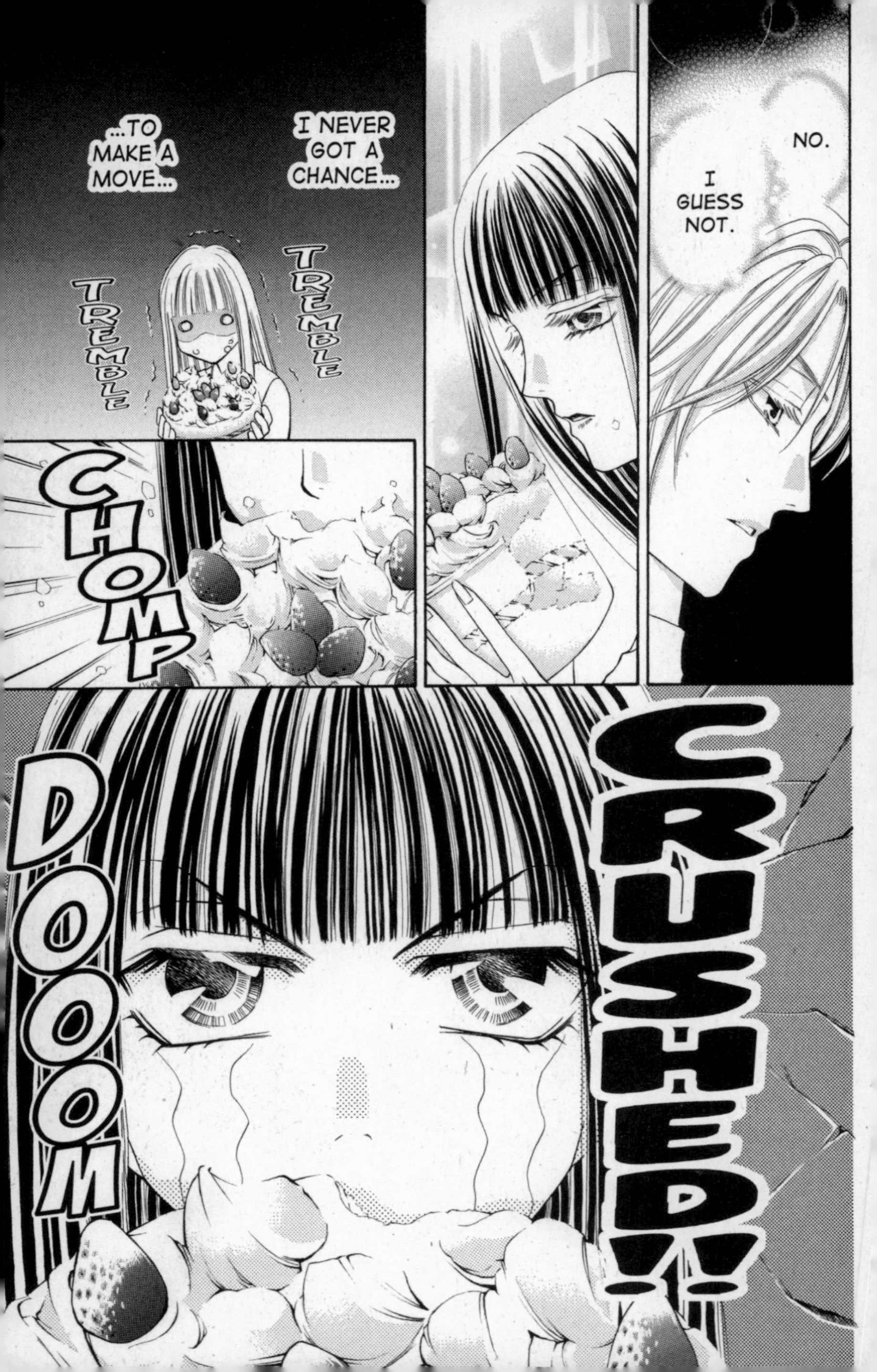
NO.
I GUESS NOT.
I NEVER GOT A CHANCE...
...TO MAKE A MOVE...
TREMBLE
TREMBLE
CHOMP
CRUSHED!!
DOOOOM

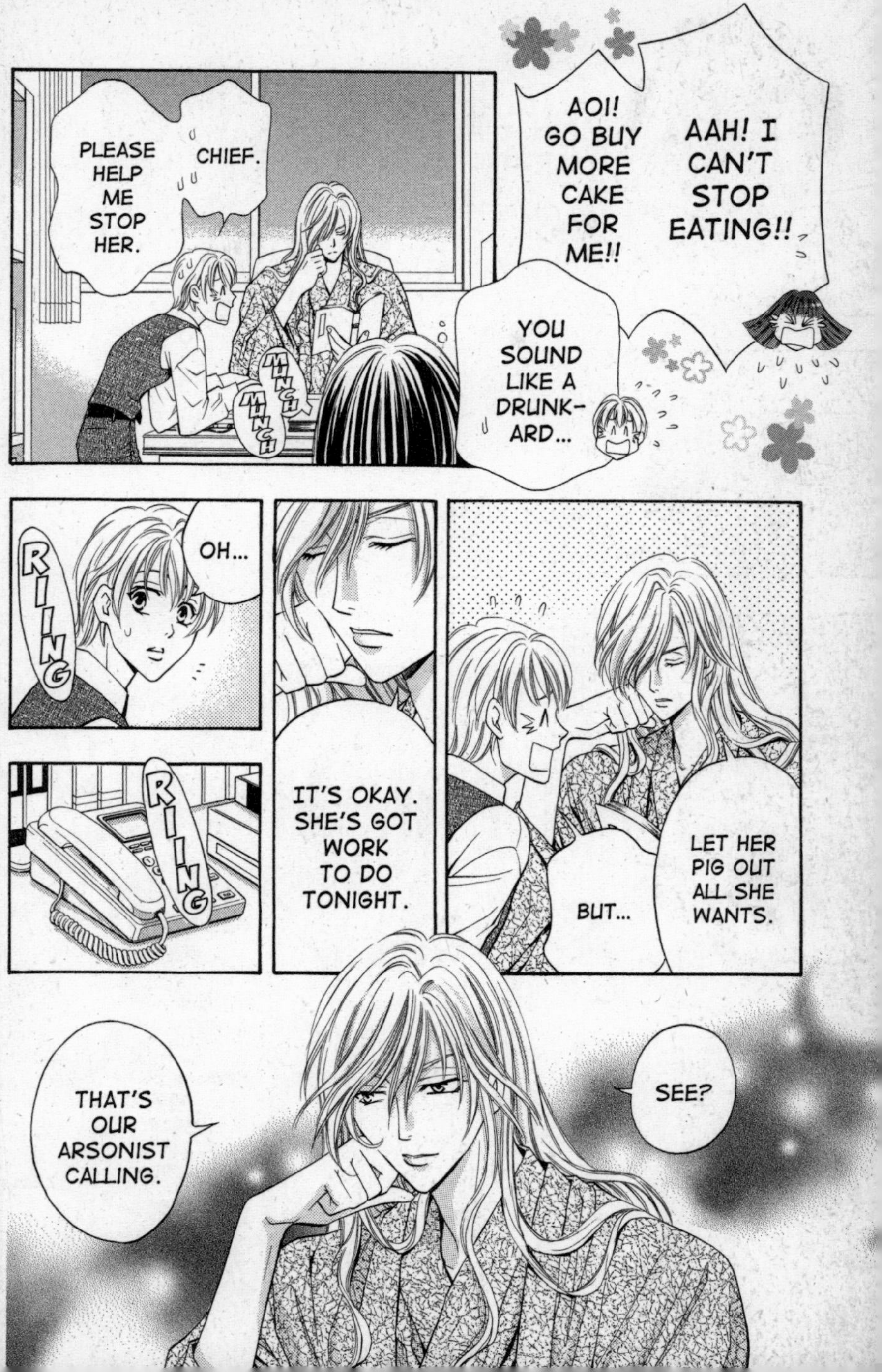
AAH! I CAN'T STOP EATING!!
AOI! GO BUY MORE CAKE FOR ME!!
YOU SOUND LIKE A DRUNK-ARD...
CHIEF.
PLEASE HELP ME STOP HER.
MUNCH
MUNCH
LET HER PIG OUT ALL SHE WANTS.
BUT...
IT'S OKAY. SHE'S GOT WORK TO DO TONIGHT.
OH...
RIING
RIING
SEE?
THAT'S OUR ARSONIST CALLING.

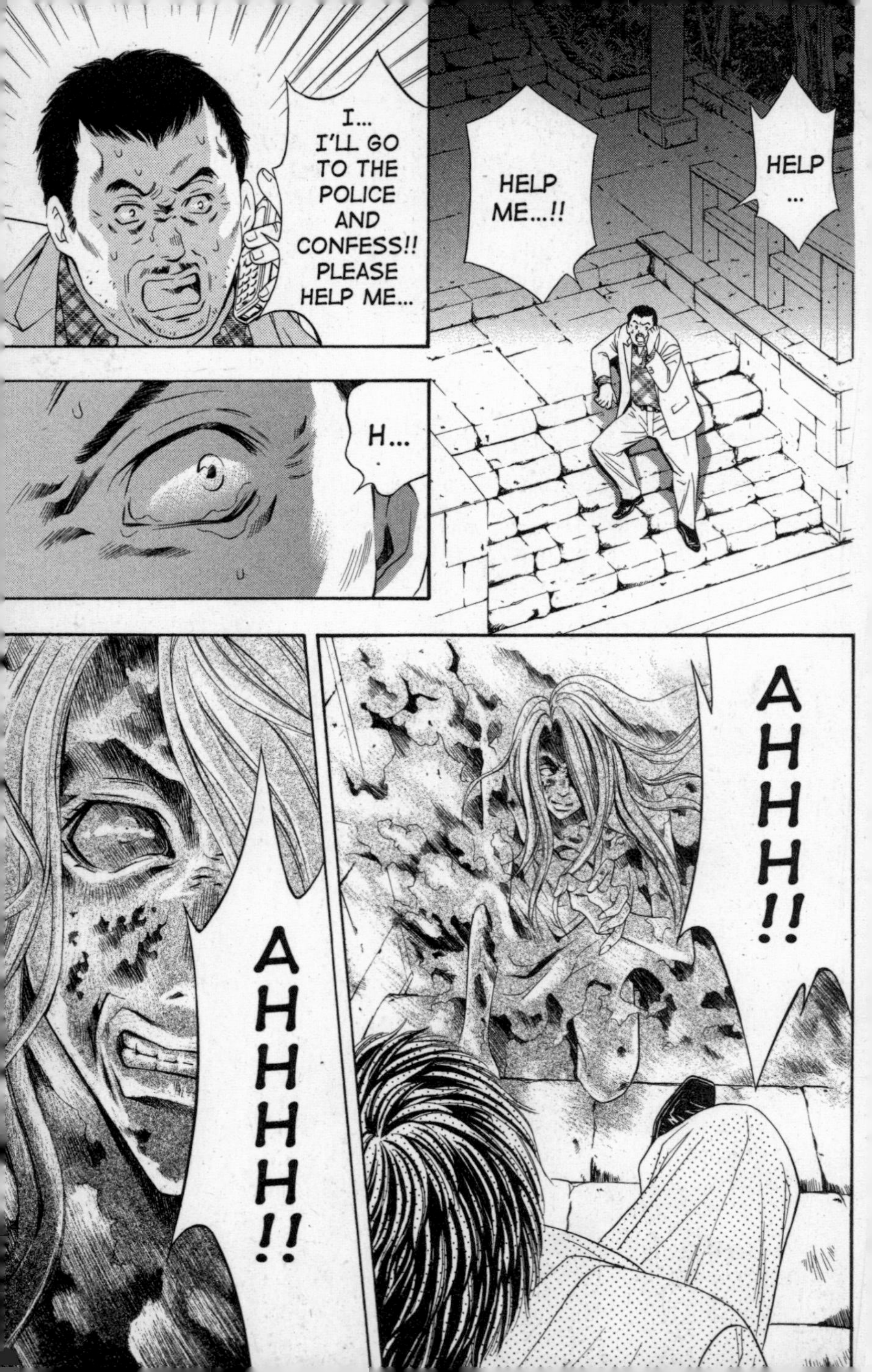
HELP ...
HELP ME...!!
I... I'LL GO TO THE POLICE AND CONFESS!! PLEASE HELP ME...
H...
AHHH!!
AHHHH!!

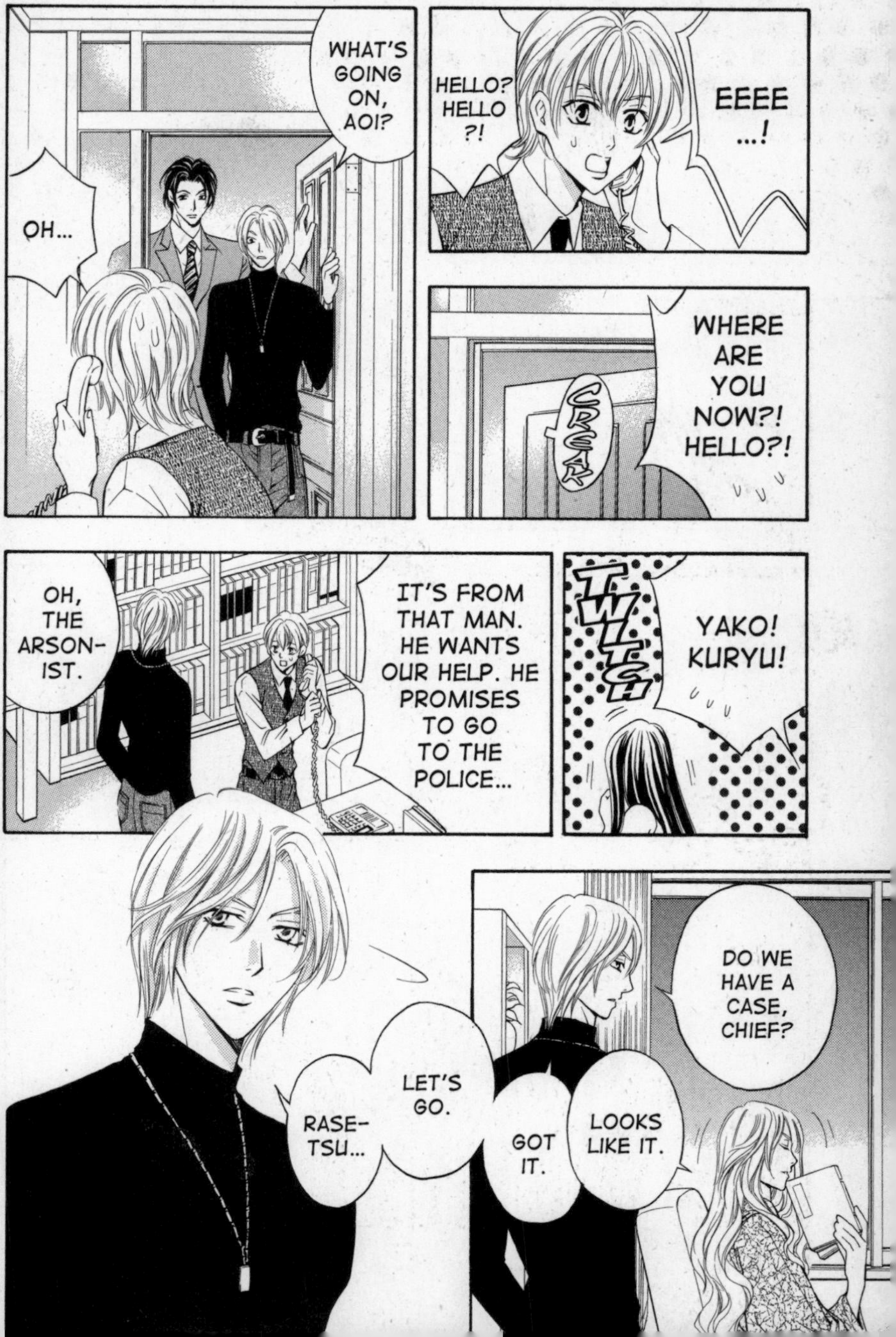
EEEE...!
HELLO? HELLO?!
WHERE ARE YOU NOW?! HELLO?!
CREAK
WHAT'S GOING ON, AOI?
OH...
YAKO! KURYU!
TWITCH
IT'S FROM THAT MAN. HE WANTS OUR HELP. HE PROMISES TO GO TO THE POLICE...
OH, THE ARSON-IST.
DO WE HAVE A CASE, CHIEF?
LOOKS LIKE IT.
GOT IT.
LET'S GO.
RASE-TSU...

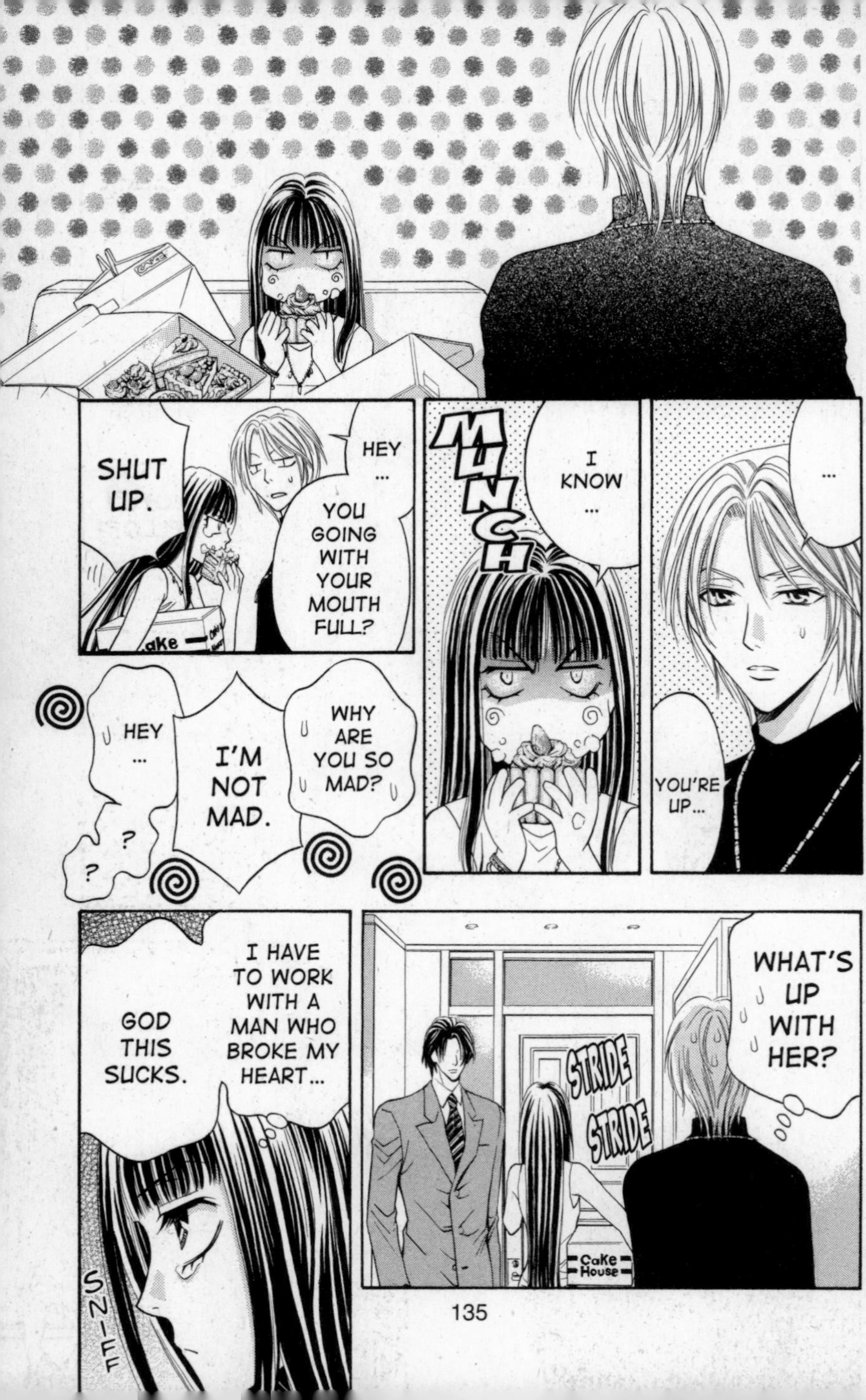
...
YOU'RE UP...
MUNCH
I KNOW ...
HEY ...
YOU GOING WITH YOUR MOUTH FULL?
SHUT UP.
CaKe
WHY ARE YOU SO MAD?
I'M NOT MAD.
HEY ...
? ?
WHAT'S UP WITH HER?
STRIDE STRIDE
CaKe House
I HAVE TO WORK WITH A MAN WHO BROKE MY HEART...
GOD THIS SUCKS.
SNIFF

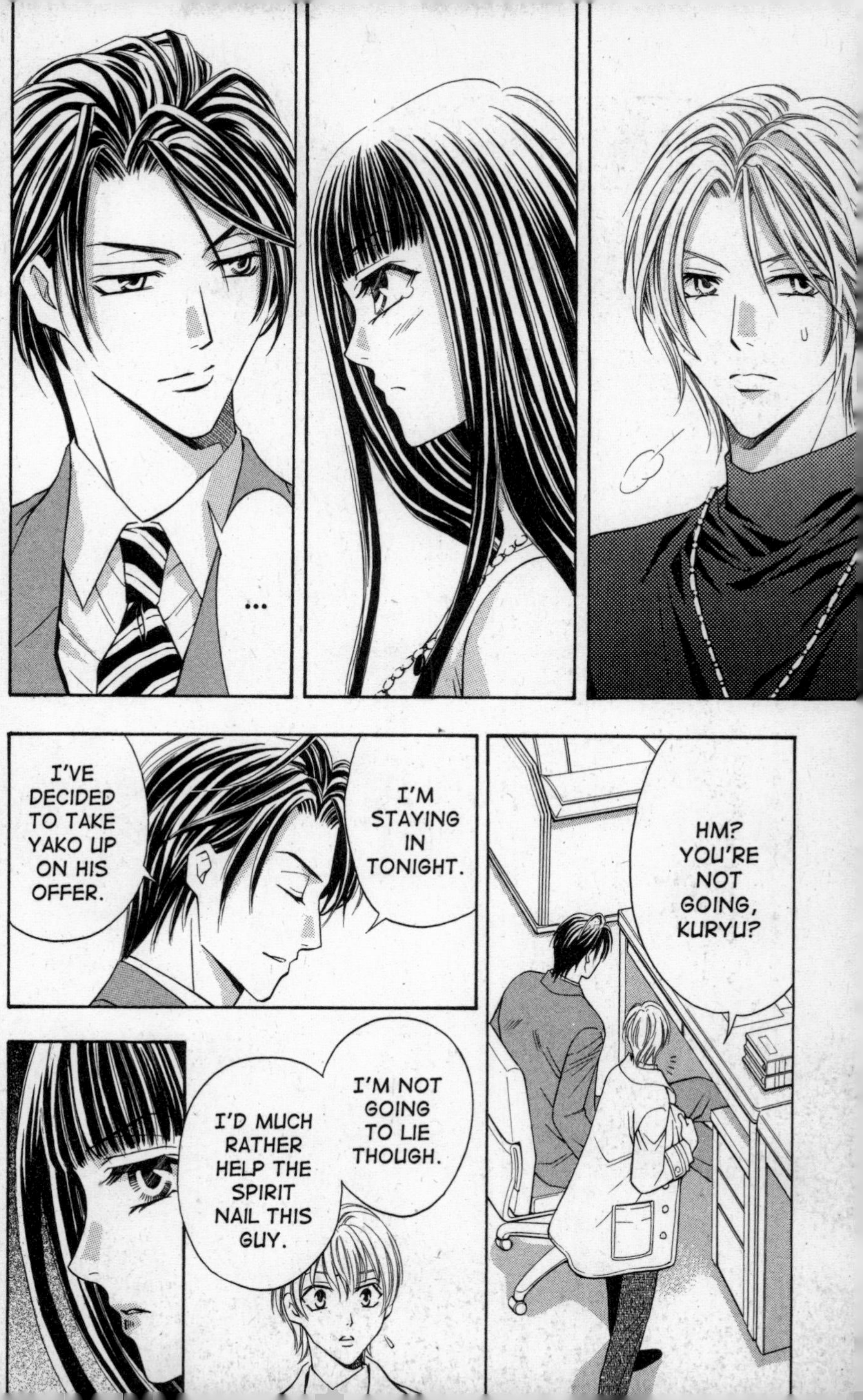
...
HM? YOU'RE NOT GOING, KURYU?
I'M STAYING IN TONIGHT.
I'VE DECIDED TO TAKE YAKO UP ON HIS OFFER.
I'M NOT GOING TO LIE THOUGH.
I'D MUCH RATHER HELP THE SPIRIT NAIL THIS GUY.

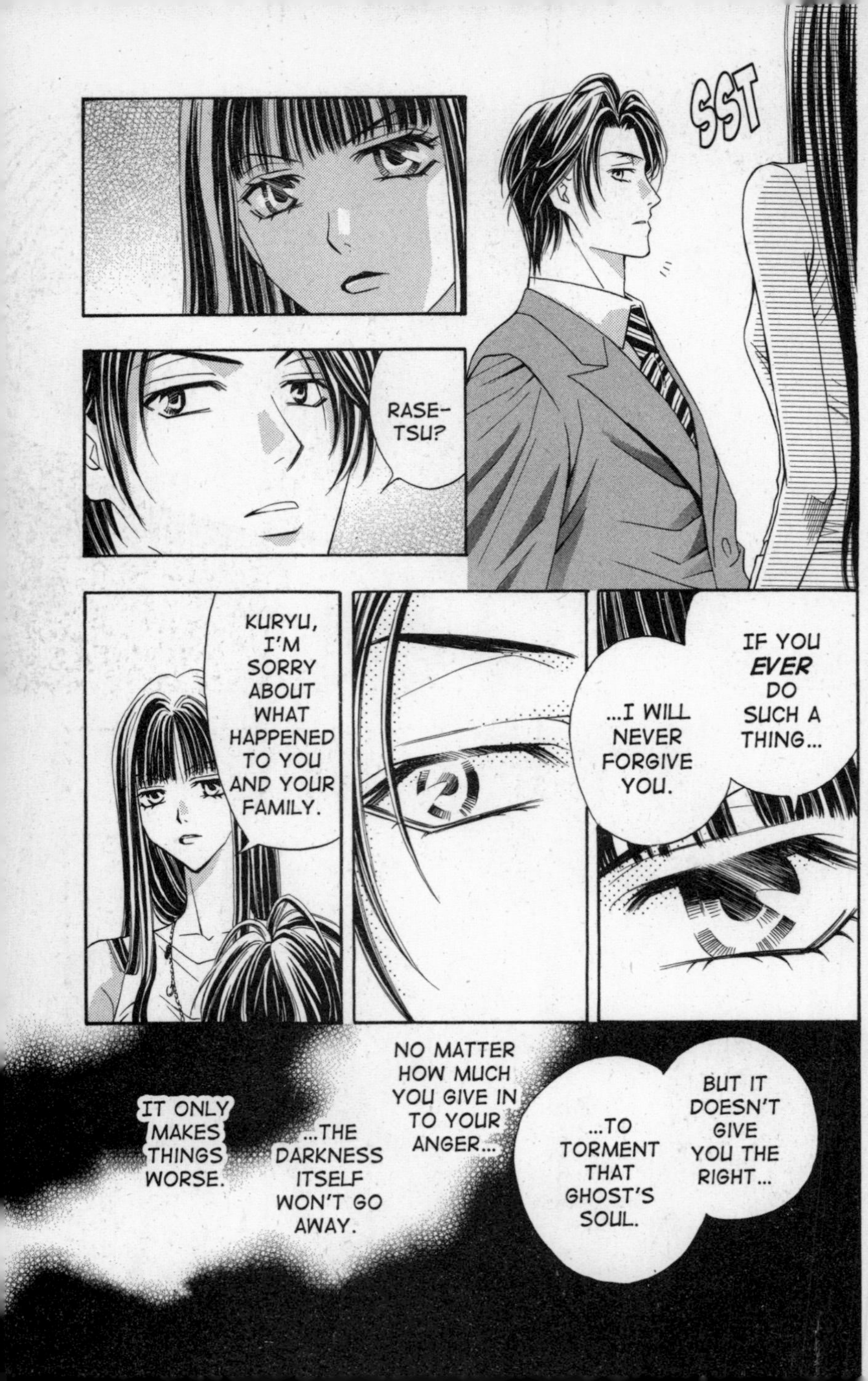
SST
RASETSU?
IF YOU *EVER* DO SUCH A THING...
...I WILL NEVER FORGIVE YOU.
KURYU, I'M SORRY ABOUT WHAT HAPPENED TO YOU AND YOUR FAMILY.
BUT IT DOESN'T GIVE YOU THE RIGHT...
...TO TORMENT THAT GHOST'S SOUL.
NO MATTER HOW MUCH YOU GIVE IN TO YOUR ANGER...
...THE DARKNESS ITSELF WON'T GO AWAY.
IT ONLY MAKES THINGS WORSE.

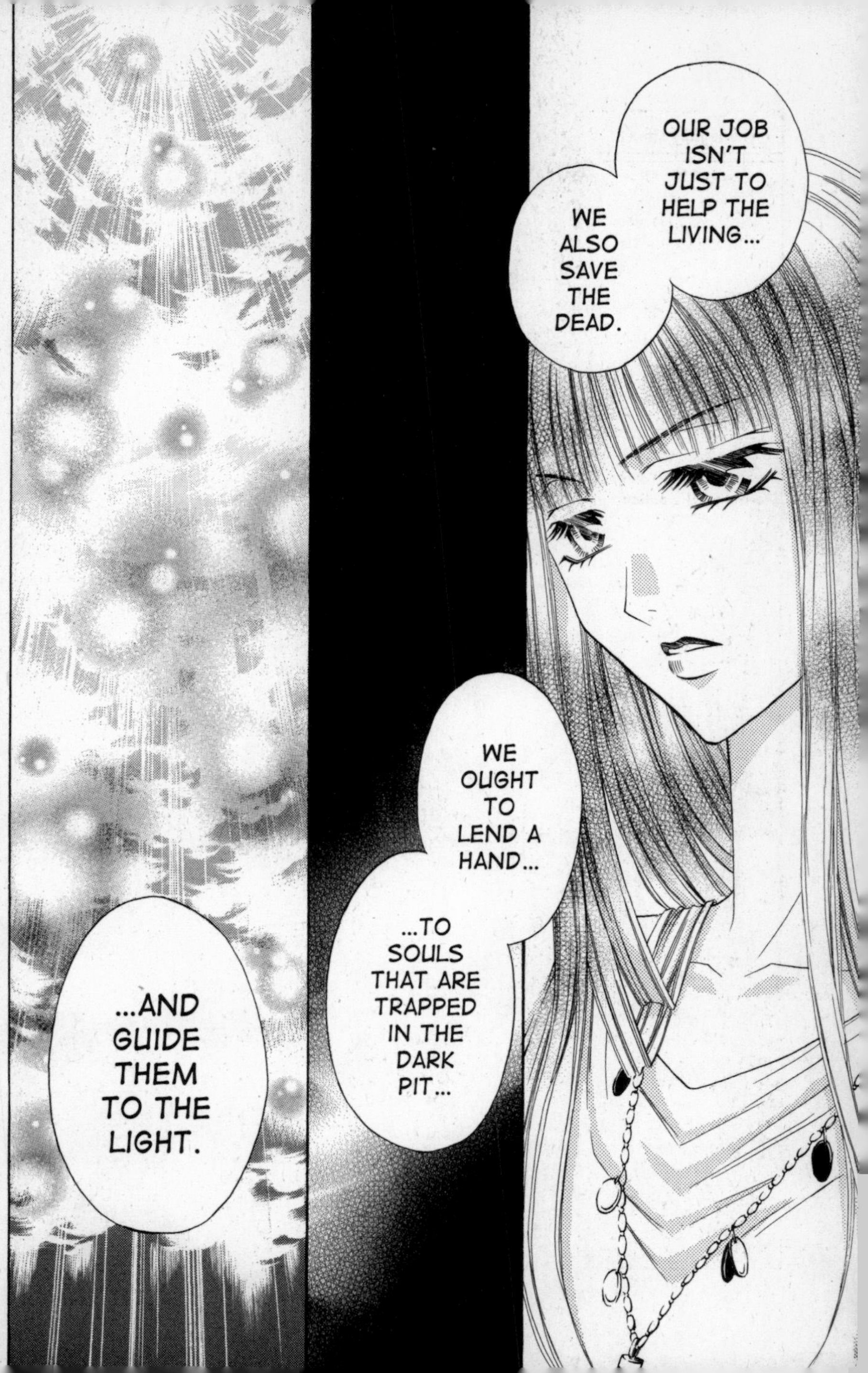
OUR JOB ISN'T JUST TO HELP THE LIVING...
WE ALSO SAVE THE DEAD.
WE OUGHT TO LEND A HAND...
...TO SOULS THAT ARE TRAPPED IN THE DARK PIT...
...AND GUIDE THEM TO THE LIGHT.

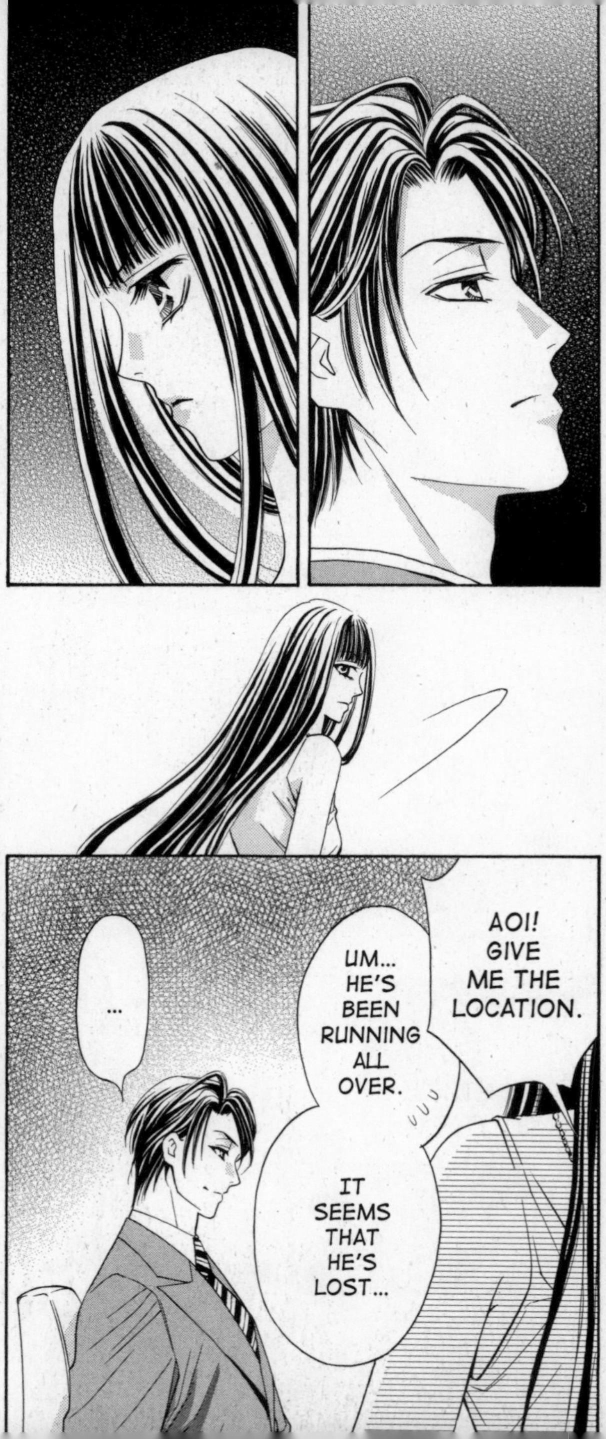
AOI! GIVE ME THE LOCATION.
UM... HE'S BEEN RUNNING ALL OVER.
IT SEEMS THAT HE'S LOST...
...

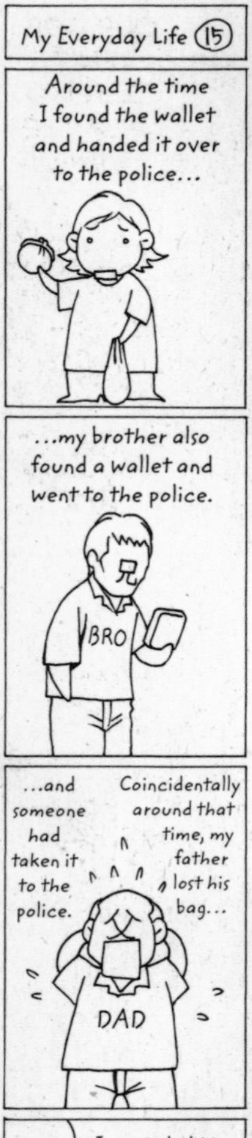
My Everyday Life 15
Around the time I found the wallet and handed it over to the police...
...my brother also found a wallet and went to the police.
BRO
Coincidentally around that time, my father lost his bag...
...and someone had taken it to the police.
DAD
I reminded him that he'd gotten his bag back because of our series of good acts.
Buy me some-thing.
Not an act of good-will.

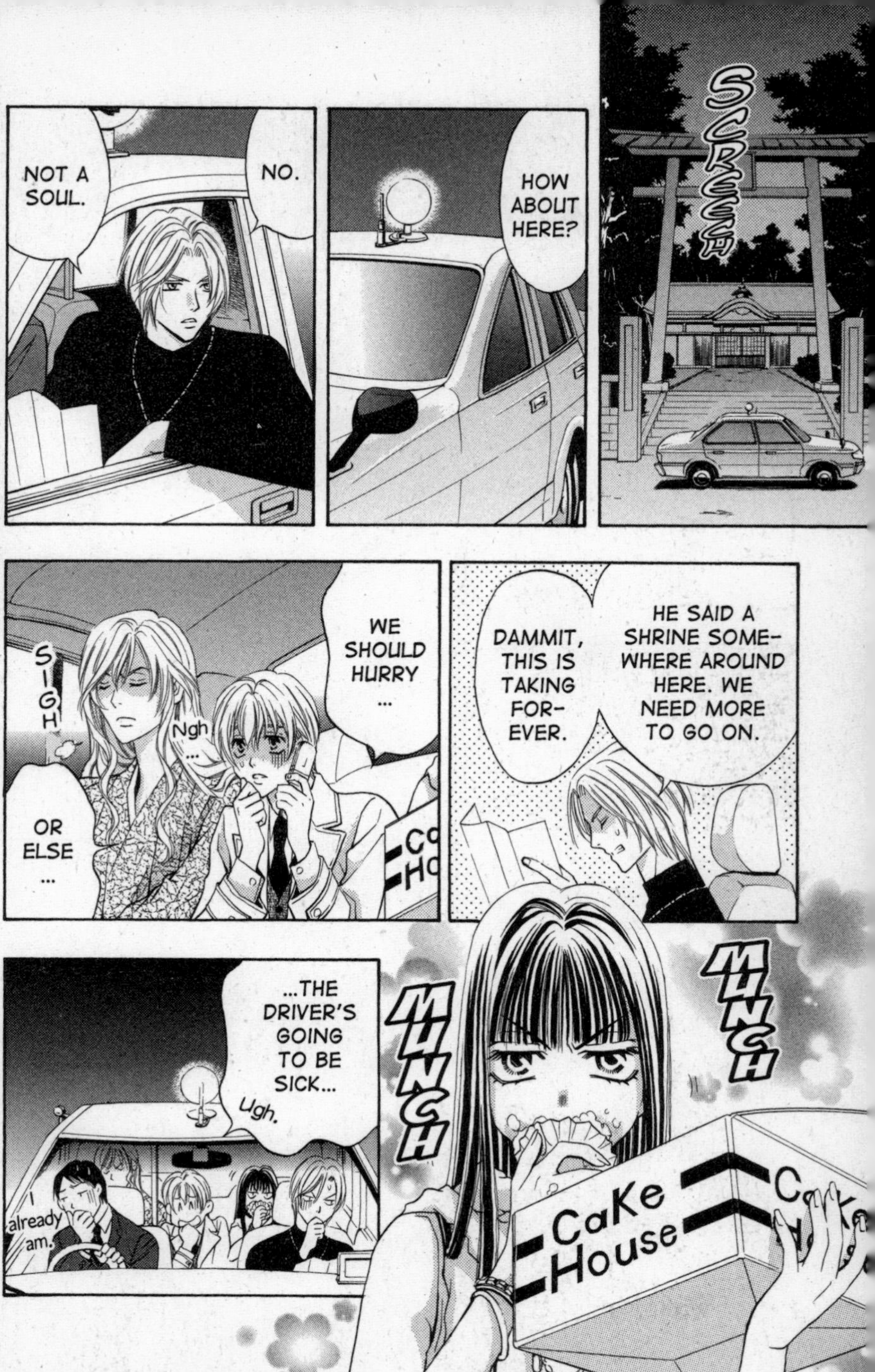
SCREECH
HOW ABOUT HERE?
NO.
NOT A SOUL.
HE SAID A SHRINE SOME-WHERE AROUND HERE. WE NEED MORE TO GO ON.
DAMMIT, THIS IS TAKING FOR-EVER.
WE SHOULD HURRY...
SIGH
Ngh...
OR ELSE...
MUNCH
MUNCH
CaKe House
...THE DRIVER'S GOING TO BE SICK...
Ugh.
I already am.

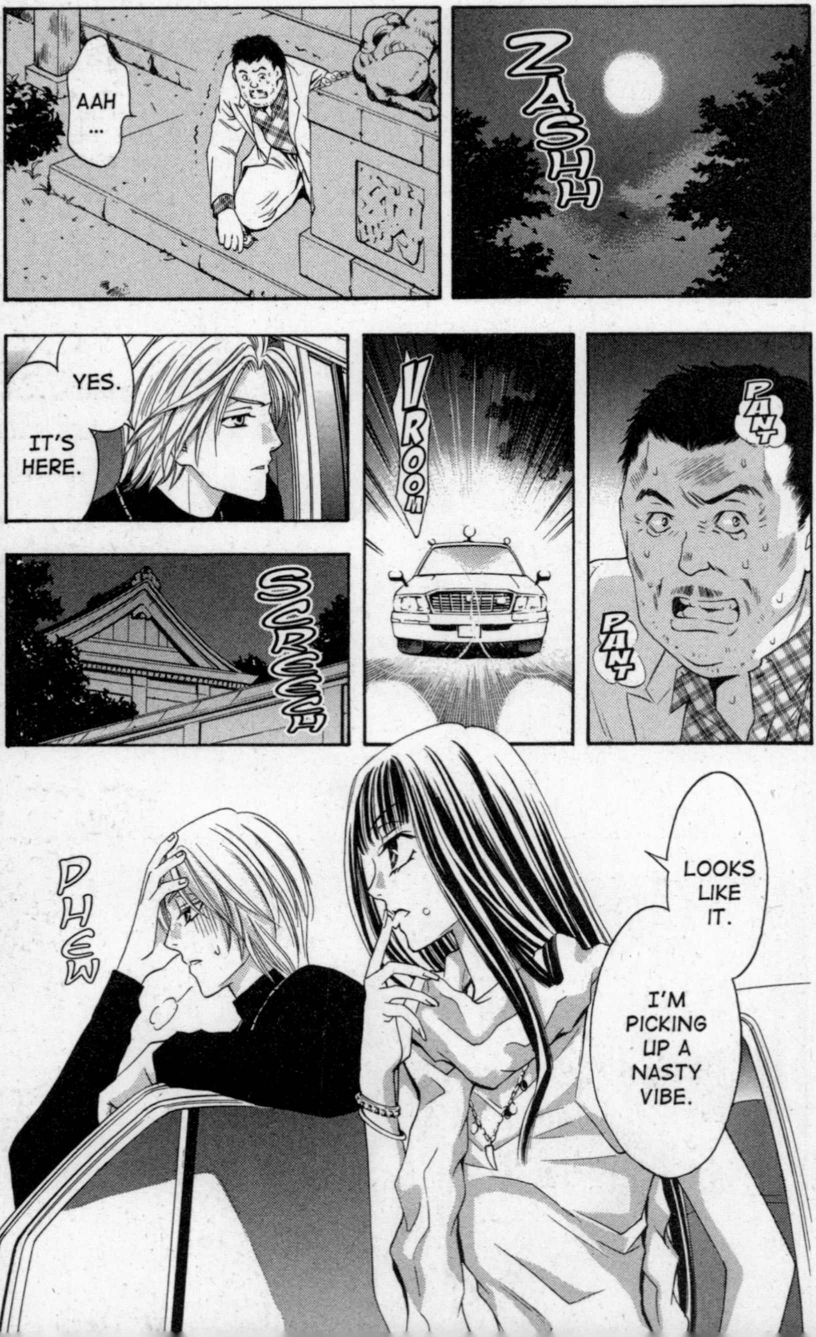
ZASHH
AAH ...
PANT
PANT
VROOM
YES.
IT'S HERE.
SCREECH
LOOKS LIKE IT.
I'M PICKING UP A NASTY VIBE.
PHEW

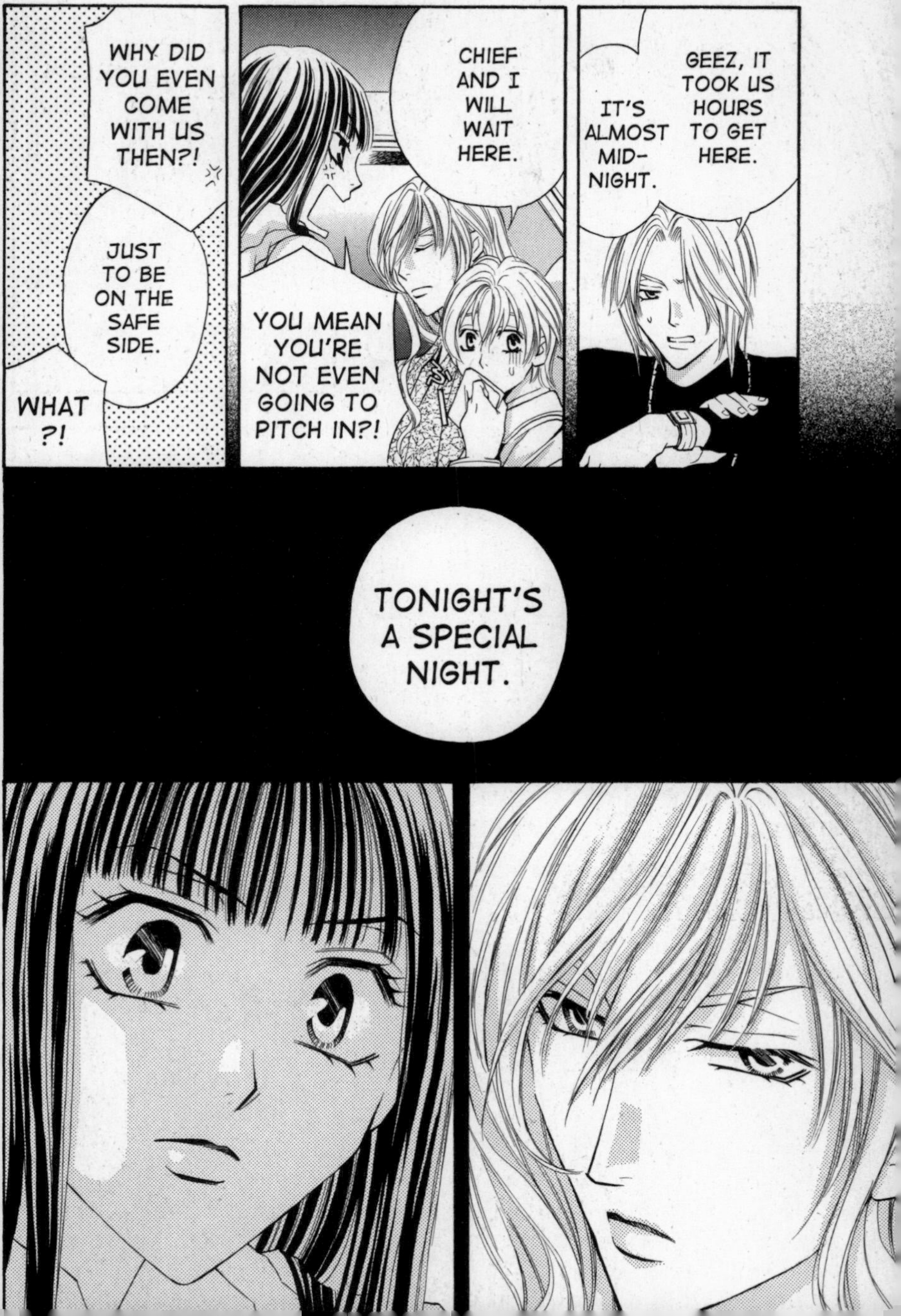
GEEZ, IT TOOK US HOURS TO GET HERE.
IT'S ALMOST MID-NIGHT.
CHIEF AND I WILL WAIT HERE.
YOU MEAN YOU'RE NOT EVEN GOING TO PITCH IN?!
WHY DID YOU EVEN COME WITH US THEN?!
JUST TO BE ON THE SAFE SIDE.
WHAT?!
TONIGHT'S A SPECIAL NIGHT.

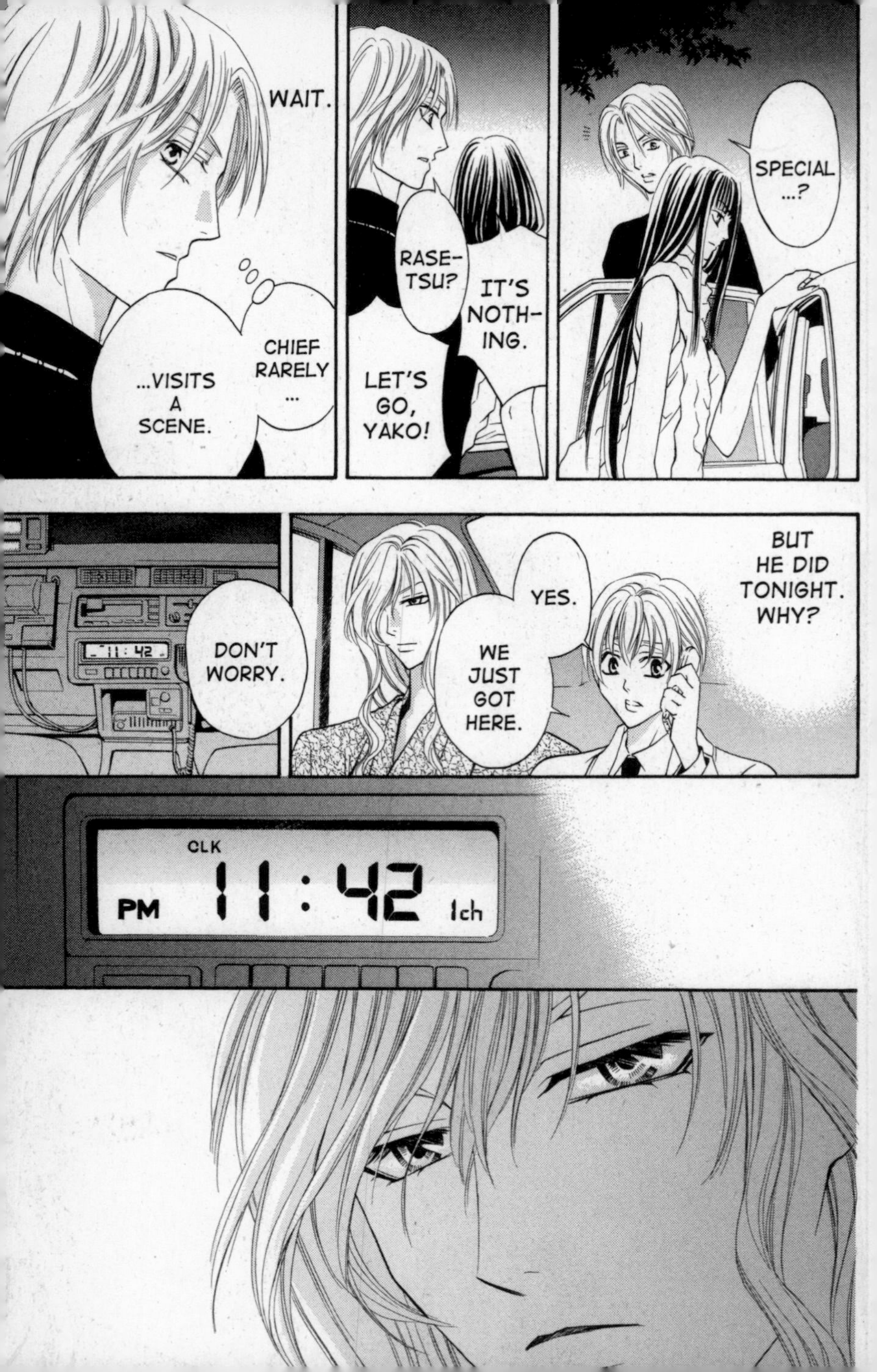
SPECIAL ...?
RASE-TSU?
IT'S NOTHING.
LET'S GO, YAKO!
WAIT.
CHIEF RARELY ...
...VISITS A SCENE.
BUT HE DID TONIGHT. WHY?
YES.
WE JUST GOT HERE.
DON'T WORRY.
CLK
PM 11:42 1ch

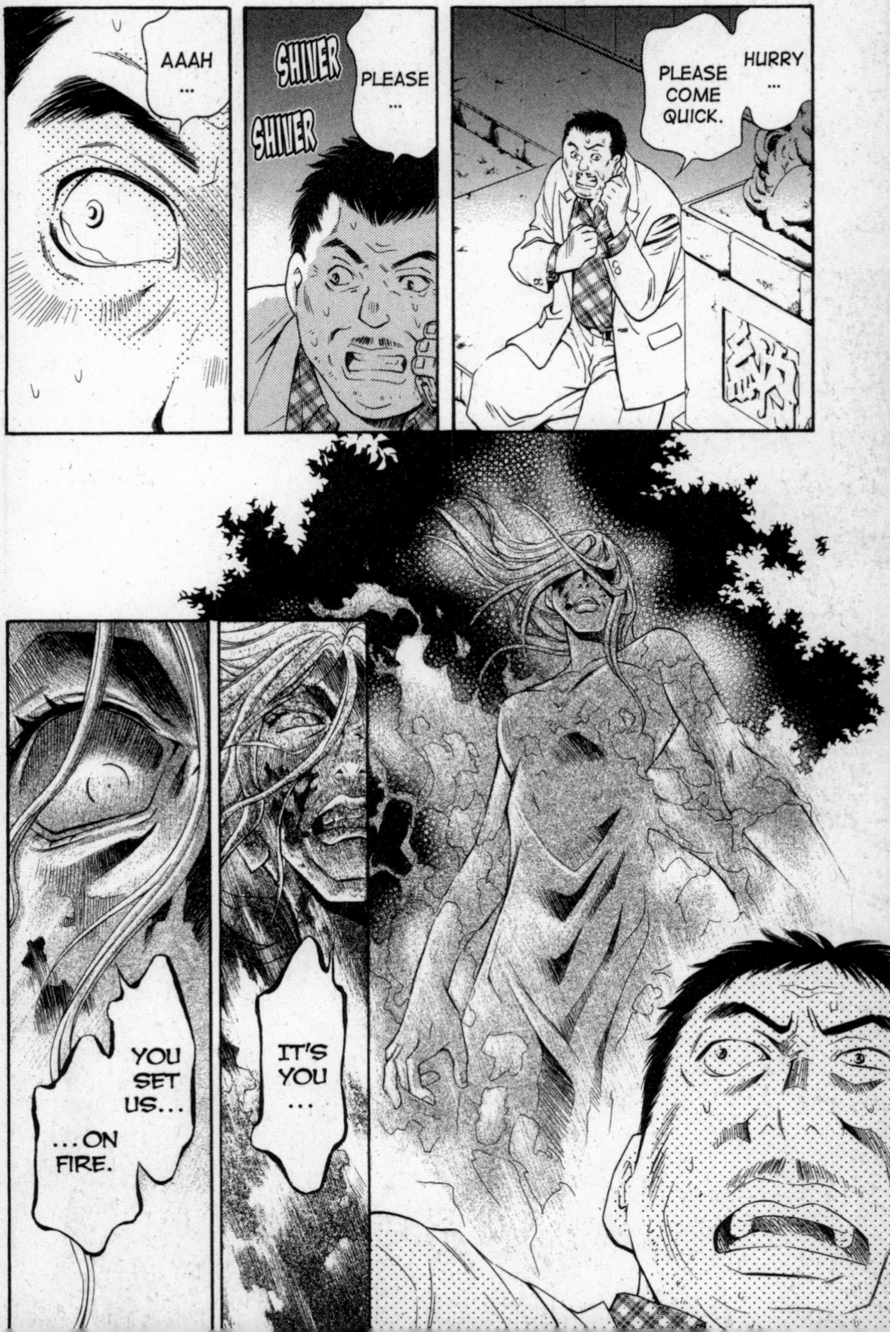
HURRY ...
PLEASE COME QUICK.
PLEASE ...
SHIVER
SHIVER
AAAH ...
IT'S YOU ...
YOU SET US...
...ON FIRE.

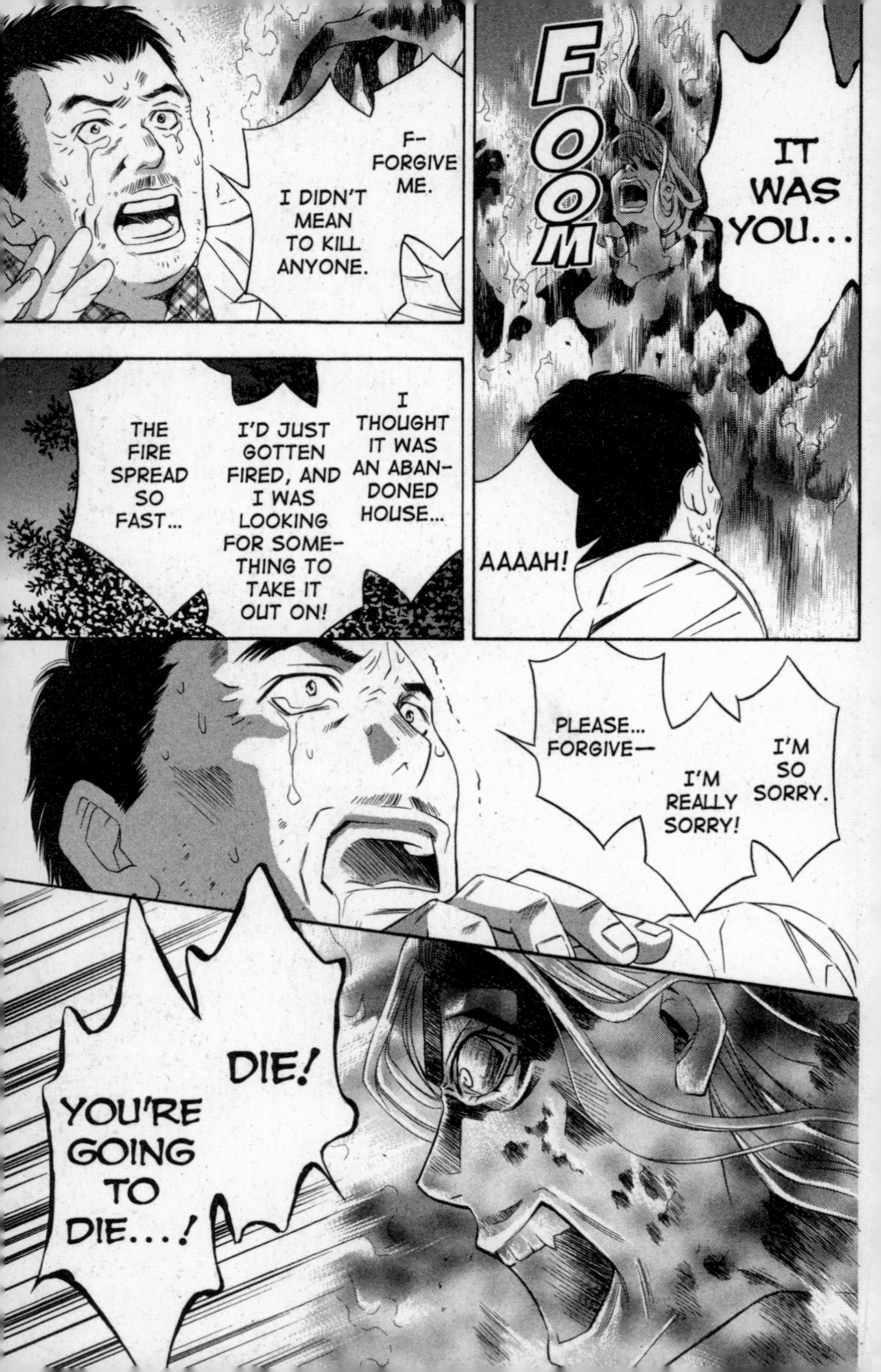
IT WAS YOU...
FOOM
AAAAH!
F-FORGIVE ME.
I DIDN'T MEAN TO KILL ANYONE.
I THOUGHT IT WAS AN ABANDONED HOUSE...
I'D JUST GOTTEN FIRED, AND I WAS LOOKING FOR SOMETHING TO TAKE IT OUT ON!
THE FIRE SPREAD SO FAST...
I'M SO SORRY.
I'M REALLY SORRY!
PLEASE... FORGIVE—
DIE!
YOU'RE GOING TO DIE...!

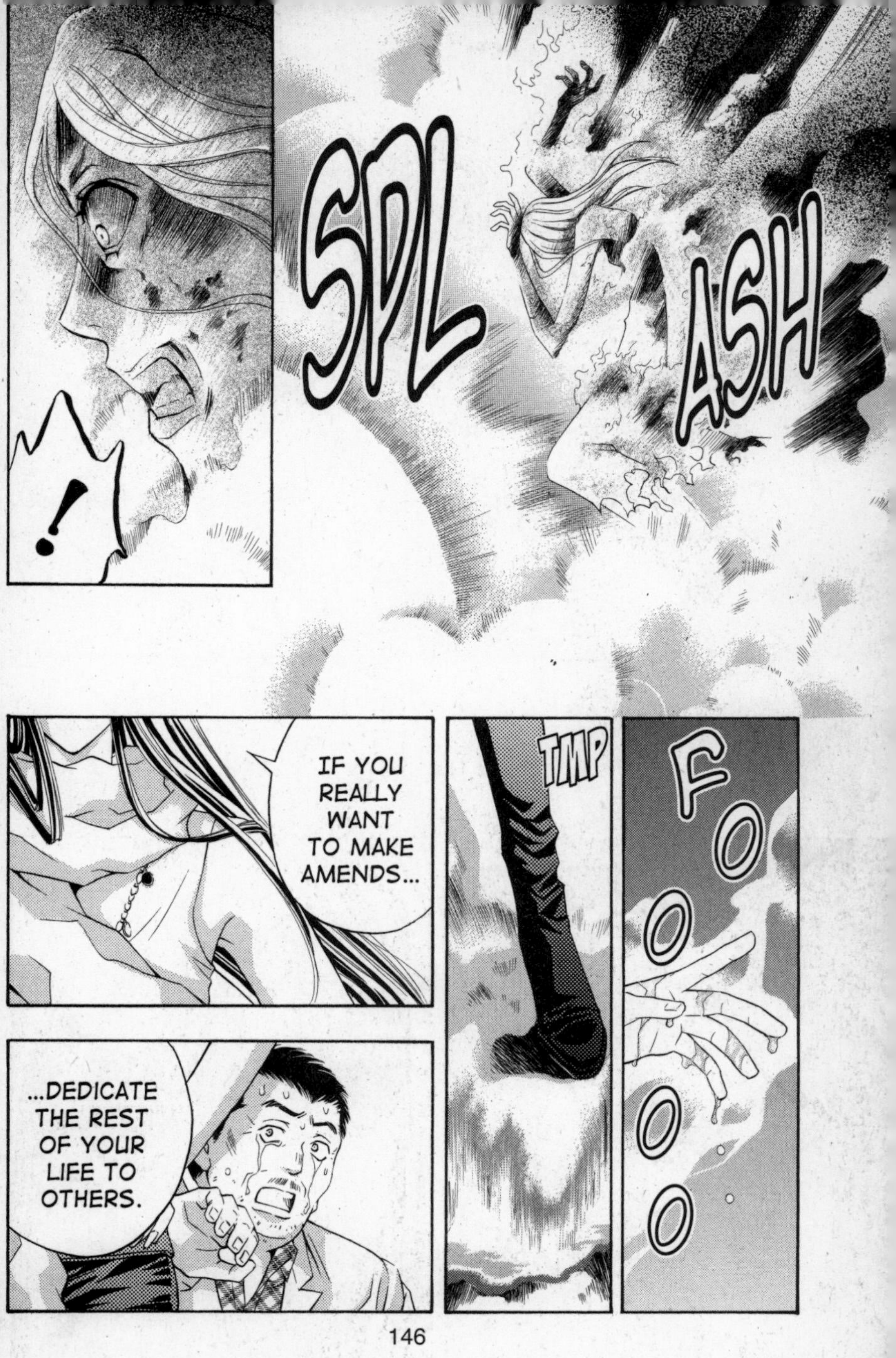
SPL
ASH
!
FOOOOOO
TMP
IF YOU REALLY WANT TO MAKE AMENDS...
...DEDICATE THE REST OF YOUR LIFE TO OTHERS.

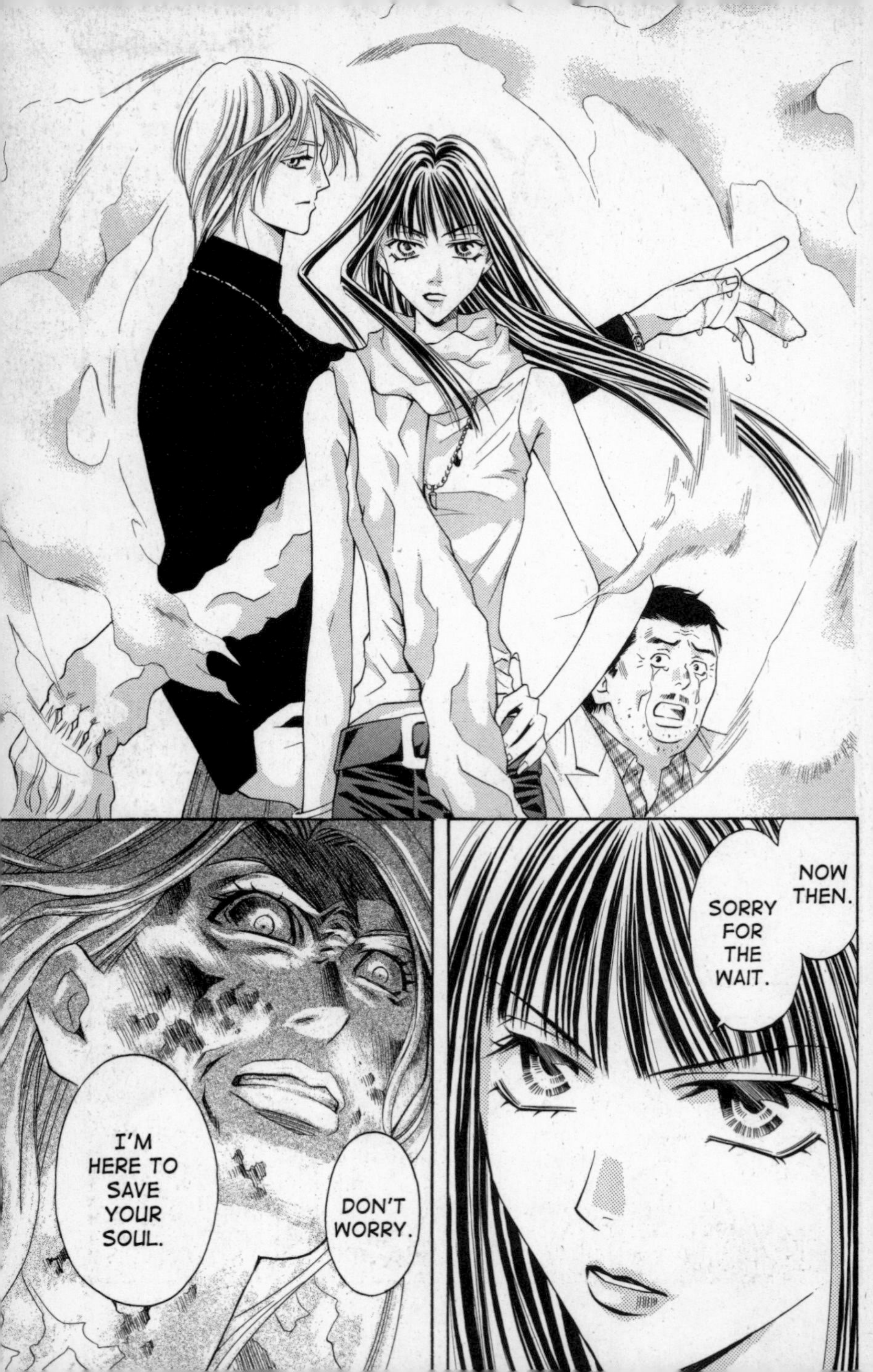
NOW THEN.
SORRY FOR THE WAIT.
DON'T WORRY.
I'M HERE TO SAVE YOUR SOUL.

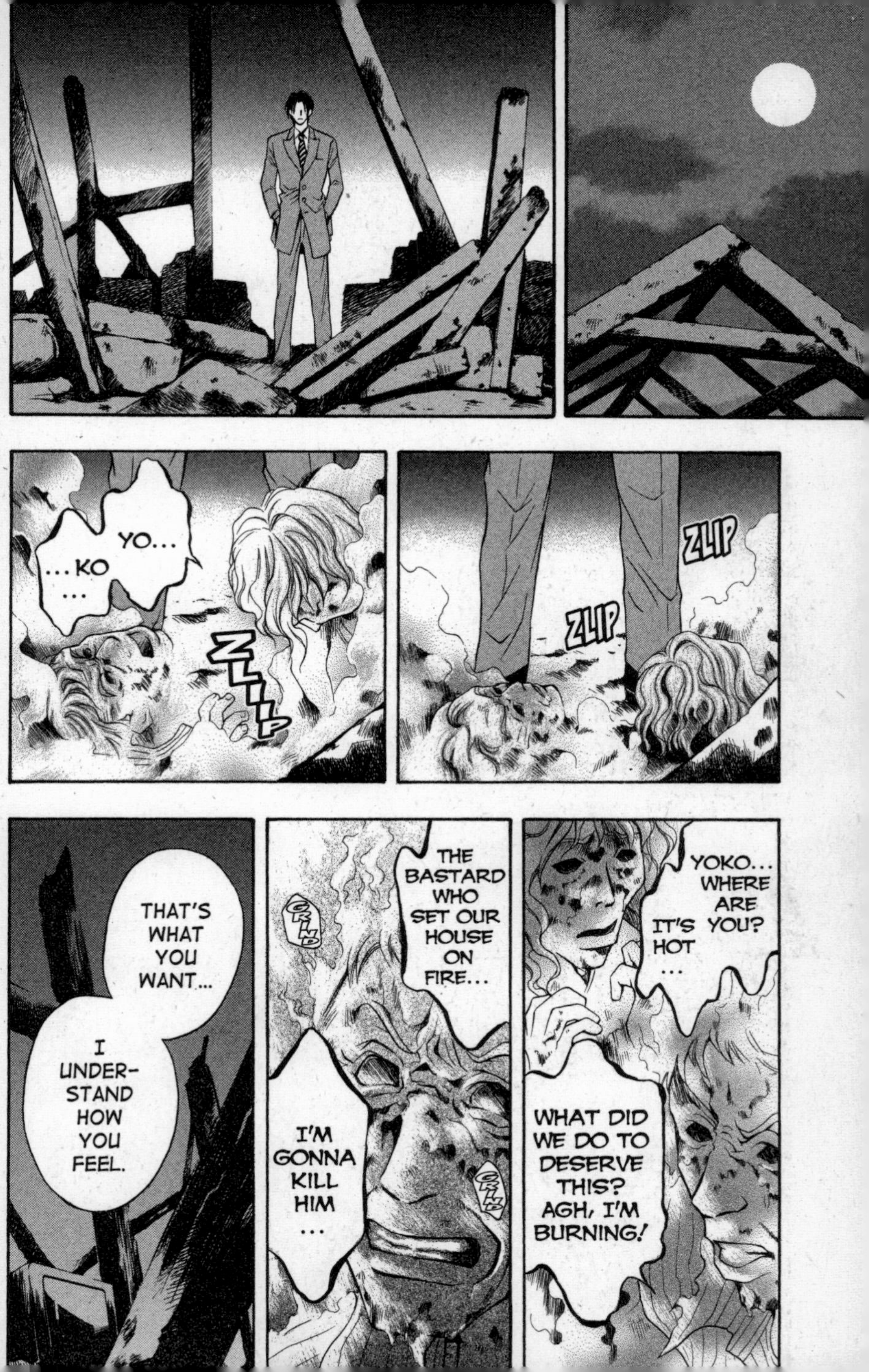
ZLIP
ZLIP
YO… …KO …
ZLIIP
YOKO… WHERE ARE YOU?
IT'S HOT …
WHAT DID WE DO TO DESERVE THIS? AGH, I'M BURNING!
THE BASTARD WHO SET OUR HOUSE ON FIRE…
GRIND
I'M GONNA KILL HIM …
GRIND
THAT'S WHAT YOU WANT…
I UNDER-STAND HOW YOU FEEL.

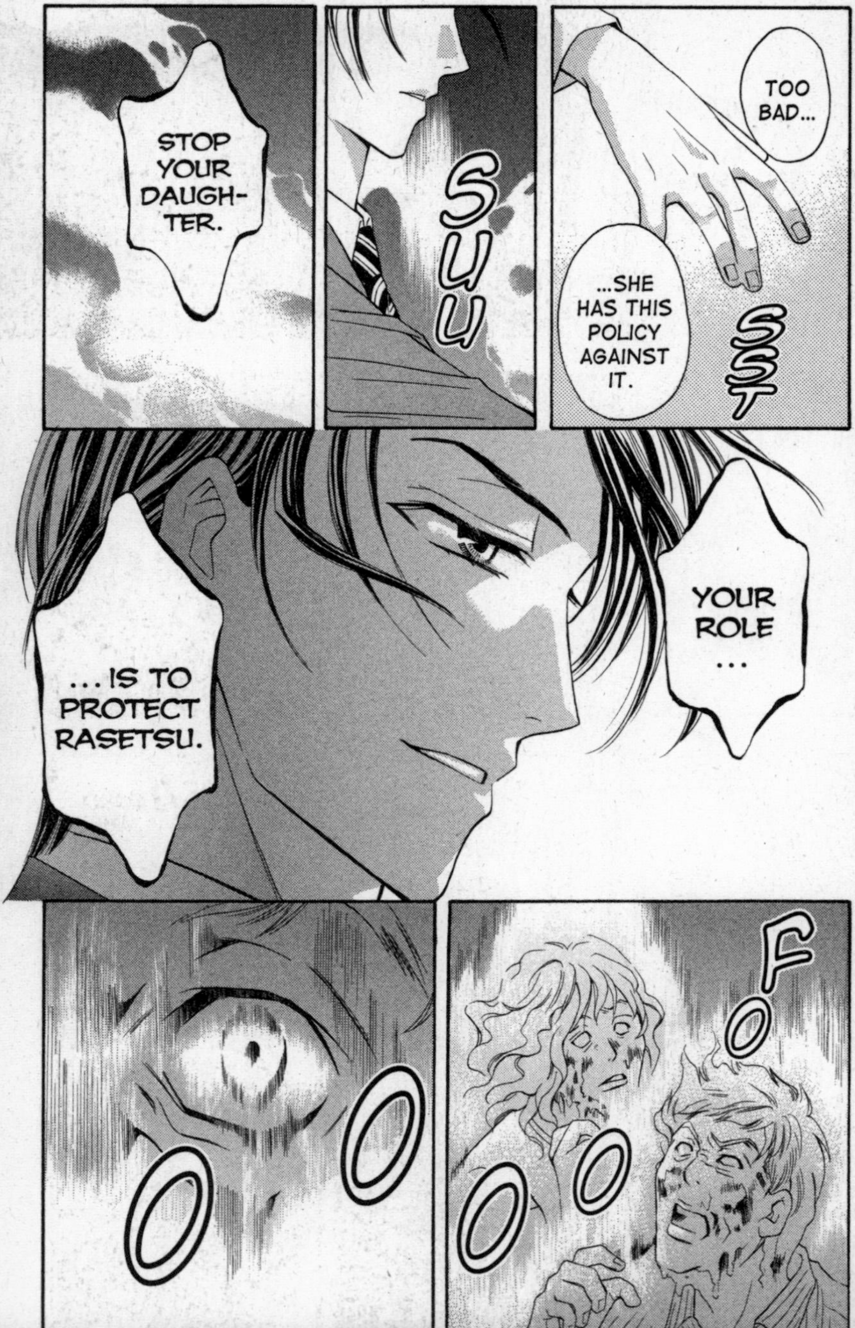
TOO BAD...
...SHE HAS THIS POLICY AGAINST IT.
SST
SUUU
STOP YOUR DAUGH-TER.
YOUR ROLE ...
...IS TO PROTECT RASETSU.
FOOO
OO

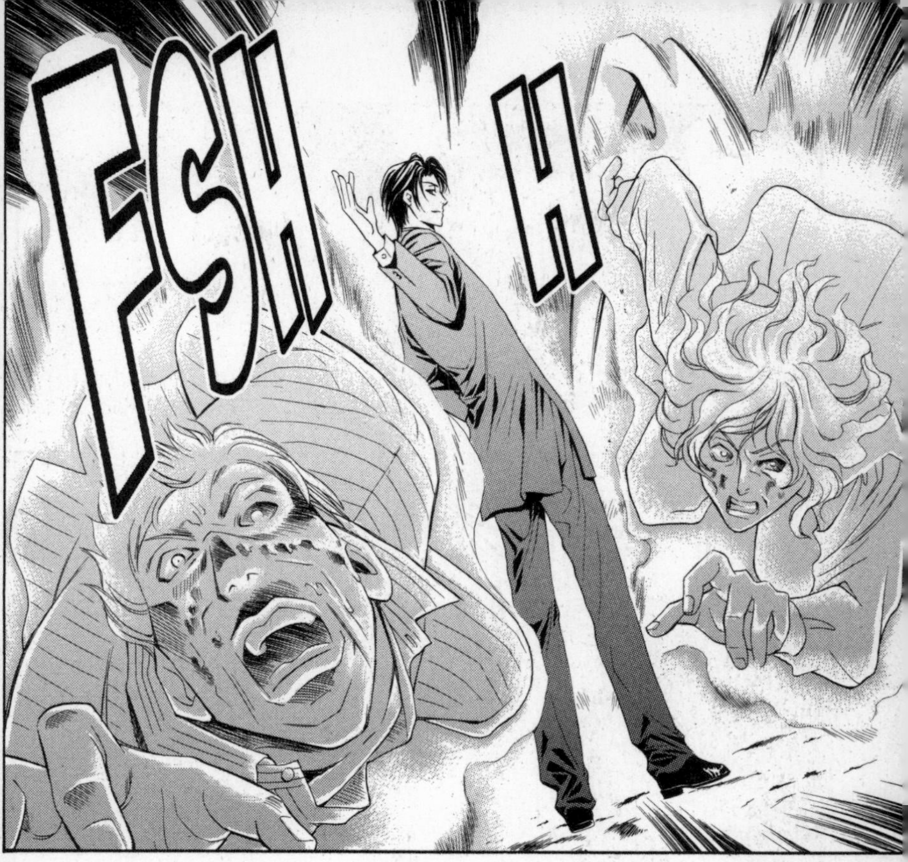
FSHH
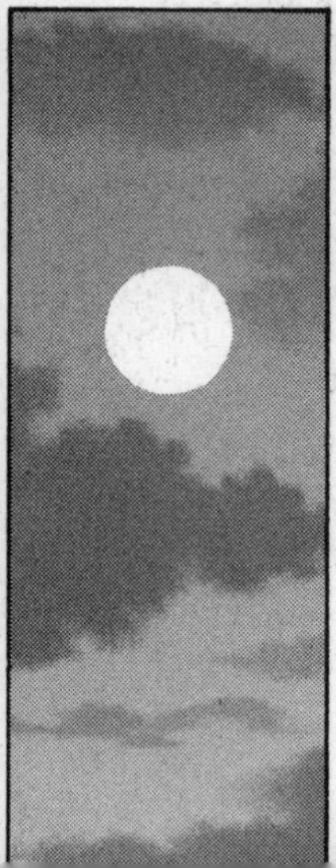
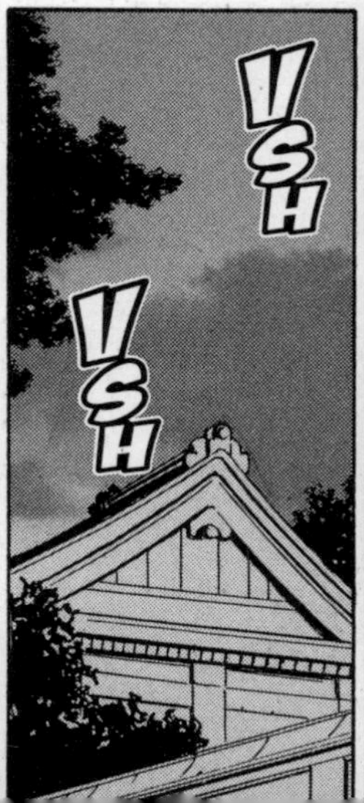
VSH
VSH
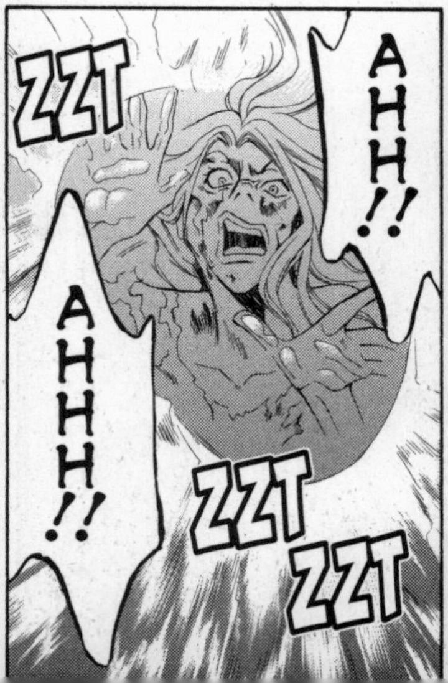
AHH!!
ZZT
AHHH!!
ZZT
ZZT

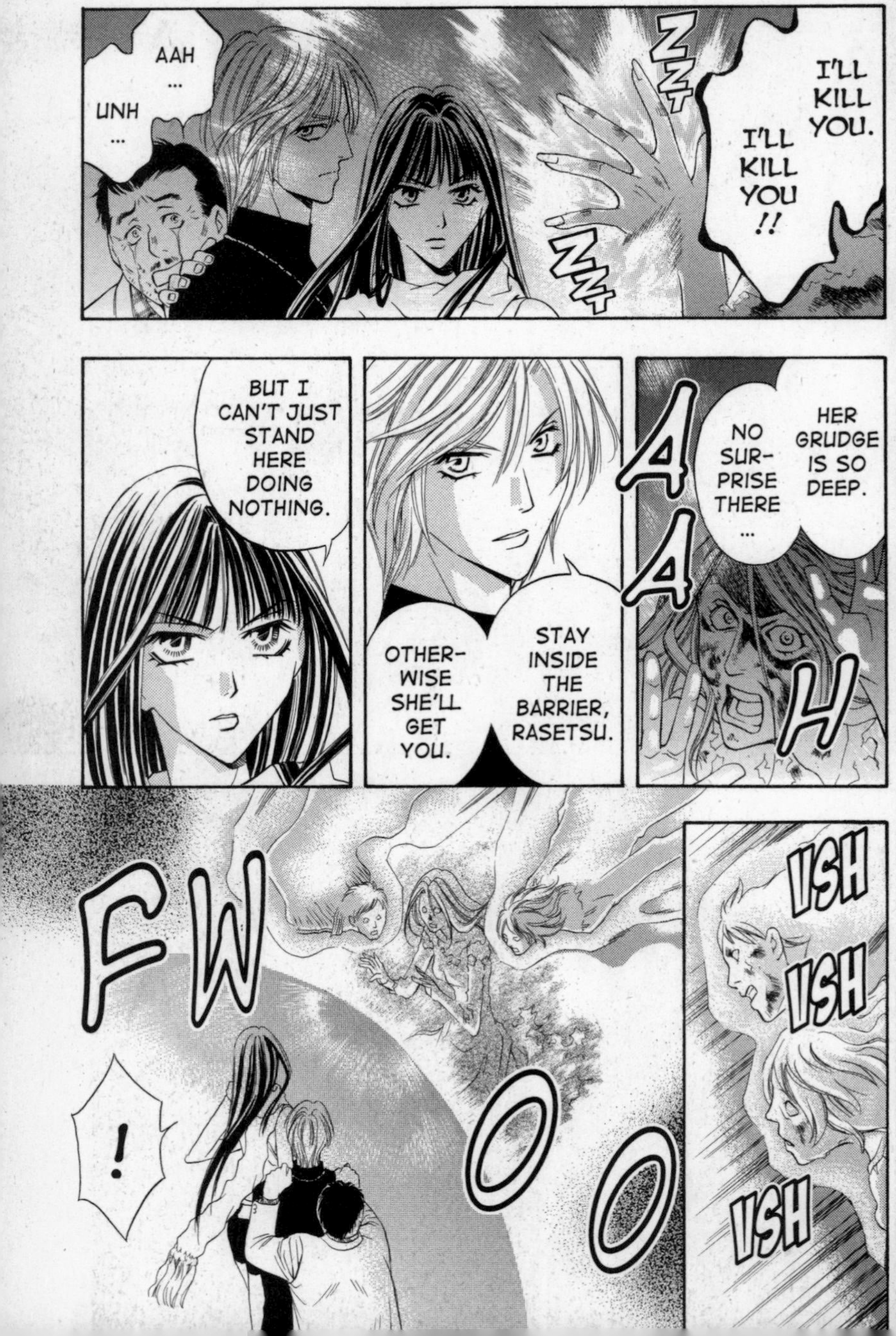
I'LL KILL YOU.
I'LL KILL YOU !!
ZZZT
ZZZT
AAH ... UNH ...
HER GRUDGE IS SO DEEP.
NO SUR-PRISE THERE ...
AAAH
STAY INSIDE THE BARRIER, RASETSU.
OTHER-WISE SHE'LL GET YOU.
BUT I CAN'T JUST STAND HERE DOING NOTHING.
VSH
VSH
VSH
FWOOO
!

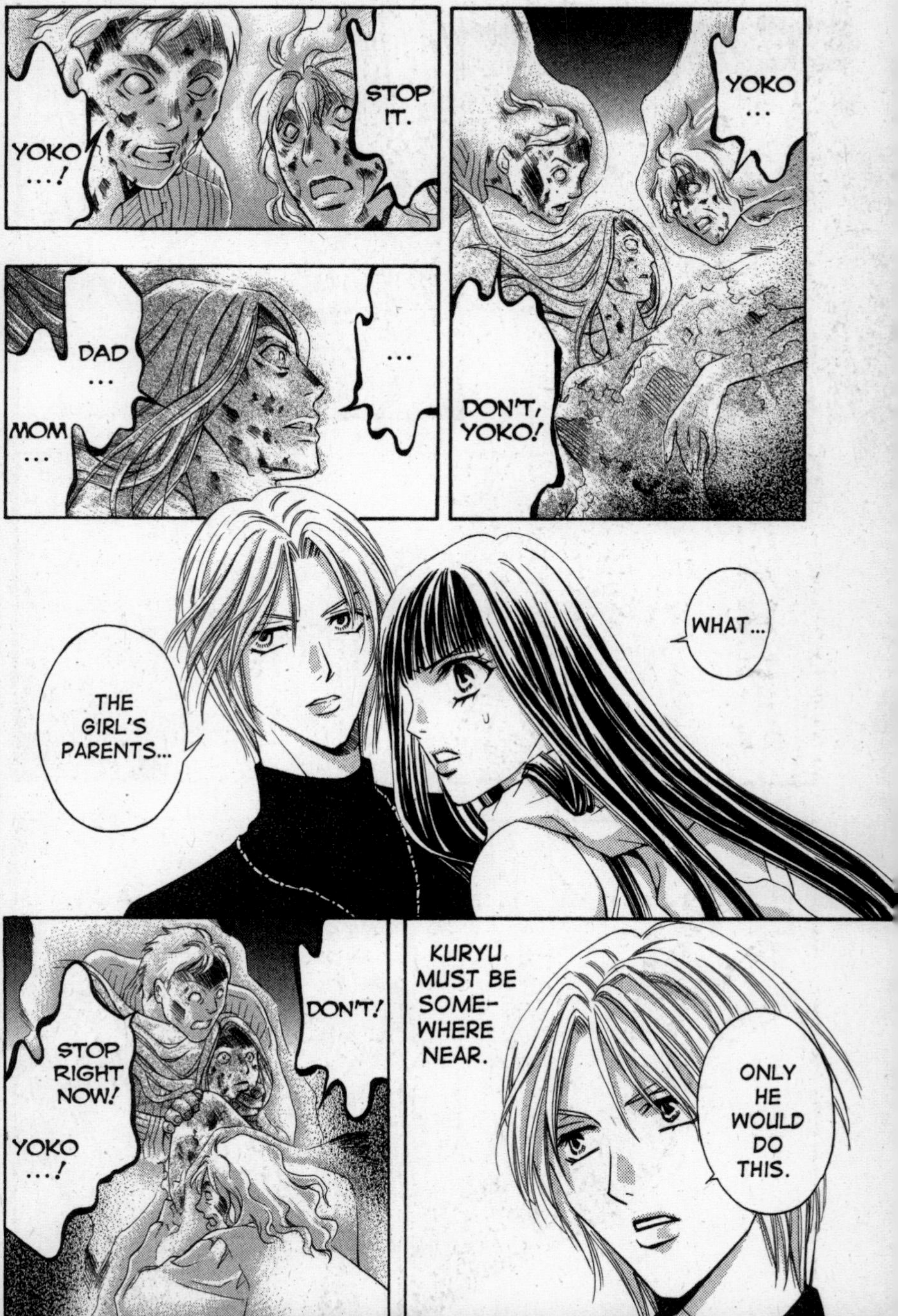
YOKO ...
DON'T, YOKO!
STOP IT.
YOKO ...!
...
DAD ...
MOM ...
WHAT...
THE GIRL'S PARENTS...
KURYU MUST BE SOME-WHERE NEAR.
ONLY HE WOULD DO THIS.
DON'T!
STOP RIGHT NOW!
YOKO ...!

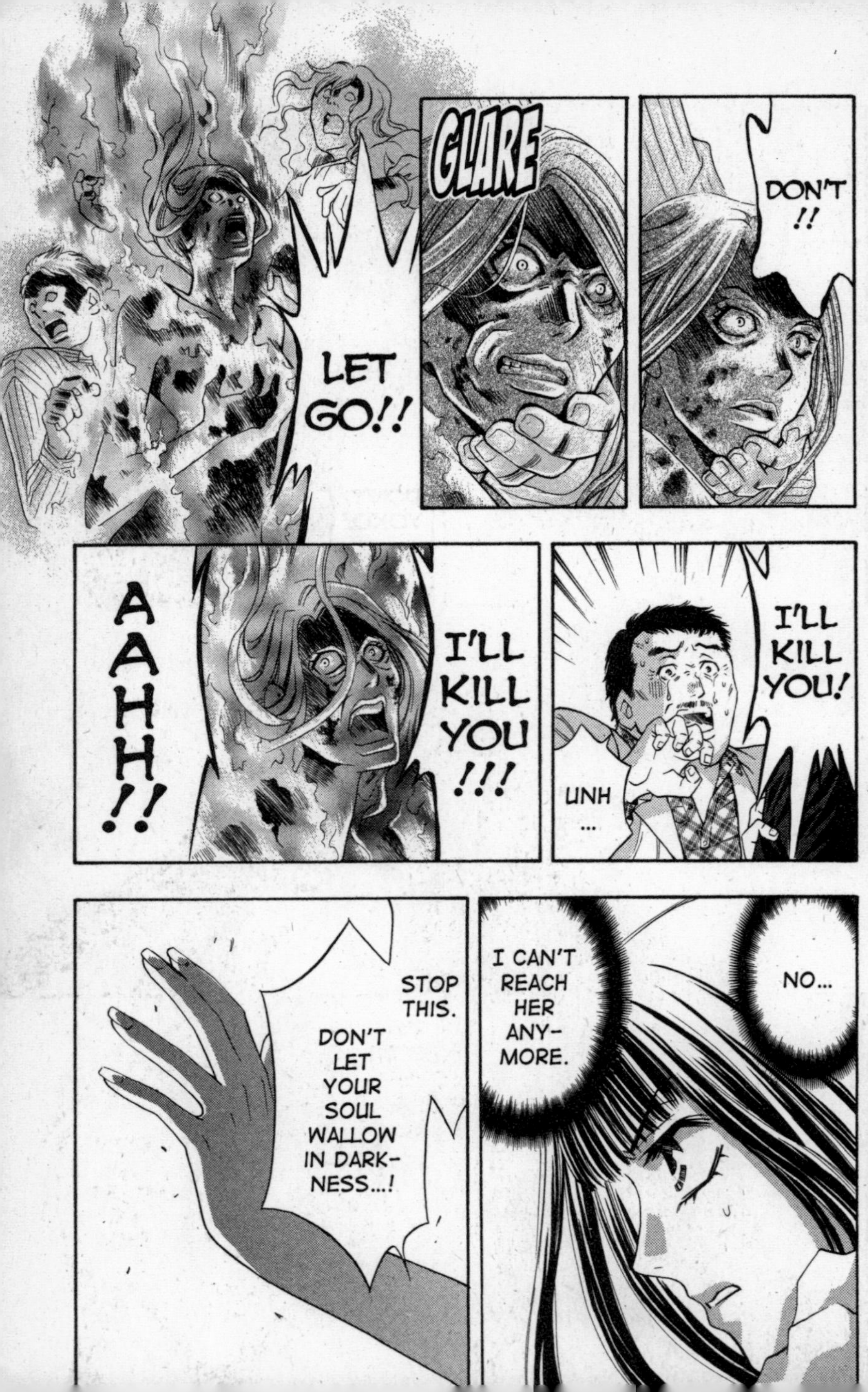
DON'T !!
GLARE
LET GO!!
I'LL KILL YOU!
UNH ...
I'LL KILL YOU !!!
AAHH!!
NO...
I CAN'T REACH HER ANY-MORE.
STOP THIS.
DON'T LET YOUR SOUL WALLOW IN DARK-NESS...!

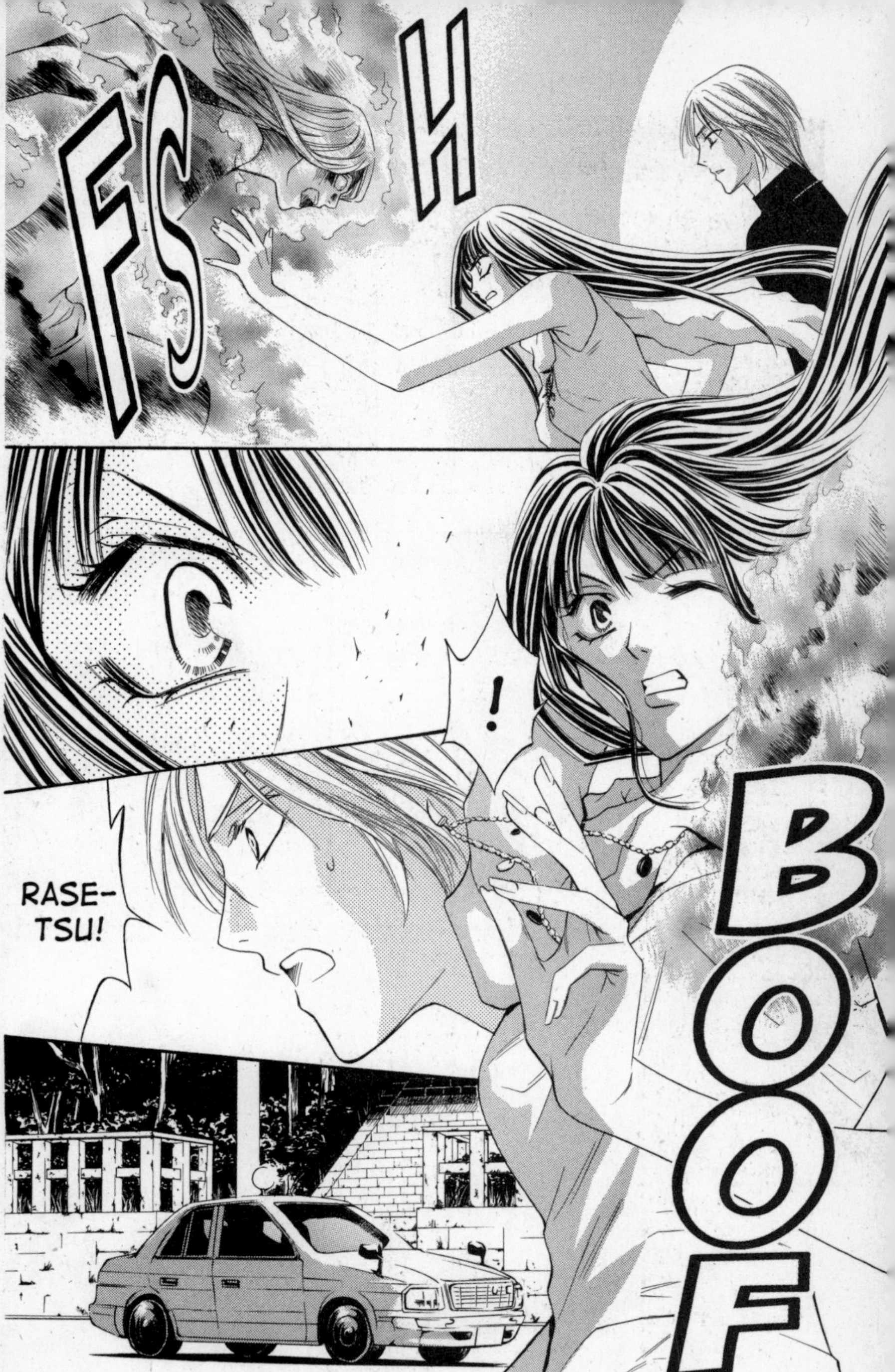
FSSH
!
BOOOF
RASE-
TSU!

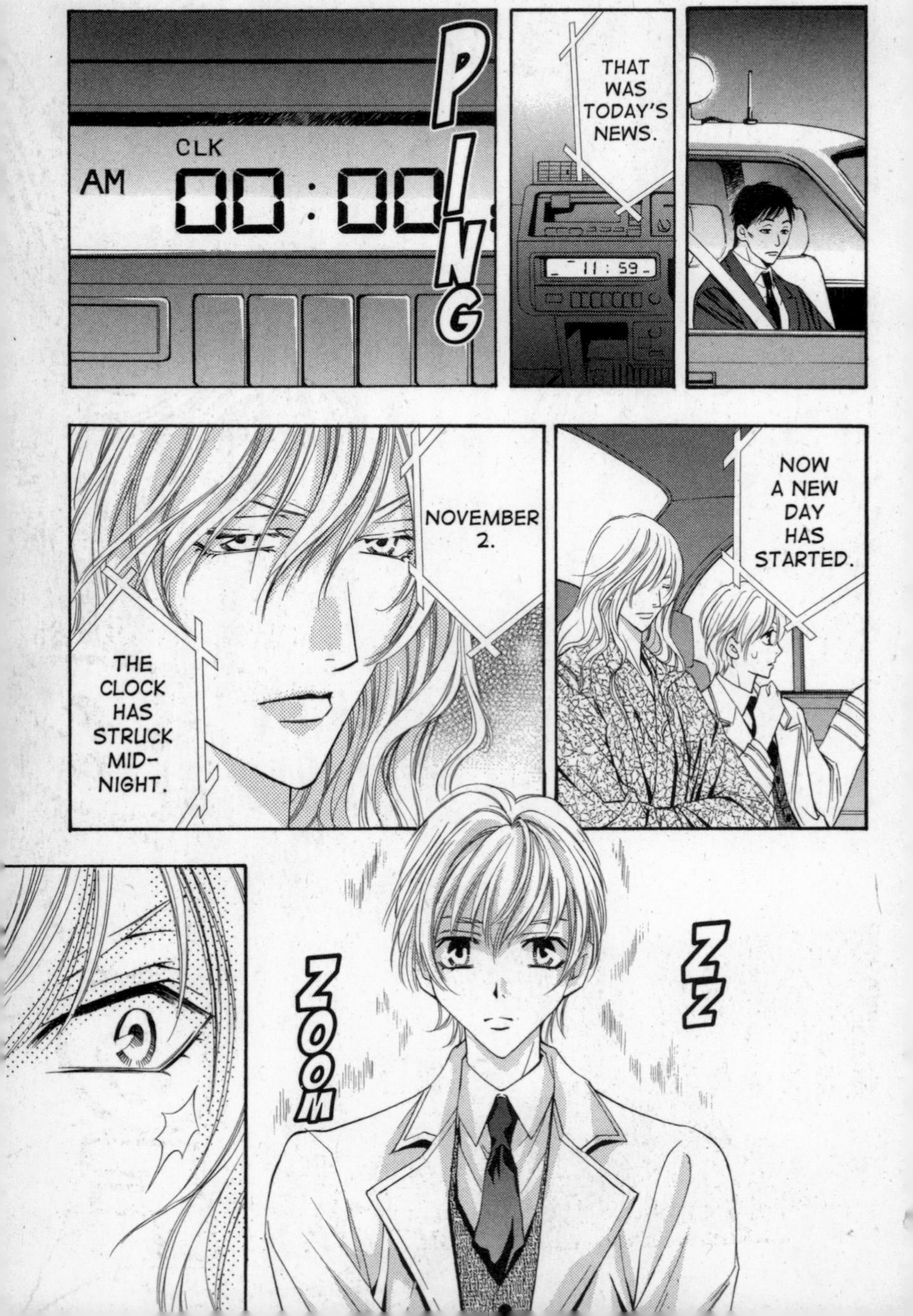
THAT WAS TODAY'S NEWS.
PING
CLK
AM
00:00
NOW A NEW DAY HAS STARTED.
NOVEMBER 2.
THE CLOCK HAS STRUCK MID-NIGHT.
ZZ
ZOOM

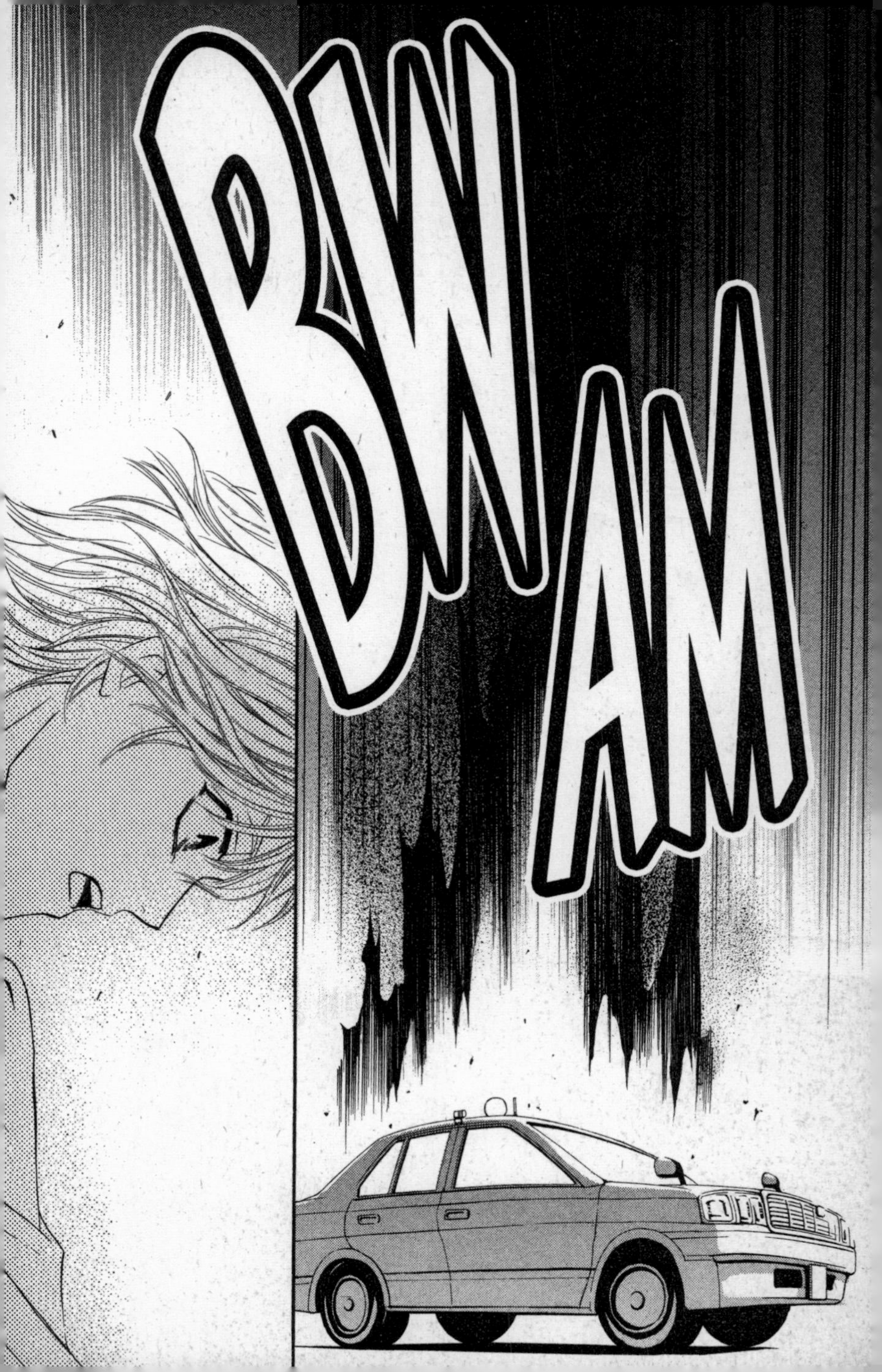
BWAM

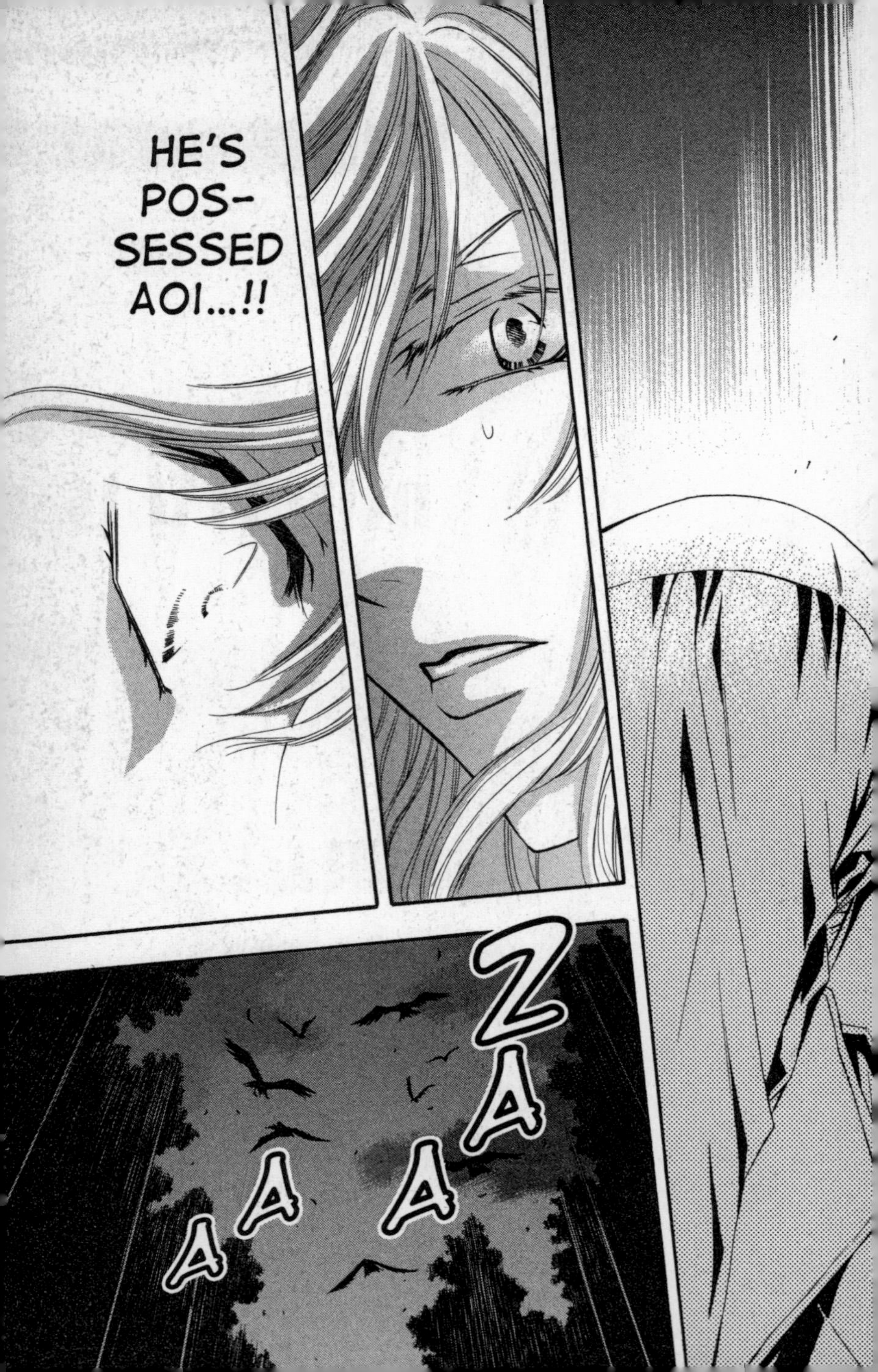
HE'S POS-SESSED AOI...!!
ZAAAAA

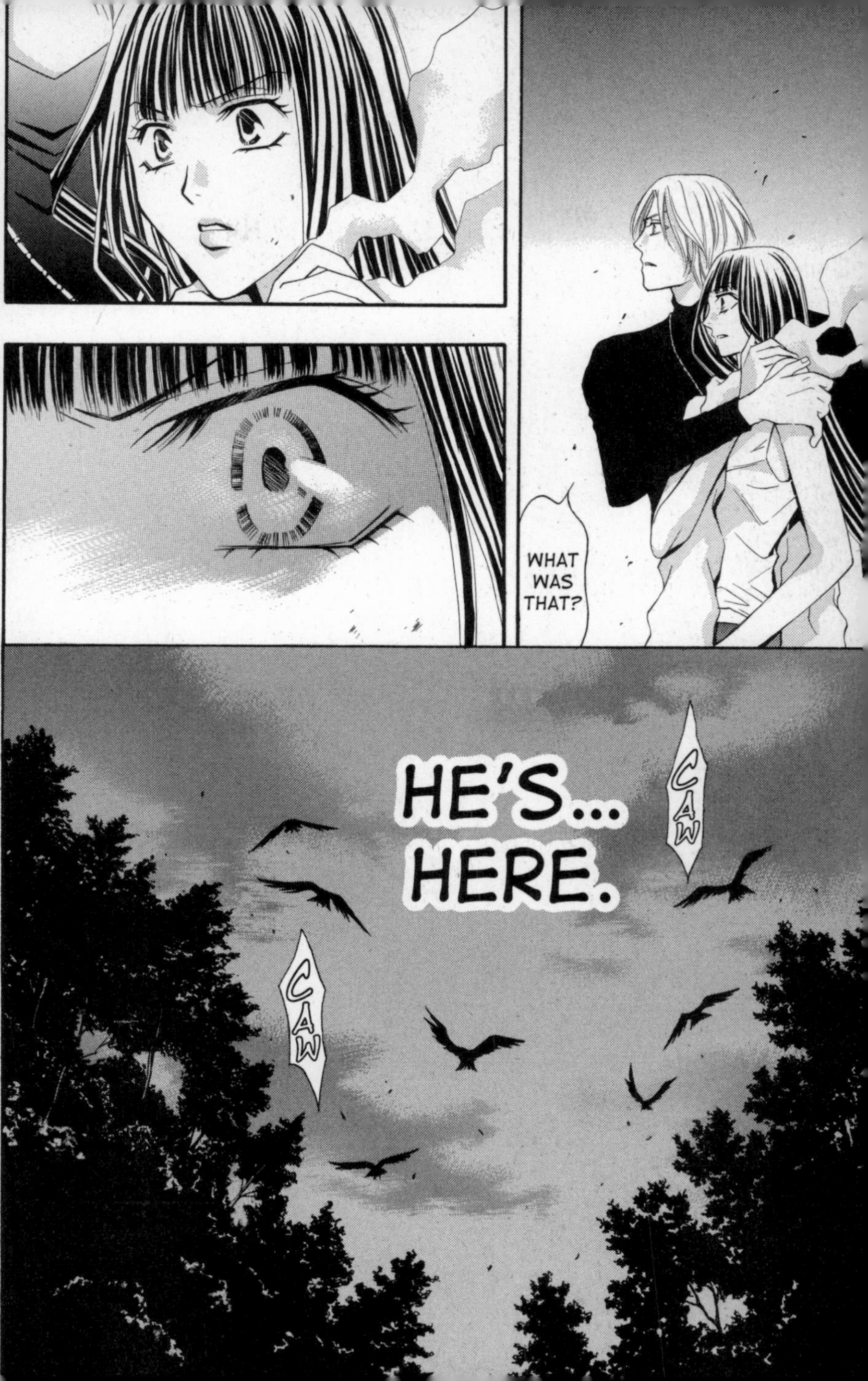
WHAT WAS THAT?
CAW
HE'S... HERE.
CAW

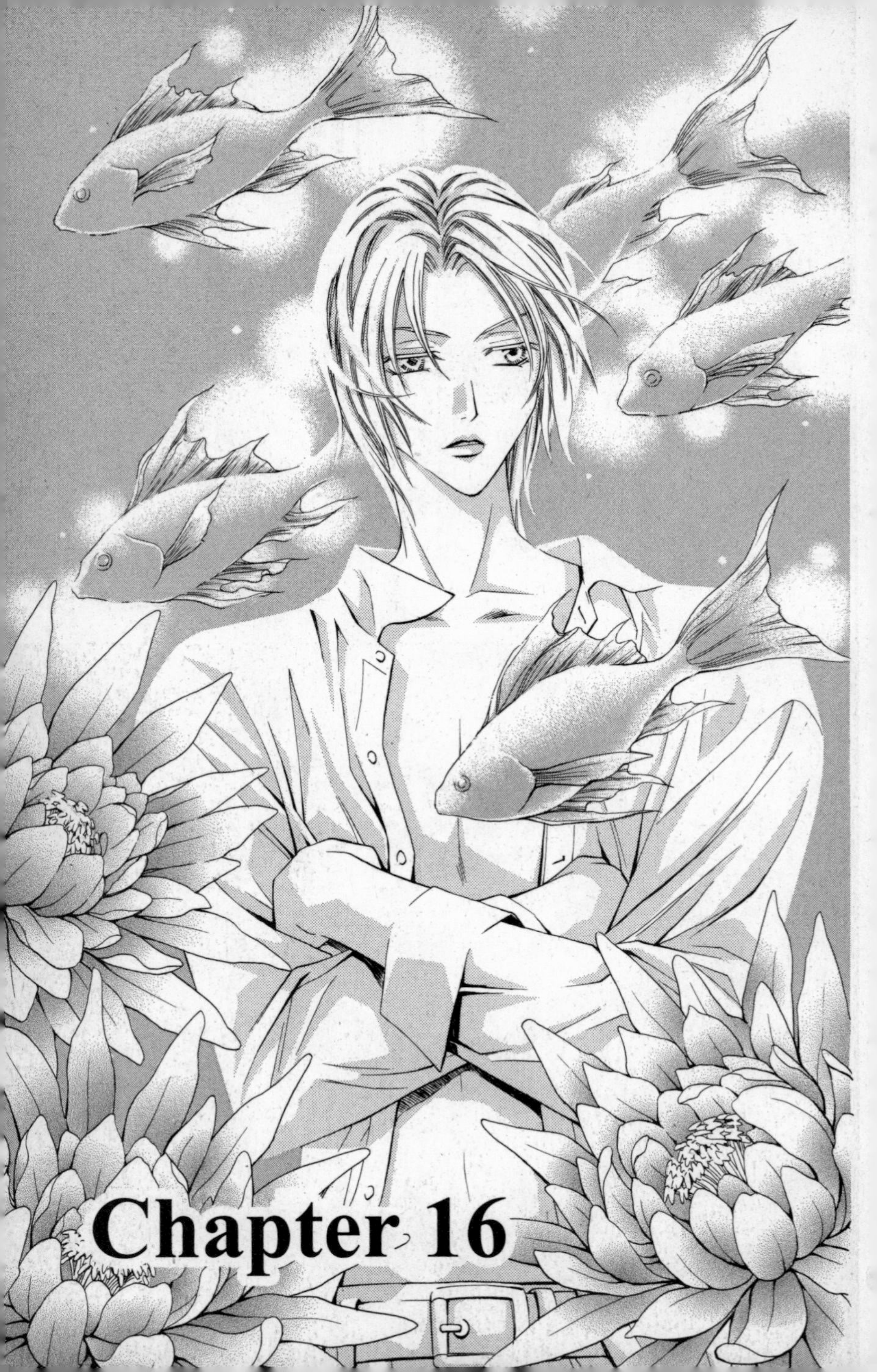
Chapter 16

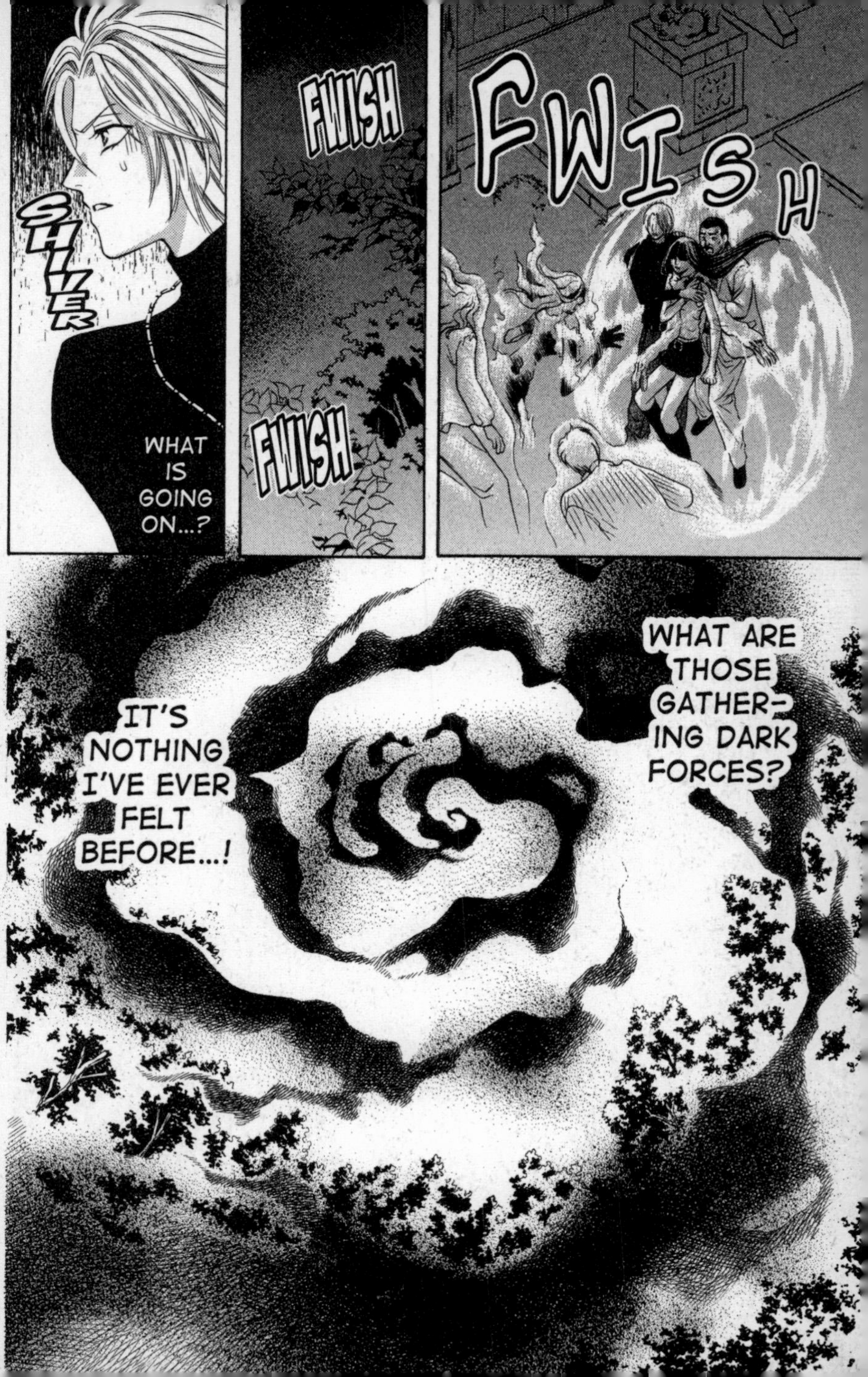
FWISH
FWISH
FWISH
SHIVER
WHAT IS GOING ON...?
WHAT ARE THOSE GATHER-ING DARK FORCES?
IT'S NOTHING I'VE EVER FELT BEFORE...!

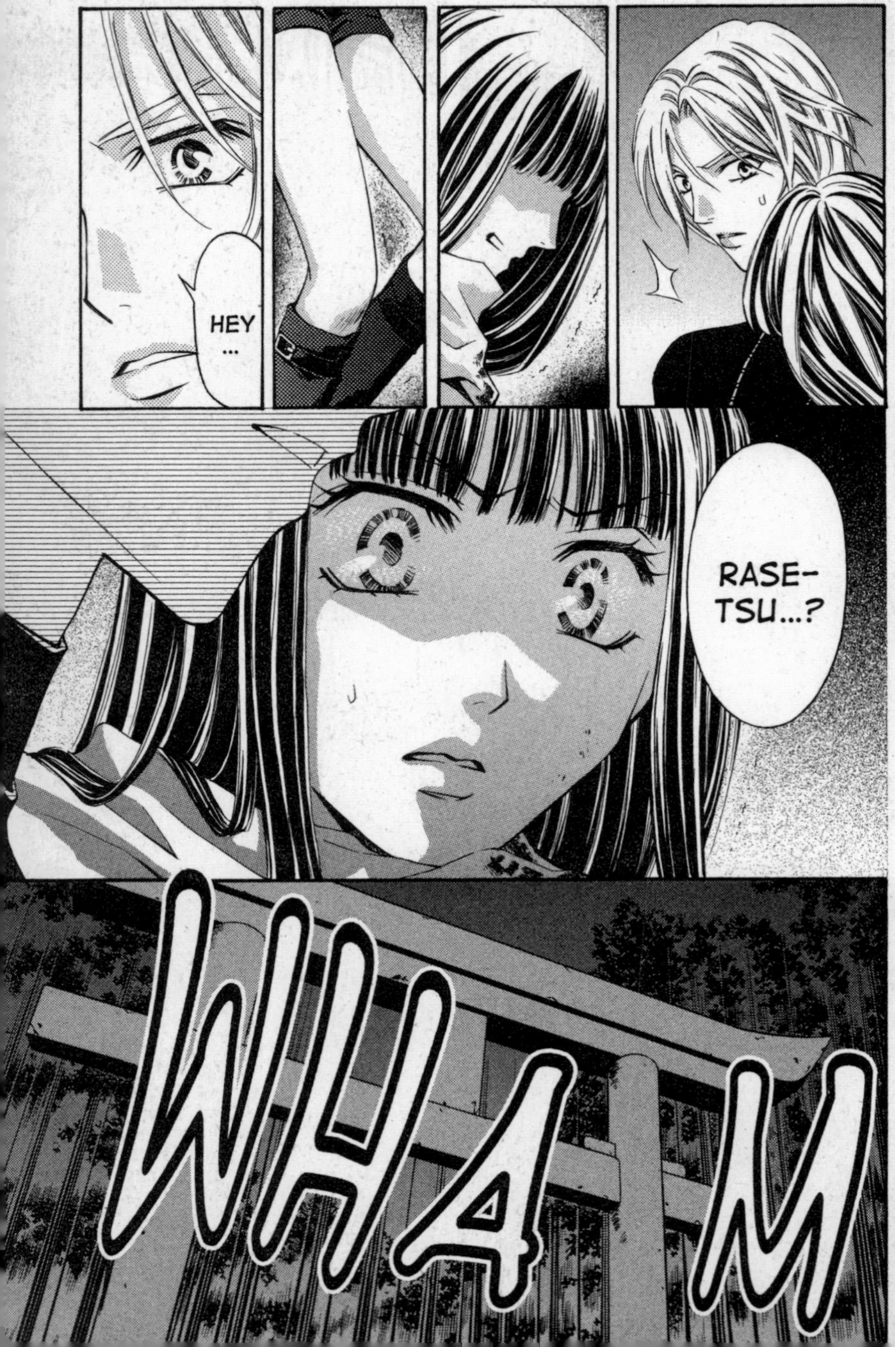
HEY ...
RASE-TSU...?
WHAM

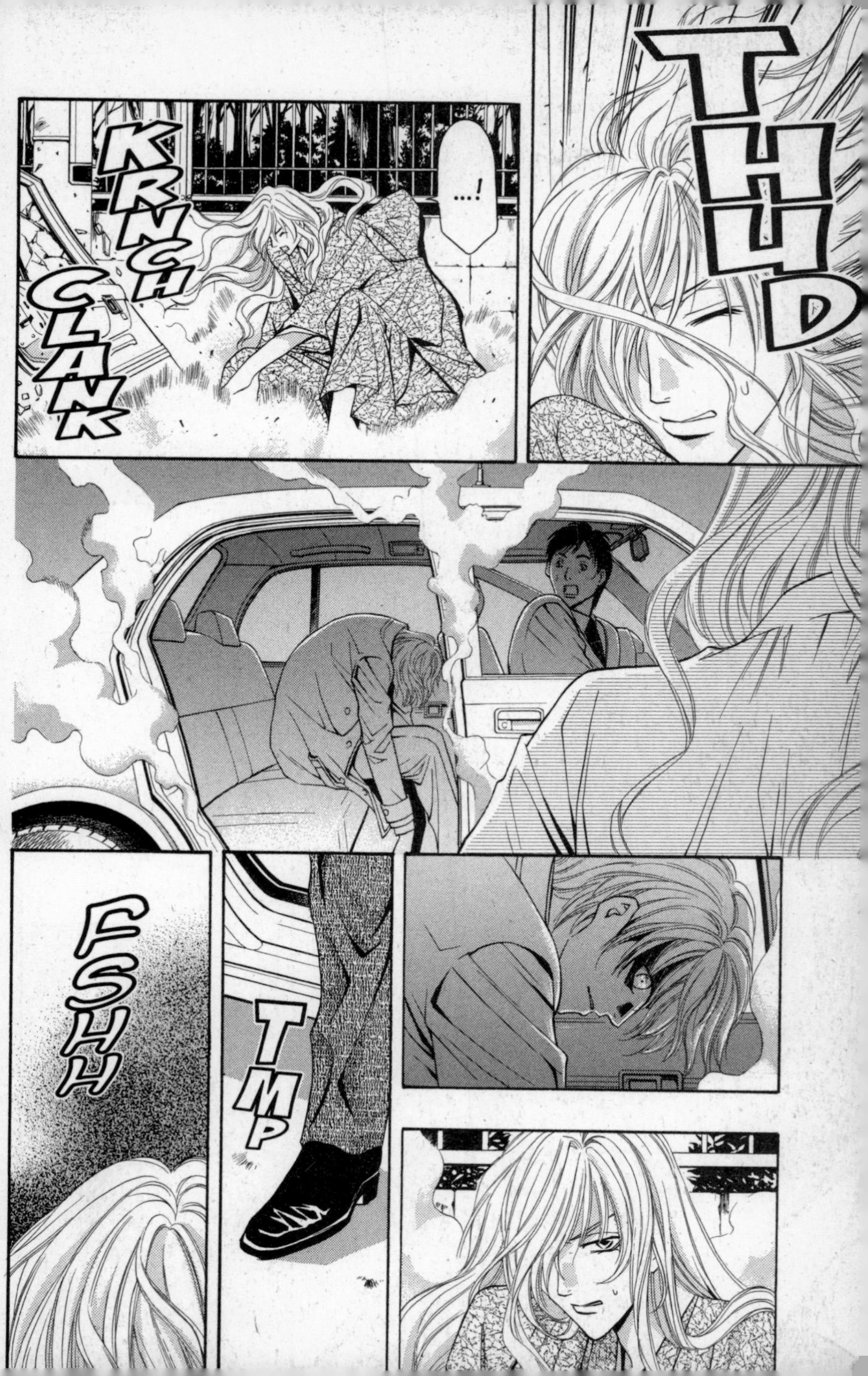
THUD
...!
KRNCH
CLANK
TMP
FSHH

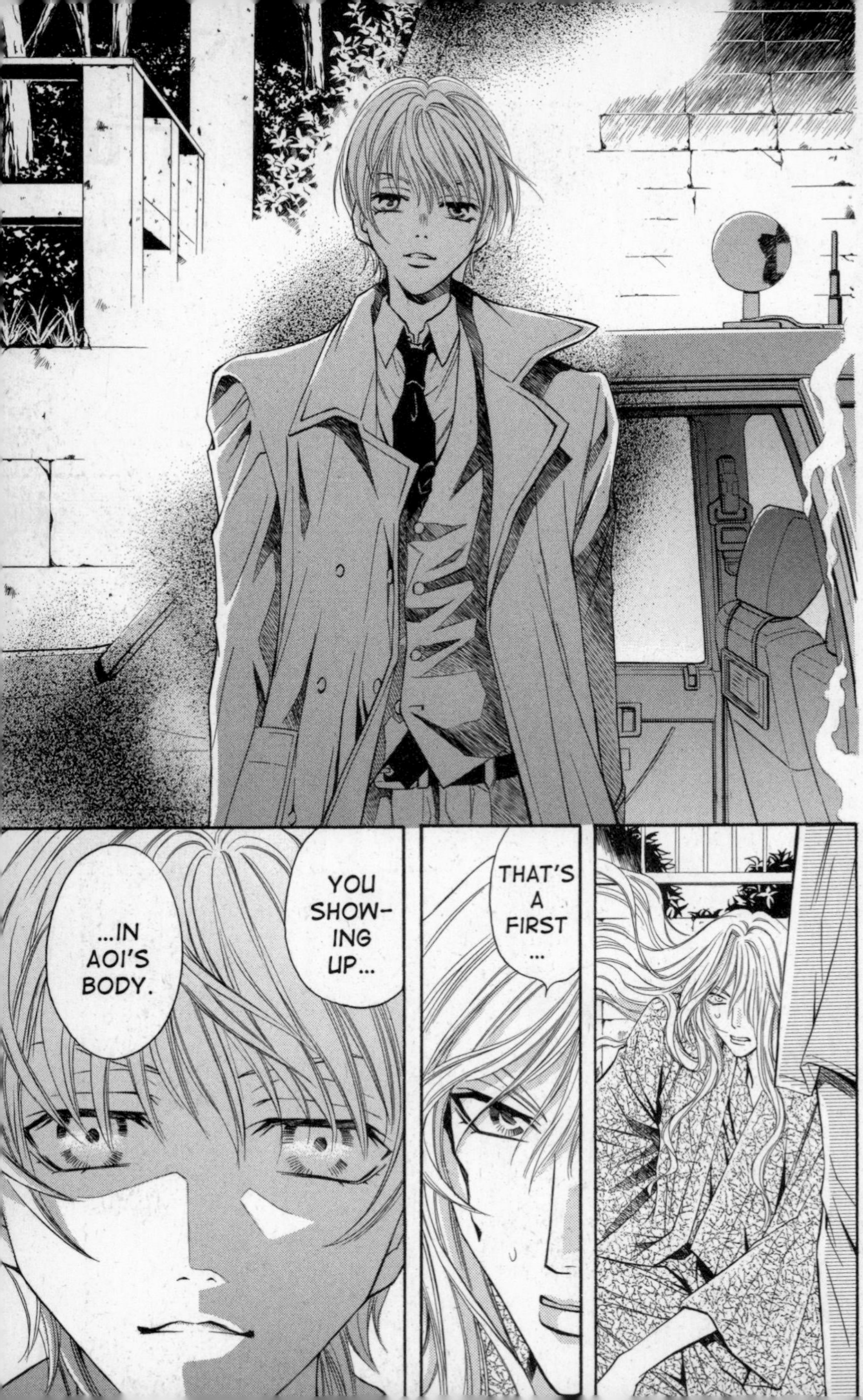
THAT'S A FIRST ...
YOU SHOWING-ING UP...
...IN AOI'S BODY.

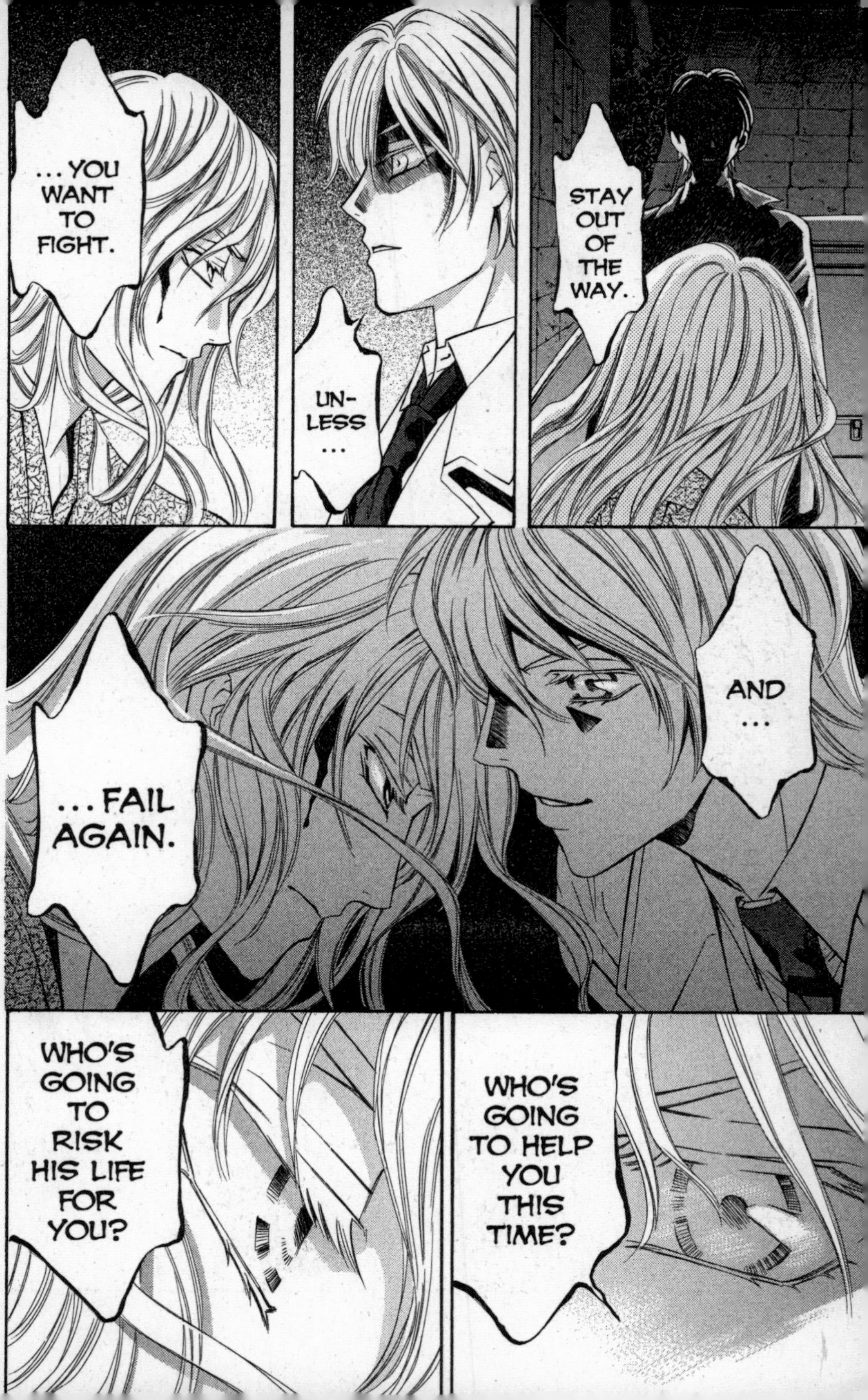
STAY OUT OF THE WAY.
UN-LESS ...
... YOU WANT TO FIGHT.
AND ...
... FAIL AGAIN.
WHO'S GOING TO HELP YOU THIS TIME?
WHO'S GOING TO RISK HIS LIFE FOR YOU?

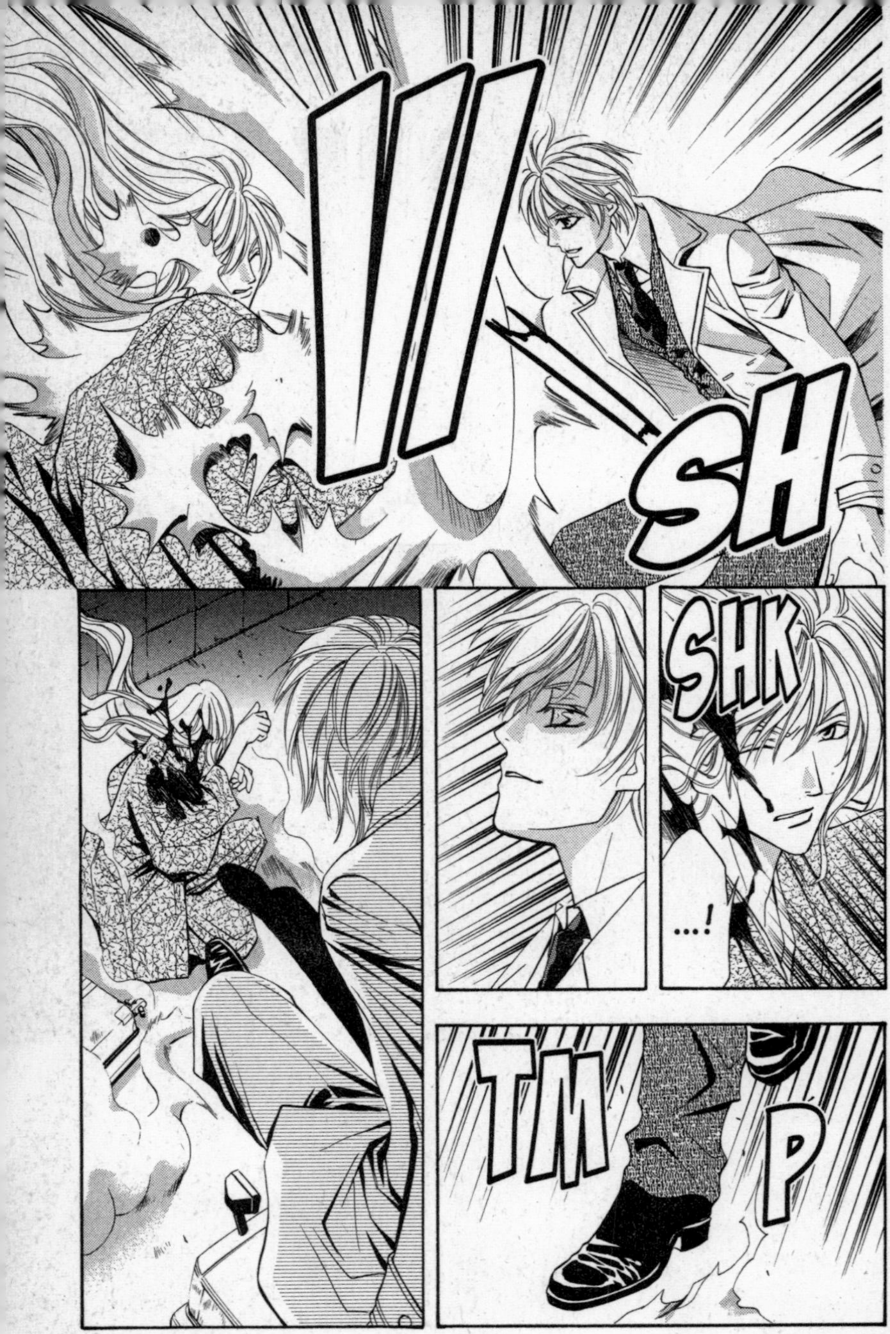
SH
SHK
...!
TM
P

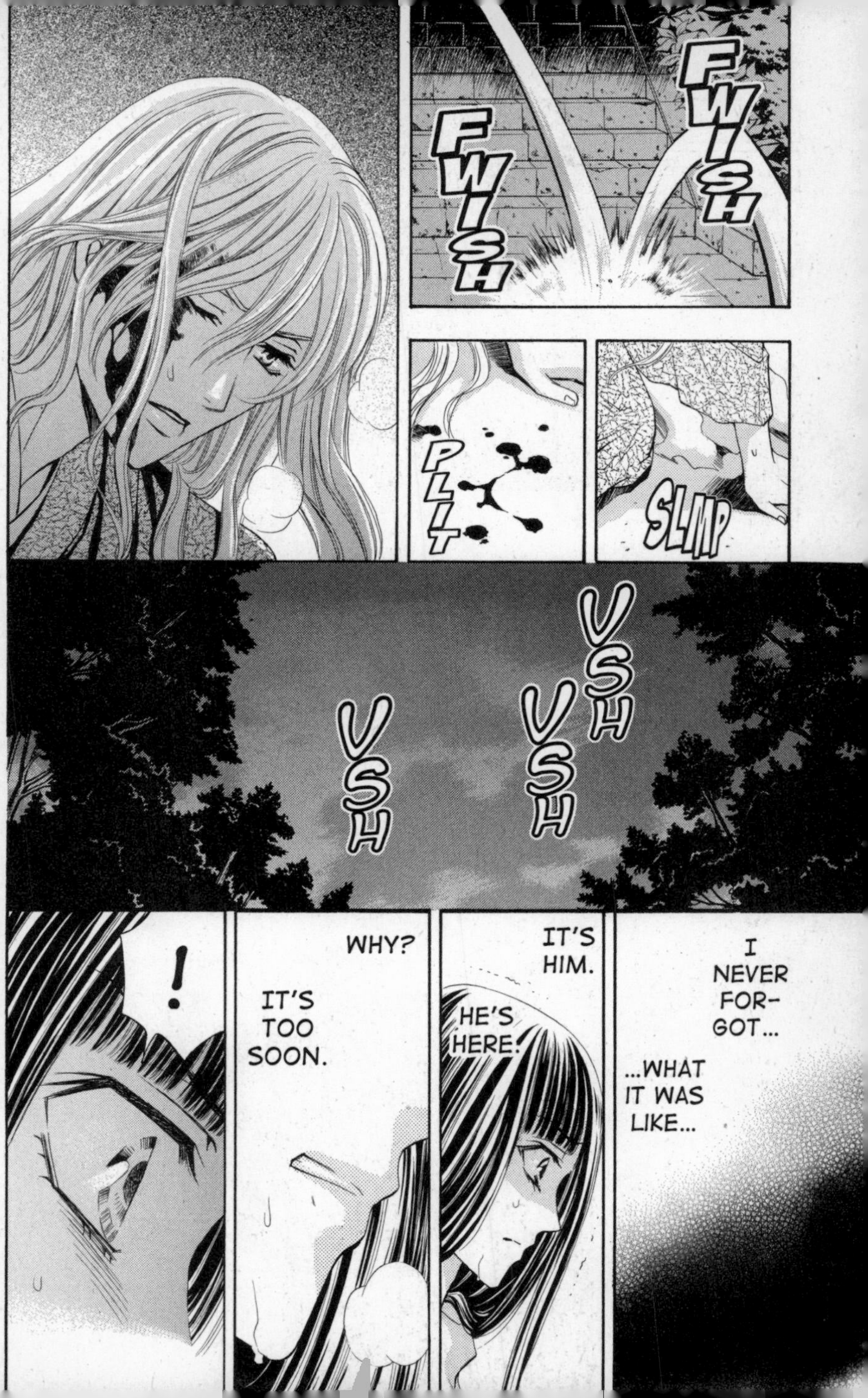
FWISH
FWISH
SLMP
PLLT
VSH
VSH
VSH
I NEVER FOR-GOT...
...WHAT IT WAS LIKE...
IT'S HIM.
HE'S HERE.
WHY?
IT'S TOO SOON.
!

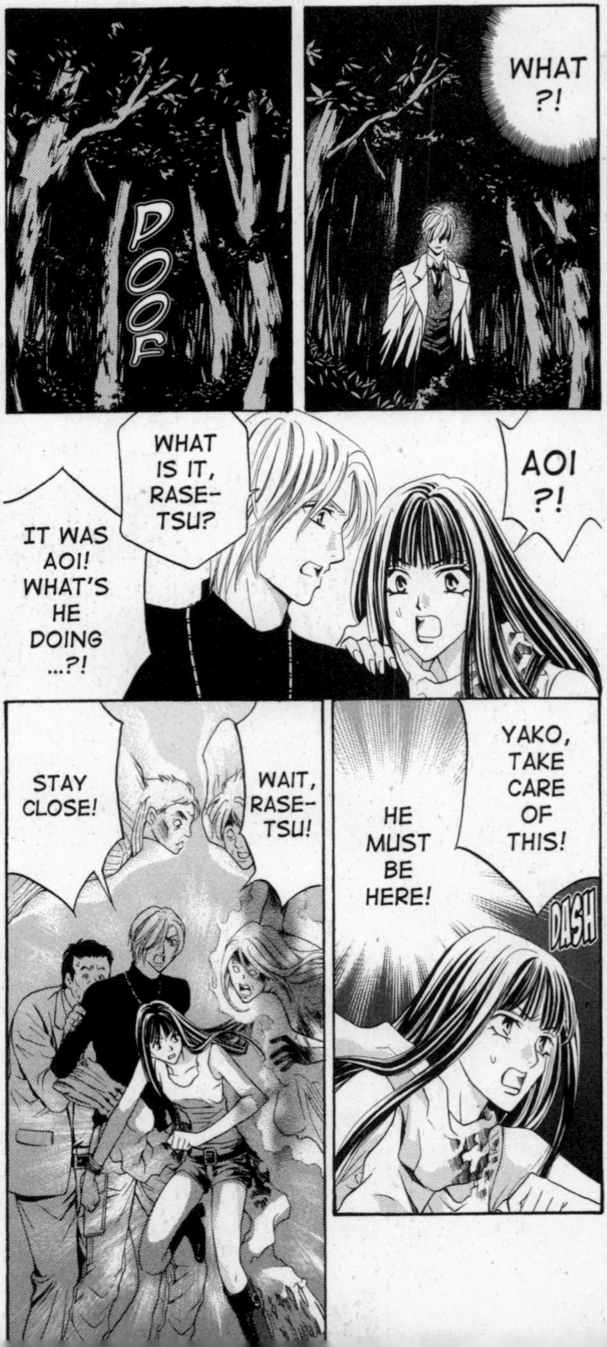
WHAT ?!
POOF
AOI ?!
WHAT IS IT, RASE-TSU?
IT WAS AOI! WHAT'S HE DOING ...?!
YAKO, TAKE CARE OF THIS!
HE MUST BE HERE!
DASH
WAIT, RASE-TSU!
STAY CLOSE!

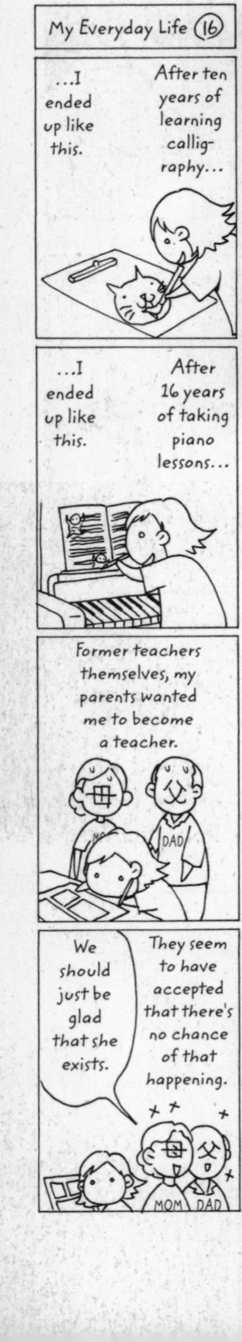
My Everyday Life 16
After ten years of learning callig-raphy...
...I ended up like this.
After 16 years of taking piano lessons...
...I ended up like this.
Former teachers themselves, my parents wanted me to become a teacher.
DAD
They seem to have accepted that there's no chance of that happening.
We should just be glad that she exists.
MOM
DAD

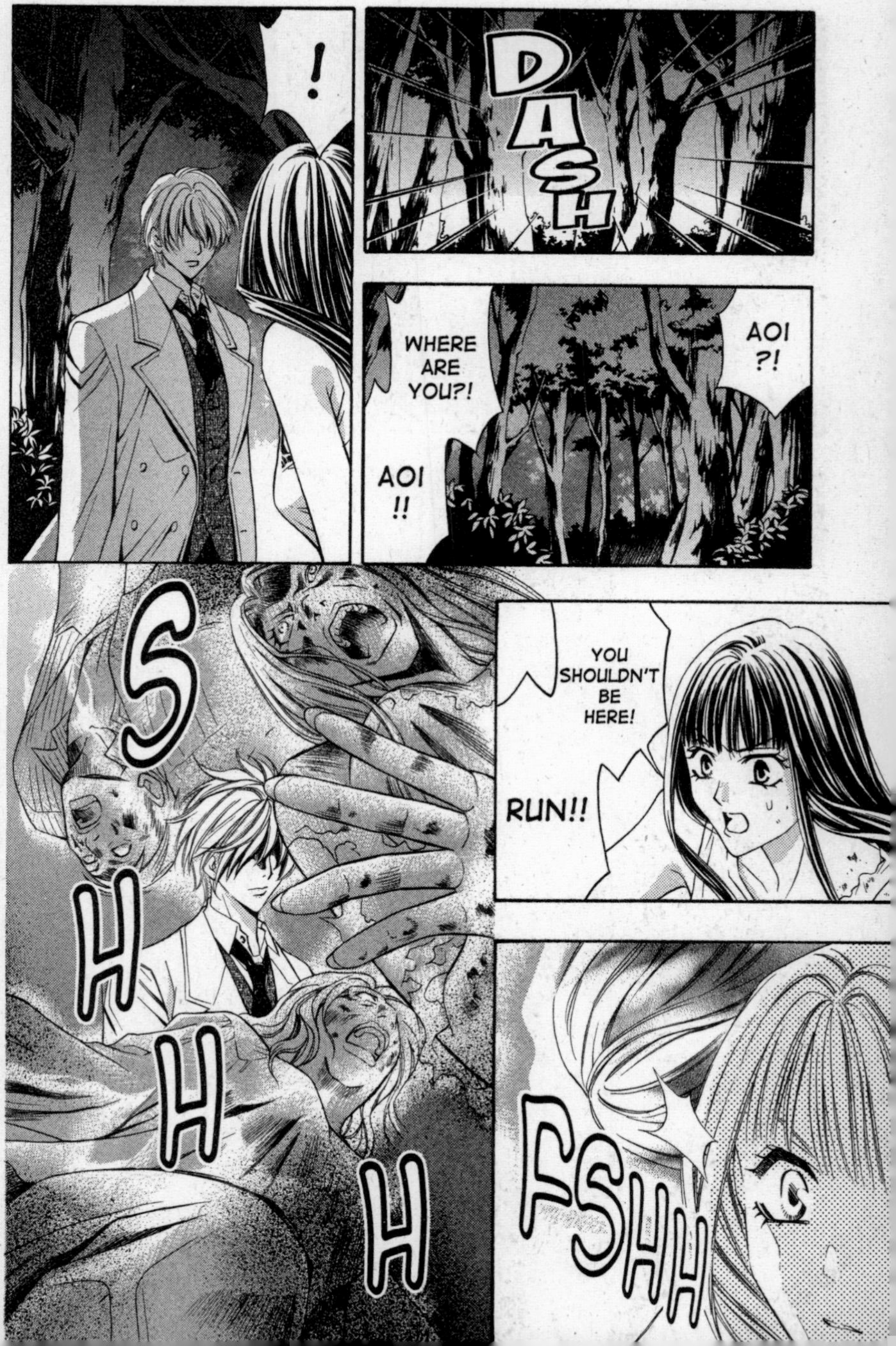
DASH
AOI ?!
WHERE ARE YOU?!
AOI !!
!
YOU SHOULDN'T BE HERE!
RUN!!
FSHH
SHHH

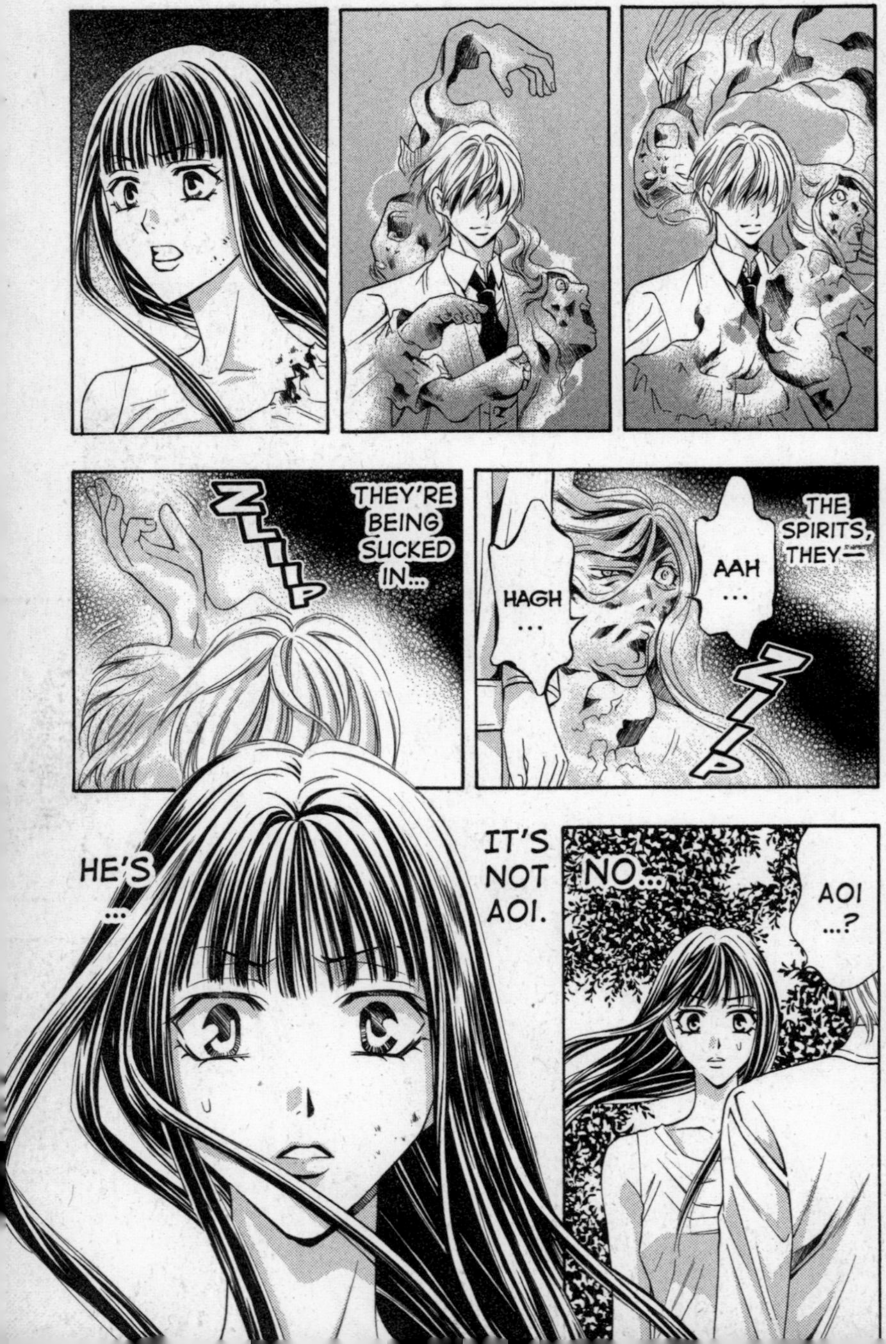
THE SPIRITS, THEY—
AAH ...
HAGH ...
ZIIIP
THEY'RE BEING SUCKED IN...
ZLIIIP
AOI ...?
NO...
IT'S NOT AOI.
HE'S ...

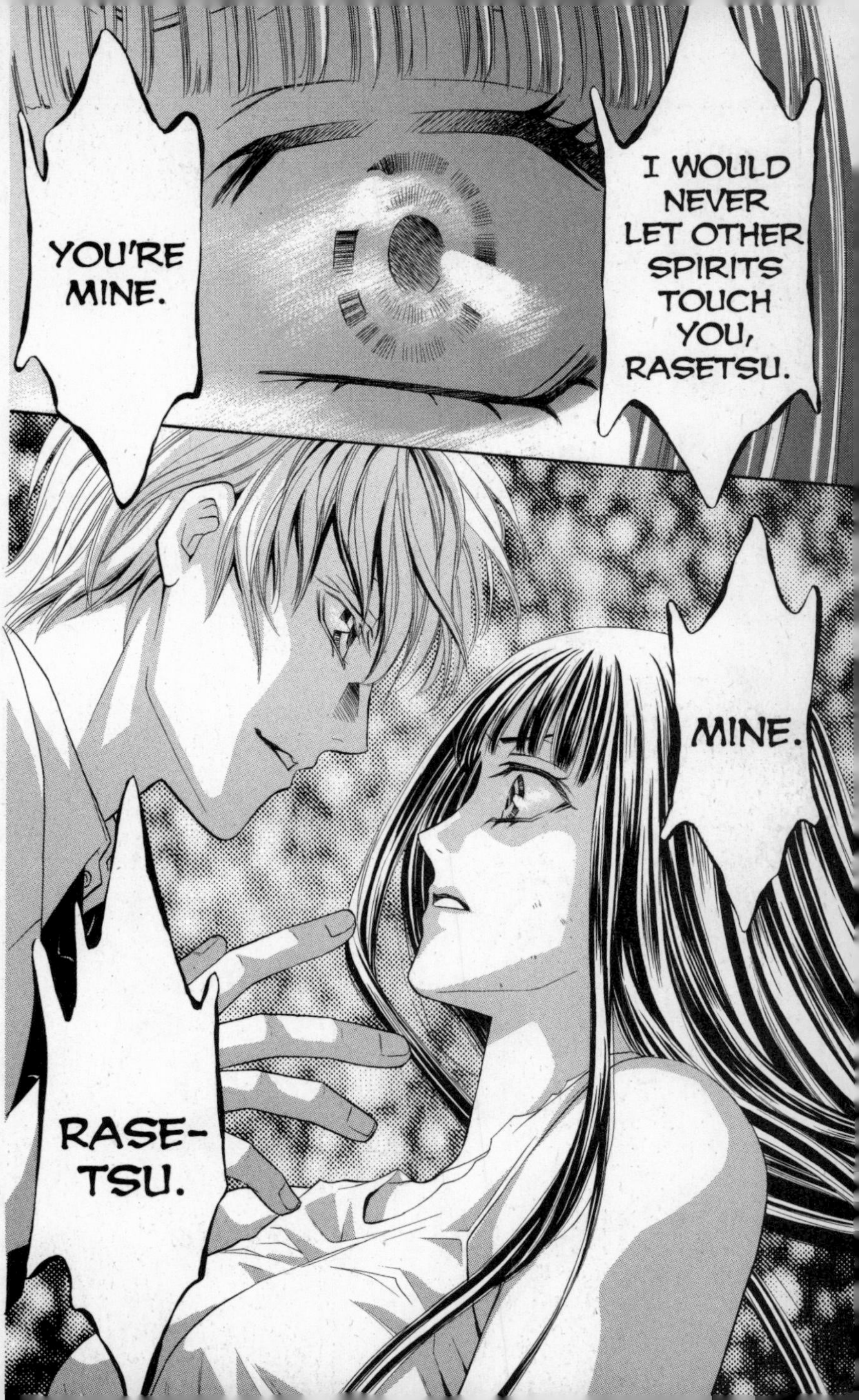
I WOULD NEVER LET OTHER SPIRITS TOUCH YOU, RASETSU.
YOU'RE MINE.
MINE.
RASE-TSU.

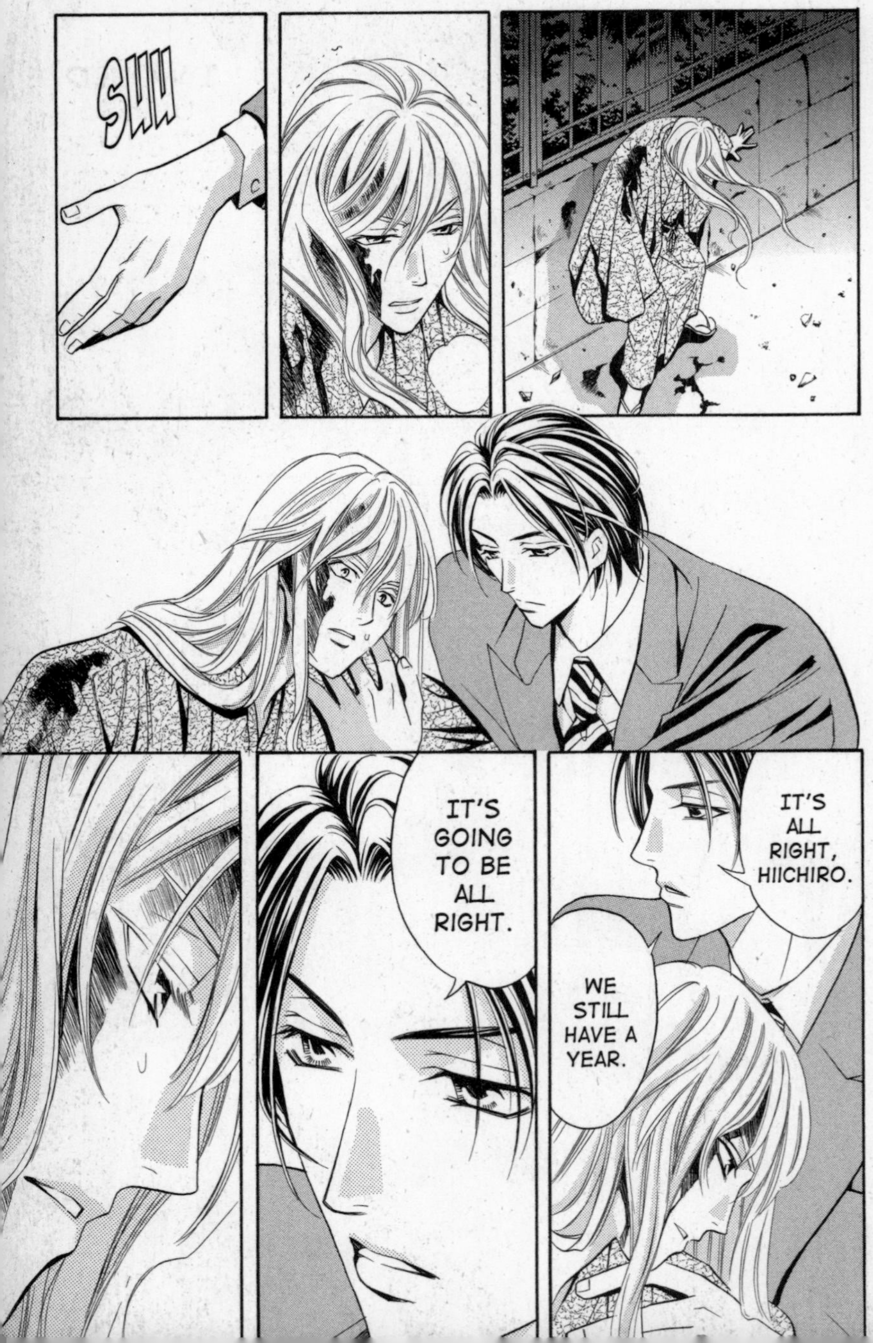
SHU
IT'S ALL RIGHT, HIICHIRO.
WE STILL HAVE A YEAR.
IT'S GOING TO BE ALL RIGHT.

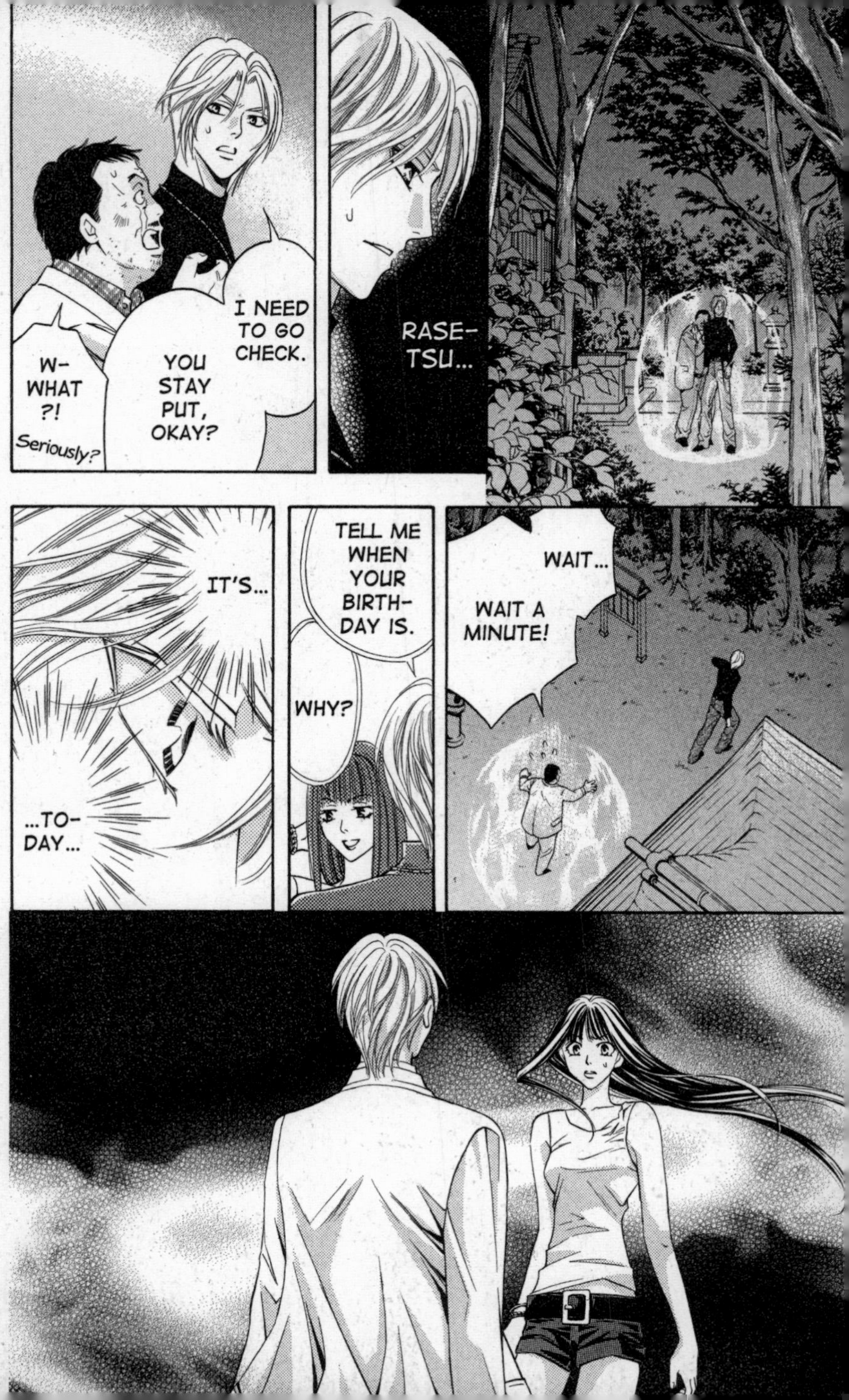
RASE-TSU...
I NEED TO GO CHECK.
YOU STAY PUT, OKAY?
W-WHAT?!
Seriously?
WAIT...
WAIT A MINUTE!
TELL ME WHEN YOUR BIRTH-DAY IS.
WHY?
IT'S...
...TO-DAY...

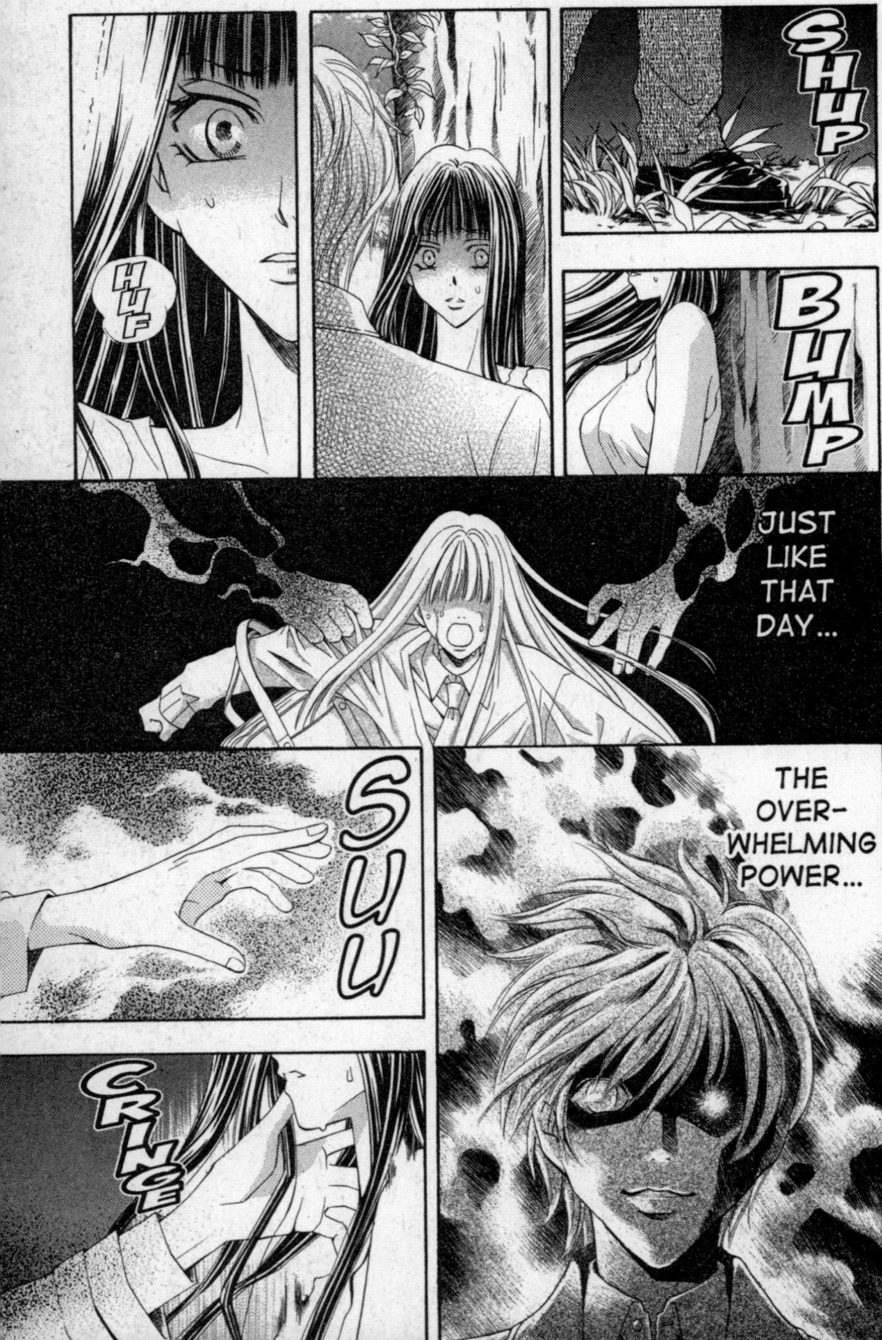
SHUP
BUMP
HUF
JUST LIKE THAT DAY...
THE OVER-WHELMING POWER...
SUUU
CRINGE

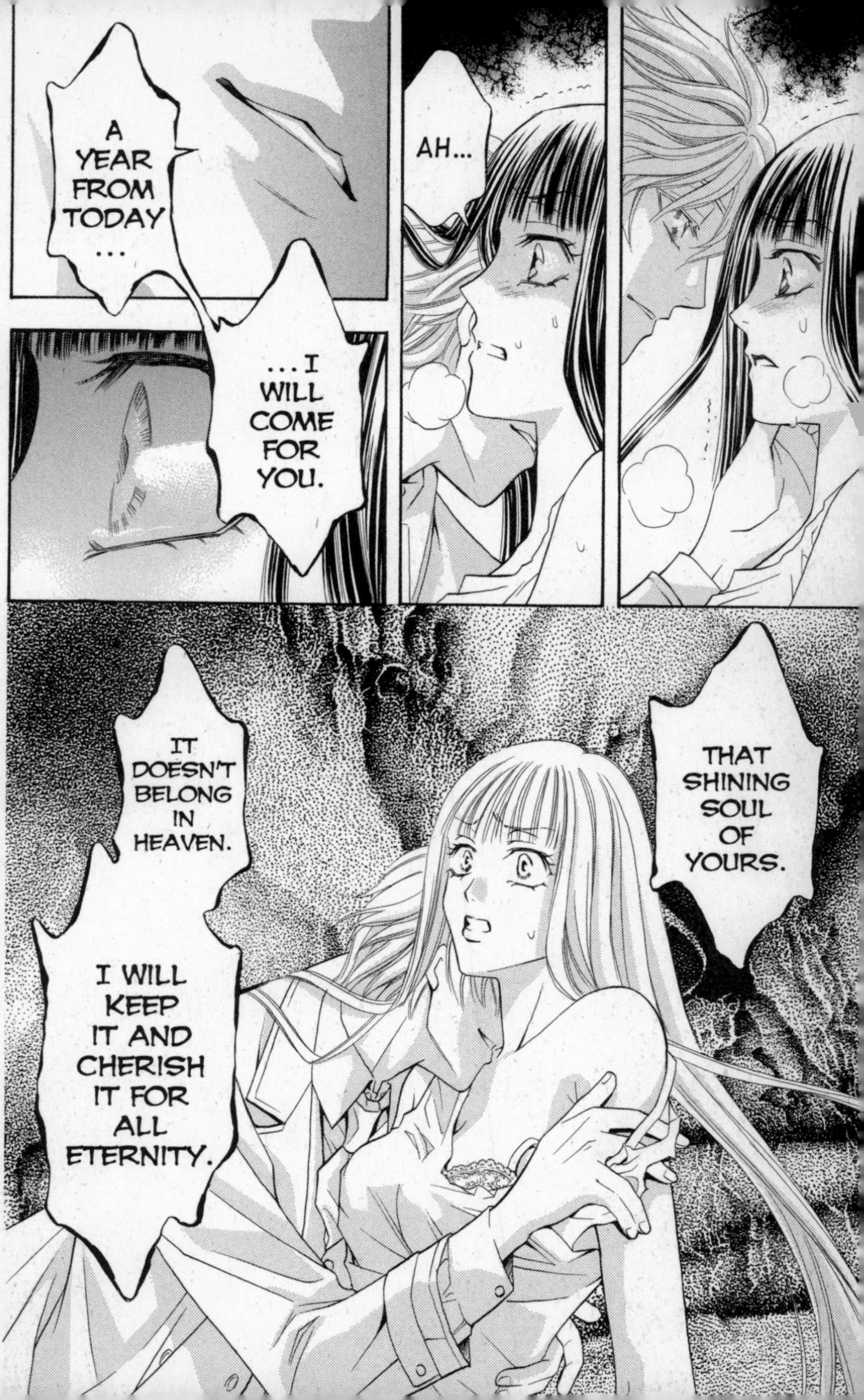
AH...
A YEAR FROM TODAY ...
...I WILL COME FOR YOU.
THAT SHINING SOUL OF YOURS.
IT DOESN'T BELONG IN HEAVEN.
I WILL KEEP IT AND CHERISH IT FOR ALL ETERNITY.

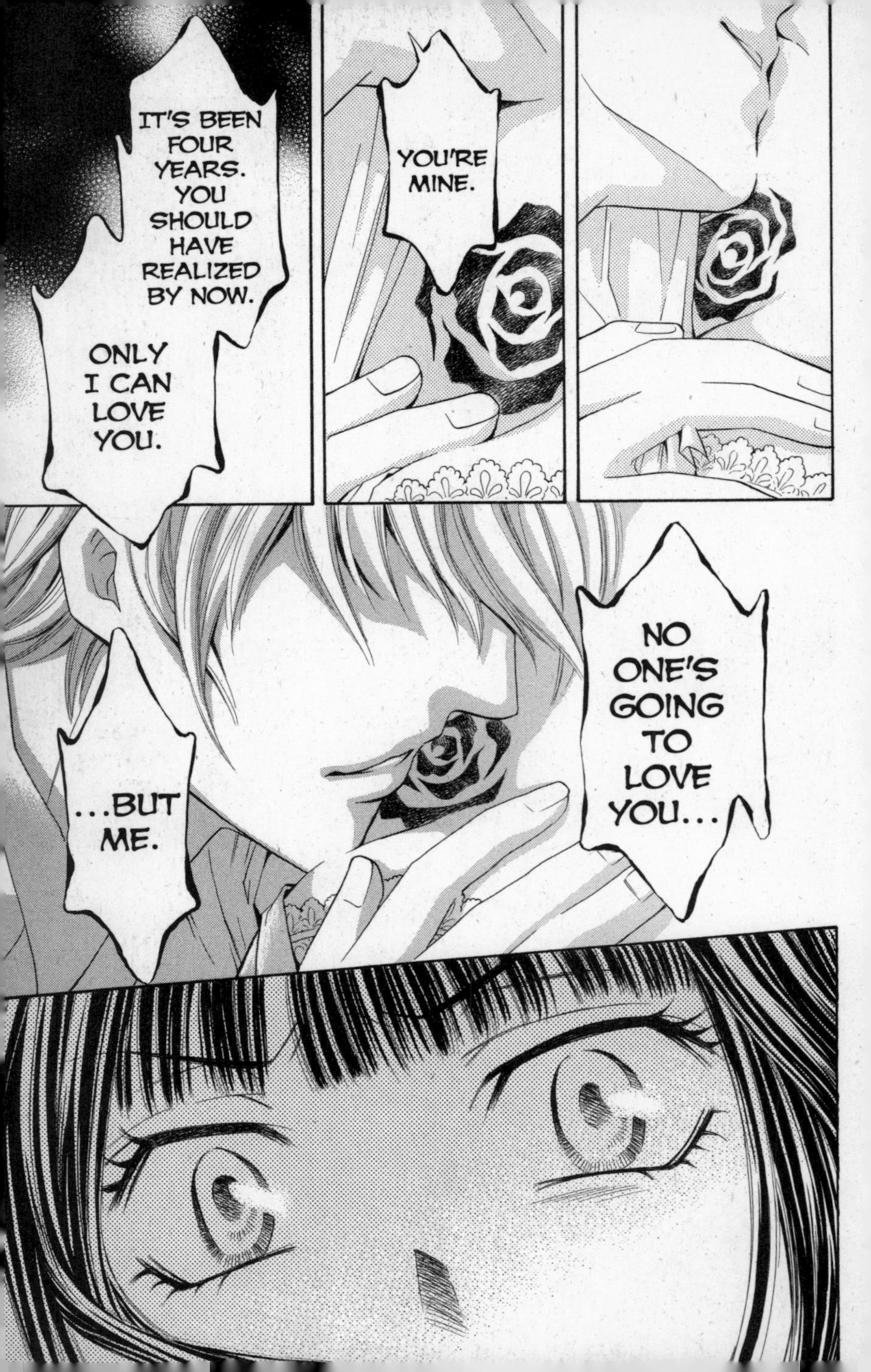
YOU'RE MINE.
IT'S BEEN FOUR YEARS. YOU SHOULD HAVE REALIZED BY NOW.
ONLY I CAN LOVE YOU.
NO ONE'S GOING TO LOVE YOU...
...BUT ME.

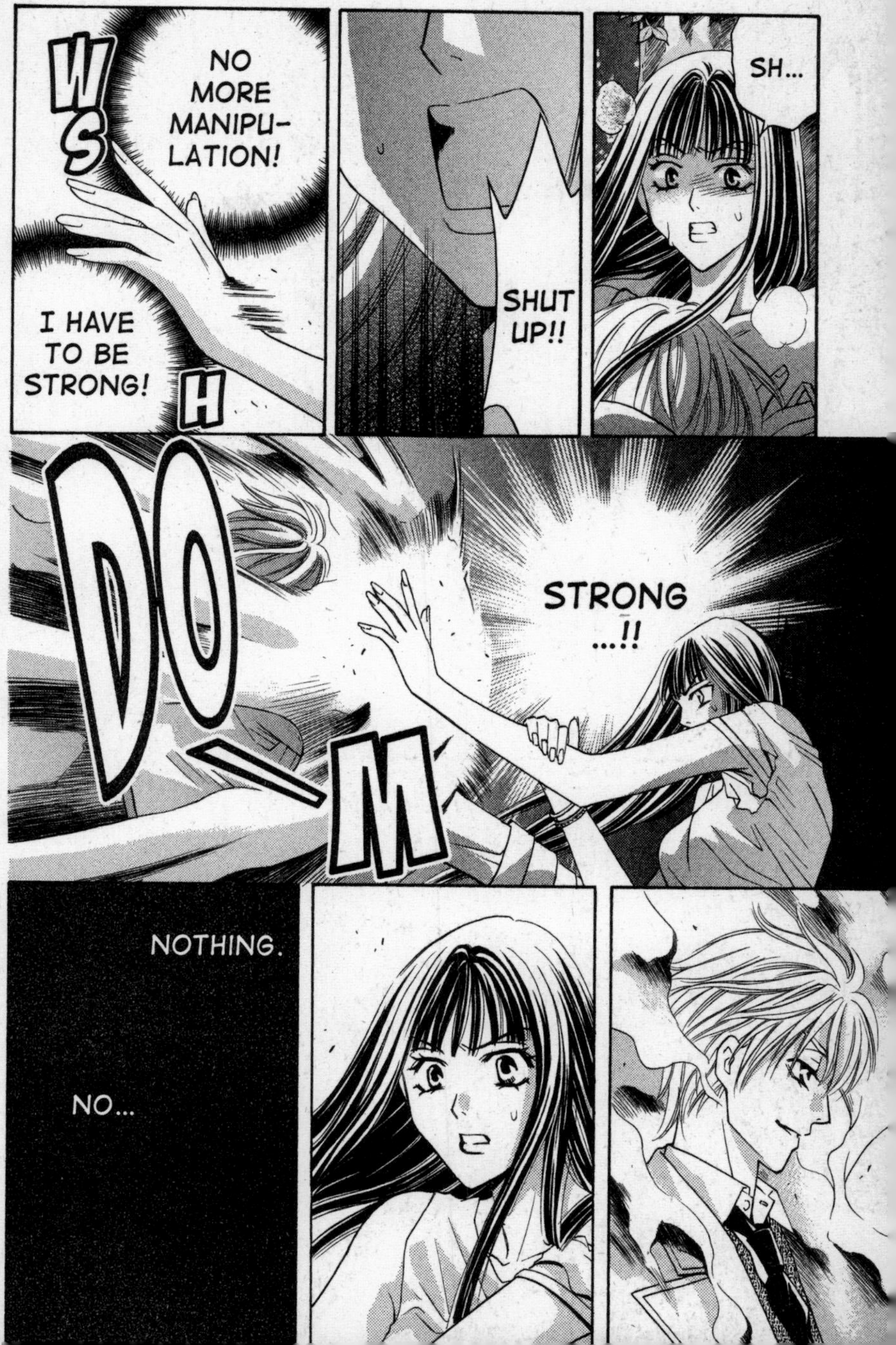
SH...
SHUT UP!!
NO MORE MANIPULATION!
I HAVE TO BE STRONG!
WSH
STRONG ...!!
DO-M
NOTHING.
NO...

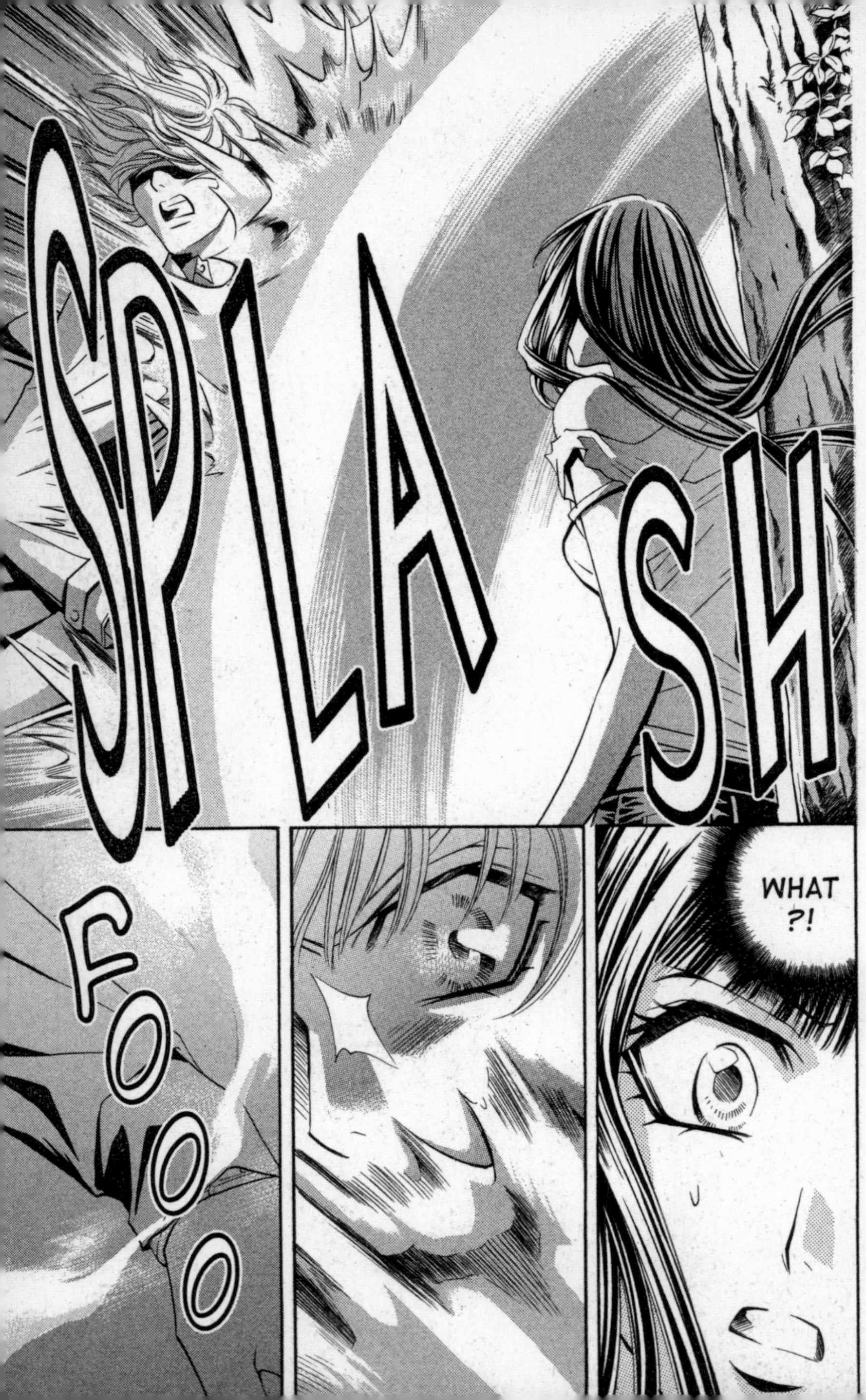
SPLASH
WHAT ?!
FOOOO

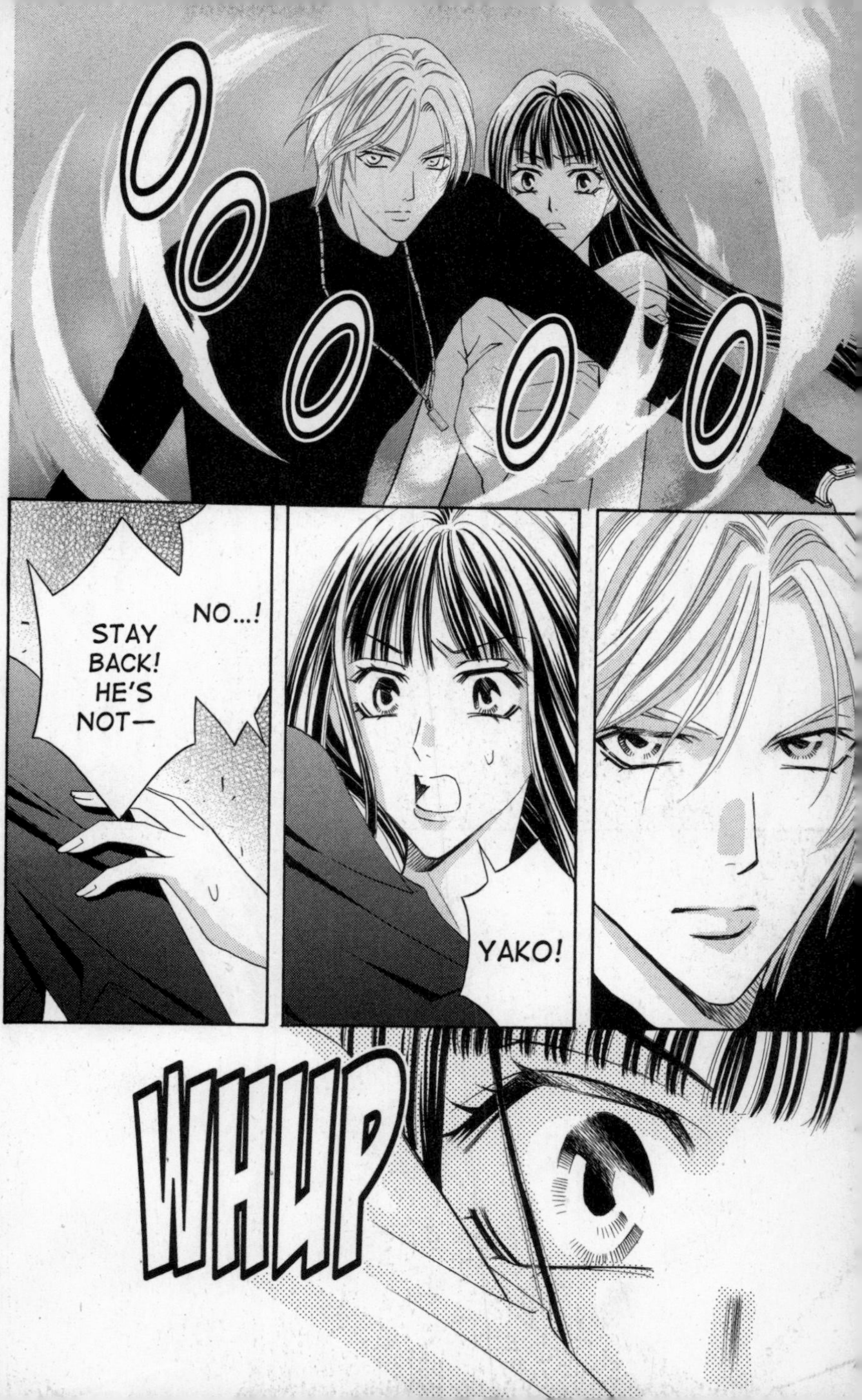
YAKO!
NO...!
STAY BACK! HE'S NOT—
WHUP

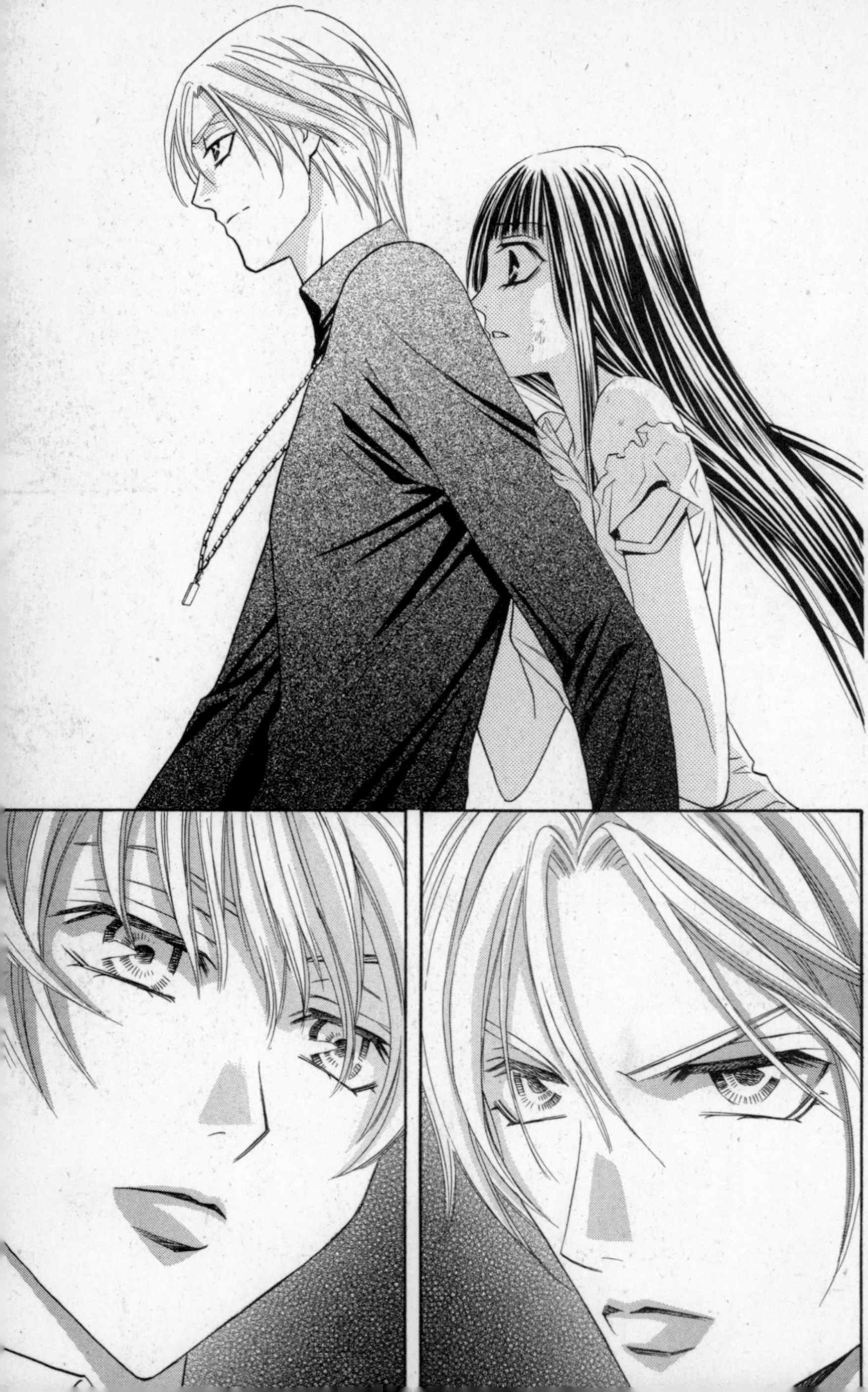

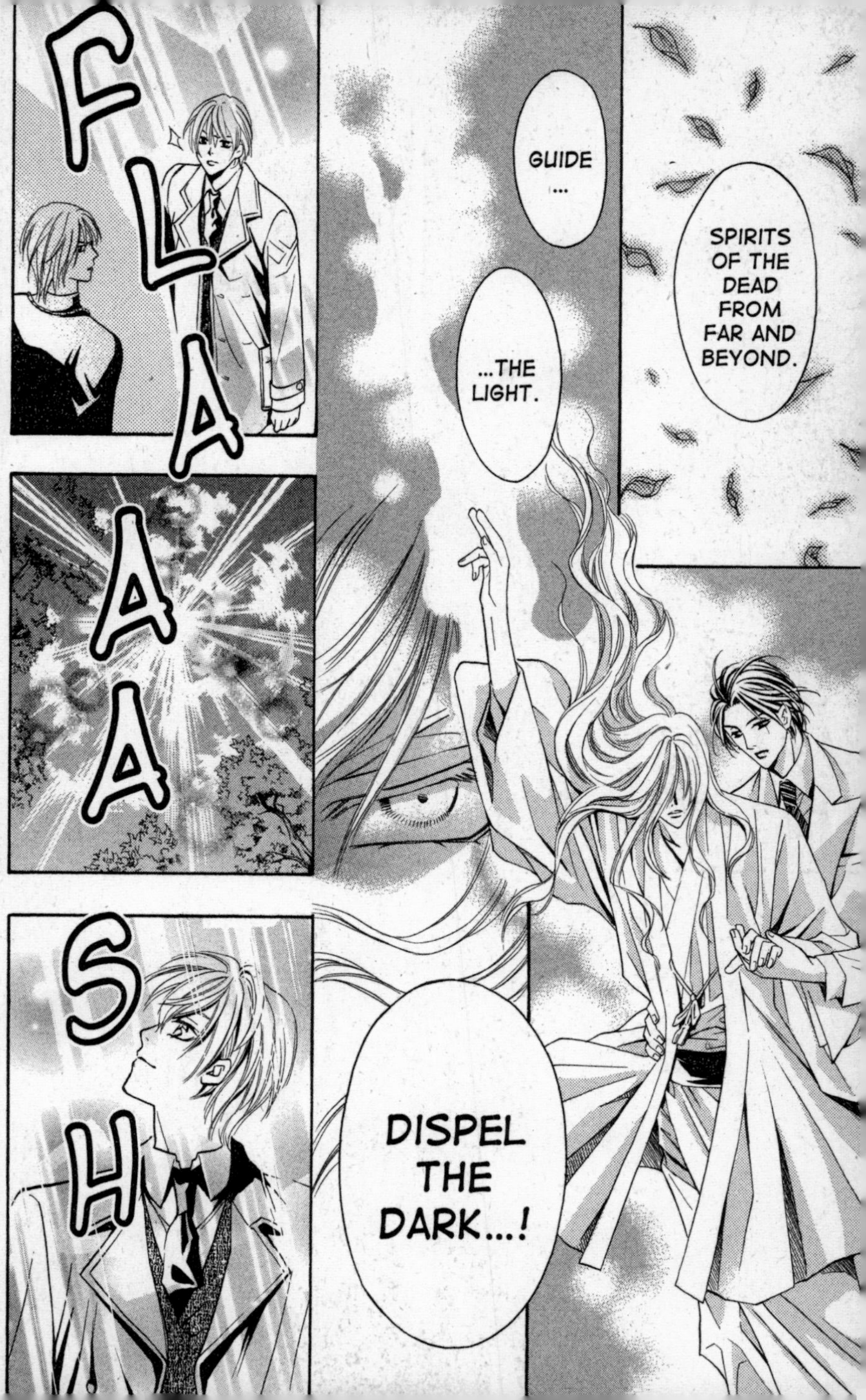
SPIRITS OF THE DEAD FROM FAR AND BEYOND.
GUIDE ...
...THE LIGHT.
DISPEL THE DARK...!
FLAAASH

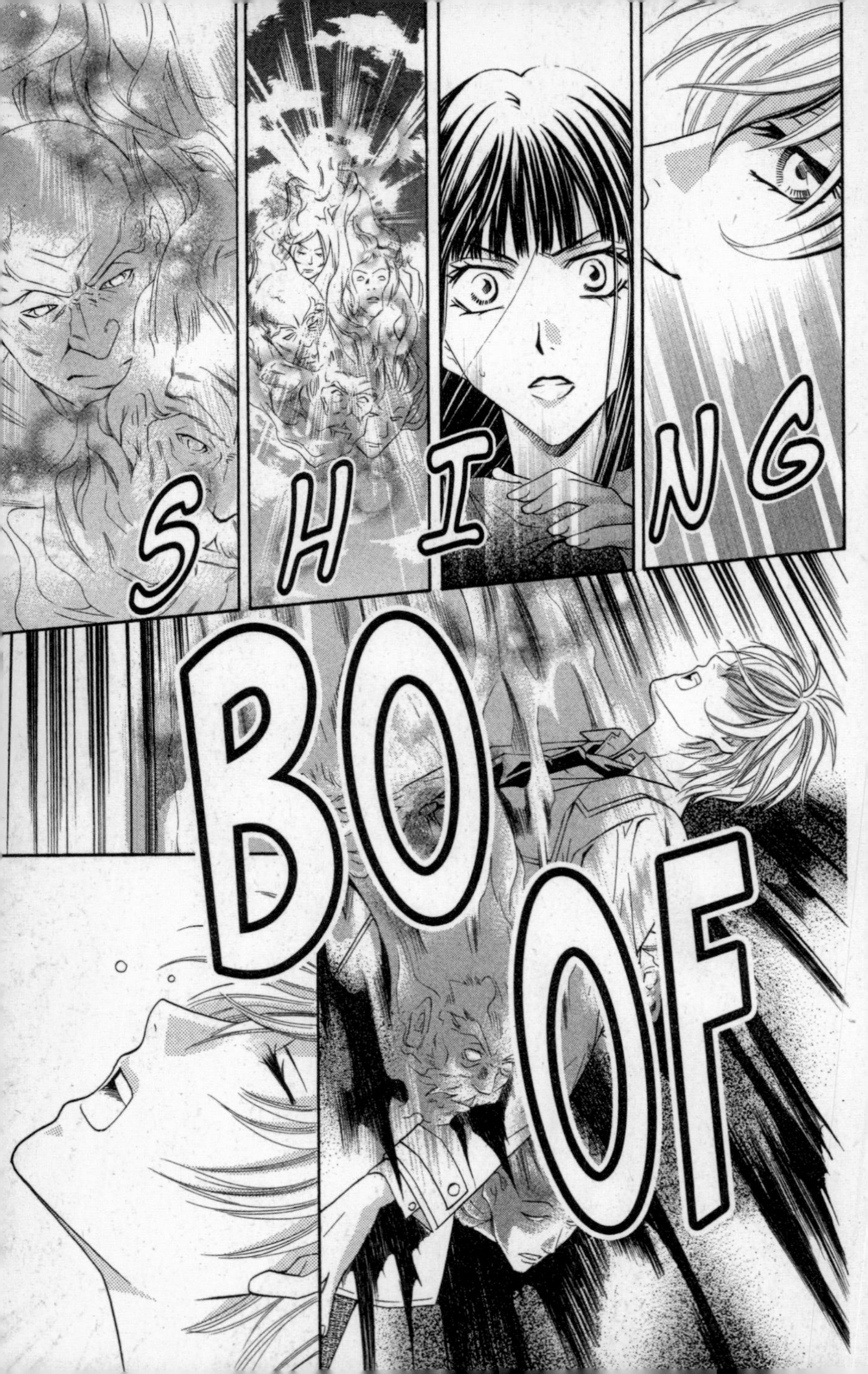
SHING
BOOF

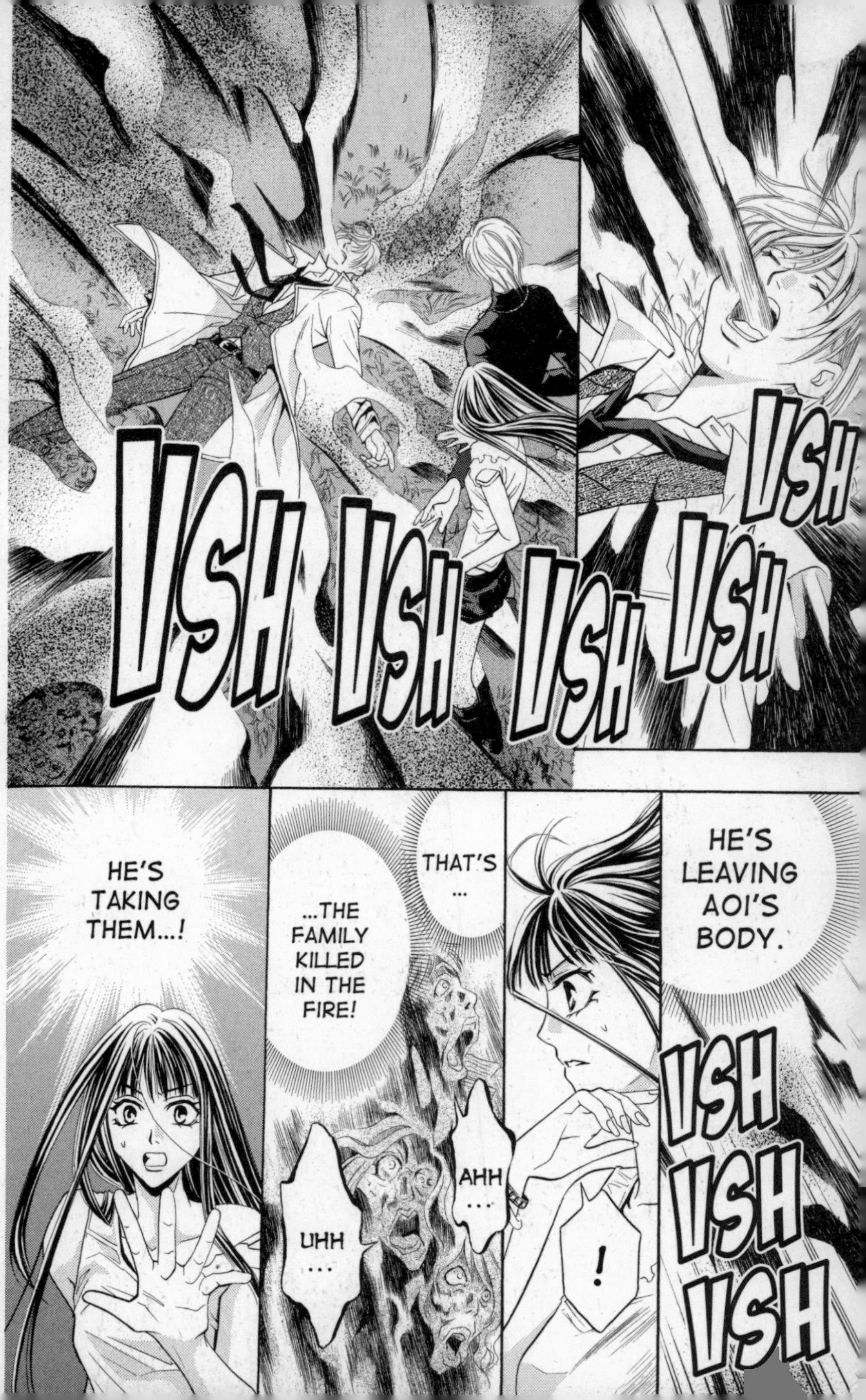
USH
USH
USH
USH
USH
USH
HE'S LEAVING AOI'S BODY.
USH
USH
USH
!
THAT'S ...
...THE FAMILY KILLED IN THE FIRE!
AHH ...
UHH ...
HE'S TAKING THEM...!

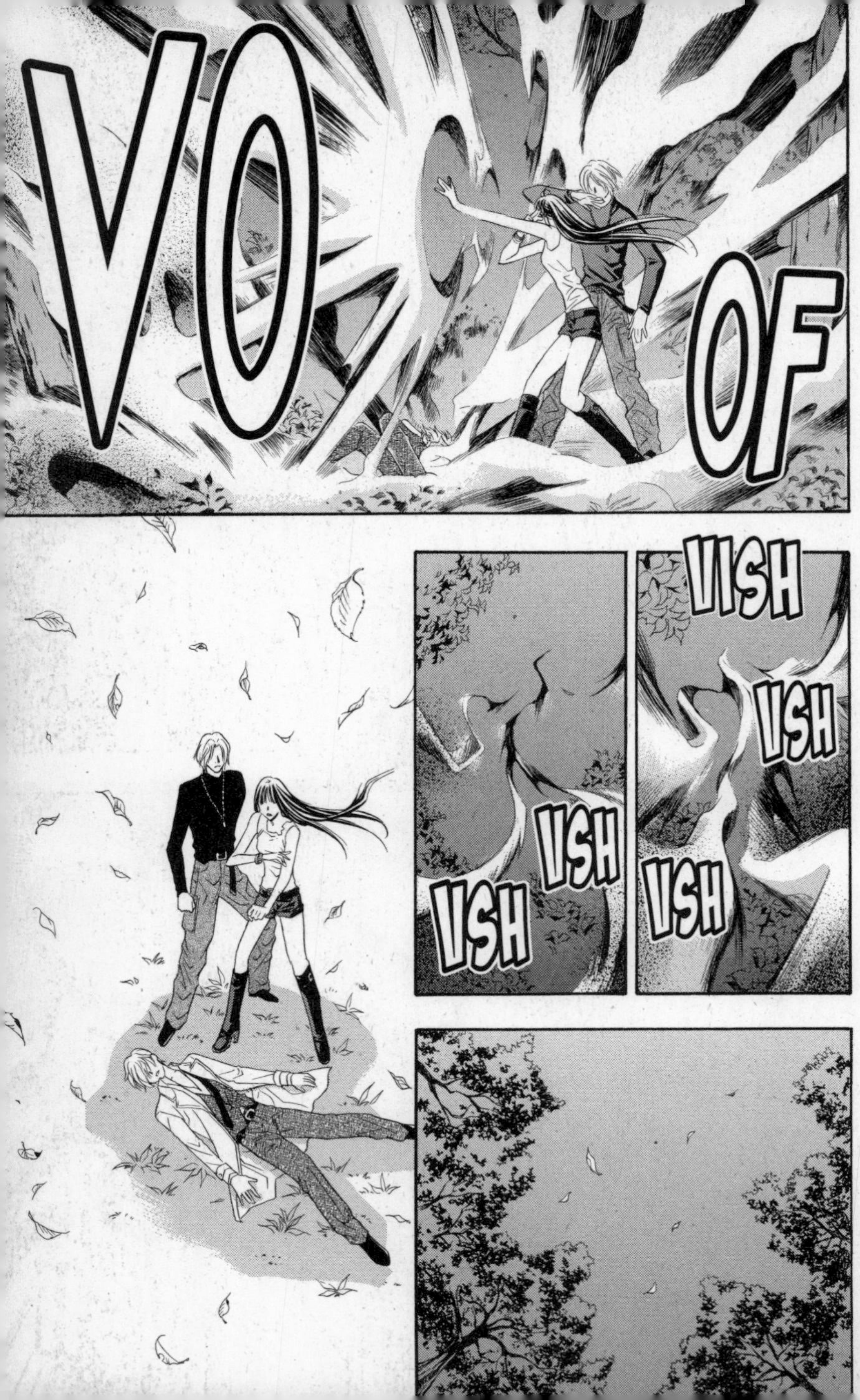
VO OF
VISH
VSH
VSH
VSH
VSH

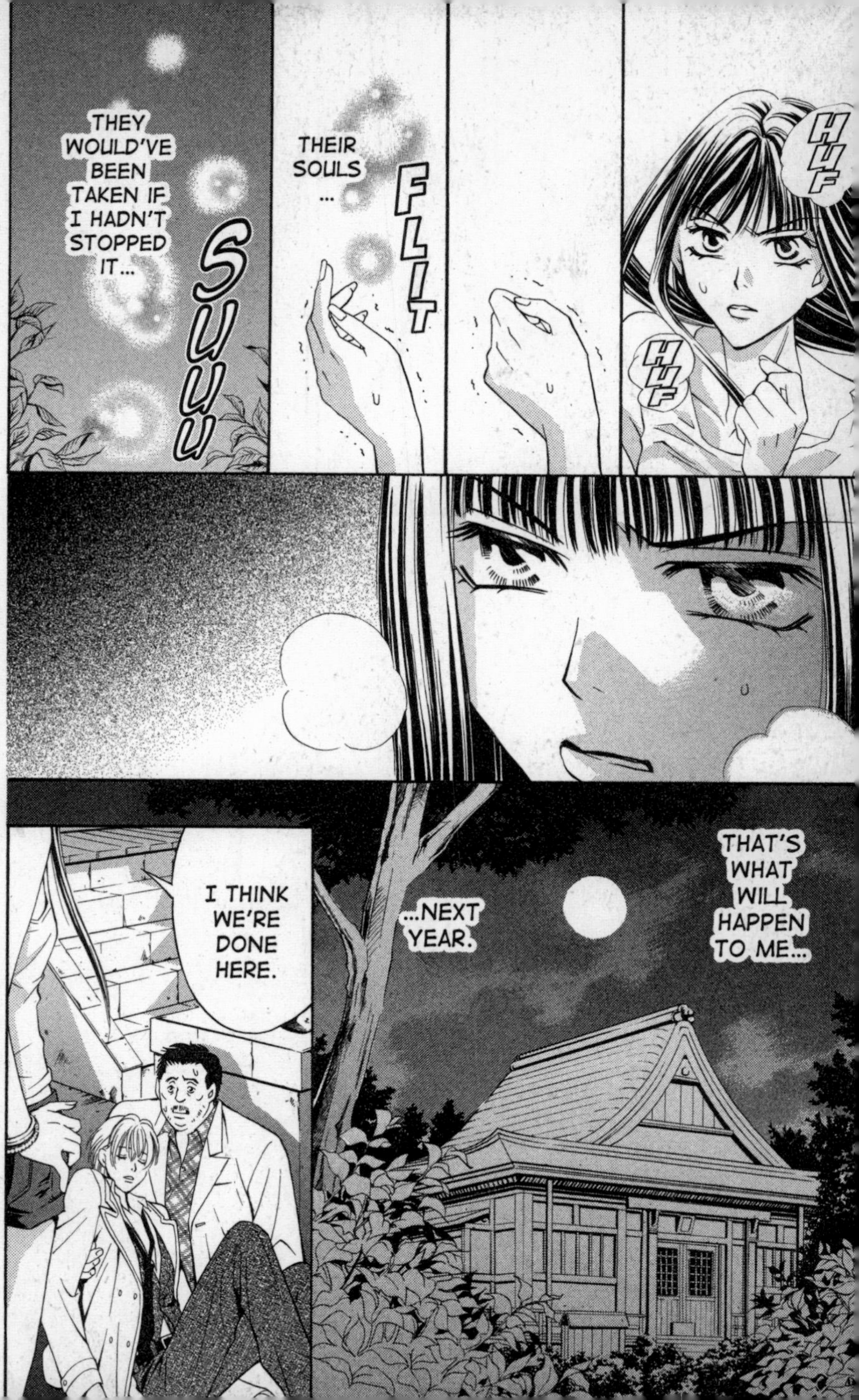
HUF
HUF
THEIR SOULS ...
FLIT
THEY WOULD'VE BEEN TAKEN IF I HADN'T STOPPED IT...
SUUUU
THAT'S WHAT WILL HAPPEN TO ME...
...NEXT YEAR.
I THINK WE'RE DONE HERE.

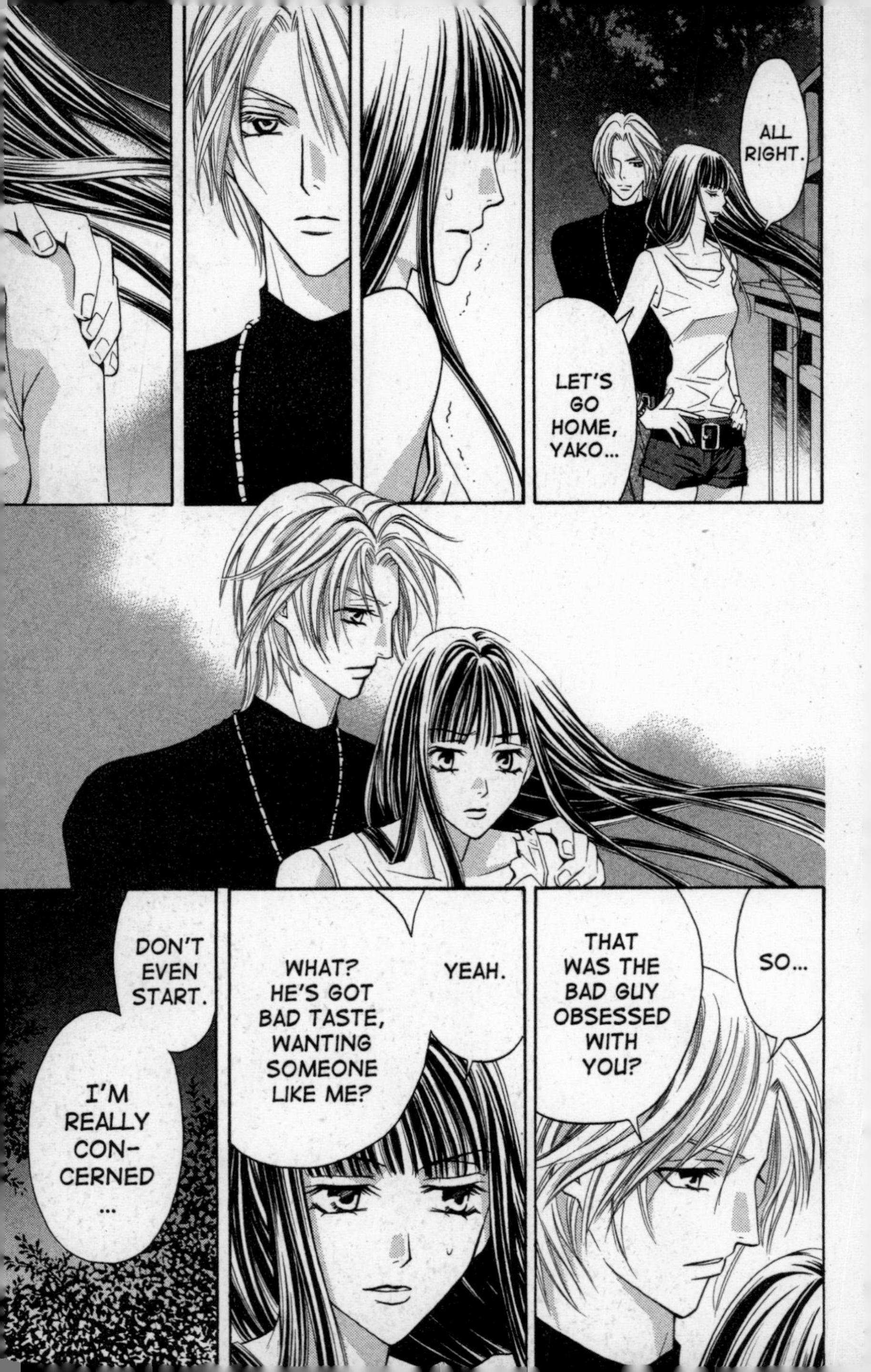
ALL RIGHT.
LET'S GO HOME, YAKO...
SO...
THAT WAS THE BAD GUY OBSESSED WITH YOU?
YEAH.
WHAT? HE'S GOT BAD TASTE, WANTING SOMEONE LIKE ME?
DON'T EVEN START.
I'M REALLY CON-CERNED ...

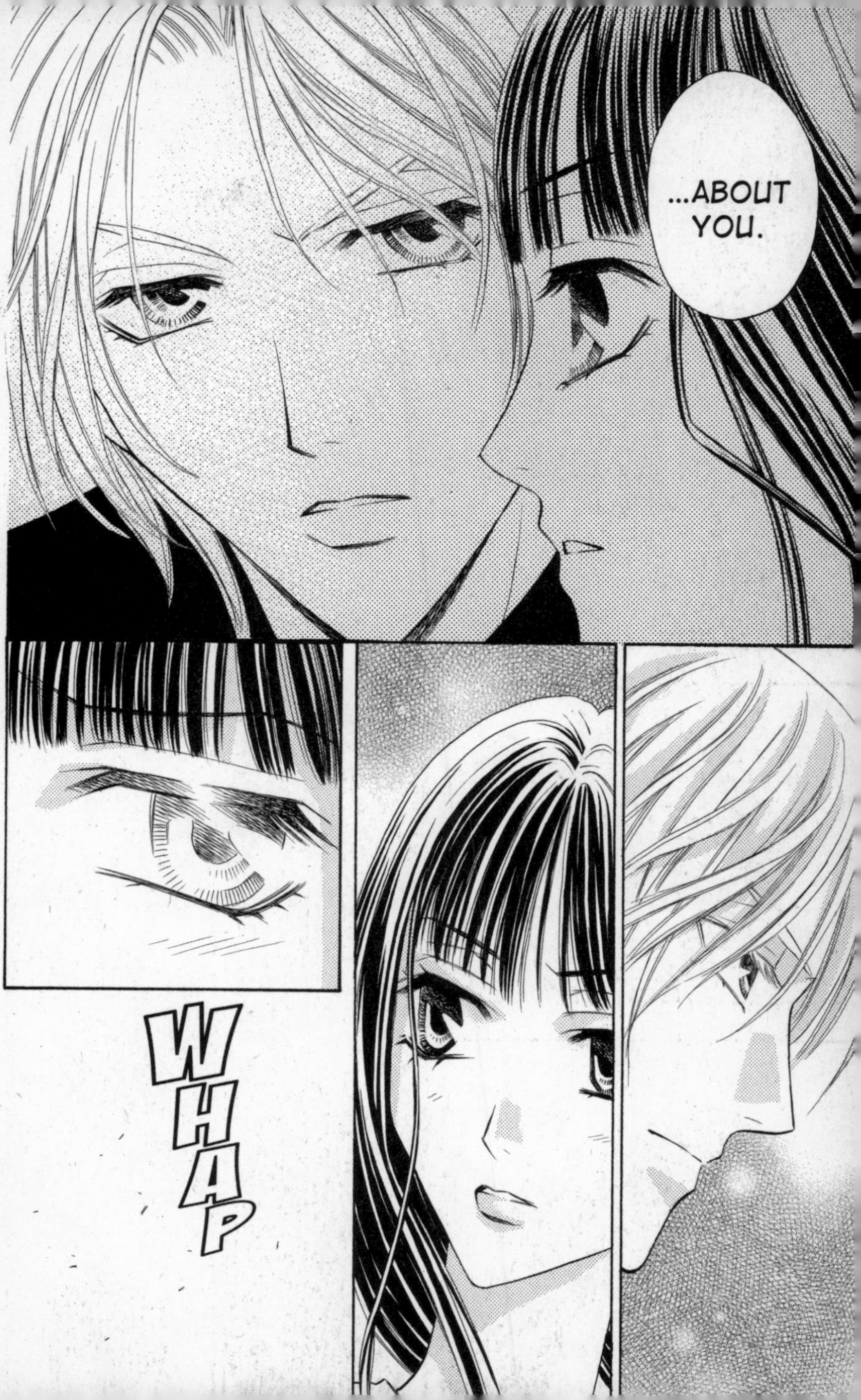
...ABOUT YOU.
WHAP

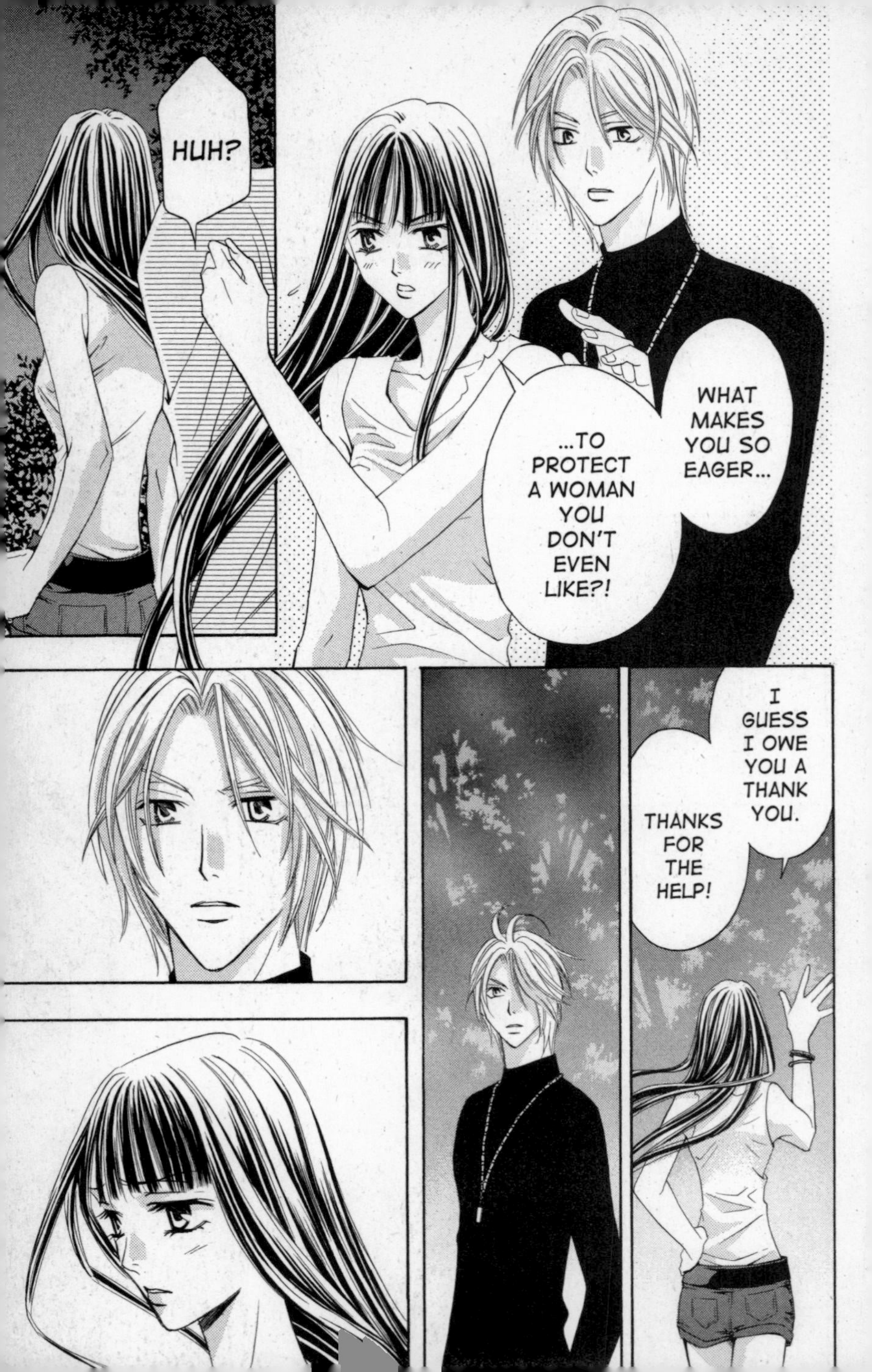
WHAT MAKES YOU SO EAGER...
...TO PROTECT A WOMAN YOU DON'T EVEN LIKE?!
HUH?
I GUESS I OWE YOU A THANK YOU.
THANKS FOR THE HELP!

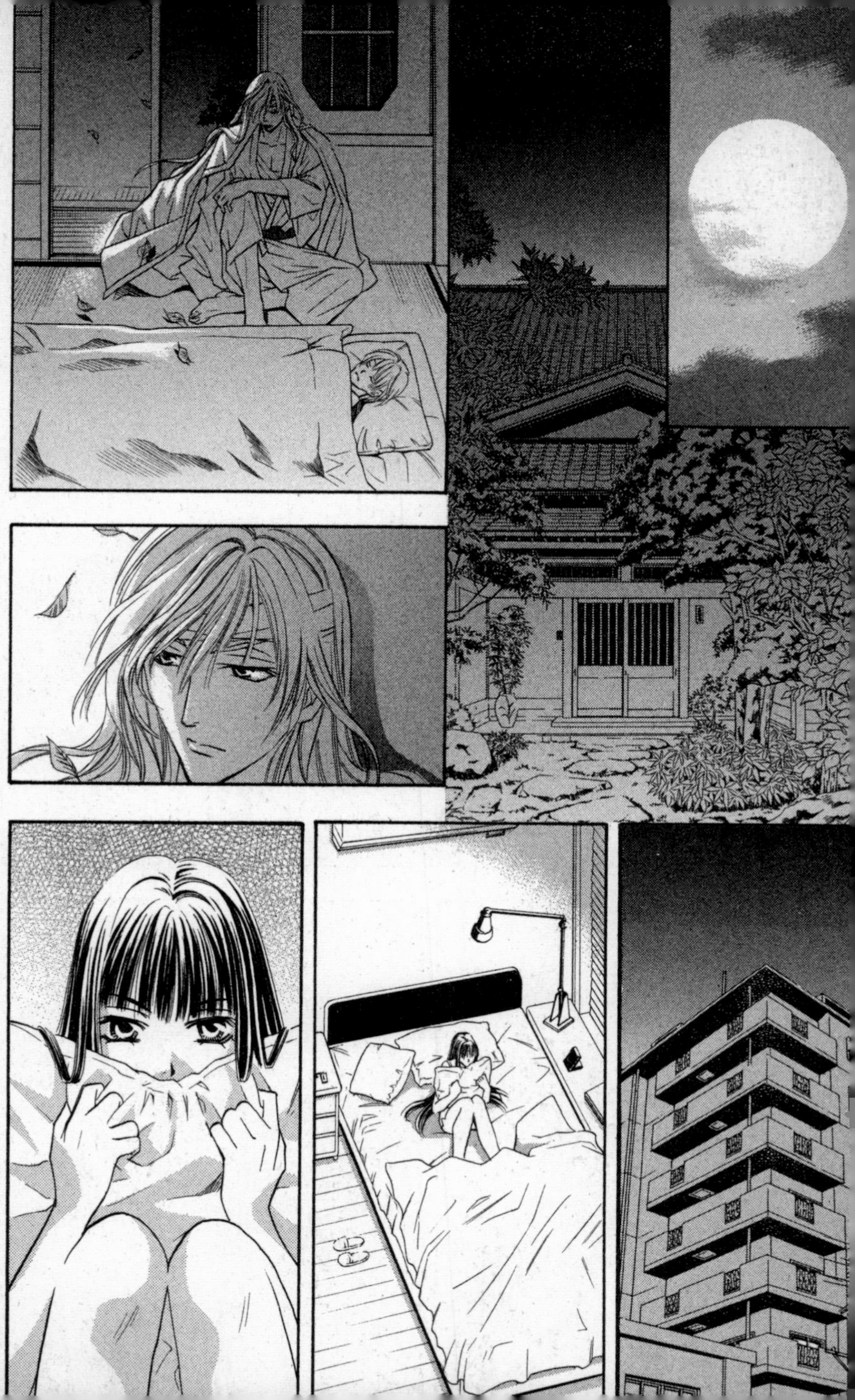

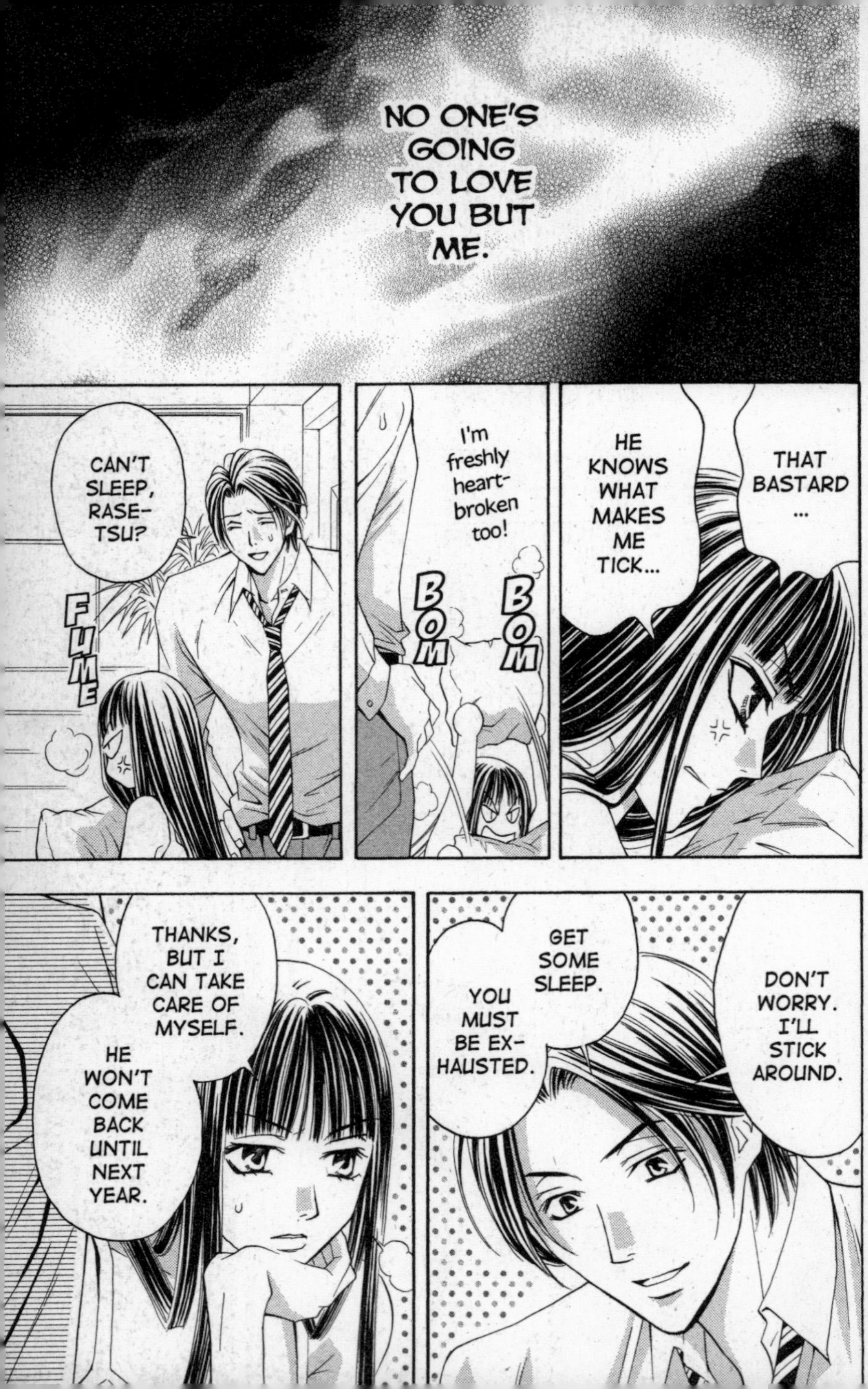
NO ONE'S GOING TO LOVE YOU BUT ME.
CAN'T SLEEP, RASE-TSU?
FUME
I'm freshly heart-broken too!
BOM
BOM
HE KNOWS WHAT MAKES ME TICK...
THAT BASTARD ...
THANKS, BUT I CAN TAKE CARE OF MYSELF.
HE WON'T COME BACK UNTIL NEXT YEAR.
GET SOME SLEEP.
YOU MUST BE EX-HAUSTED.
DON'T WORRY. I'LL STICK AROUND.

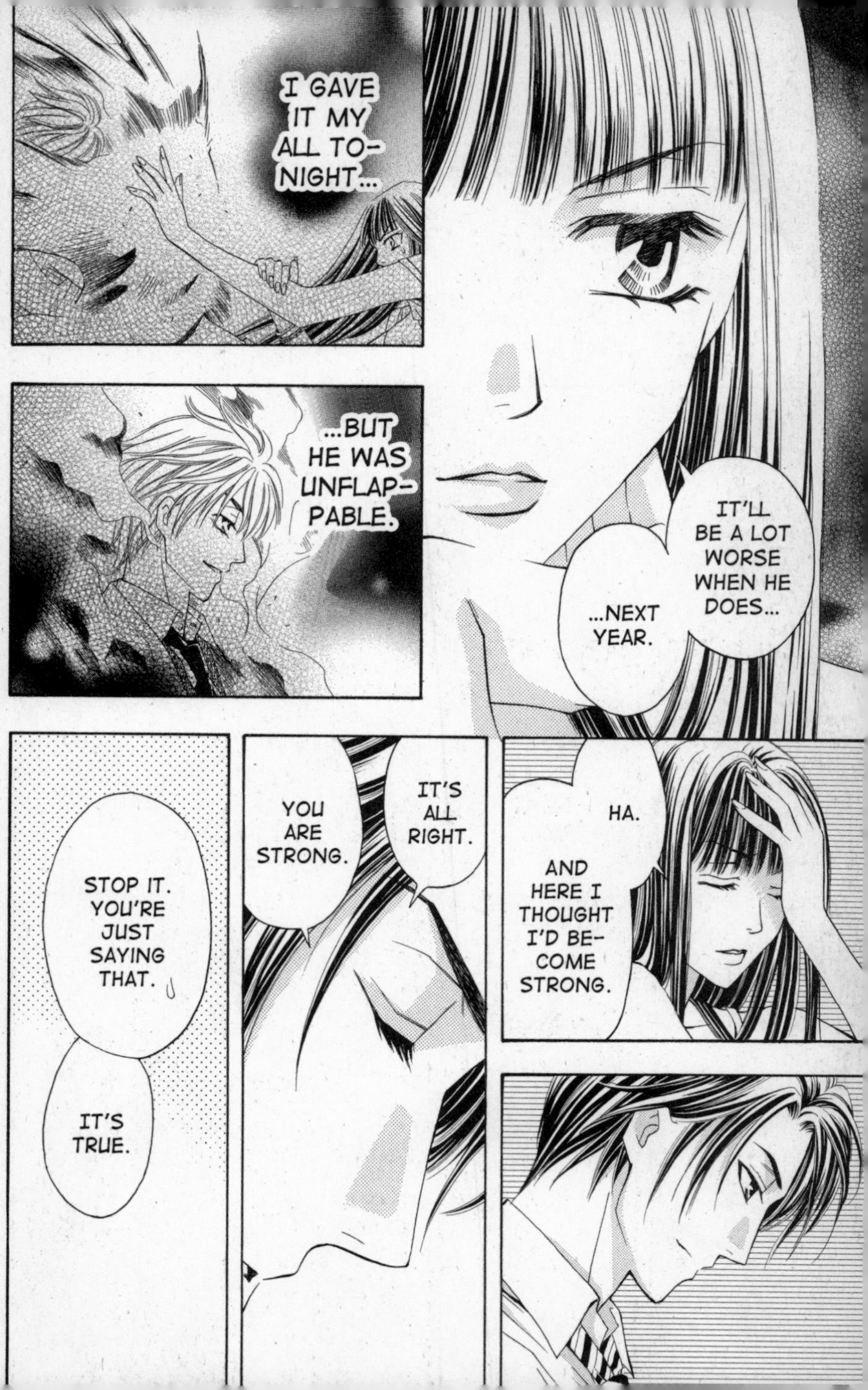
IT'LL BE A LOT WORSE WHEN HE DOES...
...NEXT YEAR.
I GAVE IT MY ALL TO-NIGHT...
...BUT HE WAS UNFLAP-PABLE.
HA.
AND HERE I THOUGHT I'D BE-COME STRONG.
IT'S ALL RIGHT.
YOU ARE STRONG.
STOP IT. YOU'RE JUST SAYING THAT.
IT'S TRUE.

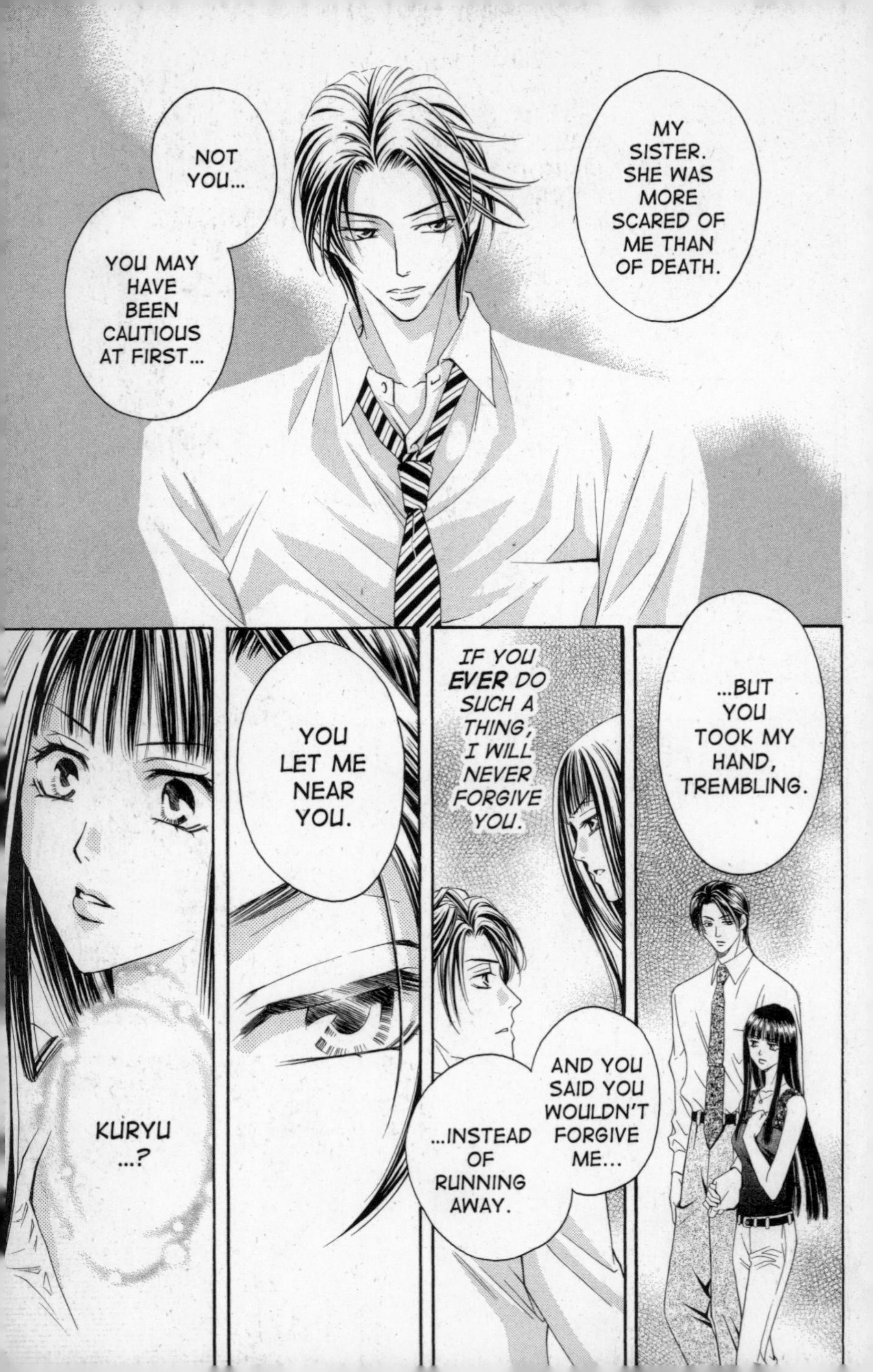
MY SISTER. SHE WAS MORE SCARED OF ME THAN OF DEATH.
NOT YOU...
YOU MAY HAVE BEEN CAUTIOUS AT FIRST...
...BUT YOU TOOK MY HAND, TREMBLING.
IF YOU *EVER* DO SUCH A THING, I WILL NEVER FORGIVE YOU.
AND YOU SAID YOU WOULDN'T FORGIVE ME...
...INSTEAD OF RUNNING AWAY.
YOU LET ME NEAR YOU.
KURYU ...?

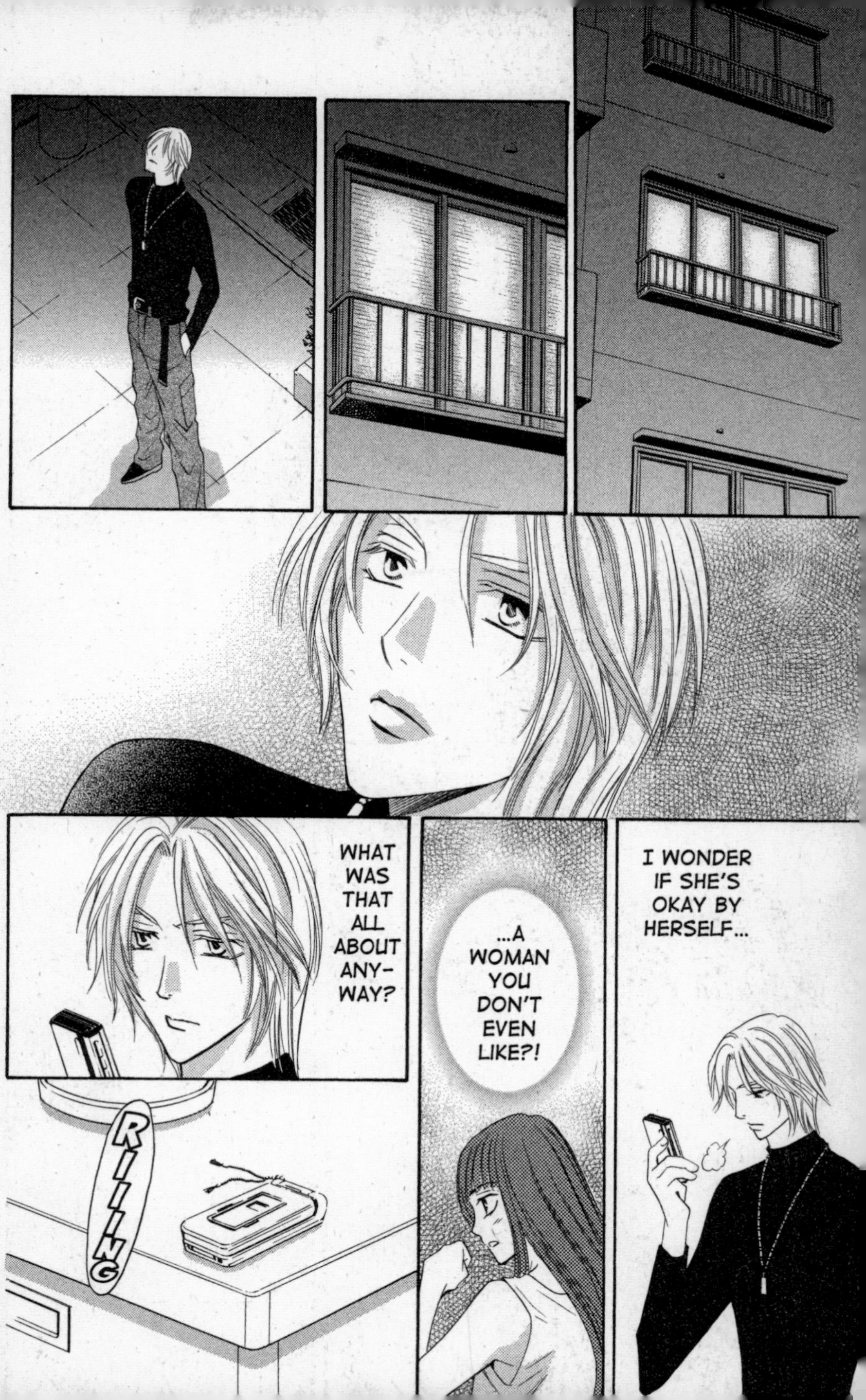
I WONDER IF SHE'S OKAY BY HERSELF...
...A WOMAN YOU DON'T EVEN LIKE?!
WHAT WAS THAT ALL ABOUT ANY-WAY?
RIIIING

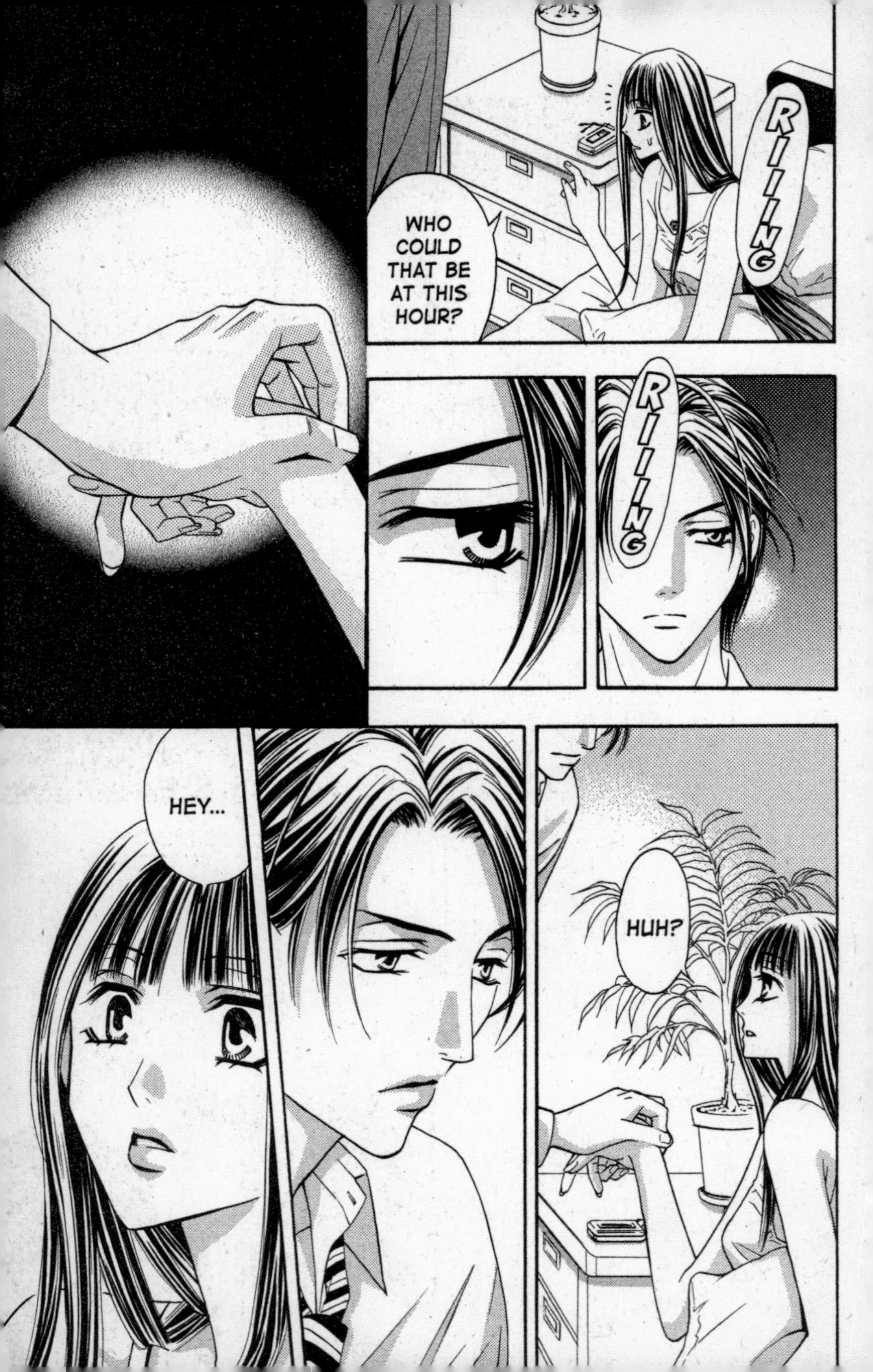
RIIING
WHO COULD THAT BE AT THIS HOUR?
RIIING
HUH?
HEY...

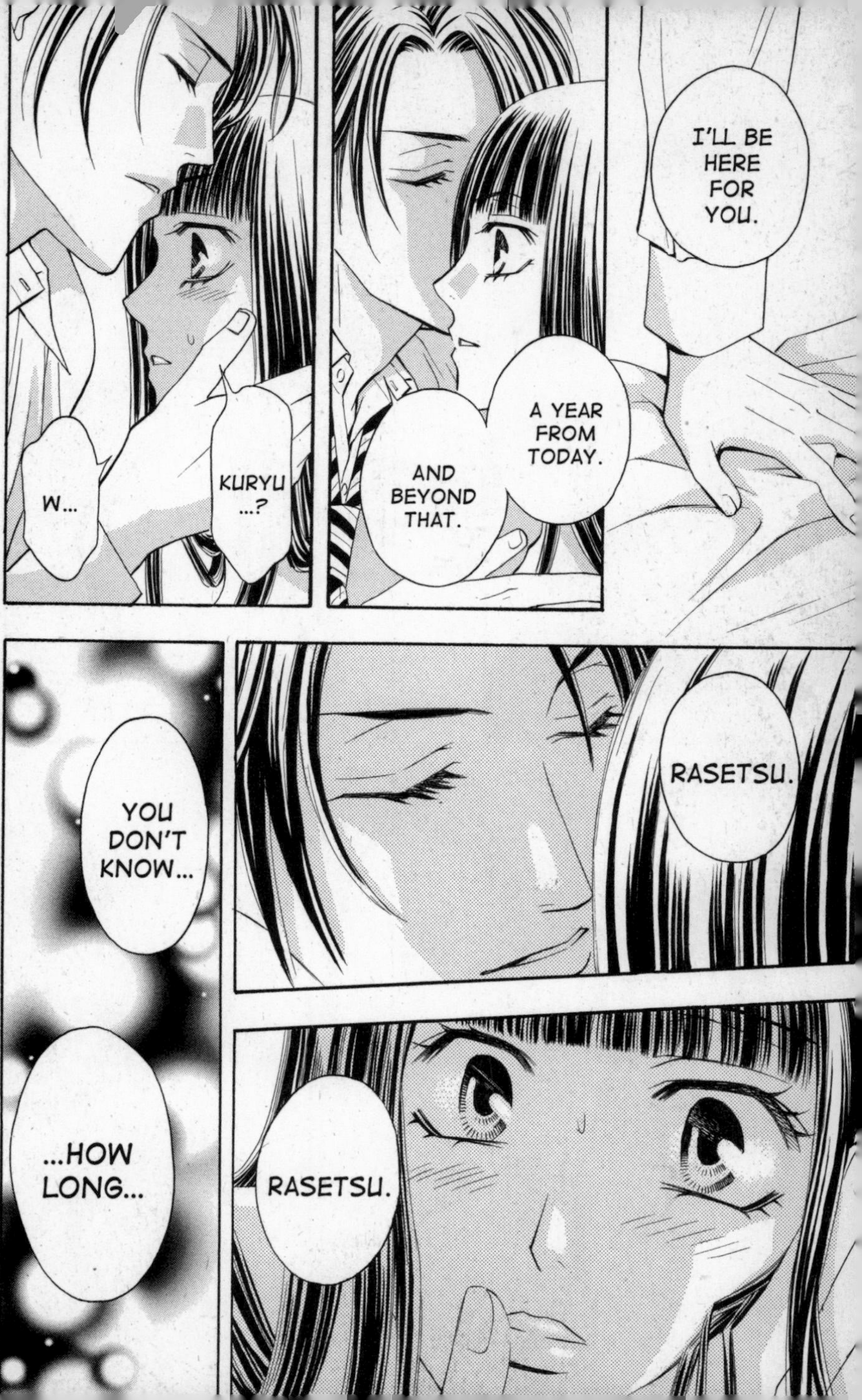
I'LL BE HERE FOR YOU.
A YEAR FROM TODAY.
AND BEYOND THAT.
KURYU ...?
W...
RASETSU.
RASETSU.
YOU DON'T KNOW...
...HOW LONG...

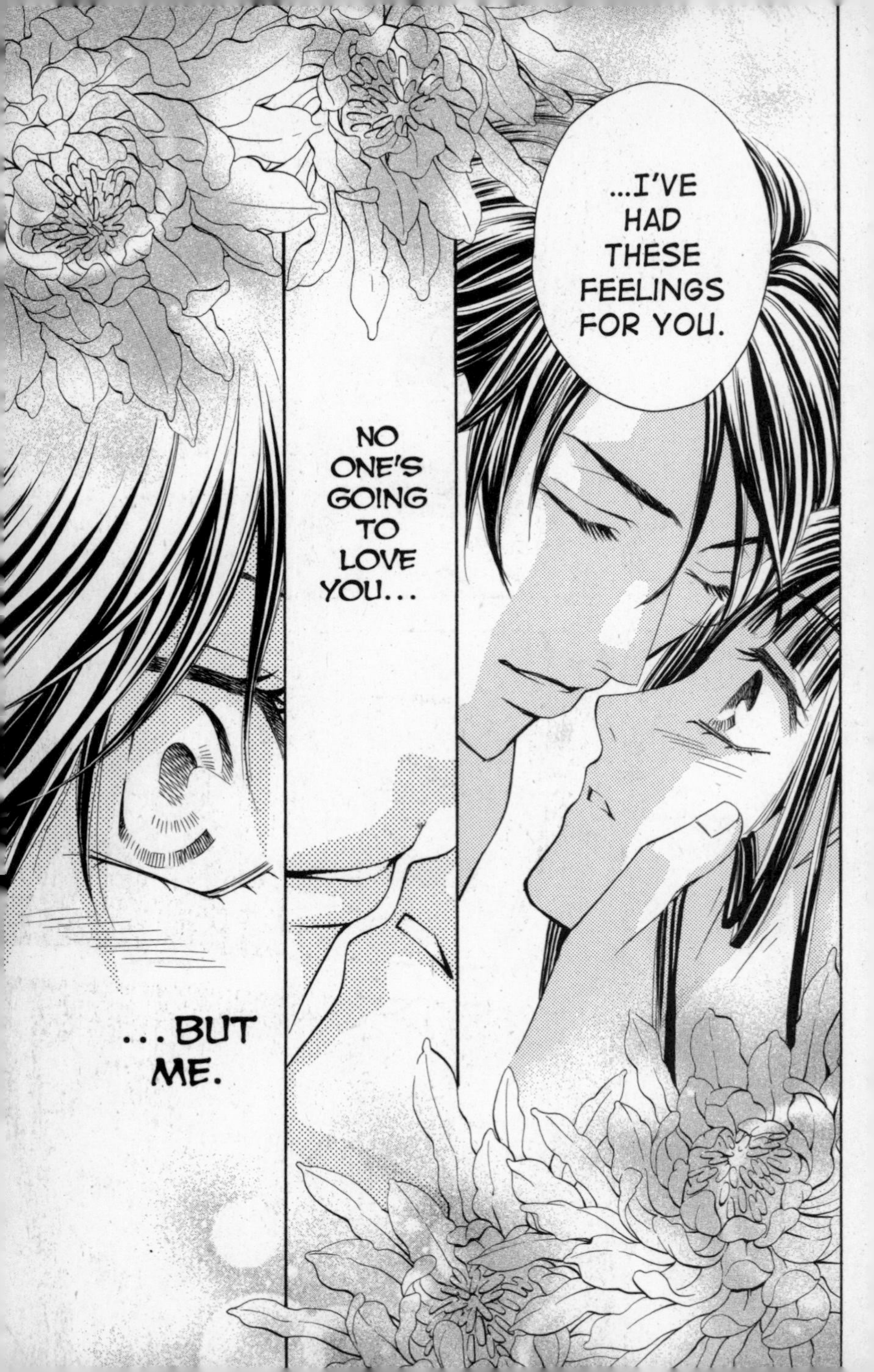
...I'VE HAD THESE FEELINGS FOR YOU.
NO ONE'S GOING TO LOVE YOU...
...BUT ME.

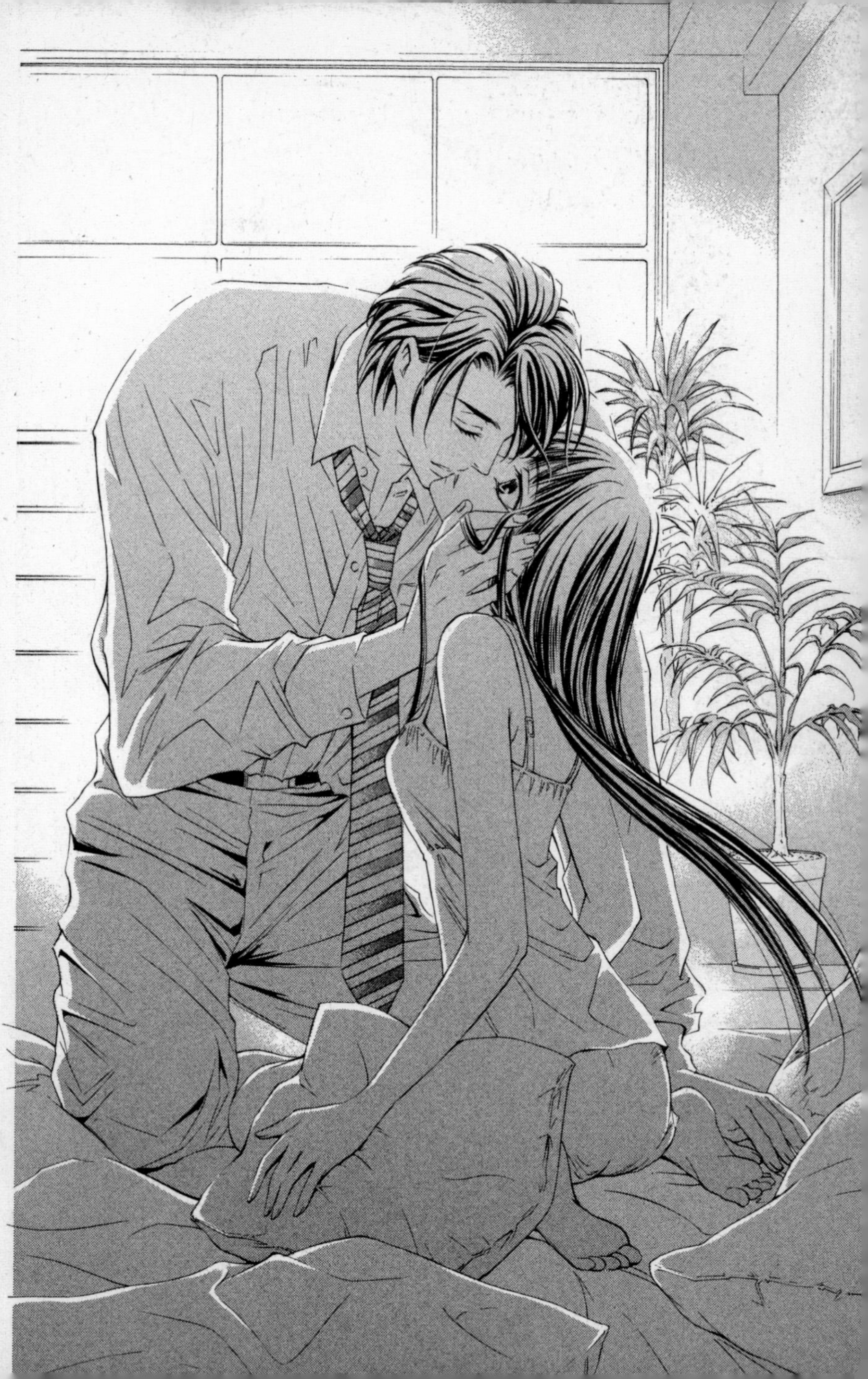

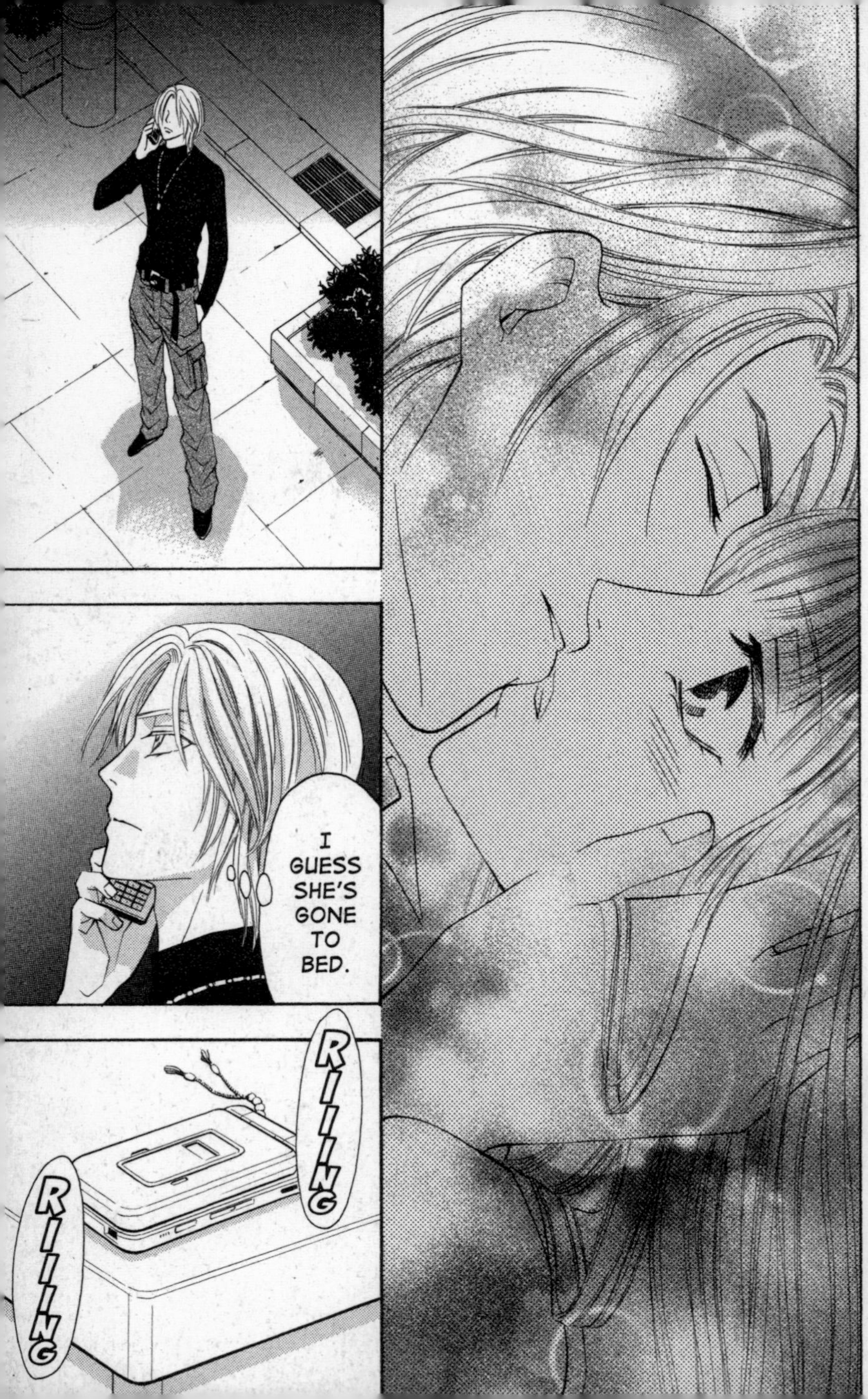
I GUESS SHE'S GONE TO BED.
RIIIING
RIIIING

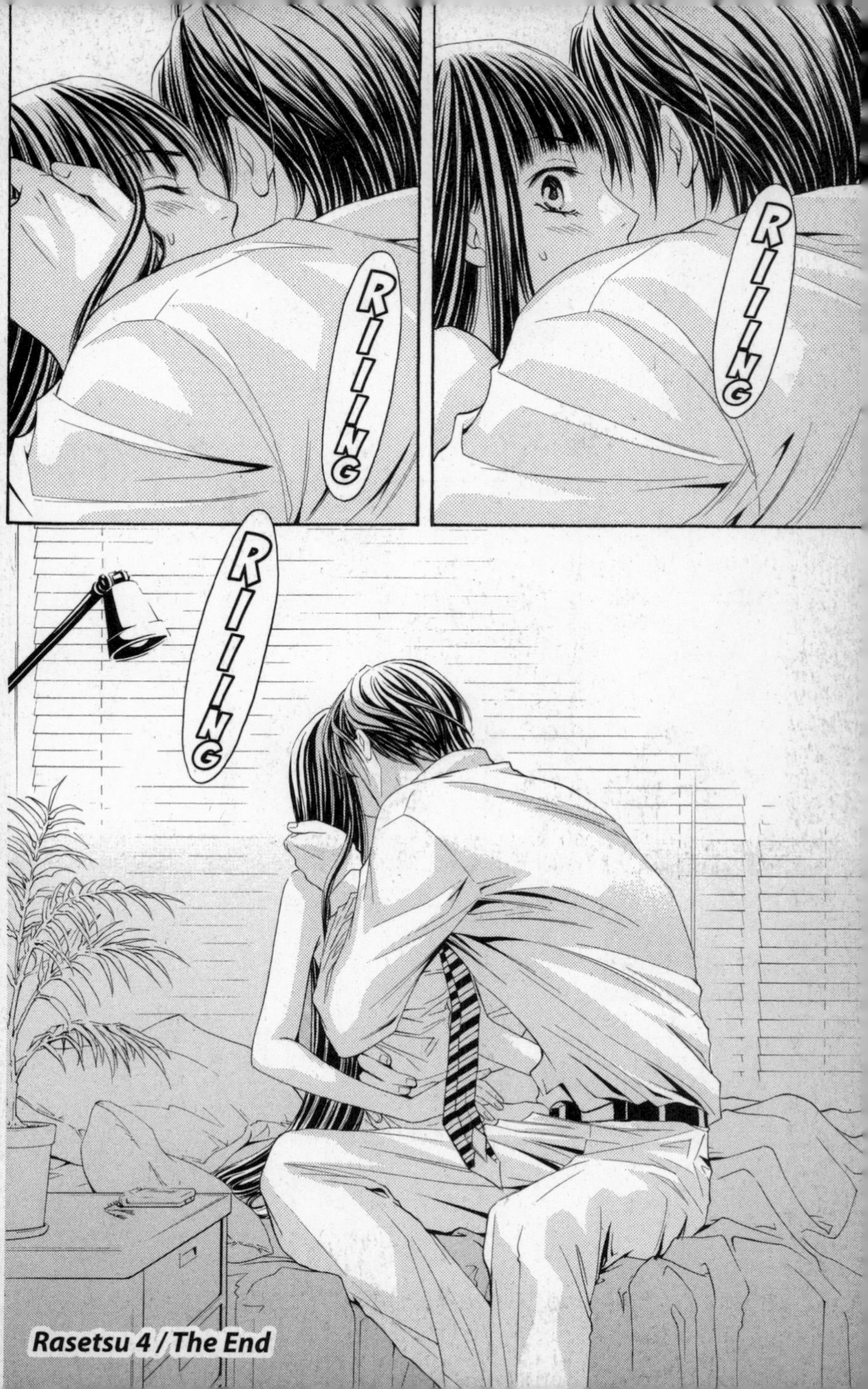
RIIIING
RIIIING
RIIIING
Rasetsu 4 / The End

BONUS MANGA
AOI'S MEMOIR

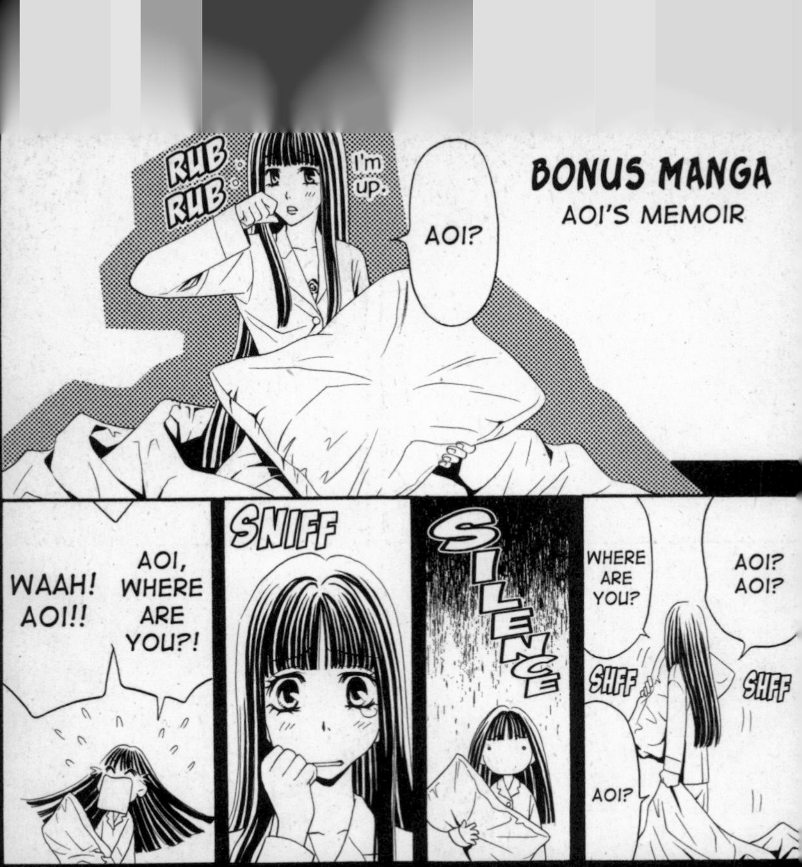
AOI?
I'm up.
RUB RUB
AOI? AOI?
WHERE ARE YOU?
SHFF
SHFF
AOI?
SILENCE
SNIFF
AOI, WHERE ARE YOU?!
WAAH! AOI!!

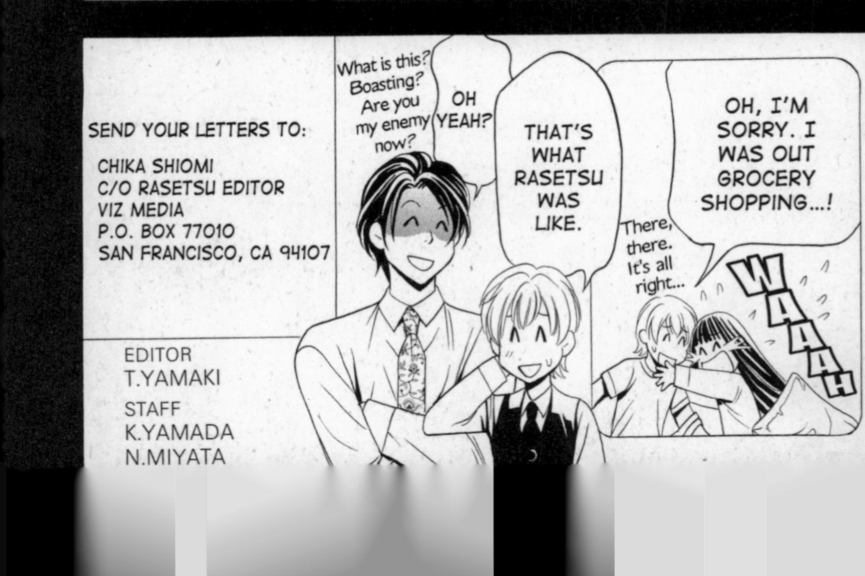
OH, I'M SORRY. I WAS OUT GROCERY SHOPPING...!
WAAAAH
There, there. It's all right...
THAT'S WHAT RASETSU WAS LIKE.
OH YEAH?
What is this? Boasting? Are you my enemy now?

SEND YOUR LETTERS TO:

CHIKA SHIOMI
C/O RASETSU EDITOR
VIZ MEDIA
P.O. BOX 77010
SAN FRANCISCO, CA 94107

EDITOR
T.YAMAKI

STAFF
K.YAMADA
N.MIYATA

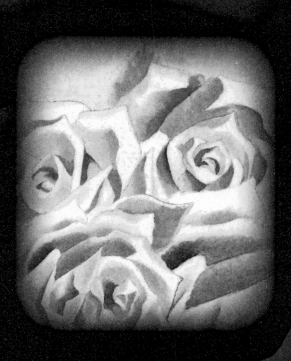

Chika Shiomi lives in Aichi Prefecture, Japan. She debuted with the manga *Todokeru Toki o Sugitemo* (Even if the Time for Deliverance Passes), and her previous works include the supernatural series *Yurara*. She loves reading manga, traveling and listening to music. Her favorite artists include Michelangelo, Hokusai, Bernini and Gustav Klimt.

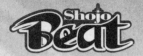

RASETSU
VOL. 4
Shojo Beat Edition

STORY AND ART BY
CHIKA SHIOMI

Translation & Adaptation/Kinami Watabe
Touch-up Art & Lettering/Freeman Wong
Design/Hidemi Dunn
Editor/Amy Yu

VP, Production/Alvin Lu
VP, Sales & Product Marketing/Gonzalo Ferreyra
VP, Creative/Linda Espinosa
Publisher/Hyoe Narita

Rasetsu No Hana by Chika Shiomi
© Chika Shiomi 2008
All rights reserved.
First published in Japan in 2008 by HAKUSENSHA, Inc., Tokyo.
English language translation rights arranged with HAKUSENSHA, Inc., Tokyo.

The stories, characters and incidents mentioned in this publication are entirely fictional.

Printed in the U.S.A.

Published by VIZ Media, LLC
P.O. Box 77010
San Francisco, CA 94107

10 9 8 7 6 5 4 3 2 1
First printing, March 2010

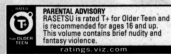

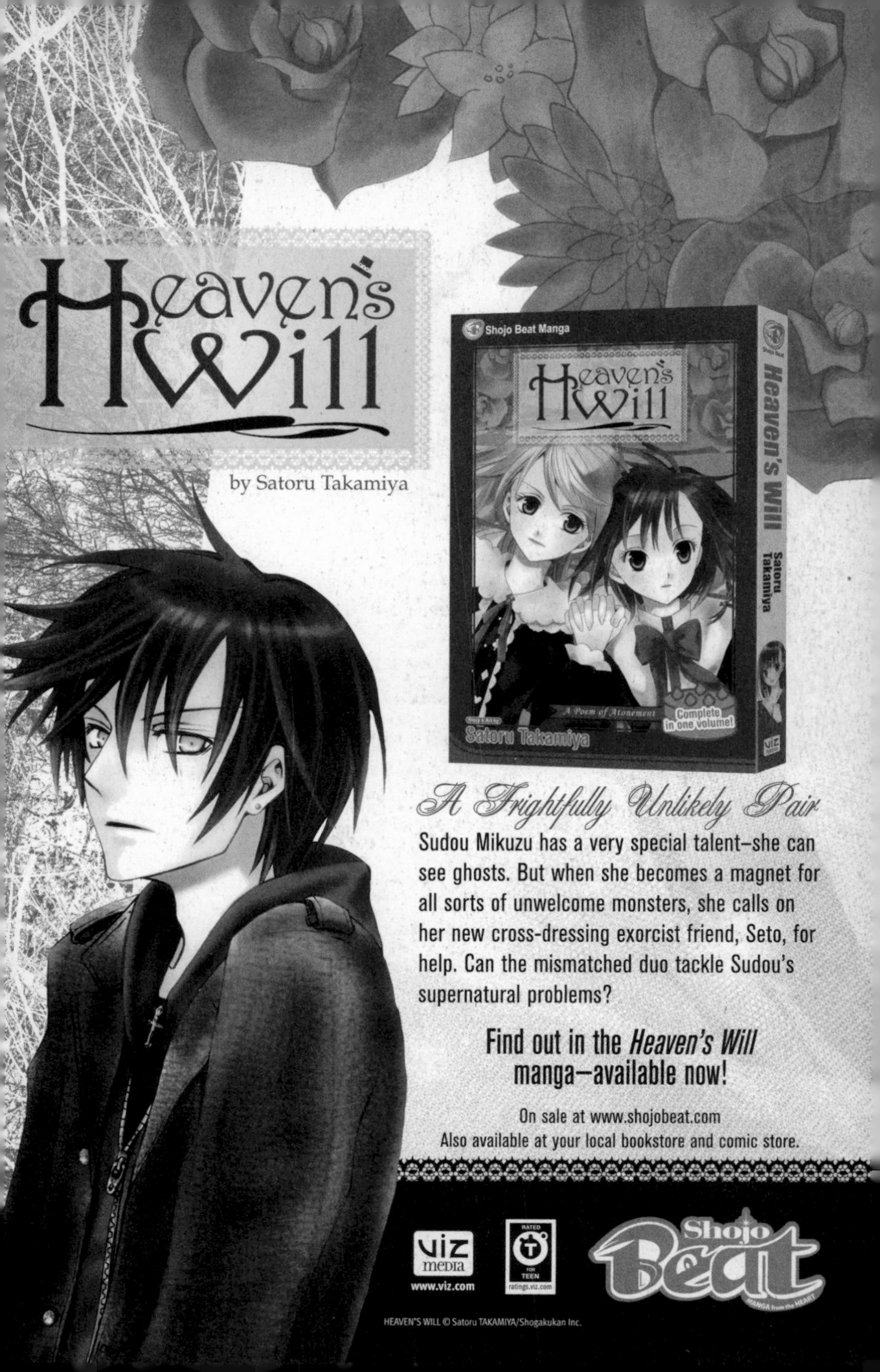
Heaven's Will
by Satoru Takamiya
Shojo Beat Manga
Heaven's Will
A Poem of Atonement
Complete in one volume!
Satoru Takamiya
A Frightfully Unlikely Pair
Sudou Mikuzu has a very special talent–she can see ghosts. But when she becomes a magnet for all sorts of unwelcome monsters, she calls on her new cross-dressing exorcist friend, Seto, for help. Can the mismatched duo tackle Sudou's supernatural problems?
Find out in the *Heaven's Will* manga—available now!
On sale at www.shojobeat.com
Also available at your local bookstore and comic store.
viz media
www.viz.com
RATED T FOR TEEN
ratings.viz.com
Shojo Beat
MANGA from the HEART
HEAVEN'S WILL © Satoru TAKAMIYA/Shogakukan Inc.

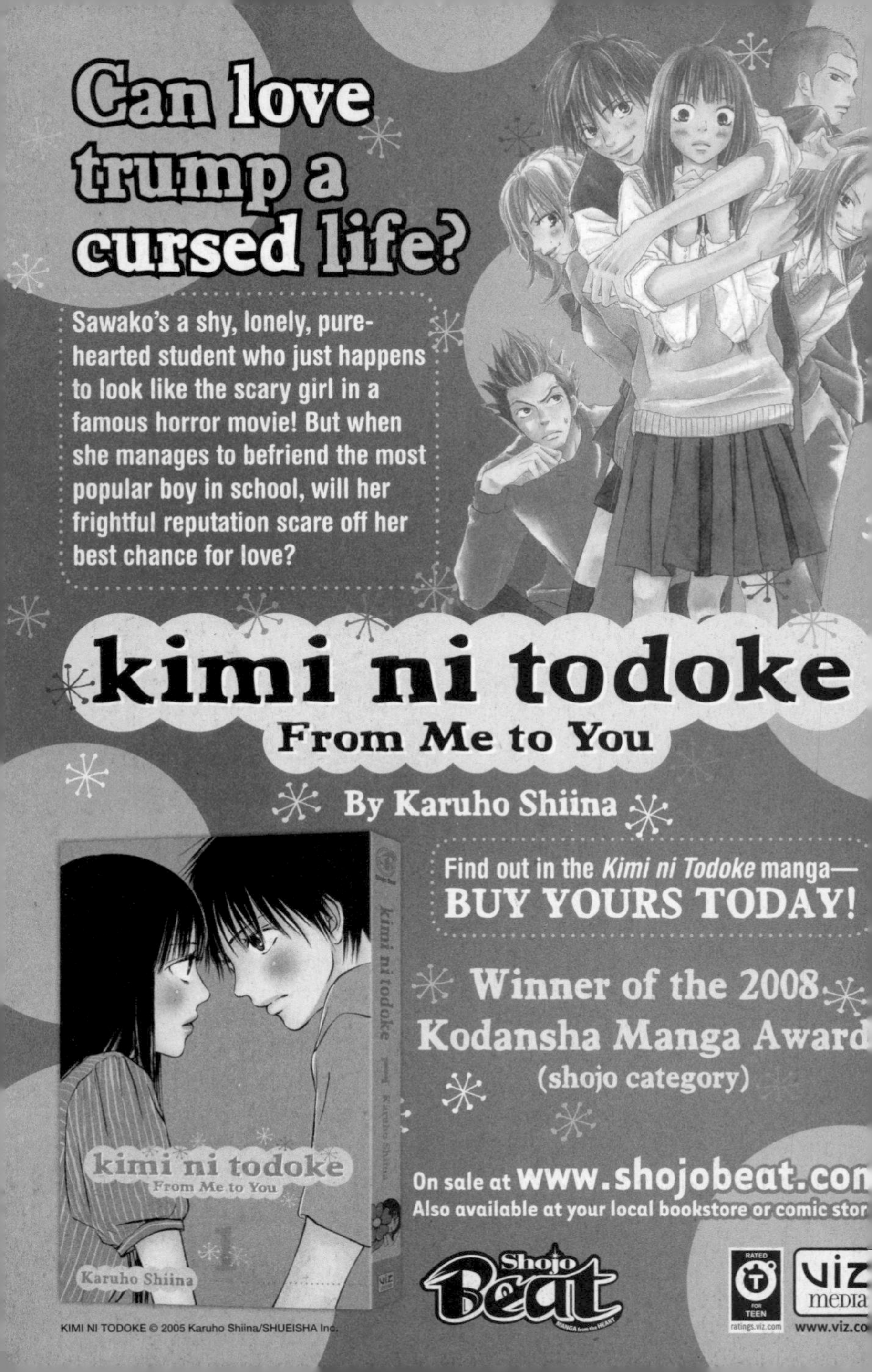
Can love trump a cursed life?
Sawako's a shy, lonely, pure-hearted student who just happens to look like the scary girl in a famous horror movie! But when she manages to befriend the most popular boy in school, will her frightful reputation scare off her best chance for love?
kimi ni todoke
From Me to You
By Karuho Shiina
Find out in the Kimi ni Todoke manga—
BUY YOURS TODAY!
Winner of the 2008 Kodansha Manga Award (shojo category)
kimi ni todoke
From Me to You
1
Karuho Shiina
On sale at www.shojobeat.con
Also available at your local bookstore or comic stor
Shojo Beat
RATED
T
FOR TEEN
ratings.viz.com
VIZ media
www.viz.co
KIMI NI TODOKE © 2005 Karuho Shiina/SHUEISHA Inc.

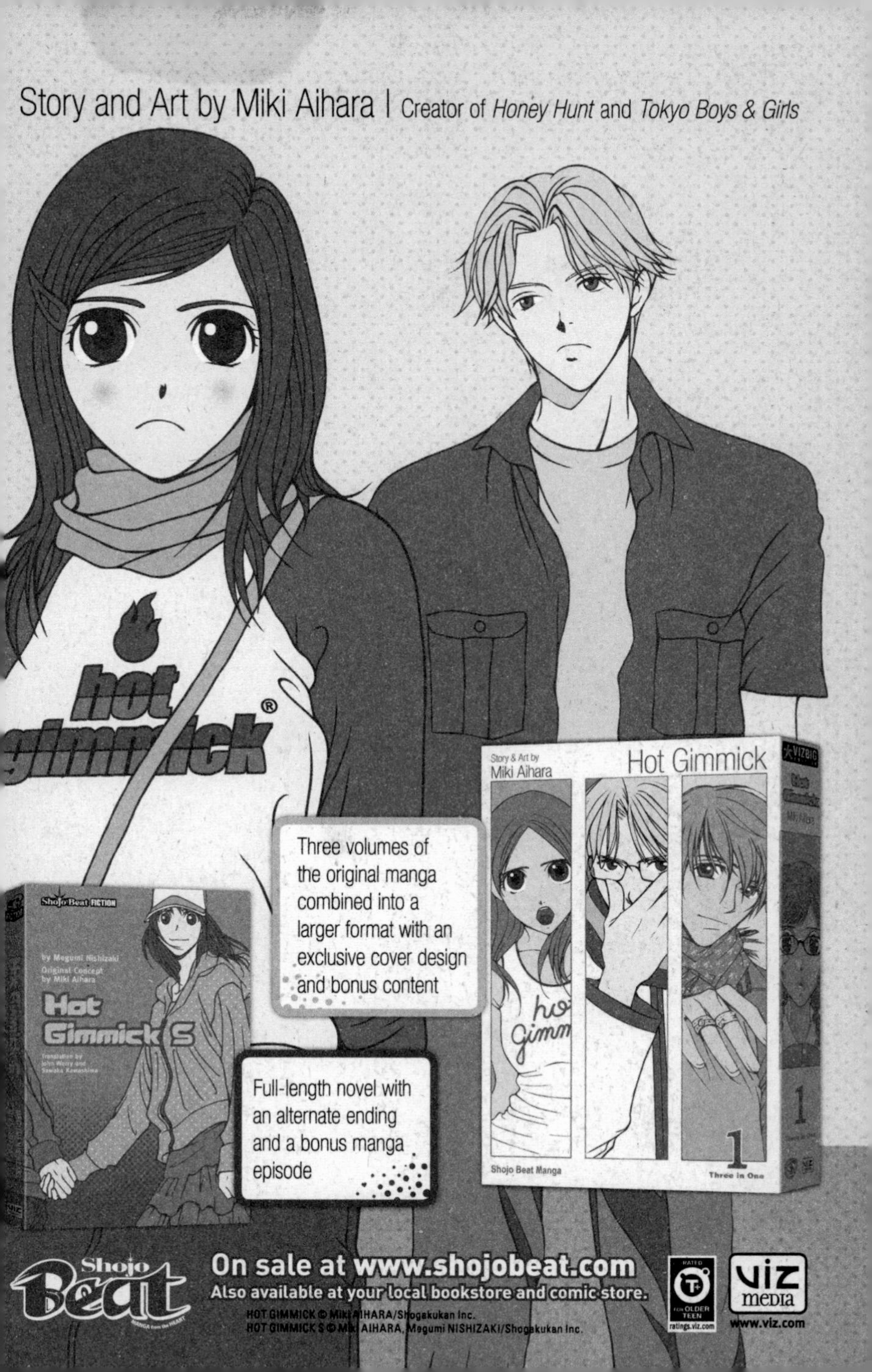
Story and Art by Miki Aihara | Creator of Honey Hunt and Tokyo Boys & Girls
hot gimmick®
Shojo Beat FICTION
by Megumi Nishizaki
Original Concept by Miki Aihara
Hot Gimmick S
Three volumes of the original manga combined into a larger format with an exclusive cover design and bonus content
Full-length novel with an alternate ending and a bonus manga episode
Story & Art by Miki Aihara
Hot Gimmick
1
Shojo Beat Manga
Three in One
Shojo Beat
On sale at www.shojobeat.com
Also available at your local bookstore and comic store.
HOT GIMMICK © Miki AIHARA/Shogakukan Inc.
HOT GIMMICK S © Miki AIHARA, Megumi NISHIZAKI/Shogakukan Inc.
RATED T+ FOR OLDER TEEN
ratings.viz.com
VIZ MEDIA
www.viz.com

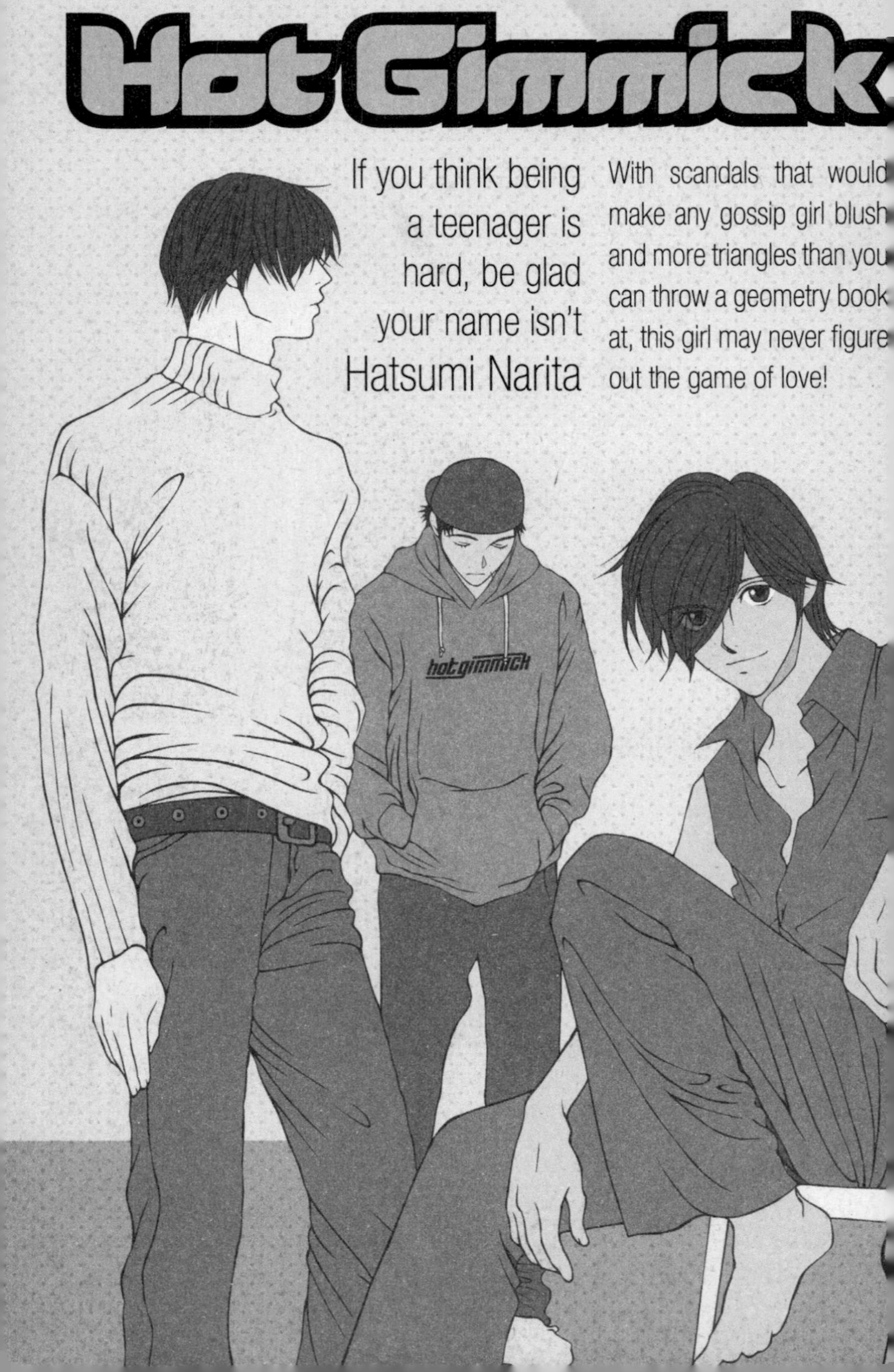
Hot Gimmick
If you think being a teenager is hard, be glad your name isn't Hatsumi Narita
With scandals that would make any gossip girl blush and more triangles than you can throw a geometry book at, this girl may never figure out the game of love!
hotgimmick

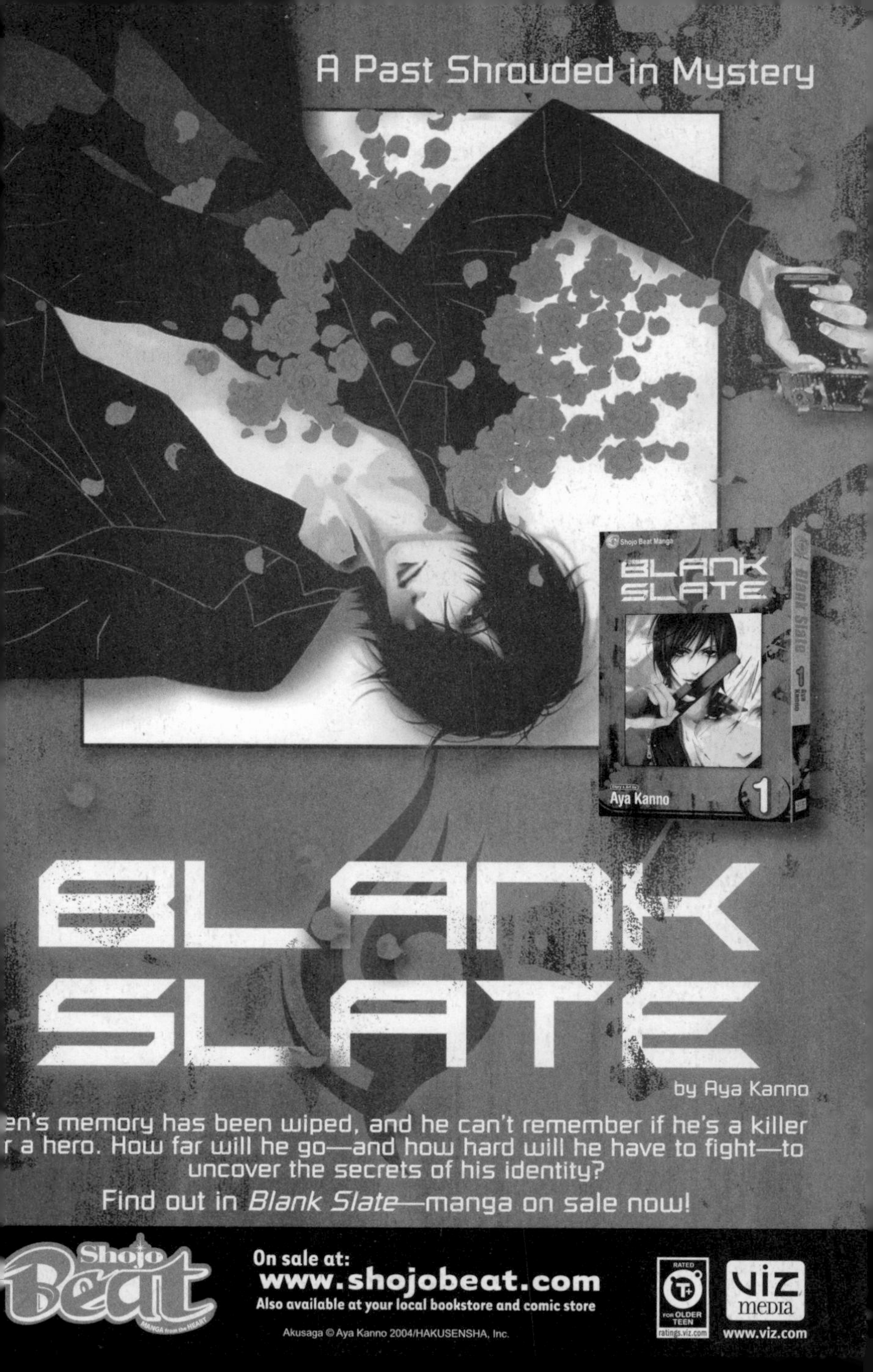
A Past Shrouded in Mystery
Shojo Beat Manga
BLANK SLATE
Aya Kanno
1
BLANK SLATE
by Aya Kanno
en's memory has been wiped, and he can't remember if he's a killer
r a hero. How far will he go—and how hard will he have to fight—to
uncover the secrets of his identity?
Find out in *Blank Slate*—manga on sale now!
Shojo Beat
MANGA from the HEART
On sale at:
www.shojobeat.com
Also available at your local bookstore and comic store
Akusaga © Aya Kanno 2004/HAKUSENSHA, Inc.
RATED T+ FOR OLDER TEEN
ratings.viz.com
VIZ media
www.viz.com

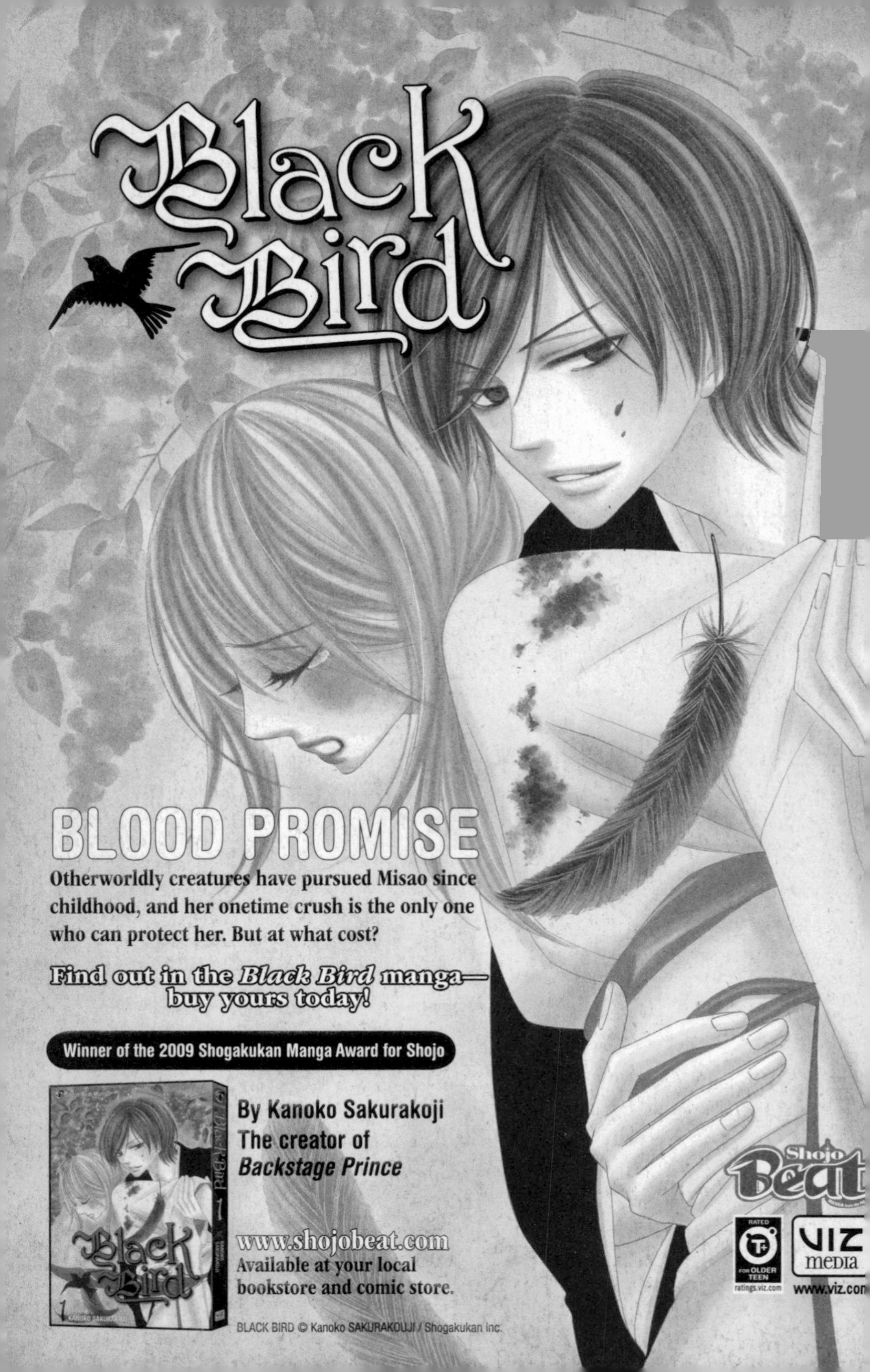
Black Bird
BLOOD PROMISE
Otherworldly creatures have pursued Misao since childhood, and her onetime crush is the only one who can protect her. But at what cost?
Find out in the Black Bird manga—buy yours today!
Winner of the 2009 Shogakukan Manga Award for Shojo
By Kanoko Sakurakoji
The creator of Backstage Prince
www.shojobeat.com
Available at your local bookstore and comic store.
BLACK BIRD © Kanoko SAKURAKOUJI / Shogakukan Inc.
Shojo Beat
RATED T+ FOR OLDER TEEN
ratings.viz.com
VIZ media
www.viz.com

Tell us what you think about Shojo Beat Manga!

Our survey is now available online. Go to:

shojobeat.com/mangasurvey

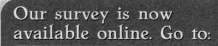

P9-BZL-265

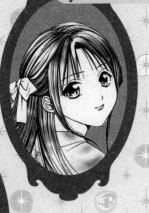

Help us make our product offerings better!

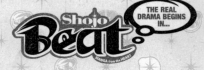